The Iron Age in Northern Britain

Unlike the Iron Age in Southern Britain, the story of which can be conveniently terminated with the Roman conquest, the Iron Age in Northern Britain has no such horizon to mark its end. The Roman presence in southern and eastern Scotland was militarily intermittent and left untouched large tracts of Atlantic Scotland for which there is a rich legacy of Iron Age settlement, continuing from the mid-first millennium BC to the period of Norse settlement in the late-first millennium AD.

The Iron Age in Northern Britain is essentially a story of continuity through change over nearly two millennia. It examines the impact of the Roman expansion northwards, and the native response to the Roman occupation on both sides of the frontiers. It traces the emergence of historically recorded communities in the post-Roman period and looks at the clash of cultures between Celts and Romans, Britons, Angles, Picts and Scots.

Northern Britain has too often been seen as peripheral to a 'core' located in southern or south-eastern England. Here Dennis Harding attempts to show that Northern Britain was not peripheral in the Iron Age: it simply belonged to an Atlantic Europe mainstream different from southern England and its immediate Continental neighbours.

Dennis Harding is Abercromby Professor of Archaeology and a former Vice-Principal at the University of Edinburgh. He has been involved in fieldwork in Northern Britain, including excavation and air-photography (for which he held a private pilot's licence), for more than thirty years. He is a fellow of the Royal Society of Edinburgh.

The Iron Age in Northern Britain

Celts and Romans, natives and invaders

D. W. Harding

Routledge
Taylor & Francis Group

LONDON AND NEW YORK

First published 2004
by Routledge
2 Park Square, Milton Park, Abingdon, Oxon OX14 4RN

Simultaneously published in the USA and Canada
by Routledge
270 Madison Avenue, New York, NY 10016

Routledge is an imprint of the Taylor & Francis Group

Typeset in Garamond by
Keystroke, Jacaranda Lodge, Wolverhampton
Printed and bound in Great Britain by
TJ International Ltd, Padstow, Cornwall

British Library Cataloguing in Publication Data
A catalogue record for this book is available from the British Library

Library of Congress Cataloging in Publication Data
Harding, D. W. (Dennis William)
  The Iron Age in northern Britain : Celts and Romans, natives and invaders /
  D.W. Harding.
    p. cm.
  Includes bibliographical references and index.
  ISBN 0–415–30149–1 (hardback : alk. paper) – ISBN 0–415–30150–5 (pbk. : alk. paper)
  1. Iron age–Great Britain. 2. Celts–Great Britain. 3. Romans–Great Britain.
  4. Great Britain–Antiquities. I. Title.
  GN780.22.G7H316 2004
  936.1–dc22   2004002803

ISBN 0–415–30149–1 (hbk)
ISBN 0–415–30150–5 (pbk)

To the postgraduate students of the Edinburgh 'school' of Scottish archaeology, 1984–2004

Contents

Figures

Preface

The present study is the cumulative result of a personal involvement in Iron Age archaeology in Britain over the past fifty years. At the same time it does not claim to be the last word, or even the writer's last word, on the subject. In fact, the absence hitherto of a general synthesis of the Iron Age in Northern Britain is a measure of the relative neglect until recent years by professional archaeologists of the Iron Age north of the Trent, and the long-standing dominance of Wessex and southern England in British prehistoric archaeology.

The writer began his career in Wessex, directing his first excavation on Cranborne Chase in 1958. Early field experience as a student volunteer had been mainly on Roman sites, at Lullingstone villa, at Verulamium with Sheppard Frere, and in Wales at the fort of Castell Collen in Radnorshire. Working as a schoolboy on a native Romano-British settlement at Studland, Dorset and subsequently on the Dark Age site at Dinas Powys and on a Medieval castle in North Wales had stimulated interests beyond Roman Britain. Directing the excavation at Pimperne in Dorset in the early sixties, and meeting Professor Christopher Hawkes there before going up to Oxford, confirmed a career in Iron Age studies, leading to postgraduate research at the Oxford Institute of Archaeology and a first appointment in the Ashmolean Museum.

Appointment to a lectureship at Durham in the mid-1960s began my drift north, and introduced me to a host of fieldworkers, professional and amateur. Among many whose excavations and surveys I visited in the field I recall especially the late Don Spratt and his colleagues in Cleveland and the North York Moors, and Denis Coggins and Ken Fairless in Upper Teesdale. My postgraduate students of that time also included Aidan Challis, Rob Young, Rowan Whimster and the late Peter Scott, all of whom made significant contributions to the archaeology of Northern Britain. Above all, literally, I explored northern England and beyond from the air, and have a debt of gratitude to Denis Ord and Ray Selkirk in particular, who compensated for my shortcomings as a pilot and navigator on many occasions.

Translation to Edinburgh in the mid-1970s led to widening interest in the Northern and Western Isles, and from the early 1980s the Edinburgh University Department of Archaeology has been regularly engaged in fieldwork in the Outer Hebrides, based upon its field centre at Calanais. This, one of the richest archaeological landscapes in Britain, had been largely neglected since the Rockets Galore rescue programme in the 1950s, but with first the Edinburgh initiative, followed within a year or two by the Sheffield SEARCH programme, that deficit has in part at least been rectified. The Northern Isles by contrast had for many years attracted colonial expeditions from the south, and in recent years have benefited from important programmes of field research sponsored by Bradford and Birmingham Universities. Again my debt to colleagues is almost limitless. In my continuing aerial surveys, George Ballingall was a tower of strength. And a succession of research students from Edinburgh University created what has sometimes deprecatingly been called the 'Edinburgh School'. At the risk of being invidious by selection, I must record a special debt to Patrick Topping, Ian Armit, Simon Gilmour, Mike Church, Andy Heald, Jon Henderson, Chris Burgess and Mel Johnson among many others who suffered the midges. Among colleagues in the Scottish Commission, I recall with pleasure and affection field trips in the company of Roger Mercer, Strat Halliday and Diana Murray. From the University of Edinburgh Geraint Coles and Nick Dixon deserve my grateful thanks, and I wish to record also my appreciation to Professor Ian Ralston and former colleagues from the Centre for Field Archaeology. I also owe a debt of gratitude to many individuals from local societies and museums throughout Northern Britain who have generously allowed me access to their collections or introduced me to their local landscapes.

The importance of the Iron Age in Northern Britain is now better recognised than it was thirty years ago. The Western Isles perhaps still remain something of an Ultima Thule to the archaeological establishment of the Golden Triangle. When lecturing once in London on work in west Lewis, I showed a map of Europe, with a circle inscribed upon it in which the centre was London, and the arc passed through west Lewis. I remarked that the circle also passed through the Pyrenees, Milan and Berlin, and that, like these places, in west Lewis the first language was not English. I recall the chill of the reception, which suggested that the audience regarded the speaker, though once from Wessex, as having 'gone native' on another heath. I recall a further occasion in Yorkshire, when I expressed my pleasure at coming down to lecture in the Midlands, an observation that nearly triggered a barrage of cloth caps and wellie boots; so I am mildly surprised to see this region now referred to in publication as Central Britain.

My purpose in writing this book, therefore, has been twofold. The first is to attempt a synthesis, however inadequate, of that part of Britain that contains the majority of significant Iron Age remains, but which has too often in the past received scant or insufficient acknowledgement in previous studies. The second is to place on record my debt to many colleagues and former pupils, whose help has aided me and whose support has encouraged me, in all the years that I have been travelling north. Archaeology may not be the path to fame and fortune, but as my Geordie navigator once observed, as we climbed away from the airfield on a beautiful, sunny morning in crystal-crisp visibility, 'it certainly beats workin''.

D. W. Harding
Gullane, June 2003

Part I

Legacy of the past

Chapter 1

Introduction
The archaeological framework

The chronological framework

Any regional or chronological synthesis should begin by defining its chronological and spatial parameters. Those parameters need not be regarded as having significance beyond limitations of convenience, though one might prefer wherever possible to adopt meaningful boundaries or chronological horizons to ones that are purely arbitrary. Furthermore, chronological thresholds that might be applicable to one region of Northern Britain will not necessarily or automatically be apposite for other regions, compounding the problems of devising a workable system of classification and terminology.

For Southern Britain the situation, superficially at any rate, is not so acute: at least there the Roman Conquest serves as *terminus ante quem* for studies of the Iron Age. It could be argued, of course, that the native response to conquest was integral to an understanding of Iron Age communities, and that Britain under Roman occupation should be regarded as an important sequel to an understanding of pre-Roman Iron Age society. But as a threshold of convenience AD 43 has at least some historical validity. There is no comparable historical threshold for the Iron Age of Northern Britain. The Romans may have established a permanent frontier across the Tyne–Solway isthmus in the late first and early second centuries, but their occupation of southern Scotland was intermittent, amounting to little more than eighty years in all. Beyond the Forth–Clyde line Roman influence was still more limited, and in Atlantic Scotland it was virtually non-existent.

For much of the Atlantic north and west there is no historically defined break in the sequence of Iron Age settlement from the second half of the first millennium BC until the Norse settlements of the later first millennium AD. Important changes can certainly be observed in the settlement sequence, notably from the 'monumental' phase of architecture, represented by brochs or 'complex Atlantic roundhouses', into the non-monumental period of building represented by 'cellular' and related structures. But there is no clear archaeological evidence to associate this progression with any radical change in population or culture. For these regions, therefore, it makes sense archaeologically to consider the 'long' Iron Age, in which 'early' represents a span of time that in Southern Britain would cover the whole of the pre-Roman Iron Age, and 'late' is applied to the first millennium AD from around its second quarter. Some authorities have preferred to adopt the threefold system of early, middle and late Iron Ages, in which the 'middle' component almost invariably constrains the occupation of brochs to a limited span of two or three centuries around the turn of the millennium. Partly because of that artificial constraint on the dating of Atlantic roundhouses and their antecedents, the simple division between 'early' and 'late' is here preferred. There is, however, at present no universally accepted scheme, and the date-spans offered by different authorities differ quite significantly. In any event, with the now routine application of radiometric dating, and a shift away from the older cultural-historical paradigm, complex classifications are no longer a priority of archaeological synthesis. On these grounds alone, the simplest and most flexible system is probably to be preferred.

In the eastern lowlands of Scotland a simple early–late division of the Iron Age will serve, so long as we recognise that not all changes in field monument or artefact types need have been synchronous, and that these changes may still have taken place within an essential framework of continuity. Field monuments such as souterrains, popularly regarded in their classic stone-built form as Pictish, are largely abandoned in eastern Scotland by the third century, though elsewhere in Scotland and Atlantic Europe they may have a longer currency. Continuity of settlement, despite disruptions, was almost certainly a keystone of the archaeology of southern Scotland and the Borders too. In the post-Roman centuries these regions were not immune from external influences or even intrusive settlement, but unlike the later Norse settlements, these are not so readily distinguishable, in terms of distinctive settlements and burials or diagnostic material types, from the native communities with which they interacted. Claims may be made for recognising innovative settlement types among the Anglian settlers of south-eastern Scotland, but in the west it is generally recognised that the historically recorded Gaelic settlement of Dalriadic Scots is very hard to equate with any innovative class of archaeological evidence, structural or material. It would thus be very hard to exclude consideration of these areas in the first millennium AD from any discussion of the Iron Age in Northern Britain. In southern Scotland as in northern England the Roman period may stand as the interface between 'earlier' and 'later' Iron Ages.

A starting date for the Iron Age around the seventh or sixth centuries BC is just as arbitrary as any historically derived horizon, and could lead to an interminable and ultimately fruitless debate regarding the beginnings of iron technology and when it impacted significantly upon communities in later prehistory. The origins of iron technology in Europe can certainly be traced back to the second millennium BC, with significant occurrences of iron artefacts in the Urnfield culture of the later Bronze Age in Central and Western Europe. For Britain, and more especially for Northern Britain, the incidence of iron artefacts or evidence of iron working is extremely limited, so much so that less than forty years ago the eminent Roman archaeologist Eric Birley was still proclaiming the view, which his tutor R. G. Collingwood had espoused, that the Bronze Age in northern England had continued uninterrupted down to the Roman conquest. As a label of convenience the point at which Northern British prehistory becomes 'Iron Age' in any meaningful sense hardly matters. But as an indication of the level of control that Iron Age communities could exercise over resources, some locally available but others necessitating longer-distance communications and access to supplies, the presence or absence of metalworking and its products may be an important measure of power or wealth. Students of the Iron Age in Northern Britain habitually refer to the presence on settlement sites of copper or bronze working as an index of social status, only very occasionally discussing the role of metalworking or metalworkers within the social hierarchy. Limited though the evidence may be, knowledge of iron technology was probably current in Northern Britain from around the mid-first millennium BC or slightly earlier, as in Southern Britain. So the term 'Iron Age' here is shorthand for a period of a thousand years and more, from at least the mid-first millennium BC to the later first millennium AD.

The structure of the following chapters, therefore, is based essentially on a broad division, justified on archaeological grounds wherever possible, between the earlier Iron Age and later Iron Age, the comparative adjectives being used simply to underscore the essential continuity of settlement. Between the two is a consideration of the Roman interlude, and its impact upon those limited regions of Northern Britain upon which it registered. In most treatments of the 'long' Iron Age, an astonishing methodological volte-face is performed by archaeologists as they move from the earlier Iron Age to the later Iron Age. Having treated the former in anonymous, sub-Childean cultural terms, they turn without explanation to discuss the later Iron Age communities of Scotland and northern England as Picts, Angles, Britons and Scots in the context of named kings, named sites and dated events, all derived from documentary sources, as if the archaeology had suddenly been relegated to a supporting role in amplifying recorded history. It is not my purpose in challenging this long-established practice to deny the value of documentary sources, nor indeed of linguistic, numismatic, onamastic or epigraphic sources, in reaching a better understanding of early societies. I do, however, object to the tacit assumption that documentary sources are in some way more reliable than archaeological evidence, particularly where the two might be in apparent conflict, and to the implication that history as a discipline is more rigorous in its methodology than is archaeology. In attempting to articulate its theoretical principles beyond the 'common sense' paradigm, archaeology may have engulfed itself in a morass of jargon and some pretentious and vacuous writing, but its basic principles for evaluating artefacts in context have been long established, and are as fundamental as those used by historians in evaluating their documents. One of the attractions of archaeology is its inter-disciplinary character, and the relevance of related disciplines, including history, in the social, economic and cognitive reconstruction of past communities should be an asset rather than a liability. But these sources too must be subjected to the methodological scrutiny of the discipline concerned, and not simply used as a basis for unsupported assertion, as too often are ethnographic or theoretical models derived from other disciplines when used by archaeologists.

The geographical context

If our chronological parameters have necessarily to remain flexible, what of our geographical limits? Since the Act of Union, Northern Britain has been a euphemism for Scotland, but in the present context that political border makes no archaeological sense, and plainly our remit must also include parts of northern England, at least for the pre-Roman period. Crucially relevant is the territory assigned in documentary records to the Brigantes, whether or not this proves archaeologically to be a meaningful entity. Archaeological distributions show a divide between coin-using societies in southern England and their non coin-using neighbours to the north, and might support a provisional boundary somewhere along the Trent, and looping around the southern Pennines towards the Wirral peninsula. It would be absurd to exclude Yorkshire, Durham and Northumberland on the one hand, or Lancashire and Cumbria, however intractable its Iron Age has hitherto proved, on the other, from any treatment of Northern Britain in the Iron Age. For the period of the Roman occupation, and more especially for any consideration of the question of 'Romanisation', these regions will also be crucial. For the post-Roman period, on the other hand, it is necessary to impose some limitations, and it is not here proposed to extend into a consideration, for example, of Anglian northern England, except in so far as it intrudes into the native 'British' areas of southern Scotland.

In view of the importance of the Irish Sea as a means of communication with other regions of Atlantic Europe, it follows that our study should include the Isle of Man, too frequently neglected in studies of the British Iron Age. A major programme of excavation was achieved during the Second World War by Gerhard Bersu, the excavator of Little Woodbury in the late 1930s and of Traprain Law among other Scottish Iron Age sites in the immediately post-war years, whilst he was interned there as an alien. But the Isle of Man has not featured prominently in British Iron Age studies in more recent years. North of Hadrian's Wall Piggott (1966) extended Hawkes' (1959) scheme of provinces and regions to include Tyne–Forth, Solway–Clyde, North-Eastern and Atlantic Provinces, a model which has proved remarkably resilient. Its most obvious limitation was its apparent presumption that major rivers and estuaries formed cultural boundaries, rather than serving potentially to unite the communities on opposite shores. Whilst this might be challenged in the cases of the Tyne, Forth, Solway and Clyde, it must be acknowledged that the communities who could see each other's shores across the Moray Firth show archaeologically very little evidence of inter-communication. A second limitation of Piggott's scheme was that it effectively ignored Perthshire and the significant distribution of crannogs and land-based duns of the central Highlands. The unity or diversity of Atlantic Scotland as a cultural province will also need to be examined in due course.

In fact, we should hardly expect any static scheme of geographical provinces to serve as a means of articulating the dynamic processes of cultural progression over a millennium or more. Necessity demands some division of the material for convenience of discussion, but the option preferred here is drawn from the basic geological and physiographical divisions of Scotland, which, unlike northern England, create broadly diagonal zones across the landmass. The geological zones of the Midland Valley and the Southern Uplands themselves evidently include subtle regional variables which will locally have affected settlement patterns, whilst climatic variables between east and west introduce further factors that will have impinged upon settlement. Over time, too, patterns of human settlement will have been subject to dynamic change for a variety of reasons, not least those imposed by human rather than environmental constraints. Nevertheless, these broad divisions may be preferred in the presentation and evaluation of the archaeological data for want of other, more compelling regional groupings.

The nature of the archaeological evidence

Archaeological evidence can be divided into three broad categories. *Artefacts* are represented by material remains such as pottery, personal ornaments, weapons or tools. *Sites*, including fortifications, domestic buildings or tombs, might also be regarded as artefacts on a larger, non-portable scale. A third category, *ecofacts*, include environmental evidence of, or relevant to, human occupation. The Iron Age in Northern Britain could be characterised as site-dominated, that is to say that the classification and interpretation of the evidence has been largely based upon field monuments – hillforts, homesteads, brochs, long-cist cemeteries or whatever – rather than by artefact assemblages. Accordingly prehistorians have written about the 'Castle Complex', the 'Hownam Culture' or the 'Arras Culture', but never of a cultural grouping designated by a material type. The point is not simply semantic, because the choice of definitive trait also determines the significant thresholds for interpretation. What is taken to matter in Atlantic Scotland, for example, is when monumentality in broch construction gives way to non-monumental cellular building, not when a given style of pottery or metal type is replaced by another, which may not be a coterminous event at all. Environmental archaeology has likewise always been subordinated to a supporting role. No one has yet proposed a classification of the Northern British Iron Age based on the 'Spelt wheat Zone' as opposed to the 'Barley Zone', though this distinction might be argued as having as great a significance as have differences in structural types.

The relative abundance of settlement sites, however, tends to obscure the fact that those that survive archaeologically may represent only part of the original settlement spectrum. Monumental stone forts and brochs have an obvious durability, as have any settlements with upstanding earthwork enclosures. Even where these have been obliterated by generations of agriculture, earthworks may be traced through air-photography. Yet archaeologically arbitrary development such as road construction continues to expose sites, the ephemeral nature of which has left no trace on the surface or from the air. Discussions of the social hierarchy of brochs, duns and wheelhouses in Atlantic Scotland, or presumptions of a 'trend towards enclosure' in the lowlands and Borders, may be based upon only a very partial selection of evidence that happens to have survived. Factors affecting survival may be many, not least the building materials used and the method of construction, but the dice of survival is obviously loaded against sites that have no enclosing works, or which may have been occupied seasonally or temporarily, or with buildings lacking substantial or earth-fast foundations.

Similar strictures could be applied to funerary sites. Archaeologists, vexed by the absence of formal cemeteries for much of the Iron Age in Northern Britain, resort to explanations that would leave no archaeological trace, such as cremation and scattering, as a possible dominant rite. But where there is an identifiable rite, such as the square-ditched barrow cemeteries of eastern Yorkshire, this is assumed to be the norm rather than just one selective mode of disposal. Chariot burials are regarded as high-status tombs, while burials that have minimal grave-goods are tacitly assumed to be of lesser status. Given their numbers, Arras cemeteries plainly come closer to a 'norm' than most Iron Age burials. But they might still represent a selective section of society, and other rites of disposal like cremation and scattering might still have been the regular practice for a significant part of the population. In earlier prehistory, long barrows and chambered tombs are widely accepted as a standard means of burial, notwithstanding the fact that the total known numbers could not accommodate more than a fraction of the total population of the Neolithic. If it is accepted that they were a very particular form of élite burial within a wider spectrum of practices then it follows that the norm has still to be identified archaeologically. As ritual and ceremonial monuments it is possible that disposal of the dead was not even their primary purpose, but just one of the associated rites.

Artefacts too are subject to differential survival, depending upon what they are made of and the matrix and circumstances in which they were deposited. The contrast between the material assemblages from the land-based and underwater excavations of the island dun and its associated structures at Loch Bharabhat in west Lewis (Harding and Dixon, 2000) was striking and instructive. Pottery survived from both land and underwater contexts in broadly equal measure, but it was only in the anaerobic conditions underwater that organic artefacts and materials survived, including a range of domestic utensils that seldom survive on dry-land sites. Perishable materials such as wood, leather or textiles were evidently used as containers and for other purposes, doubtless throughout the Northern British Iron Age. From dry-land contexts at Dun Bharabhat by contrast no bone survived, so that stone artefacts and pottery were virtually the only indicators of domestic culture. In fact, the range and quality of ceramics in the Iron Age of Atlantic Scotland, by contrast to most other regions of Northern Britain and Ireland, which are virtually aceramic, is remarkable. In other parts of the Old World, aceramic cultures are hardly known in societies as advanced as those of the Iron Age, so that the contrast in Northern Britain demands some explanation.

In contrasting the Iron Age material assemblages of the British Isles (and of Ireland) with those of Continental Europe we should remember that the better-preserved and more distinctive Continental assemblages are derived from *cemeteries* rather than from settlement sites. Not only are the prospects of survival of intact artefacts in graves far greater than in domestic contexts, but it is also possible that grave-goods were in other respects special or different from those in domestic circulation. The apparent poverty of material assemblages from Britain, including Northern Britain, in contrast to those of Continental Europe may therefore reflect the contrasting contexts of deposition rather than cultural isolation from the presumed 'mainstream' of Continental Europe.

Archaeologists by convention order their sites and artefacts into classes or types as the first step in the process of interpretation. There is nothing fundamentally wrong with this procedure, since it enables the evidence to be examined, like with like, and spatial distributions to be compared and contrasted. The problem arises in the subjective assessment of likeness, and determining which traits are important in making meaningful comparisons. At the level of defining cultural assemblages, attempts have been made in the past to distinguish between *descriptive* types, those basic structural or artefactual types that are characteristic of the cultural group under examination, but which may equally be common to several or many different cultures, and *diagnostic* types, that is, those which are exclusive to a particular cultural group, and therefore uniquely proclaim its presence. The latter are obviously in one sense more useful than the former, in that they are strictly definitive. But the definition of a cultural group should nevertheless embrace a combination of the two, since the diagnostic types may be so specific as to be less commonly represented in the cultural assemblage as whole. Typological classification can become a straitjacket, however, a construct of what scholarship at one point in time regards as important. In broch studies in particular, the emphasis in the past was almost exclusively on architectural typology, to which the complexities of plan and construction were particularly amenable.

The cultural model developed by Gordon Childe quite expressly assumed that archaeological distributions, defined by recurrent structural or artefactual types, should be coterminous with prehistoric ethnic groups or historically recognised populations. In practice population dynamics and interaction with neighbouring groups over time would obscure any simplistic patterning, even if the cultural model were tenable in principle. It is then perhaps surprising that, for Northern Britain, archaeologists can still express concern at the absence of distinctive structural or artefactual types within the assumed territory of historically inferred settlement of Dál Riata from the fifth century AD or thereabouts. In Alcock's much-quoted phrase, they apparently came without luggage, so that there is no diagnostic Dál Riata distribution. This is hardly surprising, of course, considering that they seem to have no diagnostic luggage in their homeland of origin, which is not to say that there were no significant social or political groupings in Northern Ireland from which the alleged settlers derived. It might, on the other hand, suggest that the settlement of Dál Riata was not so much a demographic movement as the estab-lishment of a ruling political élite, or indeed that the historical record was a metaphor for the culmination of a process of cross-channel inter-action that had been in progress over many generations.

Within Northern Britain there are certainly some regional distributions that can be distinguished archaeologically, though it is arguable whether any would have lived up to Childe's requirement of recurrent associations. The square-ditched barrow cemeteries of eastern Yorkshire accord most closely to the model, but even here it is one type that dominates, with associated material types regularly represented that are not exclusive to the region. Brochs, or Atlantic roundhouses, are certainly distinctive of the Atlantic north and west, but the ceramic assemblages of the Northern and Western Isles reflect independent local fashions, so that cultural unity across the Atlantic province would be hard to sustain. With the aid of place-names it might be possible to identify a 'Pictish' territory in eastern Scotland, but its correlation with archaeological types and distributions is far from straightforward.

In addition to diagnostic and descriptive artefacts, a third category of *exotic* types has been identified (Clarke, 1971), the value of which as cultural or chronological indicators has perhaps been over-rated in the past. Samian pottery or E-ware of the sixth century AD are exotic, in that they are not indigenous products but foreign imports, and may assist in dating the context in which they are found because their own chronology is more reliably established. In a different sense, prestige items, especially unique artefacts, may be regarded as exotic, but their value archaeologically may be limited in that, despite their intrinsic interest, they are hardly typical of a community at large. Unfortunately, exotic items of either kind may have been treasured and curated over many generations, and the 'heirloom factor' is still much debated, especially where individual finds rather than widespread distributions are concerned.

Aspects of environmental change

Most archaeological studies of post-glacial environmental change in Northern Britain concentrate understandably upon the geomorphological changes in the Late Glacial and Early Holocene, and in particular the effects of isostatic uplift and eustatic sea-level rise between *c.* 9000 and 6000 BP. It is generally assumed that these processes would have slowed down by the Neolithic, and would have stabilised by the Iron Age. Even so, there is evidence of continuing effects of some consequence in various parts of Northern Britain, from the Humber estuary or the Mersey (Tooley, 1974) to the Northern and Western Isles (Ritchie, W., 1985). In the Western Isles sea-level rise since the Neolithic has been estimated as being up to 5 metres, with major consequences for the western coastal settlements of the southern islands. Elsewhere marine incursion may have continued to erode the coastline as late as the Norse period. Within the Calanais area of north-west Lewis, for example, sub-peat field boundaries that may still have been in use in the first millennium BC extend today into the waters of Loch Ceann Hulavig, suggesting that a later prehistoric agricultural landscape may have been flooded by marine incursion as late as the Iron Age. For the Northern and Western Isles, therefore, establishing the extent of the land-mass available for settlement and evaluating continuing changes in coastal geomorphology are essential prerequisites to an informed understanding of Iron Age settlement patterns.

A major factor affecting the land available for settlement in Northern Britain is the spread of blanket peat, the extension of which is induced by a wetter environment, but which cannot be correlated simply with climatic deterioration, still less with a single horizon of climatic deterioration. The spread of peat demonstrably took place in different regions and localities at different rates, and for a variety of different environmental and anthropogenic factors. In parts of northern and western Scotland areas formerly under cultivation were evidently abandoned, the soils becoming waterlogged and encouraging peat growth at a relatively early stage, in others as late as the first millennium BC or into the first millennium AD. The Neolithic fields at Scord of Brewster on Shetland (Whittle et al., 1986) were subsequently engulfed by peat growth, though whether as a result of local pedological and hydrological factors, perhaps triggered by cultivation practices themselves, or of their abandonment, remains arguable. By the first millennium BC wider climatic changes eventually induced the concentration of later settlement within the coastal regions of Shetland. In the Western Isles, peat expansion in some areas was evidently quite late, resulting in a similar coastal distribution of Iron Age settlement. At Borve, north Lewis, the broch is now isolated in a peatland landscape, its foundations and presumably any associated agricultural landscape buried in more than a metre of peat growth since the Iron Age.

Ambient temperature and length of ripening season would also have been significant factors in the viability of cultivation in antiquity. Length of growing season may not have been a serious constraint in north-eastern England (van der Veen, 1992), but in the Western Isles it must have brought cereal cultivation much closer to the borders of marginality. The abandonment of Bronze Age agricultural landscapes in upland Perthshire, and perhaps even of cord-rig cultivation in the Border hills, has been taken as evidence of a climatic deterioration towards the end of the Bronze Age, and this deterioration, though part of a more complex picture than once supposed, is still widely accepted. The quality of soils themselves, and the extent to which Iron Age communities were actively engaged in manuring and soil improvement, are plainly important considerations. Modern assessments of soil quality, relative to arable production or rough pasture, have limited applicability to conditions in the Iron Age, in which different subsistence requirements and a lower level of agricultural technology may have made viable areas of land that would not be amenable to modern farming. The survival of Mediaeval and earlier agricultural landscapes, in parts of northern England and northern and western Scotland that are now rated as suitable only for rough grazing, is adequate testimony to this point.

Among the more dominant environmental issues of relevance to the Iron Age in Northern Britain are the twin questions of forest or woodland clearance and its concomitant, the intensification or more accurately the 'extensification' of agriculture. Various episodes of forest clearance and regeneration have been identified for different periods since the Neolithic in Northern Britain. The Western Isles are generally regarded as a treeless landscape, apart from limited areas of coppice, from an early date, though pine stumps still visible in the peatlands stand testimony to former forests. The range of dispersal of tree pollen in the prevailing south-westerlies of the Western Isles makes palynological absence an uncertain criterion, and it is quite probable that timber resources were carefully managed, for example, in smaller, sheltered locations along the east coast of Lewis and Harris. On the other hand, the clear evidence for re-use of North American or Scandinavian driftwood (Church, 2002) indicates that no source of supply could be neglected. South-west Scotland and north-western England on the other hand may have been substantially forested throughout the Iron Age, though modern research suggests that extensive forest clearance and extensification of agriculture in northern England preceded the Roman occupation (van der Veen, 1992). Though doubtless the Roman frontier armies would have placed additional demands upon the native population for grain supplies, therefore, we should not automatically link this historic context with any observed increase in agricultural production.

Van der Veen's research has highlighted some of the methodological problems in the study of cereal pollen, plant macro-fossils and plant species as indicators of agricultural regimes. There may still be problems in the identification of cultivated and wild cereals, especially in small quantities, and more recent work on samples from well-preserved environments in the Western Isles suggests that there may yet be issues of taxonomy to be resolved. More especially, however, questions relating to site taphonomy and what stage in the production process samples represent have qualified any simplistic interpretation of the evidence. Not only is it necessary to recognise which stage is represented in order to validate inter-site comparisons, but recognising the nature of the assemblage is essential to determining whether the community was cereal-producing or simply a consumer of grain produced elsewhere. What survives from most archaeological sites is commonly fireside waste, which may be indicative only of secondary preparation of foodstuffs. Cereal analyses nevertheless have indicated a significant contrast between Iron Age practice in northern England and Scotland. Spelt wheat, which widely replaced emmer in Southern Britain from the late Bronze Age, was evidently introduced into north-eastern England shortly thereafter, and was widely represented before the end of the pre-Roman Iron Age. Scotland, especially in the Atlantic north and west, remained a barley monoculture throughout the Iron Age. Whether the reasons for this contrast were environmental or cultural is an issue that will need to be addressed as research progresses.

Faunal analysis until recent years was too often limited to a simple list of species present, perhaps with relative percentages, though these were not always reliably determined by an agreed methodology. This has been characterised as the 'so they ate sheep, then' approach, since that was about the extent of the contribution to an understanding of the faunal economy. As with the study of cereals and plant macro-fossils, the environmental archaeologist has too frequently been expected to salvage insights retrospectively from arbitrarily recovered assemblages, rather than having an input into excavation strategy from the outset. One of the major problems in reconstructing the Iron Age economic base in Northern Britain is assessing the relative importance of agriculture and pastoralism. Both may be evidenced in site assemblages, and, without succumbing to Piggott's 'Celtic cowboys' model, we may still incline towards a belief in the predominance of pastoralism. How communities managed their stock or distributed the products, however, remains largely unclear, though occasionally it may be possible to see hints of differential distribution of collective resources. In west Lewis the high percentage of red deer at Beirgh and Cnip, matched in Great Bernera at Bostadh, contrasts with the dominance of cattle at Dun Vulan in the south. In fact it seems possible that the Lewis communities collectively managed wild herds to a greater degree than was hitherto imagined. What is abundantly clear is that the local Iron Age population was well provided for by a range of different resource options, some of which were hardly exploited at all. The absence of shell-fish and the predominance of inshore species among the fish-bones from sites in the Western Isles suggest that there was no need to venture into boats for deeper water fishing, which even until recent times was abundantly accessible to small boats. Contrary to the image of marginal subsistence, enhanced by the depression of Highland and Island communities under a harsher regime of land-ownership in more recent times, the archaeological evidence for the Iron Age in Atlantic Scotland indicates a sound economic basis with a diversity of potential resources.

Taphonomy and retrieval

Taphonomy, or the study of the nature of archaeological deposition and its interpretation, is crucial to any meaningful reconstruction of past societies. Unless interpretation, whether technological, economic, social or cognitive, is based upon a rigorous evaluation of the evidence and its context, it can never be more than creative fiction, an exercise in theo-retical reconstruction divorced from the archaeological data-base. This is not to suppose that there is such a thing as objective archaeological 'fact' that is not in some measure prejudiced by the research strategy or subjective observation of the archaeologist. However accurately observed or recorded, *what* we observe or choose to record will inevitably be selective from the infinite data-resource, according to the questions that we bring to the investigation. Each generation of archaeologists has its own agenda of questions, and there need be no *a priori* assumption that a more recent agenda invalidates or supersedes an earlier one, though it might be expected to refine or qualify earlier agendas.

A simplistic popular misconception is that archaeology, notably through excavation, provides an insight into everyday life of past societies, an archaeological 'window on the Iron Age' to parallel that opened up by documentary history. In practice there can be very few instances in which excavation affords such a window on everyday life in the past: a settlement engulfed by volcanic eruption or a shipwreck in deep water might be examples. Otherwise what survives for the archaeologist to uncover is at best only as much as ancient communities chose to leave behind when a site was abandoned, and even that residual assemblage will have been diminished by the effects of environmental erosion and material deterioration. To assume that whatever material assemblage is found within the confines of a building represents the cultural assemblage of the occupants, and that it may be used to infer the activities in which they were engaged, without reference to the circumstances in which those deposits were laid down, risks serious misrepresentation of the evidence.

Stratigraphy is plainly fundamental in ensuring that a sequence of occupational episodes is accurately distinguished, but taphomony is equally crucial in determining whether deposits may reasonably be regarded as associated, redeposited or residual, whether representative of primary or secondary episodes of activity. Such principles may be regarded as so elementary as to be unworthy of repetition, though study of even modern, professional excavation reports might suggest the contrary. Obtaining a suite of radiocarbon dates is no substitute for stratigraphic excavation, indeed would be a wasted resource without it.

Unfortunately on many upland sites in Northern Britain surviving stratigraphy is minimal, as indeed may be the material assemblage. As we shall see, dating of early Iron Age settlements in northern England in particular has long been inhibited by the lack of associated artefacts, and by, for example, an over-dependence on a scrap of samian from a secondary context. By contrast, some settlements in the Northern and Western Isles display long site sequences, in the case of Beirgh, west Lewis or Old Scatness, Shetland, spanning as much as a thousand years. In some instances it may be clear that early excavators failed to distinguished between primary and secondary occupation, in terms of both structural and artefactual remains. In other instances the secondary phases of occupation may have been so slightly built by comparison to the monumental Atlantic roundhouses that their ephemeral walls were easily confused with collapsed debris from the primary structures.

Where site sequences have been recognised, this is almost invariably through structural changes, either in the enclosing palisades and earthworks of hillforts or in the super-imposed remains of successive house foundations. In the case of enclosed settlements, it is then too often assumed that the sequence of enclosure must correlate with the occupational sequence within, overlooking the possibility of intervals of occupation in which the enclosure works were not maintained. Similarly, there is a natural inclination for archaeologists to assume that changes in material culture will accord with major changes in the structural sequence of a settlement. At Beirgh, for example, there are four major building horizons, broch, roundhouse, cellular buildings and finally a figure-of-eight structure. During this sequence there are also significant changes in pottery styles, and possibly in other artefact types. But there need be no presumption that these changes were coterminous with the structural changes, nor indeed that the site sequence is best described and interpreted in terms of the structural sequence, rather than in terms of the artefactual sequence.

Even assuming a site's stratigraphy to be reasonably clear, which is seldom the case on Iron Age settlements, identifying the nature of individual deposits can be contentious. A thick deposit of organic material containing potsherds and abundant animal bone may be classified as an occupational deposit, but this hardly explains its presence within a domestic building. Are we really to imagine that the occupants wallowed ankle-deep in malodorous domestic refuse, or is it not more likely that this represents accumulated midden material introduced when the building was still upstanding, but as a roofless ruin? Does the presence of crucible and mould fragments indicate metalworking *in situ*, or in the absence of other industrial debris, must we conclude that this material was introduced from elsewhere? If so, what was the nature of this deposit, and is it reliably associated with any specific structural or chronological horizon? What actually constitutes a floor level in such settlements? Areas of paving, or the foundations of a hearth, may indicate the level of a floor surface, but these are not invariably present and certainly not necessarily uniform in composition or extent.

Attempts have been made in recent years to interpret activity areas within settlement structures on the basis of artefact distributions, focussing attention directly on the taphonomic issue (LaMotta and Schiffer, 1999). Distributional concentrations in pottery sherds and other artefacts have been interpreted as evidence of functional divisions between working areas and sleeping or storage areas of house interiors; but everything depends upon the context of the artefacts, since the distribution may reflect survival patterns rather than patterns of activity. Residual material, incorporated into the core of wall-fillings, constructional post-packing or in floor foundations, plainly has no bearing on the actual occupation and use of the building. Deposition during the principal occupation of a building, whether through deliberate deposit, casual discard or unretrieved loss, would have an obvious relevance to our interpretation of that occupation, but if the building was periodically cleaned, this primary material might well be removed. Where the occupational surface is founded on or near to bedrock, as is the case in many upland sites, primary deposits are likely to have been obliterated by generations of secondary occupation. The life-cycle of a building need not end with the termination of its primary function. 'Post-abandonment' use could take a variety of forms, most obviously for ancillary activities or simply as dumps, which may result in significant perturbation of earlier deposits. Recent research at Cladh Hallan and elsewhere in South Uist, using advanced techniques of sampling with a view to demonstrating the differential spatial use of buildings along the lines put forward by Fitzpatrick (1994) for Southern Britain, has demonstrated the crucial importance of distinguishing between occupational and post-abandonment deposits. The conclusion of one recent study (Young, M., 2002) was that artefactual distribution had very little direct correlation with the functional use of space, which was more likely to leave traces in terms of micro-refuse or more especially in physical and chemical signatures in the soil. A similar conclusion regarding micro-refuse seems to be implied by the evidence from Old Scatness, where a lack of correlation between the date of construction of buildings and the deposits filling them suggested thorough clearing of material at the end of the building's use.

Northern Britain in Ancient Europe

Childe's *The Prehistory of Scotland* of 1935 was the first major synthesis of the Scottish evidence since Anderson's half a century earlier, and it began a resurgence in the 'European' view of Scottish prehistory which had been espoused by Daniel Wilson, Robert Munro and John Abercromby. Following Childe in the Abercromby chair at Edinburgh University, Piggott certainly saw this as the beginning of a new enlightenment after a prolonged Dark Age of introspective isolation:

> Scottish archaeology, after the brilliant lead given by such as Anderson, Munro, Abercromby and James Curle, had moved into a distressing period of isolation. Excavation and field techniques were at a shockingly low level, and out of touch with contemporary developments south of the Border, while comparative studies were similarly stultified and parochial. This led to an unfortunate climate of thought prevailing, in which Scottish prehistory was regarded as something *sui generis*, inaccessible and strange, couched in a secret language of broch and wag, weem and dun, and not to be regarded as part of the wider British scene. Too often English distribution maps were made which faded out around the line of Hadrian's Wall, and the uncritical acceptance as an immutable law of Fox's generalised thesis . . . of a Highland and Lowland Zone, led inevitably to the relegation of Scotland as a peripheral area, so retarded chronologically and culturally as to render it an Ultima Thule without significance to the main stream of British or European prehistory.
>
> (Piggott, S., 1966: 2)

Re-reading this passage, and especially its final sentence, we might be forgiven for wondering whether the greater parochialism lay north or south of the Border. So pleased was Piggott with the rhetorical cadences of this assessment, however, that he quoted its main thrust verbatim in a retrospective review nearly twenty years later (Piggott, S., 1983: 5). In fact, much as the extract above may have amused an Edinburgh New Town dinner party in the 1960s it hardly stands up to detailed scrutiny. First of all, Anderson stood for the 'nationalistic' viewpoint that archaeology, like charity, should begin at home, and to that extent represented the opposite opinion to that of Munro and Abercromby. Second, we might wonder who were the models of enlightened excavation practice and field techniques south of the Border in the opening decades of the twentieth century? Field standards between Pitt-Rivers and Wheeler south of the Border left much to be desired, as they did in Scotland.

For Piggott the charge of parochialism was, of course, implicit in the idea that Scottish prehistory could in any aspect be *sui generis*. Nowadays such a notion would not excite condemnation. With the decline in diffusionism as a universal explanation of culture change, independent development is regularly seen as a likely process governing settlement patterns and cultural fashions. This is not to regard Scottish prehistory as isolated or insulated from developments elsewhere, merely to avoid the assumption that innovation could only be triggered as a result of external impulses, such impulses invariably in the earlier twentieth century being seen as transmitted from regions further south, with a Continental 'mainstream' beyond. Today the concept of Scotland in Ancient Europe, to parody a political slogan, can accommodate relationships, unilateral or reciprocal, between Scottish prehistory and neighbouring regions without denying the distinctive and sometimes unique character of the Scottish evidence.

Diffusionism was fundamental to Piggott's generation, and is graphically represented in Robert Stevenson's map of Iron Age metalwork in Scotland (Stevenson, R. B. K., 1966: Fig. 2), in which arrows bringing immigrants or mobile artefacts remind one of the maps produced by the hyper-diffusionists of the early twentieth century. Diffusionism as an explanation of culture change frequently carried with it the corollary of time-lag, allowing several generations or even centuries for ideas to be transmitted from core to periphery. This concept was implicit in Fox's Highland/Lowland geographical model, summarised in his well-known dictum that in the lowlands of Britain, south and east of the Jurassic Ridge, new cultures were *imposed*, whereas in the Highlands new cultures were *absorbed* (Fox, 1932/38: 34).

In the diffusionist model it was axiomatic that Mediterranean and Middle Eastern societies represented the cradle of civilisation, in relation to which north-west Europe in general and Northern Britain in particular were peripheral and culturally retarded. European prehistory was seen essentially in terms of the sequence of Urnfield Bronze Age through Hallstatt to La Tène Iron Age, itself underpinned by contacts with the Mediterranean world. The Central European bias was further reinforced by the dependence for establishing a chronological framework on contact with the more securely dated cultures of the Mediterranean world, with which at second or third hand, and with due allowance for time-lag, the Iron Age of north-western Europe and Britain might be linked through citing 'parallels' in material culture. With the advent of absolute dating techniques, and no longer dependent upon typological analogies, the relationship between Atlantic Europe and Central or Northern Europe on the one hand, and the Mediterranean on the other, can be reviewed afresh, without any presumption of priority in the nature of those inter-relationships.

For Northern Britain, external communication by sea was as important as contact over-land, and in particular the western seaways seem likely to have served as a major artery of contact between Scotland, Ireland, western Britain and Brittany, with longer distance networks beyond that. Pytheas the Greek (Hawkes, 1977; Cunliffe, 2001) was surely not the only adventurer who sailed these western waters, and we may expect that sea-borne communication, whether by short coastal networks or longer ocean-going expeditions, must have been the norm over much of prehistory and into the early historic centuries. Prevailing weather conditions doubtless made such ventures seasonal, and climatic deterioration or volcanic traumas may have curtailed such activities for prolonged periods. Recognising such communications archaeologically has always proved controversial. Comparisons between the brochs and duns of Atlantic Scotland and the stone-built cashels of south-western Ireland are superficially attractive, just as, in a much earlier period, the practice of communal burial in megalithic tombs prompts obvious comparisons between Brittany, Ireland, Scotland and western Britain. Yet in both cases detailed analysis suggests quite independent regional development. On the other hand, fragments of E-ware or Continental glass from sites in south-west Scotland and Ireland in the seventh century AD are actual imports, testifying to direct or secondary contacts along the western seaways. Whether these contacts resulted in actual migration, or the annexation of one region by the ruling élites of another, is hard to argue on archaeological evidence alone. But the archaeological evidence might cause us to qualify received assumptions, based upon historical documents, whose cryptic records might easily compress into a single symbolic episode a more complex process that in reality was accomplished over a longer period of time.

Archaeology and history

For an older generation of archaeologists, trained in history or classics, archaeology was naturally regarded as an extension of the discipline of history into the preliterate ancient past. R. G. Collingwood had famously described archaeology as the 'handmaid of history', and this remained the prevailing view until the dawn of the 'New Archaeology' in the late 1960s. Christopher Hawkes (1948) certainly believed that archaeology was a branch of historical scholarship, and had no hesitation in declaring that it was not a subject in its own right, but belonged within the broader disciplinary framework of history. Neither Collingwood nor Hawkes would have implied that archaeology was any less rigorous methodologically than history, however, though their research questions inevitably were coloured by their historical perspective.

Archaeology is sometimes described as *text-aided* or *text-free*, depending upon whether the period under review is one for which documentary sources are available. The terms are slightly ambiguous, the one implying that the presence of documentary sources is an asset, the other perhaps suggesting that the archaeologist, liberated from the constraints of historical evidence, is free to indulge his own theoretical perspectives. Archaeological evidence and historical sources are complementary, but should each be evaluated according to the criteria of their respective disciplines. As Hachmann (1976) argued in the context of the presumed Belgic invasion of south-eastern Britain, apparently alluded to by Caesar, 'solving a specifically archaeological problem by reasoning directly from a literary source is never a correct procedure. Conversely, a problem posed specifically by literary sources can have no satisfactory solution through arguments based exclusively on archaeological material.' The archaeology of Northern Britain, especially of the first millennium AD, has been substantially *text-led*, with the evidence of archaeology forced to comply with the historical agenda. Why are symbol-stones always described as *Pictish* symbol-stones? Is their ethnic origin proclaimed on the carvings themselves? Do documentary sources ever claim that Picts carved stones? The association between symbol-stones and Picts was made by Daniel Wilson (1851), and was only very belatedly adopted by Joseph Anderson (1881; Allen and Anderson, 1903), who rightly recognised the unsubstantiated nature of the equation.

There could be no clearer demonstration of the subordination of archaeology to recorded history than Wheeler's (1954) identification of the Stanwick fortifications in north Yorkshire as the site of Venutius' resistance against Rome, based upon Tacitus' account of events in the third quarter of the first century AD. Archaeological evidence for the dating of the presumed structural sequence was tenuous at best, but it was the dating and explanation of Site H, the supposed southern entrance of Phase 3, that is solely dependent upon the historical connection. Discovering that there was no causeway between ditch terminals, which is the invariable hallmark of an Iron Age entrance, nor any trace of structures in timber or stone flanking the entrance passage, the excavator concluded improbably that the work of construction was halted by a sudden emergency, and the causeway dug away in a makeshift attempt at securing the defences. But what could have been this emergency? Given the total absence of dateable artefacts from any part of the Phase 3 enclosure, the entire interpretation hinged upon matching a structural anomaly of doubtful archaeological authenticity with the historical record. Following Tacitus, Wheeler chose the campaign of AD 71–74 initiated by the governor Petillius Cerialis against Venutius and the Brigantes as the crucial crisis, and advanced his interpretation, not as a tentative hypothesis, but as self-evident fact.

> The inference from all this is scarcely in doubt. During the cutting and building of the principal surviving entrance . . . a sudden alarm stopped the work. As an emergency measure, the causeway was cut away, so that the ends of the unfinished ditches were joined up, thus isolating the intended gateway and turning it into a defensive strong-point. . . . Not a single potsherd was recovered from the whole site; no appreciable traffic had ever passed this way to or from the great enclosure. The picture of frustration is complete. . . . We can almost see the tribesmen toiling vainly at their gate, almost hear the Ninth Legion tramping up from its new fortress at York to one of its rare victories.
>
> (Wheeler, 1954: 15–16, 23)

More recent excavators have suggested a quite different interpretation of the site, that it was occupied by a pro-Roman faction engaged in amicable trade in Roman products with their southern neighbours. Changing fashions in interpretation, of course, need not invalidate the older view. But in this instance the older view lacked any shred of credible archaeological evidence to complement the historical record.

The quest for Venutius, or for Vespasian's legions at Maiden Castle, was symptomatic of the historical approach to archaeology, of which more exotic or fanciful examples were Schliemann's search for Agamemnon at Mycenae, Woolley's discovery of the Flood of Genesis at Ur, the equation of the Neolithic walls of Jericho with Joshua's trumpeteers, or the quest for Arthur's Camelot at South Cadbury. There is, of course, nothing inherently unacademic in equating archaeological sites with historically named places, assuming that the evidence stands up to rigorous scrutiny. Many Roman locations in Britain are very well authenticated, for example, but the identification of native sites from Ptolemy's *Geography* or early historic sites from Bede are very much less secure, including some that are now part of received wisdom. The fact is that the archaeological agenda has moved on: locating the site of Mons Graupius will tell us very little about the political, social, economic or cognitive systems of the protagonists in that historical event. There is, of course, every reason for adopting an inter-disciplinary approach in which the evidence of archaeology, documentary history, place-names, epigraphy and numismatics can all contribute to a better understanding of past societies and events. But the evidence of each should be independently evaluated by the criteria of that discipline before any attempt at correlation can be legitimately undertaken.

Northern Britain and the Celtic question

Through the 1990s, prompted by publicity linked to the 1991 Venice exhibition 'I Celti', some English archaeologists launched a campaign of deconstruction, arguing that there was no sound evidence for a pan-European ethnic population of Celts, and still less that any inhabitants of Britain had been Celts. It is certainly true that archaeology alone cannot demonstrate the presence of Celts in Britain, which was formerly inferred on historical and linguistic grounds. But the issue in this case is not so much deferring to historical and linguistic evidence in preference to archaeological evidence; it is a debate over the interpretation of historical and linguistic evidence itself. The Celtic 'myth' has recently been portrayed as an invention of linguists and ethnologists from the sixteenth century and later, with no firm basis in archaeology and precious little in ancient documentary sources (Collis, 1997; Chapman, 1992; James, 1999). It is true that the definition of the language group from which Irish, Scottish Gaelic, Welsh and others were descended as Celtic was a relatively late development, but that does not make the languages or their speakers a modern invention. Nor does it follow that the only proper usage of the term 'Celtic' should be linguistic. When Hecataeus and Herodotus in the sixth and fifth centuries BC wrote about the Celts, and Ephorus in the fourth century listed them together with Scythians, Indians and Ethiopians as one of the barbarian neighbours of the Greeks, they may have been somewhat vague or even schematic in their geography, but they plainly were describing what they perceived as actual ethnic groups. None of the classical sources could be regarded as trained ethnographic observers, and several like Diodorus, Strabo and Caesar drew extensively on the Posidonian tradition for what at times amounts to little more than formulaic descriptions of barbarians. Caesar at any rate was familiar with both Gaul and Southern Britain, though his ethnographic observations are unlikely to have been seriously researched beyond the purposes of his military and political campaigns.

Critics of the 'Celtic model' point out that no classical writer ever referred to Britain as Celtic: both Strabo and Caesar, for example, refer to Britain and its inhabitants as Britons. For Caesar Celtica was one, possibly the largest, of his threefold divisions of Gaul, whilst in Strabo's *Geography* Celtica lay parallel to the island of Britain across the Channel. This tells us little about the ethnic status of Britain, which is not the central topic of discussion, though a parenthetic digression in Caesar's diaries (*de bello Gallico*, V, 12–14) stresses the similarity of the south-eastern British tribes and their Gaulish neighbours. Part of the difficulty lies in the meaning of the terms Keltoi/Celti, and indeed of Galatae and Galli, all of which appear to have been used as supra-tribal names, and even to have been interchangeable. So, for example, Polybius, writing in the second century about the battle of Telemon, refers to the Boii, Insubres and Taurisci as 'Celts', suggesting that there may have been a hierarchy of names, the choice of which might well depend upon the context in which a given population was being described. The uncertainty remains whether any of these names were what the native communities called themselves, even where those names are linguistically Celtic.

The correlation between linguistic evidence and archaeological cultures and distributions is a vexed issue. The equation of Celts, whether ethnically or linguistically defined, with La Tène archaeological material is plainly an oversimplification and has too readily been assumed in the past. It is true that La Tène assemblages are found widely through north Alpine Central and Western Europe, broadly coincident at least in part with the distribution of Celtic languages in antiquity, as inferred from place-names, personal names and cognate evidence. But La Tène material culture is extremely diluted in the quantity and number of definitive types in Southern Britain by comparison with Continental Europe, and for large parts of Northern Britain is virtually non-existent. In Ireland the 'La Tène' assemblage is almost exclusively of insular manufacture, including some types that are not represented in Continental Europe. Furthermore the La Tène distribution in Ireland has a bias towards the northern two-thirds of the country, suggesting that there must have been a non-La Tène Iron Age counterpart in the south and west. Evidently not of indigenous origin, the La Tène of Ireland is still of uncertain external origin (Raftery, 1984).

The fact that the term 'Celtic art' has regularly been used to describe what should more accurately be called La Tène art has compounded the confusion, but is otherwise a distraction from the main issue. La Tène art is simply one aspect of the study of La Tène material culture, which helps to clarify some of the external connections of and influences upon the La Tène assemblage. It does nevertheless show a particular concern with some of those themes, such as personal wealth and ornament, weaponry and martial equipment, and feasting and the aristocratic drinking service, all of which the ancient texts suggest were pre-occupations of Celtic society. The evidence of archaeology, however, indicates that these concerns ante-date the appearance of La Tène culture by at least half a millennium, since they are abundantly represented in the Urnfield culture of the later Bronze Age.

The fact that Hecataeus and Herodotus could allude to Keltoi in the sixth and fifth centuries BC might indicate that their existence was already well established by that time, and by any reckoning, therefore, the La Tène culture of north Alpine Europe is too late in the archaeological sequence to qualify as the archaeological counterpart of the earliest Celtic-speakers in Europe. Renfrew's challenging suggestion (1987) that Celtic languages were first introduced into Western Europe by the same agencies that introduced Neolithic farming practices has not met with general acceptance among Celtic linguists, and the strongest candidate therefore as the earliest Celtic speakers is still those peoples who are represented archaeologically by the practice of Urnfield cremation. Of course there are extensive regions of Atlantic Europe on which the Urnfield tradition made no impact, but where there were instead other distinctive archaeological traits, notably in their metalworking industries, which indicate a network of relationships along the Atlantic seaways. Any simplistic equation between Celtic speakers and archaeological cultural groups or distributions, therefore, is unlikely to be evident from the complex and dynamic development of later prehistoric communities in Central and Western Europe over half a millennium or more.

The issue of correlating archaeological and linguistic evidence for European Celts is likely thus to be incapable of simple resolution, but the debate may be conveniently summarised:

> If the material distributions identified by archaeologists coincide broadly in time and space with the evidence adduced by linguists, and if one can discern no evidence for subsequent population incursions or linguistic superstrata, then it would not be an unreasonable inference that the makers or users of the material assemblages were speakers of those languages, whatever label they are given. Indeed, the economic hypothesis that absence of evidence for complexity constitutes *prima facie* evidence for simplicity is one which should be as familiar to archaeology as it is to other disciplines. Such a coincidence can certainly be sustained at the time of the Roman conquests of Gaul and Britain. The plausibility of backward inference becomes more contentious as one attempts to go further back in time, but is not the crux of the current debate. Whether these people, or groups of people, and the language or languages they spoke can be equated with the people named as Celts by Herodotus (or Caesar) is ultimately undemonstrable, since they were not a literate society and left no record of who they were or what they called themselves. Yet it is difficult to imagine who else the ancient sources were referring to, if not the makers and users of the cultural assemblages at the given time and place.
>
> (Harding and Gillies, forthcoming, b)

To what extent, then, might Northern Britain be regarded as 'Celtic' in the Iron Age in any of the senses considered here? In linguistic terms it may be regarded as such, at any rate from the early Iron Age and Roman periods, and probably from an earlier period still. Archaeologically it may be hard to justify the use of the terms Hallstatt or La Tène to describe the material culture of the Iron Age in Northern Britain; indeed where La Tène artefacts do occur they might well be regarded as 'exotic' in the primary sense described above. But since it has been argued that the equation between La Tène material culture and Celticity in any other sense can only have been partial at most, this need not exclude Northern Britain from the Celtic realms. In any event, defining the Iron Age of Northern Britain in terms other than those of the Central European Urnfield-Hallstatt-La Tène sequence would be an exercise that is long overdue.

Part 2

The earlier Iron Age

Chapter 2

Brigantia and northern England

The conventional view of northern England in the Iron Age has been largely determined by historical sources dating from the Roman occupation. Tacitus, whose account formed the basis of Sir Mortimer Wheeler's interpretation of Stanwick, states that the territory of the Brigantes was *reputedly* the most populous in the entire province (*Agricola*: 17), and Ptolemy, writing in the second century AD, explicitly reported that Brigantia extended from sea to sea. Wheeler certainly assumed a single tribal group or at least a confederation of tribes with a paramount king or queen, and later commentators in general have likewise assumed that Brigantia was in some sense a meaningful entity. Cunliffe (1991: 189) questioned the 'Brigantian confederacy' model, but still acknowledged the primacy of the Brigantes over their client neighbours.

Rivet and Smith's (1979: 279) suggestion that the term Brigantes itself was no more than a descriptive name for 'highlanders', given to them by incomers, is a timely warning against equating Roman identifications with native identities. But the fact remains that its use in the name of the cantonal centre at Aldborough (*Isurium Brigantium*) suggests that it was recognised as a group identity under the Roman occupation. Furthermore, there are dedications along and beyond the northern frontier to the goddess Brigantia, whom Ross (1970: 151–2, 160–1) interpreted as the tribal deity of the Brigantes, commonly associated with water sources and cognate to the Irish Brigid. As regards the nature and geographical extent of Brigantia in the Roman period, Ptolemy's list of nine centres certainly suggests a regional structure, though only four of these sites, *Vinnovion* (Binchester, Co. Durham), *Caturactonion* (Catterick, N. Yorks), *Isurion* (Aldborough, Yorks) and *Eboracon* (York) can be securely identified. Of the others, *Calagon, Rigodunon, Olicana* and *Camulodunon*, none is convincingly located west of the Pennines. To the west the *portus Setantiorum* and to the east the *sinus portuosus Gabrantovicum* have been taken to indicate tribal sub-septs of the Brigantes, though the Gabrantovici ('horse-riding warriors') sounds like another descriptive name rather than a native identity. Other *pagi* might be inferred, such as the Carvetii of the north-west, whose centre at Carlisle acquired *civitas* status in the third century.

The case for a unified or confederated Brigantian state, dominated by a ruling paramount dynasty, is therefore far from secure. The territory of the Brigantes may have been exaggerated, and in reality centred only in the eastern Pennines and the Vale of York, around their tribal capital at Aldborough. The Eden valley could have been the territory of the Carvetii, centred on Carlisle, and to the south bordering on the Setantii of north Lancashire. These latter evidently made a lesser impact upon the documentary record, but need not on that account be relegated to client groups of a dominant Brigantia. The account documented in Roman history may be a rationalisation of a much more complex system in which local communities had their own distinctive identities. As Higham suggested (1986: 149) 'the North on the eve of conquest may have been as fragmented as was Wales during much of the early medieval period.'

The archaeological evidence is still more complex to interpret, not least because of the inherent problems of dating sites to the pre-Roman period. For the Brigantes to be credible as a powerful unitary entity in the first century AD we must assume its genesis in the preceding centuries of the Iron Age, if not much earlier still. Over half a millennium or more we should not necessarily expect cultural boundaries to remain static, making 'ethnic' patterns still more difficult to read. The problem for the past century has been to identify archaeologically sites and material assemblages that can be assigned to these preceding periods. In Hawkes' classic scheme (1959/1961: Fig. 1) northern England north of the Trent included his Eastern and Pennine provinces. Beyond that sketched definition, the Pennine province thereafter rated mention only once, in a footnote. Thirty years later the situation was seemingly not much better. Summarising the evidence, excluding the Arras complex of eastern Yorkshire, Cunliffe's (1991: 101) conclusion from 'the sparse material culture and the apparent paucity of settlements is that the population of northern England was small compared with the south'. West of the Pennines in Lancashire, even allowing for poor survival in the archaeological record, Haselgrove (1996: 64) admitted that the Iron Age population was probably lower than elsewhere in the north. The most populous group in Britain was proving frustratingly elusive archaeologically.

The problem really, of course, is not a paucity of sites, but a paucity of adequately dated sites. Prior to the routine application of radiocarbon dating, dependence upon material associations for dating was bound to prove inadequate in contexts that are largely aceramic, as in the earlier Iron Age of much of northern England. In fact, as Challis showed some years ago (Challis and Harding, 1975), and others have confirmed since (Willis, 1999), northern England is by no means totally aceramic, though much of the domestic pottery appears to be of relatively late date. Earlier communities were presumably aceramic by choice, using containers made from perishable materials such as wooden vessels, leather bottles, wicker baskets or textile bags. Conventionally this was seen as the hallmark of mobile pastoralists or at least of communities for which transhumance was an important tradition, but whether this explanation will serve in this instance must depend upon a closer analysis of the archaeological evidence for economy and society in the Northern British Iron Age. Ireland and the Isle of Man, like Wales, northern England and much of lowland Scotland, is largely aceramic, and in Northern Britain it is the Hebrides, and to a lesser degree the Northern Isles, that stand out as the exception. As Raftery (1995b) noted for Ireland, the problem is compounded by the fact that preceding periods have developed ceramics, both domestic and funerary, so that the abandonment of pottery by the mid-first millennium BC, if that was the case, was conscious and deliberate, presumably signifying some radical change in food preparation and consumption. It has been suggested that poorly fired and friable fabrics might not survive, especially if exposed to ploughing, but in this case we might still expect some contexts, such as pits or ditches, to yield occasional insights into the original extent of the ceramic assemblage. The only realistic conclusion is that Iron Age communities in these regions were indeed largely aceramic, and by choice.

One important respect in which communities of northern England differed from their southern neighbours was in making no use of coinage. The Brigantian tribes can hardly have been unaware of this development, since Corieltauvian coins and hoards are found north of the Trent, in the immediately bordering zones (Hunter, F., 1997: Illus. 5), where some accommodation to neighbouring practice is unsurprising. Beyond this, however, the tail-off in the distribution is marked, and those finds that are indeed authentic losses in antiquity must represent exotic imports rather than having any bearing upon a monetary economy. Surprisingly, the number of Gaulish coins equals those minted in Britain, suggesting direct contact with the Continent rather than secondary redistribution from the south of England. Possible explanations might include gift-exchange, diplomatic liaisons, marriage dowry, mercenary payments or indeed the movement of refugees. The absence of local coinage among northern communities need not signify insufficient social or political development. A dispersed pattern of settlement and an economy in which pastoralism was undoubtedly a significant if not dominant element, on the other hand, were doubtless factors in what amounts to a conscious rejection of, or lack of a perceived need for, a monetary economy.

Important though pastoralism undoubtedly was, we can now be confident that Piggott's (Piggott, S., 1958a) model of primitive pastoralists was misplaced, and that there were extensive areas of the northern coastal plains and valley lowlands where cereal cultivation would have been an important component of the economy. Self-evident as this might seem to anyone familiar with agricultural patterns in Northern Britain from more recent times, it has taken a good deal of research (e.g. Van der Veen, 1992) to dispel the image of the footloose Celtic cowboy ranging over rough pasture in a state of pastoral nomadism. The absence of storage-pits in the north of Britain was immaterial, since above-ground storage would have been more practical. Likewise the apparent absence of field-systems and other evidence of an organised agricultural landscape was inevitably exaggerated, in northern England as in southern Scotland, through the difficulties of assigning extant remains to their correct chronological horizon. *Pace* Frere (1967: 55 and still 1998: 42; Haselgrove, 1984: 15) there is no good reason to believe that Caesar's allusion to the peoples of the interior as not growing corn but living on milk and meat (*de bello Gallico*: V, 14) was an accurate reflection of Brigantian economy. In the first place it is a formulaic denigration of barbarians (cf. Webster, 1999), applied equally to the Germans (*dbG*: IV, 1 and again VI, 22) and later in similar terms by Cassius Dio (*Epitome*: 76, 12, 1–5) to the Caledones and Maeatae of the barbarian North. In the second place there is no reason to suppose that Caesar had any informed knowledge of, or serious interest in, an 'interior' part of Britain quite so far north.

As to the geographical divide and contrast in political and agricultural base, the legacy of Fox's Highland/Lowland division of Britain, with the economic rider of Piggott's Woodbury–Stanwick economic model, still underlies most standard assessments of the British Iron Age:

> When Aulus Plautius founded the Fosse frontier in the years AD 44–7 he was simply emphasizing a geographical and political truth. Britain could be divided into two parts about a line drawn along the Jurassic ridge from Lincoln to Lyme Bay. To the south and east lay a densely settled region with authority centralised about oppida and with a subsistence economy depending to a large extent on the production of grain. To the north and west settlement was more scattered and in places sparse, there was little centralisation of power and, while cereals were widely grown, there appears to have been a greater reliance on stock rearing.
>
> (Cunliffe, 1991: 213; not as misquoted in Bevan, 1999: 2)

A more subtle geographical contrast was that drawn by Haselgrove (1999: 257) within northern England about the central axis of the Pennines. To the west there was a far greater proportion of upland to lowland, the climate would have been wetter, and in consequence pastoralism doubtless dominated over arable cultivation in the local economies. To the east a mixed agricultural economy would certainly have been practical and has been amply demonstrated in the lowlands from the Vale of York to the Tyne. These two provinces were also exposed to quite different external contacts, on the east from south-eastern England and across the North Sea coastline from the Continent, to the west from the Irish Sea and the western seaways. The role of these two natural routes of access was undoubtedly instrumental in forming the complex character of Iron Age communities and their material culture in Northern Britain. The importance of the western seaways has often been stressed, though archaeologically it is difficult to demonstrate a coherent community of culture in the Irish Sea zone or beyond. The eastern route of access, and the southern North Sea crossing from the mouth of the Rhine, may well have resulted in more direct impulses into north-eastern England in the Iron Age, though again we should beware simplistic explanations of what is often very limited evidence. These differences and factors contingent upon them undoubtedly influenced the patterns of Roman colonisation and native response in northern England, and it would be surprising if they had not created regional variations in social and economic circumstances throughout the first millennium BC.

The Humber to the Tees

The Humber and the river Trent have long appeared to be a significant boundary in terms of archaeological distributions (Challis and Harding, 1975), whether or not it corresponded to a coherent ethnic or cultural boundary in the Iron Age. Seaborne access north was open not only through the Humber estuary, but up the eastern coast of Yorkshire, where the pottery and associated artefacts from Staple Howe (Fig. 2.1; Brewster, 1963) and Devils Hill (Brewster, 1981), with older finds from Scarborough (Fig. 2.2; Smith, R. A., 1927), display what Haselgrove (1984: 14) has termed a 'North-west European Hallstatt Interaction Sphere'. Earlier commentators like Burgess (1974: 213), with less regard for current academic correctness, saw the coastal–riverine distribution of Hallstatt C weaponry and high-status metalwork of Hallstatt C–D type up the eastern coast of England and into Scotland as 'a classic raiding pattern' rather than the product of trade or exchange. In the older convention the finds of 1861 from Ebberston of a bronze sword of Gündlingen type with human bones, together with a second sword probably from the same site, would have been interpreted as burials of colonising Hallstatt warriors. Likewise the barrow from Aldro (Challis and Harding, 1975: 42–3, Fig. 20), including among its fragmentary bronzework a ferrule comparable to those found in late Hallstatt wagon graves in West Central Europe, might be seen as evidence of direct contact from the Continent. We certainly need not exclude the possibility of some immigrant groups, though the absence of a regular burial rite of Continental Hallstatt type argues against extensive incursions. Insular pottery, including jars with finger-impressed ornament which characterised Cunliffe's West Harling–Staple Howe style zone, sometimes referred to as 'Hallstatt' in Britain, has rather less in common with Central European Hallstatt wares than it has with coarse pottery of the later Bronze Age and earliest Iron Age in the Low Countries.

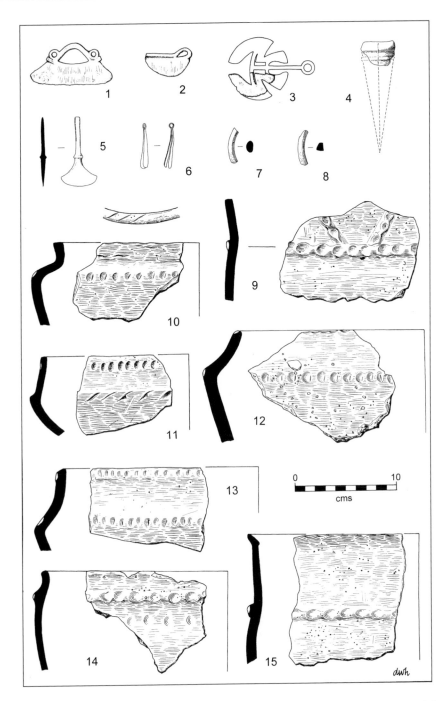

Figure 2.1 Pottery and other artefacts from Staple Howe, Yorkshire. 1–3, bronze razors; 4, bronze socketed axe; 5, bronze chisel or leather-worker's knife; 6, bronze tweezers; 7–8 jet or shale bracelets; 9–15 pottery. Drawings by D. W. Harding, 1–8 adapted from Brewster (1953), 9–15 courtesy of the British Museum.

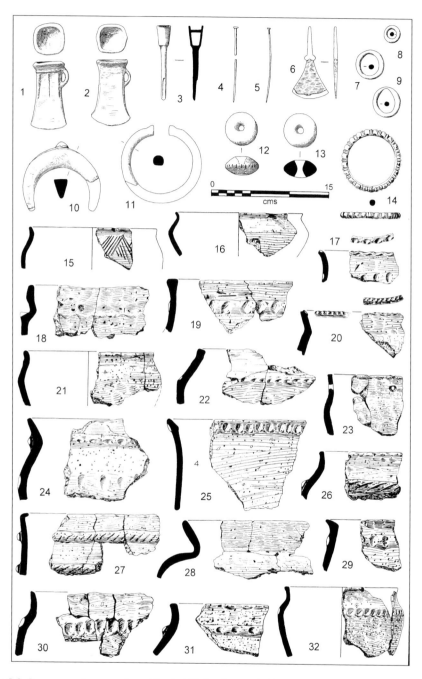

Figure 2.2 Bronzes and pottery from Castle Hill, Scarborough, Yorkshire. 1–2, bronze socketed axes; 3, bronze socketed gouge; 4–5 bronze pins; 6, bronze tanged chisel, or leather-worker's knife; 7–9, bronze rings; 10–11, jet and shale ornaments; 12–13, pottery spindle-whorls; 14, bronze bracelet; 15–32, pottery. Drawings 1–13 by D. W. Harding, adapted from Wheeler (1931); drawings 14–32 by A. J. Challis, reproduced by kind permission.

The Staple Howe settlement (Fig. 2.3, 1), a palisaded or stockaded enclosure, which underwent structural modifications on at least two occasions, could have spanned a period between the eighth and sixth centuries BC. The circular or sub-circular huts of rather irregular post-built construction were not at all comparable to the large, symmetrical plans of the early Iron Age in Wessex, but were more akin to the middle Bronze Age tradition of the South Downs, like Plumpton Plain and Itford Hill, or their counterparts in the Netherlands at Nijnsel and elsewhere (Harding, 1973). The bronzes (Fig. 2.1, 1–3) were not closely tied to the structural sequence, nor to the site's single radiocarbon date (2400+/– 150 BC: BM-63, for grain from an internal quarry hollow). The double-looped bronze razor (Fig. 2.1, 2) is certainly a Central European Hallstatt type, but its closest parallels are from Belgium, while the single-looped razor (Fig. 2.1, 3) has analogies in the Nordic series of the later Bronze Age. The third, fragmentary razor (Fig. 2.1, 1), reconstructed as resembling the example from Kinleith, Midlothian, is evidently an insular form without known Continental parallels. By contrast, the leather-worker's knife (Brewster, 1963: Fig. 61, 5) is an Atlantic Late Bronze Age type, and the scrap of socketed axe (ibid.: Fig. 62, 9) likewise may indicate activity on the site at this period. The bronze tweezers (ibid.: Fig. 61, 4) could well be part of a late Bronze Age domestic assemblage, though the type is not strictly diagnostic, and is certainly found in Continental Iron Hallstatt contexts. Jet bracelets (ibid.: Fig. 66) likewise are not diagnostic, but could date from the late Bronze Age. The assemblage could include survivals, but the combination of late Bronze Age types with innovative Hallstatt forms is not uncharacteristic of hoards of this transitional phase, like Llyn Fawr in Glamorgan (Fox and Hyde, 1939) or Horsehope, Peeblesshire (Piggott, S., 1953b).

Finger-tip decoration along shoulder and rim of coarse ware jars is not uncommon in the Southern British Iron Age, and need not imply more than a broad compatibility with wider North-West European fashions. The use at West Harling, Norfolk, on the other hand, of vertical finger impressions, an ornamental skeuomorph perhaps of the rivets of sheet-bronze vessels, and of random finger-tip ornament to create a rusticated effect on the body of the jar is more closely reminiscent of the styles of the Low Countries. Pottery similar to that from Staple Howe, from Castle Hill, Scarborough, was unfortunately not closely associated with either the late Bronze Age bronzes (Fig. 2.2, 1–6) nor the bronze bracelet with ribbed mouldings of Continental Hallstatt type (Fig. 2.2, 14) that was found nearby, but has also been seen as the product of contacts with the European mainland around the seventh century BC (Challis and Harding, 1975). In fact, both pottery and metalwork would not be inconsistent with communication and traffic between the communities bordering the southern North Sea basin. The scale of this interaction, however, should not be over-estimated. The total sum of Hallstatt metalwork of Continental derivation in Britain is minimal compared to the range and quantity of types represented in the cemeteries or even settlements of Central Europe, and is certainly not amenable in Britain to the recognition of successive sub-phases of Hallstatt C and D.

The location of the Staple Howe and Devil's Hill stockaded settlements on outlying spurs at the interface between the upland Wolds and the lowlands of the Vale of Pickering is suggestive of strategic control of both agricultural environments. It is generally assumed that in later prehistory the Wolds would have been used primarily for pastoralism, in this instance with arable agriculture concentrating in the lowlands to the west, where a broadly contemporary open settlement has been identified at Heslerton (Powlesland

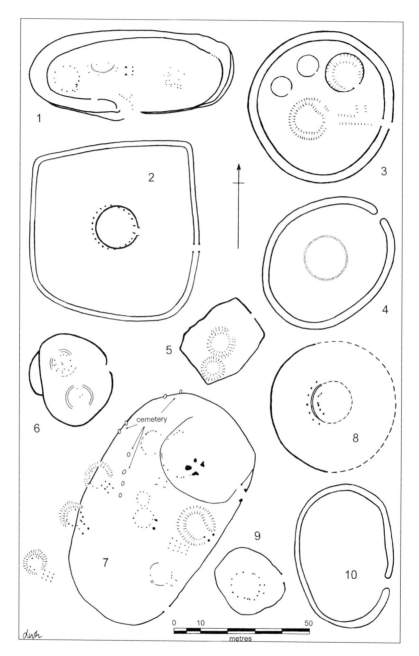

Figure 2.3 Plans of palisaded settlements. 1, Staple Howe, Yorkshire; 2, West Brandon, Co. Durham; 3, High Knowes, Alnham, Northumberland; 4, Gray Coat, Roxburghshire; 5, Greenbrough, Roxburghshire; 6, Glenachan Rig, Cardon, Peeblesshire; 7, Dryburn Bridge, East Lothian; 8, Bannockburn, Stirlingshire, homestead 1; 9, Knapps, Kilmacolm, Renfrewshire; 10, Gibb's Hill, Dumfriesshire, phase IV. Drawings by D.W. Harding, adapted from Brewster (1963), Jobey (1962), Jobey and Tait (1966), RCAHMS (1956), Mercer (1987), Feachem (1959), Triscott (1982), Rideout (1996), Newall (1956), RCAHMS (1997).

et al.,1986). Already from the later Bronze Age the landscape in this region was dominated by linear dyke-systems, and pit-alignments, dividing up the land for agricultural segregation and perhaps for the purposes of indicating community ownership and identity. Sometimes these earthworks are double or multiple, reinforcing their imposition of order on the landscape. Trackways too, defined by bank and ditch, extend along the dry valleys or lead towards networks of smaller fields. This systematic division of the landscape implies not only considerable resources of manpower to build, but a social hierarchy in which there was the required authority to create and implement this structure.

In field monuments there is not much evidence for social hierarchy. Though Grimthorpe (Stead, 1968), with its timber-framed rampart, may have been in occupation in the early first millennium BC, hillforts in the conventional sense are not a major element in the archaeological landscape of the Wolds. The fortified enclosure at Thwing (Fig. 2.4; Manby, 1980) may indeed have enjoyed a special status, but its duration and significance remain uncertain, being based upon a single radiocarbon date giving a *terminus post quem* at the end of the second millennium for the construction of its rampart. The double-ditched plan with opposed entrances, reminiscent of a class 2 henge monument of the late Neolithic, is most closely matched by the South Ring at Mucking, Essex, which yielded uncalibrated radiocarbon dates in the early first millennium BC. Though a special, even ritual, function might be inferred, the associated assemblages from each site appear to be entirely domestic in character. But the lesson is clear, that models of settlement or social hierarchy based upon the example of Wessex or southern England generally are likely to be wholly inappropriate to other parts of Britain.

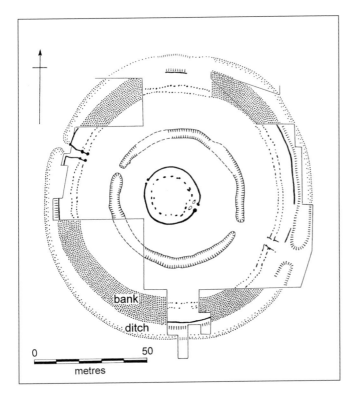

0   50
metres

Figure 2.4 Paddock Hill, Thwing, Yorkshire, outline plan. Drawing by D. W. Harding, adapted from Bewley (1994).

The decline in importance of the Wolds appears to coincide with an increase in settlement in adjacent regions like the Vale of York. To the west is the remarkable site of Dalton Parlours, south of Wetherby (Wrathmell and Nicholson, 1990). Though the earliest Iron Age settlement appears to have been characterised by roundhouses within a sub-rectangular enclosure, the subsequent aggregation of additional, irregular enclosures with roundhouses, in which the focus of settlement apparently shifted, is unusual. Unusual too is the extent of the site, and of the surrounding fields, linear dykes and trackways, some of which, though dating remains uncertain, may be expected to have their origins in the Iron Age. In the later second or third centuries AD the site was occupied by a suite of Roman buildings, raising the prospect that its pre-Roman status was in some measure perpetuated under the occupation. There are some problems with this interpretation, however, to which we shall return later. For the present, the importance of Dalton Parlours lies in its longevity of occupation in the Iron Age, which may have been underestimated because of the undiagnostic nature of the pre-Roman material assemblage. The existence of no less than five major phases of pre-Roman enclosure itself argues for a long occupation. Preceding phase 1 was a yet earlier feature along the southern boundary of the site, which would not be inconsistent with a palisaded settlement of the early–mid-first millennium BC. The radiocarbon dates are less than conclusive regarding the site's beginnings. One, however, from a phase 3 roundhouse, suggests a span around the third quarter of the first millennium BC for a relatively advanced stage in the occupational sequence.

The roundhouses themselves, which display both ring-groove and post-hole construction, range in size from 9 to 11 metres in diameter, with just one at 17 metres attaining or exceeding the size of the largest Wessex roundhouses (Fig. 2.5, 1). With up to three times the internal floor area of the smaller houses, discounting any upper or mezzanine capacity, this may represent an instance of status being reflected in differential house size. In fact this largest house appears also to be among the earliest structures on the site, though its continuing existence into phase 2 is suggested by the way that the northern ditch of a later enclosure bends to accommodate its presence. It was itself apparently unenclosed, unlike the classic north-eastern homesteads of the West Brandon kind. The smaller houses, by contrast, are all enclosed, though not every enclosure contained evidence of structures. The houses from Dalton Parlours are again unusual in having two entrances, either diametrically opposed or nearly so in most cases (Fig. 2.6, 1–2). The largest roundhouse is the exception, with its two entrances at half past ten in relative disposition. Though two entrances have been recognised elsewhere, the pattern is not as common as might be expected, considering the obvious advantages in terms of internal light or shelter from wind.

It would be tempting to see in the Dalton Parlours sequence a shift in social pattern from the single large roundhouse to the smaller roundhouses within their individual enclosures. Where more than one house plan was recovered within an enclosure there is no positive evidence of contemporaneity, and in some cases clear evidence from overlapping plans that they were not. The existence of separate but apparently contemporary house-enclosures, however, implies social units in which domestic space and perhaps land-holding were separately identified rather than communal, as might be inferred from the village enclosures of the Border region for example.

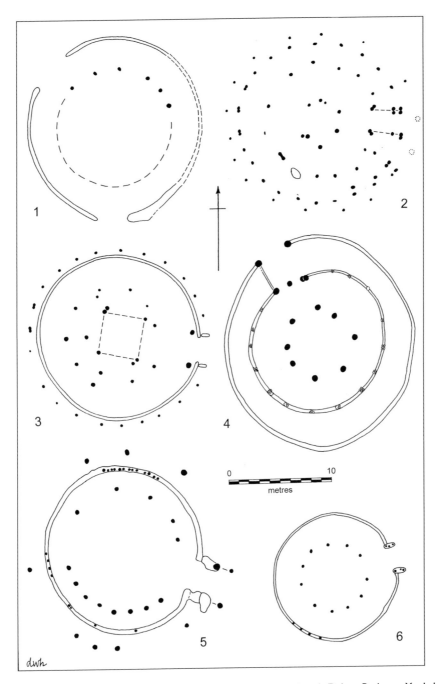

Figure 2.5 Large roundhouses of posthole or ring-groove construction. 1, Dalton Parlours, Yorkshire, house 5; 2, West Brandon, Co. Durham, house A; 3, West Brandon, Co. Durham, house B; 4, Scotstarvit, Fife, phase 1; 5, Bannockburn, Stirlingshire, fort house 1; 6, West Plean, Stirlingshire, house 2. Drawings by D. W. Harding, adapted from Wrathmell and Nicholson (1990), Jobey (1962), Bersu (1948), Rideout (1996), Steer (1956).

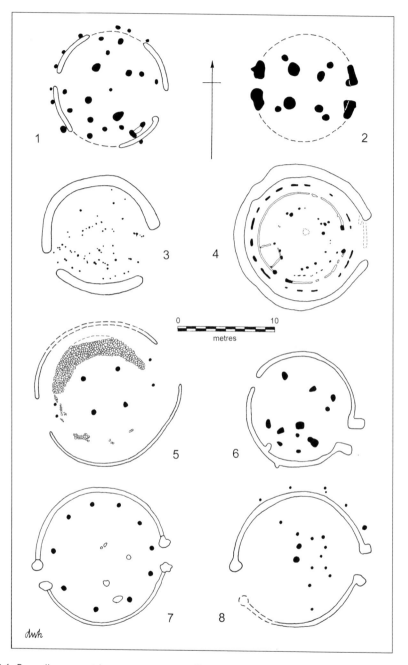

Figure 2.6 Roundhouses with two entrances and/or central four-post settings. 1, Dalton Parlours, Yorkshire, house 3; 2, Dalton Parlours, Yorkshire, house 2; 3, Roxby Moor, Yorkshire, house 1; 4, Roxby Moor, Yorkshire, house 2; 5, Wolsty Hall, Cumbria; 6, Hayknowes, Dumfriesshire; 7, Rispain Camp, Wigtownshire; 8, Carronbridge, Dumfriesshire. Drawings by D. W. Harding, adapted from Wrathmell and Nicholson (1990), Inman *et al.* (1985), Blake (1959), Gregory (2001), Haggarty and Haggarty (1983), Johnston (1994).

The Arras culture

The introduction of the innovative burial rites associated with the Arras culture of eastern Yorkshire, which can be dated at earliest to the fifth century BC, evidently post-dates the abandonment of the early settlements on the Wolds. The distinctive character of these cemeteries, notably the use of barrows within enclosure ditches of square plan, makes them easily identifiable from air-survey (Fig. 2.7), and those containing the burial of two-wheeled carts or chariots, has ensured their predominance in field research over the past half-century (Stead, 1965, 1979, 1991). Investigation of contemporary settlement, on the other hand, has been comparatively neglected until recent times. A notable exception is Wetwang Slack (Dent, 1982), where the adjacent open settlement of some eighty roundhouses aligned along a linear trackway was subsequently subject to a process of enclosure by boundary ditches, which also resulted in the nucleation of the cemetery. As might be expected, the material assemblage from domestic contexts was considerably poorer than from the adjacent funerary groups. Archaeological approaches to this rich

Figure 2.7 Square-ditched barrow cemetery, Burton Fleming, Yorkshire, air-photograph. Cambridge University Collection of Air Photographs, BUJ 28, Unit for Landscape Modelling, copyright reserved.

data-set reflect the passage of time and academic fashion. In the past the principal concern was the origin of the exotic funerary rite, which bears obvious similarities to the early and middle La Tène cemeteries of the Champagne, Ardennes and Middle Rhine. The notably compact distribution of cemeteries in eastern Yorkshire encouraged a presumption that they might reflect a distinct population group, though the recent discovery of a chariot-burial at Ferrybridge indicates that outliers might yet be anticipated. Yet at the same time the fact that the cart or chariot is generally dismantled rather than buried intact, and the flexed posture of the inhumations, both distinguish the Yorkshire chariot-burials from the Continental series. Equally, the artefacts found with these burials, and in the square-ditched barrows generally, include virtually none that could be regarded as actual imports. Distinctive types like involuted brooches, with their swivel-mechanism replacing the spring of earlier La Tène types, are decidedly insular, and representative of novel technical devices found elsewhere in Southern Britain from the fourth century, but not evidently inspired from Continental Europe. The pottery series from the Yorkshire graves furthermore is plain and coarse (Fig. 2.8), with not the slightest indication of influence from the early La Tène fashions of the Champagne, where wheel-thrown vessels finely ornamented with geometric or curvilinear designs are not uncommon. To explain these absences, it will simply not suffice to suggest, as Childe might have done, that the invaders left their 'womenfolk' behind, and depended thus upon local pottery supplies.

If the Arras burial tradition was the product of immigrant communities, there still remains the question of dating the colonising episode. Relatively few finds from Yorkshire beyond a handful of La Tène 1 brooches are as early as the La Tène 1 hey-day of the Champagne cemeteries, so that an apparent time-lag of a century or more before the *floruit* of the Yorkshire series needs to be explained. Despite these significant local differences, the view that the Yorkshire cemeteries were the product of immigrant settlers, if only on a limited scale by an influential élite, has proved remarkably resilient, though pin-pointing an exact Continental homeland of the putative immigrants has proved tantalisingly elusive.

Today the agenda has shifted towards the reconstruction from burial evidence of social and cognitive systems, of which much more can undoubtedly be inferred from funerary evidence such as the Yorkshire cemeteries than from most other less well-documented sources in the insular Iron Age. An analogy in the 'long Iron Age' of Northern Britain to the appearance of a novel and distinctive burial type is the appearance of long-cist cemeteries around the Forth estuary from the fifth and sixth centuries AD. This distribution does not correlate as easily as the Arras distribution with any assumed tribal territory, but like the square-ditched barrows of the Yorkshire series they do not have convincing local antecedents. The long-cist cemeteries may have been prompted by the adoption of Christianity: apart from their orientation and absence of grave-goods, later cemeteries are closely associated with Christian sites. So the possibility should be considered that the Yorkshire cemeteries were the result, not of colonisation by settlers from north-eastern France, but of the adoption by the ruling power of innovative cult practices, introduced by 'missionaries' whose interests lay not in pottery or brooch typology but in the ritual disposal of the dead.

A final question that is seldom addressed relates to the end of these cemeteries. By the later Iron Age a new class of settlement appears, characterised by rectilinear habitation enclosures and associated fields aligned along a trackway. In some instances, such as Bell

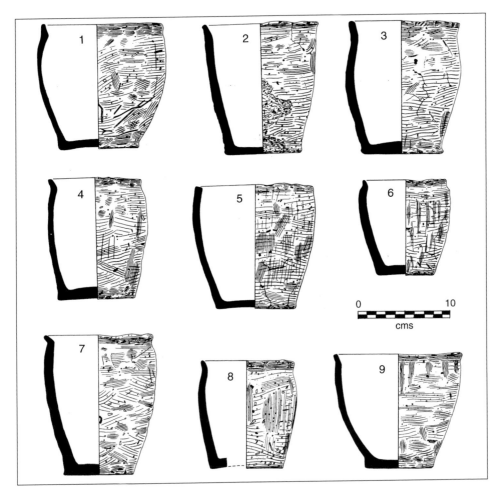

Figure 2.8 Pottery from eastern Yorkshire. 1–5, Danes Graves; 6–8, Eastburn; 9, Riggs Farm. Drawings by A. J. Challis, reproduced by kind permission.

Slack, these 'ladder settlements' actually overlie earlier cemeteries of square-ditched barrows. The demise of the cemeteries evidently took place around the first century BC, and the new settlements were developing by the first century AD, but before the Roman occupation. What, then, accounts for the disappearance of the cemeteries from archaeological visibility? Were we able to resolve this question, we might be closer to understanding the social and ideological rationale that prompted their appearance in the first place. Haselgrove (1984) advanced the suggestion that the introduction of more formal rites for the disposal of the dead could have been triggered by social stress resulting from increased pressure on land and resources, and that conversely the success of agricultural intensification strategies may have resulted in their abandonment. But if this were the case, it still hardly explains why the formalised rite should be one that most closely resembles Continental practices in the La Tène Iron Age, unless some contact took place with Continental sources.

The North York Moors

The North York Moors have a range of field monuments and settlement sites that have been investigated over a number of years, mainly by locally sponsored research projects. The high moors in later prehistory were doubtless used as summer pasture for communities whose permanent settlements were on lower-lying land, in the Vale of York or on the Tabular Hills above the Vale of Pickering. The few hillforts in the region – Eston Nab, Sutton Bank and Boltby Scar – are located peripherally to the high moors, but pivotally between the high pastures and lower lying settlements and agricultural land. The distribution of beehive querns (Hayes *et al.*, 1980) broadly corresponds to areas of good agricultural land.

Dating, as ever, remains tentative, though the negative evidence of absence, as at Percy Rigg, Kildale (Close, 1972), of material of Romano-British date in an area where there are numerous settlements that evidently were occupied in the Roman period, allows the assumption of earlier occupation. At Eston Nab, the presence of a palisaded enclosure preceding a rampart and ditch, together with the pottery assemblage from the site, would be consistent with the later Bronze Age to Iron Age dating offered by the excavator, and now offers the best local model for the late Bronze Age and earliest Iron Age material culture from the region (Vyner, 1988). The discovery beneath the rampart at Boltby Scar of gold, basket-shaped ear-rings, dateable arguably between the Beaker period and late Bronze Age (Challis and Harding, 1975: 111), provides no more than a *terminus post quem* for the construction of its defences. Spratt's analysis (1982) of the Cleave Dyke system, with which the Boltby fort was almost certainly an integral part, therefore depended perhaps a little too heavily upon the dating of the fort as evidence of the date of the dykes. Yet there can be little doubt that agricultural re-organisation and territorial demarcation of the earlier first millennium BC would afford the most appropriate context for this remarkable series of field monuments. The principal dyke, or discontinuous series of dykes, is aligned close to the north–south watershed of the Hambleton Hills, with branches extending from it periodically towards the heads of tributary valleys of the Rye to the east. The system is evidently designed to create land divisions in which both upland and lowland, water supply and peat deposits were available. The main dyke is not evidently aligned in relation to the later Hambleton Street; instead it shows a marked correlation to the liminal distribution of Bronze Age barrows, suggesting that it was a development out of an earlier, Bronze Age system of land division. It was evidently of more than one phase of construction, and research, based upon air-photographic evidence (Spratt and White, 1986), indicated that the Cleave Dyke in its earlier phase was based upon a pit-alignment rather than a continuous ditch. The longevity of use of the Boltby promontory would seem entirely consistent with this view.

To the east of the Cleave Dyke, on the Tabular Hills flanking the north side of the Vale of Pickering, is an even more extensive network of dykes (Spratt, 1989). The principal dykes run along the upper sides or into the heads of valleys, with cross-ridge dykes, possibly of later Iron Age or early Roman date, extending across spurs and valley heads. Dating is notoriously difficult to determine, and except for the dykes on Levisham Moor, which stratigraphically pre-date the Iron Age and Roman native settlement, is not yet sufficiently based upon excavated evidence. As with the Hambleton Hills system, the relationship between the dykes and earlier Bronze Age cairnfields and barrows suggests the probability of their origins in the later second millennium, though there is evidence of later re-use and adaptation at a much later date. The effect of the system, doubtless supplemented by the natural boundaries provided by topography, is to create a series of territories, or 'estates' in Spratt's terminology, each with its share of the terrain resources, and conforming quite closely to the surviving townships, except where obvious changes have been imposed upon the older system in Medieval times. There is no direct connection between the Tabular Hills system and the dyke systems of the northern Wolds, to the south of the Vale of Pickering, though the two systems might well have been in broadly contemporaneous use in the first millennium BC. It should also be noted that square-ditched barrows do occur on the north side of the Vale of Pickering, and two cart-burials, at Pexton Moor and Cawthorn Camps, are within the south-western concentration of dykes on the limestone hills. As regards the function of the dyke systems, current opinion favours their interpretation as territorial divisions, perhaps of communities for whom pastoralism was an important but not necessarily dominant element in the economy. Though the soils on the corallian limestone of the Tabular Hills are well suited to arable cultivation, some enclosures in proximity to the dyke systems might argue for pastoral activities. The major dykes of the Scamridge system, on the other hand, are of a different scale order, and would have required a much greater effort and resource for their construction. Spratt saw them as tribal or political boundaries in the first instance, but their subsequent modification indicated their adaptation into the wider and more general system of 'estate' boundaries.

Levisham Moor (Hayes, 1983) shows a similar pattern of dykes with barrows or cairn-fields of presumptively Bronze Age date on the higher moors. This important complex of earthworks includes enclosures that were evidently used for domestic occupation, some that possibly served as paddocks, and one that certainly was the focus of an iron-working industry. Some of these may represent infilling secondary to the establishment of the basic dyke system. In close proximity were fields of 'brickwork' pattern defined by stony banks that could well be the remnants of an earlier agricultural system, later obliterated by the intrusion of Medieval rig-and-furrow. The site is generally assigned to the later Iron Age and Romano-British periods. Roman pottery from Enclosure A certainly suggests contemporary occupation. Apart from a fragment of late first or second century glass bangle, however, Enclosure B otherwise produced no clearly Roman types among a significant assemblage of native pottery. By contrast, the absence of definitively Roman pottery from Enclosures C and D argues strongly for an earlier occupation of these sites. Hayes recognised that the 'native' forms could have been in fashion from the third century BC to the later Roman period. On the basis of the pottery forms alone, there seems to be no good reason for denying the possibility that this complex settlement was in use from the early first millennium, when the dyke system was first established. Once again dating has inevitably been retarded because the only *diagnostic* types are those from the site's Roman occupational horizon. It is simply not credible that these sites were not in use in the early and middle Iron Age, just because the archaeologically diagnostic material acts as a magnet, polarising our attention on either the later Bronze Age or Romano-British phases.

Along the northern fringes of the North York Moors, among numerous settlements of the Roman native phase, are several sites for which an earlier Iron Age date is probable. Principal among these is the nuclear settlement at Percy Rigg, Kildale (Close, 1972), essentially an unenclosed cluster of roundhouses, though perhaps located within a larger terrain enclosure. Its five principal houses almost certainly represent two or three phases of construction, of which the latest have stone wall-foundations surviving to several courses. Each house was surrounded by a drainage trench, or network of trenches that may have embraced ancillary working areas. The houses, averaging 6 or 7 metres in internal diameter, had thick stone walls and paved floors, generally with a central hearth. Their stone foundations might have prompted their dating to the Roman period, but the coarse pottery from the site, the predominance of saddle querns over a single rotary quern, and the absence of diagnostically Roman material, argues for an earlier occupation. In fact, if the querns are indicative of arable agriculture, then it is hard to imagine that farming at 270 metres would have been viable as late as the period to which the site has conventionally been assigned. A sub-square enclosure a little over a mile to the west on Great Ayton Moor (Tinkler and Spratt, 1978), by contrast, was regarded as pastoral in purpose; its enclosing bank and internal ditch is certainly suggestive of containment rather than exclusion, and the absence of querns may be significant. The single structure uncovered within the enclosure was oval in plan, with timber posts that could have supported a ridge-roof. The wall-foundations were of stone, with stone paving and central hearth, but otherwise the structural similarities with Percy Rigg are not close. Nor are the ceramic assemblages as close as might be expected in view of the sites' proximity, and it may be that they belong to quite different periods of settlement, though both probably in a pre-Roman horizon.

Further to the east, the settlement on Low Roxby Moor (Inman *et al.*, 1985) included both enclosed and unenclosed houses, again with surrounding ditches or gullies, the purpose of which appeared to be for drainage rather than to contain timber uprights of the outer wall. A notable feature of several house plans was again the existence of a secondary entrance (Fig. 2.6, 3–4), indicated either by a second break in the surrounding ditch, or by door-posts in the house plan itself. The orientation of the principal entrance was generally to the east, with the subordinate entrance between west and south-west. House 2 showed singular detail in its plan. The main wall was built of stakes, bedded into a ring-groove, continuous except for its two doorways, and describing a circle nearly 9 metres in diameter. More substantial postholes in the interior could have retained earth-fast, weight-bearing timbers to support the roof. Beyond the stake-wall was a further circle of slots, most like those from the large roundhouse at Pimperne, Dorset, which at Roxby the excavator suggested, on account of their squared cross-section, may have held sill-beams to provide external securing of eaves-supports or the heel of the main rafters themselves. Adjacent to the second entrance and projecting inwards from the stake-wall were two further lengths of gully, possibly part of some internal fixture, but in any event indicative of radial division of internal space. The radial division of internal space is doubtless integral to circular architecture, but it is a concept more expressly visible archaeologically in the context of stone buildings of the Atlantic Scottish Iron Age.

The Roxby settlement, evidently truncated by later settlement and agriculture, again probably spanned a protracted period of time, from the pre-Roman Iron Age, into the opening centuries AD at least. The single radiocarbon date might argue for a late pre-Roman Iron Age occupation, but the probability is that the site was occupied over several centuries. In its pre-Roman phase, it appears to have been for permanent rather than seasonal occupation by a community engaged in arable cultivation as well as pastoralism, in view of the pattern of cross-ploughing underlying House 1. Iron working is indicated by a bowl furnace in House 3 and smithing hearth in House 2, though in view of the relatively small quantities of debris the excavator was inclined to view this as a repair-workshop rather than a large-scale local industry. Metalworking in this instance therefore need not be a measure of high status.

Tees to Northumberland coastal plain

Longevity of the pattern of land-use has been abundantly demonstrated in Upper Teesdale, notably by fieldwork in the 1970s and 1980s by Coggins and Fairless (Coggins, 1985, 1986). Settlements range in date from the later middle Bronze Age at Bracken Rigg to the eighth century AD at Simy Folds, with early Iron Age occupation the least positively demonstrated. It seems probable, nevertheless, that the homestead at Forcegarth Pasture North originated in the later first millennium BC, since there was no Roman material present on the site, as there was at the neighbouring Forcegarth Pasture South, and the radiocarbon date (1810+/−70 BP – Har 804) came from a relatively late context. Within the enclosure a central house cluster of three conjoined rooms could have been spanned by a single roof. Unlike the Bracken Rigg houses, whose wall foundations were no more than a spread of stony rubble, these walls were properly coursed. Two internal hearths yielded evidence of iron working. There was a further separate roundhouse within the enclosure. Two further roundhouses just outside may have resulted from expansion of the settlement, or perhaps were part of an earlier, unenclosed phase of occupation. On the south side of the valley, extensive linear dykes and field enclosures indicate an ordered system of landscape division, which probably dates from the prehistoric period, though modified in later generations. Palaeobotanical evidence also indicates cereal cultivation from the Bronze Age, though pastoralism was probably always the dominant element in the economy.

In the study of lowland Iron Age settlements, enclosed sites have inevitably been predominant, if only because their earthworks afford a better prospect of survival than unenclosed sites, and they are more readily identified from air-photographic survey. Pre-eminent among enclosed sites are hillforts, commonly regarded as most typical of the period, and representing the apex of a hierarchical social order. In fact, in the Tyne-Tees region there are very few, an absence that cannot be explained on topographical grounds, nor indeed on grounds of sparse population, since lesser enclosed homesteads have been increasingly documented through air-photography and fieldwork from the early 1970s.

Enclosed settlements from the Tees to the Northumberland coastal plain may typically contain a single, centrally located large roundhouse that was presumably occupied by a nuclear family. Among older excavations, the classic site of West Brandon in Co. Durham (Jobey, 1962) still serves as a useful model. There were no radiocarbon dates, and the poverty of the material assemblage inhibits dating on that basis. On the other hand, there were no Roman finds, and the querns were saddle-querns, suggesting a dating earlier than the second century BC or thereabouts. The main enclosure (Fig. 2.3, 2) displayed two major constructional phases, the first of twin-palisaded construction, the second a single bank and ditch. That the two were successive rather than contemporary elements of a more complex enclosure was indicated by the offset alignment of their entrances. Palisades are hardly chronologically diagnostic, but they are widely represented in the Borders in the mid-first millennium BC, so that the enclosed settlement at West Brandon need not have been as late as Jobey's cautious estimate. A smaller post-ring roundhouse in the south-east corner of the site, external to the palisaded enclosure and truncated by its ditched successor, probably pre-dated both, and was tentatively assigned by the excavator to the late Bronze Age.

The central roundhouse (Fig. 2.5, 2–3), with its successive plans marginally offset, is one of the largest yet excavated, with an overall diameter of nearly 18 metres. It is also unusual in having in its primary phase no less than four concentric circles of postholes. Of these the second largest circle was interpreted as the external wall of the house, corresponding to the continuous ring-groove of the phase 2 plan. Within this was the main weight-bearing circle of postholes, conforming to the proportional range of standard roundhouse geometry. The innermost ring of House A could relate to support of the upper ring-beam, required of this scale of building (Reynolds, 1993); alternatively it could have screened a central hearth or supported spits and suspended vessels. In House B, a central setting of four posts, distinguished by their greater depth, may have served a similar function. Notwithstanding the Little Woodbury model, central four-posters are not essential for roof support, though they would have been an asset like a builder's scaffolding frame in the constructional stages, and could have been used to support a mezzanine floor or internal fittings around the hearth thereafter. Like a modern scaffolding tower, this frame could have been free-standing, so that earth-fast postholes will not necessarily survive. Nevertheless, four-post settings can vary, from the smaller, centrally located kind, as at Little Woodbury, which may have enclosed the hearth, to the larger variant, as at West Brandon, which may more probably be linked to upper superstructure. In both phases at West Brandon an outermost ring of posts was interpreted as eaves-support, though why this should have been considered necessary is unclear. Structurally these large roundhouses do not require external buttressing, though their thatched eaves might have required protection from livestock.

West Brandon, together with the comparable single homestead at West House, Coxhoe (Haselgrove and Allon, 1982), are the two sub-rectilinear enclosed sites that appear to have been abandoned before the close of the first millennium BC. They also both lie along the edge of the 125-metre contour, where, as Haselgrove (1982a) has argued, they would have been ideally located to exploit the lower pastures and water sources of the Wear valley required for cattle raising, but with access to upland grazing for sheep. It is therefore conceivable that the abandonment or relocation of these settlements was coincident with a period of agricultural intensification in the last centuries before the Roman occupation, when cereal production achieved greater prominence in the lower margins of the Tees and Wear, whilst in the Pennine valleys seasonal pastoral sites may have been exploited on a more permanent basis. This process of agricultural intensification, or extensification, would be consistent both with palynological evidence for an increase in forest clearance in the later pre-Roman Iron Age, and for innovation in cereal cultivation in parts of north-eastern England at this period.

Van der Veen's (1992) analysis of cereals from excavated sites in the Tees lowlands on the one hand, and from a group of sites north of the Tyne on the other, suggested that two significantly different crop husbandry regimes were being practised. Her Group A sites, north of the Tyne, yielded emmer, barley and some spelt wheat; the weed assemblage contained annuals rather than perennials, suggesting a considerable degree of soil disturbance, and nitrogen levels were high, indicative of manuring to enhance fertility. Group B, in the Tees valley, produced no emmer, but spelt and barley, on soils which were low in nitrogen, suggesting more intensive cropping, and in association with perennials as well as annual weeds, suggesting a relatively lower degree of soil disturbance. The relative merits of emmer and spelt wheat in terms of yields have not been closely documented experimentally, but there is evidence that the increasing dominance of spelt in the later first millennium BC was because it proved hardier, more disease resistant and more tolerant of a range of soil types than emmer. It was tentatively suggested that the cultivation of the Group A sites might have been by spade and hoe, in contrast to the plough agriculture practised in the Group B regime. The intensification of agriculture in the later pre-Roman Iron Age, witnessed in different degrees in north-eastern England, was part of a wider pattern of change, for which evidence has also been adduced for parts of Southern Britain and beyond. It was evidently not prompted initially by the Roman occupation, though the demands of the Roman army on the northern frontier would certainly have had its impact on the local economy. The causes were doubtless social as well as economic, with population expansion resulting in a need for greater agricultural production. Agricultural intensification in turn may have induced a decline in soil fertility and yields, prompting diversification in agricultural practice. Pastoralism would have been a major if not the dominant component in the agricultural economy of much of northern England, and even in a fertile belt like the Tyne-Tees region, cattle, with sheep, remained an important component of the faunal assemblages at Catcote, Hartlepool (Long, 1988), at Coxhoe and at Stanwick. With the possible exception of Ingleby Barwick there is very little evidence for field-systems in association with the homestead settlements of the Tyne-Tees region. Air-photography has on occasions located potential patterns, but these are in most cases more probably the result of periglacial frost cracking than of early agriculture.

Unenclosed settlements are, not surprisingly, more elusive than enclosed sites. Isolated ring-ditches, identified from the air, could equally be Bronze Age burials in the absence of excavation to demonstrate otherwise. Occasionally, as at Strawberry Hill, Shadforth (Haselgrove, 1980), where a ring-ditch occurs outside the polygonal enclosure, it is likely to be an Iron Age house site on grounds of similarity with two more ring-ditches inside the enclosure. But whether this indicates a separate phase of open settlement remains uncertain.

The site at Thorpe Thewles (Heslop, 1987) provides an interesting sequence of occupation, contradicting the simplistic model of a 'progresssion towards enclosure' that for many years dominated Iron Age studies in south-eastern Scotland. Here the principal enclosed phase (phase 2) was not unlike the rectangular homestead model, with a single large house at its centre. The house-type was different from either the post-ring or ring-groove variants of West Brandon, however, being defined by a broader enclosing ditch, probably a drainage ditch rather than integral to the building in the manner of the Scottish ring-ditch houses. Ancillary buildings of more than one sub-phase of construction were clustered around the principal building. In the next phase (phase 3) the ditch was evidently backfilled to allow expansion of the settlement, unenclosed and with numerous smaller roundhouses and ancillary structures. As ever, the date of the earliest occupation at Thorpe Thewles is hard to establish, but thermoluminescent dating suggests it may have been no later than the third quarter of the first millennium BC, and the presence of saddle-querns would be consistent with this assessment. The site in its later pre-Roman or early Roman occupation is remarkable for the relative wealth of its material assemblage, with a range of small personal ornaments, which included probable imports from Southern Britain or the Continent. Its nucleated layout of structures is most closely paralleled by the mid-first century AD occupation of the Tofts field at

Stanwick, and possibly by the late Iron Age and early Roman settlement at Catcote, Hartlepool.

No formal enclosure was identified at Catcote, though linear boundary gullies suggested a system of field enclosures comparable perhaps to those discovered from air-survey at Ingleby Barwick on the Tees (Heslop, 1984). The date of the native settlement on the ridge top was originally assumed to be late on account of the presence of Romano-British pottery and artefacts, but the sequence evidently began earlier in the pre-Roman Iron Age (Long, 1988), a conclusion that was endorsed by thermoluminescence dating for the adjacent downslope site (Vyner and Daniels, 1989). Both Stanwick and Catcote showed evidence of imported pottery from south-eastern England or beyond of the immediately pre-Roman period. Apart from the obvious land route through the Vale of York to the south, there is therefore the further possibility that sea-borne trade or cabotage was responsible for the introduction of these exotic goods.

Excavations and re-assessment of the Stanwick fortification in the 1980s has resulted in a major review of Wheeler's conclusions of the 1950s (Haselgrove *et al.* 1990; Welfare *et al.*, 1990; Haselgrove *et al.*, 1990). It now seems probable that the earliest Iron Age settlement, dating perhaps from a century or two before the Roman occupation, was undefended, though it may have had several small, ditched enclosures. The nearby site at Melsonby (Fitts *et al.*, 1999) was likewise an open settlement, perhaps in use as early as the third or fourth centuries BC. The principal excavated structure of this early phase of occupation was a ring-groove building some 9 metres in diameter, set concentrically within a penannular gully, which in the absence of evidence for uprights was assumed to have been for drainage. The ring-groove was shadowed internally by a fainter slot with stake-holes, together forming a ground-plan for which there are few close local parallels. It was unclear whether the penannular gully and ring-grooves were part of a single building, or representative of successive phases of construction, and the absence of hearth or internal features leaves open the question whether it was indeed a roofed domestic structure. Radiocarbon samples from the penannular gully confirmed its use in the second half of the first millennium BC, and the absence of Iron Age coarse pottery could indicate that it was abandoned before the first century BC. By the first century AD the settlement comprised a network of small ditches and gullies, and evidently shared with the larger Stanwick site the benefits of imports from the Romanised south. The extent of this 'Romanisation' of Brigantia will be considered further in due course. For the present, the importance of Stanwick and Melsonby is their demonstration of the fact that open settlements formed an integral part of the Iron Age landscape from at least the third or fourth centuries BC, so that here at least open and enclosed settlements were contemporary facets of a more complex pattern of settlement.

The Central and Southern Pennines, Lancashire and Cheshire

The relatively sparse distribution of hillforts in northern England suggests that the political, social and economic roles of southern hillforts were fulfilled in other ways in the north. Quite evidently the higher Pennines over 300 metres would have been less attractive climatically for settlement, at any rate by the first millennium, so that it is significant that Mam Tor in the Derbyshire Peak (Fig. 2.9; Coombs and Thompson, 1979), where house stances appear to have been quite densely concentrated, has yielded

Figure 2.9 Mam Tor, Derbyshire, air-photograph. Cambridge University Collection of Air Photographs, BAW 09, Unit for Landscape Modelling, copyright reserved.

radiocarbon dates indicating occupation, though not certainly fortification, in the middle Bronze Age. In the southern Pennines there are several hillforts that have timber-framed or stone-revetted ramparts including Bunbury Camp, Ball Cross and probably Wincobank (Beswick, 1987), all of which could have been constructed or occupied in the later Bronze Age or early Iron Age.

Castle Hill, Almondbury, was for many years regarded as the centre of the southern Brigantes on the eve of the Roman Conquest and identified with Ptolemy's *Camulodunon* (Richmond, 1925), an identification that was made more plausible by the false attribution of Corieltauvian coins from the Lightcliffe hoard to a find-spot at Almondbury (Allen, 1961, 260–1, 293: 261; 1963: 22–8). As a result of a series of radiocarbon dates from his later excavations Varley (1976) revised his earlier assessments and acknowledged that Castle Hill was abandoned several centuries before the Conquest. He proposed a fourfold structural sequence, for the last three of which a series of radiocarbon dates were centred in the sixth and fifth centuries BC, giving a calibrated span beginning in the first half of the first millennium BC. This re-assessment is also consistent with the thermoluminescent date for the actual destruction of the final multivallate fort. Varley's conclusion was unequivocal:

> If Almondbury ever was Camulodunum, it can only have been given its name as a tribute to that Celtic god of war whose stronghold it had been, at least in legend, and whose ancient ruins could have been a place of excursion for those stationed at Slack.
> (Varley, 1976: 130)

From the available evidence, therefore, all of the hillforts in the southern Pennines could have been abandoned by the later fifth or fourth centuries BC. Settlement remains of the second half of the first millennium BC have proved so elusive that some have argued that the region must have been depopulated in consequence of climatic deterioration of the later Bronze Age, and used only for occasional summer transhumance until the Roman occupation, when exploitation of lead deposits encouraged re-settlement on a significant scale. Palaeoenvironmental evidence, however, suggests that agricultural activity was unbroken throughout the first millennium BC (Bevan, 1999: 12–13; 2000: 148), and it is more probable that the problem lies in dating the origins of settlements that continued to be occupied in the Romano-British period.

If Iron Age settlement in the southern Pennines has been conventionally regarded as sparsely represented, in the Mersey and Ribble coastal belt until recent years it was dismissed as virtually non-existent. The geography of the region, with its natural routes of access to and from the Irish Sea, made this seem implausible, but modern development and other constraints hinder archaeological visibility. It has commonly been assumed that the region was still extensively wooded at the time of the Roman advance under Agricola, though environmental evidence may qualify this view (Schoenwetter, 1982). The paucity of known settlements is not exclusive to the Iron Age; apart from coin-hoards, evidence of settlement in the Roman period between the Mersey and the Ribble is equally sparse. Air-photographic survey in fact has now resulted in the recognition of a number of enclosed settlements, some of which, like Great Woolden Hall (Nevell, 1989) were demonstrably occupied in the Iron Age, while others by analogy most probably were. In Cheshire there is evidence for specialised activities, notably the production of salt, which through the first millennium BC was traded through North Wales and the Welsh Marches, as indicated by the distribution of briquetage, or 'Very Coarse Pottery' (VCP) (Morris, 1985). Whether hillforts played any role in the control and distribution of this resource has yet to be demonstrated, but their distribution, ringing the estuaries of the Dee and Mersey, by contrast to their almost total absence north of the Mersey, certainly implies a strategic network. Dating of these hillforts is far from firmly established. The two Cheshire forts, at Eddisbury (Varley, 1950) and Maiden Castle, Bickerton (Varley, 1935, 1936a, 1936b, 1964), apparently had timber-laced ramparts with stone facing, which may have been part of a late Bronze Age or earlier Iron Age defensive system, though probably within a longer structural sequence. The palisade underlying the prehistoric rampart at Beeston Castle (Ellis, 1993) could likewise date from the later Bronze Age.

The strategic disposition of the Cheshire hillforts around the Mersey and Dee estuaries is mirrored in lesser scale by the three known hillforts facing Morecambe Bay, Skelmore Heads, Castle Head and Warton Crag. Skelmore Heads (Powell et al., 1963) again shows a sequence from stockaded enclosure to earthwork fort, which may have included a timber box-rampart. The late Bronze Age hoard from the site is not demonstrably of the same period as the fort, but that possibility cannot be ruled out. Dating is uncertain for all three, but there is no compelling evidence for late occupation. Among the most enigmatic sites in this area is Urswick Stone Walls (Dobson, 1907), only a mile south-west of Skelmore Heads. Its dating remains uncertain, but the absence of Romano-British pottery from the early excavations argues against its occupation in the Roman period (pace Challis and Harding, 1975: 135). The fact that the enclosure walls and the dun-like walls of the principal roundhouse were constructed of stone certainly need not imply a Roman date, especially when the construction includes massive, undressed, orthostatic boulders. Finally among the Lancashire group are the hillforts of Portfield, Whalley and Castercliff, overlooking tributaries of the Ribble. The cliff-edge fort at Portfield (Beswick and Coombs, 1986) certainly had multi-period defences, with stone-revetted and timber-laced walls, but the sequence was not absolutely resolved by excavation. A late Bronze Age origin for the hillfort was inferred in part from the discovery within the enclosure of a hoard of bronzes, including two socketed axes, a tanged knife and a socketed gouge, which Longworth (Blundell and Longworth, 1967) had concluded was a bronze worker's scrap hoard, buried perhaps as late as the seventh century BC. Two gold items, a penannular tress-ring and a bracelet, nevertheless, were surely higher-status items, and if contemporary with the hillfort may indicate that site's social importance. The small, oval hillfort at Castercliff was certainly defended with stone and timber ramparts from an early date, excavations (Coombs, 1982) having produced uncalibrated radiocarbon dates centring on the mid-first millennium BC. The site evidently had a turbulent history, its inner rampart being partly vitrified and the outer remaining unfinished.

Though our knowledge of the hillforts of this region is plainly insufficient to support more than provisional conclusions, they are nevertheless not entirely without rationale. The Cheshire and Morecambe Bay distributions may well imply communities controlling access to and from the Irish Sea routes, the former with the particular asset of salt production, and the latter combining access to arable resources within reasonable proximity and upland pastures beyond. The southern Pennine group of forts is likewise a coherent distribution, each perhaps representative of a local community focus, within a broader landscape in which hillforts are not the dominant class of field monument. Ingleborough alone in this analysis stands in enigmatic isolation. What is clear, however, is that the role of hillforts in northern England does not remotely accord with the patterns observed in Wessex or southern England more generally. Here there are no 'developed hillforts' (Cunliffe, 1991: 352) dominating the later pre-Roman Iron Age; indeed on present evidence there would appear to be few if any hillforts still occupied in the later pre-Roman Iron Age.

Ingleborough (Fig. 2.10; King, 1987; Bowden et al., 1989), overlooking a tributary of the Lune in the central Pennines, is indeed exceptional. At 723 metres it is hard to conceive that this was in permanent rather than seasonal occupation, even in the later Bronze Age. Rivet (1958: 142) proposed the identification of the site with Ptolemy's *Rigodunon*, and it is true that a Castor ware sherd and coin of Antoninus Pius were found on the site. But as Challis observed (Challis and Harding, 1975: 123), it is inconceivable that the construction of this substantial 6 ha fort should have been permitted in the Roman period. The univallate enclosure is itself noteworthy for its external stone facing, combining orthostats and coursed walling. Within its core, the rampart was divided as in casemate construction with vertical slabs forming a series of compartments, a technique which may be related, though not necessarily derivatively, to timber box-ramparts. Within the interior some twenty hut-circles have been identified, though an alternative suggestion that these might have been burial cairns needs further examination. The possibility of external settlement on the terraces below the summit should also not be discounted. Whatever its date, the Ingleborough fort occupies an imposing situation atop of a series of natural steps, reinforcing its role as a symbolic focus in the landscape.

Twenty miles to the east, in Wharfedale north of Grassington, is one of the densest areas of upland field-systems anywhere in Northern Britain (Fig. 2.11). Lying between

(a)

(b)

Figure 2.10 Ingleborough, Yorkshire, air-photographs. a, landscape situation; b, ramparts and interior. National Monuments Record England, a, NMR 12065/51, SD7474/30, b, NMR 12065/34, SD 7474/13. Crown copyright

Figure 2.11
Grassington,
Yorkshire, air-
photograph of
field-system.
Cambridge
University
Collection of Air
Photographs,
K17-AC 26, Unit
for Landscape
Modelling,
copyright
reserved.

the 250 and 300 metre contours, they are made up of small, square and larger rectangular fields, with occasional settlements in which circular, stone house foundations are visible. Since the pioneer fieldwork of Raistrick (1937, 1939; Raistrick and Chapman, 1929; King, 1978) these have been assigned to the later pre-Roman and Roman Iron Age, on the basis of pottery scatters, but the expectation must be that their origins lie in the Bronze Age or early Iron Age, had we the means archaeologically to test this hypothesis.

By way of a postscript, we may note that one of the two principal hillforts on the Isle of Man also appears to have been occupied in the first half of the first millennium BC, consistent with the evidence from northern England. At over 480 metres, the hillfort of South Barrule, like Ingleborough, might appear to be too high to sustain permanent occupation, yet it contained within its inner rampart at least eighty circular house stances, one of which yielded an early date for a single radiocarbon sample from its latest occupation. Pottery, mainly simple barrel-shaped jars, could be consistent with a late Bronze Age or earliest Iron Age attribution, and certainly sets the site apart from the local Iron Age promontory forts, which are largely aceramic (Gelling, 1972). Lines of stake-holes beyond the inner rampart's ditch, apparently inclined outwards, have been interpreted as emplacements for wooden *chevaux de frise* (Harbison, 1971).

Cumbria and the north-west of England

Hillforts are likewise not a major component of earlier Iron Age settlement in north-west England. As in the Borders, the distinction between small hillfort and more substantial ditched homestead becomes an issue of semantics, since the great majority of sites are under an acre in an enclosed area. Only Carrock Fell, at over 2 hectares (5 acres) stands out as potentially on the scale of a regional *oppidum*. R. G. Collingwood (1938) thought that it could have been occupied as a major tribal centre, and that the breaks in its perimeter walls were the result of deliberate slighting of the defences by Roman forces. But its height (650 metres) and exposed location, together with the absence of any surviving surface traces of habitation, make it unlikely that it was permanently occupied, with permanent settlements doubtless favouring lower locations (Higham, 1986: 129). The settlement at Dobcross Hall (Higham, 1981) included a univallate enclosure of 3 ha in which the ditch was of defensive proportions, and which the excavator considered was probably pre-Roman, notwithstanding a subsequent phase of Romano-British activity within its inner enclosure. Among smaller enclosed sites, the triple-ditched cliff-edge enclosure at Swarthy Hall on the Solway Plain produced a single radiocarbon date from its ditch filling of 450+/−50 BC (GU-2657; Bewley, 1992), and it might be anticipated that other ditched enclosures now recognised from air-photography were built and occupied in the earlier pre-Roman Iron Age.

Nowhere in Northern Britain are the problems of identifying pre-Roman Iron Age settlement so acutely demonstrated as they are west of the Pennines. In the absence of diagnostic artefacts for the early Iron Age, the regular occurrence of scraps of Romano-British pottery or glass invariably prejudices interpretation in favour of a principal occupation in the Roman period. The relative density of settlements, either surviving above the zone of later destruction like the extensive habitations, enclosures and fields on Crosby Garrett and Crosby Ravensworth fells, or as crop-marks identified by air-photography in the Eden valley or Solway plain, makes it unlikely that the region was only sparsely settled in the immediately preceding or succeeding phases. At Crosby Garrett (Fig. 2.12) fields radiate around the Severals settlement in a way that suggests an integral system. The disposition of sites along the fell almost implies space for an original fourth focus between Severals and Intake 1 that has been subsequently over-ridden and obliterated. The problem of identifying a sequence of settlement types, successively distinctive through morphology or dateable by material associations, has remained intractable. The answer must be that 'native' settlement remained largely unchanged over a millennium or more from the mid-first millennium BC. Many sites display a degree of complexity that suggests longevity of occupation. Assuming that they originated in the pre-Roman Iron Age and remained in use throughout and beyond the Roman occupation, it is hardly surprising that superficial analysis of finds should focus upon the Roman interlude, a problem that was clearly recognised by R. G. Collingwood at Ewe Close (1933: 204). In his survey of the Crosby Ravensworth sites, Collingwood had noted the frequent occurrence of barrows of presumed Bronze Age date in proximity to 'native' settlements, a relationship which, as we have seen, has led a more recent generation of fieldworkers in the North York Moors to infer an older genesis for the landscape pattern of dykes and settlements. For Collingwood, however, there was no great dilemma in the apparent Iron Age hiatus, since he assumed that in this cultural backwater the Bronze Age continued uninterrupted until the Roman period.

Since Ewe Close (Fig. 2.13), however, has remained in the archaeological canon as the archetypal Roman 'native' homestead in the west Pennines, it is worth revisiting briefly to be clear what W. G. Collingwood actually reported. First of all, the complex of enclosures, house stances and dykes is the product of composite construction over a protracted

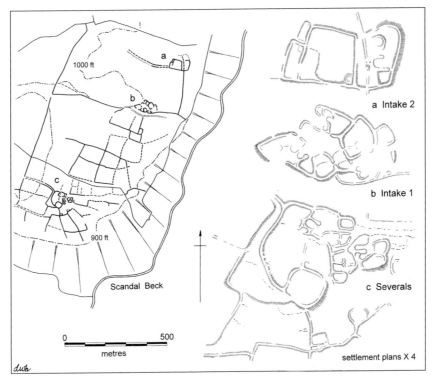

Figure 2.12 Crosby Garrett, Westmorland, plan of native settlements. Drawing by D. W. Harding, adapted from RCHME (1936).

period of time, as Jobey observed (1966b: 11). The fact that the Roman road deviated in its route from Low Borrow Bridge to Brougham in order to accommodate a pre-existing settlement at Ewe Close (RCHME, 1936: 83) need not itself require a pre-Roman date for that settlement, but it might well imply a native settlement of established importance from pre-Roman times. In fact the sub-square enclosure containing the large stone-built roundhouse is in plan not unlike Northumbrian Iron Age homesteads when detached from the encroaching network of irregular enclosures and garths, and it would be tempting to think that there could have been earlier phases of construction, whether of stone or timber or a combination of both, beneath the surviving walls and paving. W. G. Collingwood recognised that there were intrusions into the subsoil beneath the paving of the central roundhouse, which he therefore acknowledged may have been secondary. He also reported quite specifically that one of the roundhouses (K) contained no Roman material or finds whatsoever despite careful excavation, which, in the light of a number of Roman finds elsewhere within the enclosure might indicate that this building was not part of the contemporary layout. He was certainly aware of the possibility that the extant structures represented multi-period construction. While some features may have been Mediaeval or later, we should not discount the possibility of post-Roman occupation, which archaeologically could prove as elusive as evidence of pre-Roman settlement. Notwithstanding the presence of Roman pottery of second to fourth century date, the character of the settlement, however, is 'native', not just in terms of the predominance

Figure 2.13 Ewe Close, Westmorland, air-photograph from the north-east. Cambridge University Collection of Air Photographs, AQM 04, Unit for Landscape Modelling, copyright reserved.

of circular house-plans, but also in the construction of the enclosure walls, in which the use of substantial boulders, frequently described as 'set on edge', recalls the monumental enclosure at Urswick Stone Walls. The cellular structures recessed into the thickness of the enclosure walls on either side of the entrance at Ewe Close might be reminiscent of guard chambers flanking hillfort entrances in the Welsh Marches, but the cellular style of building is one which has a long pedigree in Atlantic Britain and Ireland, arguably from the later Bronze Age and certainly into the mid-first millennium AD.

The elements of the Ewe Close settlement are reflected variously in the neighbouring settlements of Crosby Ravensworth and Crosby Garrett. The combination of recti-linear enclosure with curvilinear or irregular enclosures is matched at Ewe Locks, Crosby Ravensworth, which also has a principal roundhouse located just off-centre within a rectilinear enclosure. Clusters of conjoined circular or cellular houses are found on several sites, though at Burwens some apparently conjoined houses are more probably the product of successive phases of rebuilding within a confined enclosure. The Crosby Ravensworth sites were evidently originally part of a more extensive landscape pattern, linked by a complex network of dykes. It extends across the Scandal Beck into the neigh-bouring districts of Crosby Garrett and Waitby, linking some 8 kilometres of landscape into a unitary system (Jones, 1975). Severals and the two Intake settlements at Crosby Garrett, in particular, are defined by dykes and natural topography, and linked by rectilinear fields, in a manner which argues for broad contemporaneity of use, even though the layout may have mutated over many generations.

The case for regarding the majority of settlements in Cumbria and the west Pennines as 'Roman native' must take account of the stratigraphic context of occasional dateable finds. At Yanwath Wood near Penrith (Higham, 1983), for example, abraded samian sherds and fragments of Roman glass were found *'close to the lip'* of a ditch that had evidently silted up before these scraps were deposited. The clearest demonstration of this principle is the site at Wolsty Hall (Blake, 1959). Of the three adjacent enclosures, oval, circular and rectangular, the latter two both produced clear evidence of occupation in the Roman period. In the case of the oval enclosure, by contrast, Hadrianic pottery occurred in the *upper* levels of the ditch filling, suggesting that it was long since out of use by the early second century, whilst the roundhouse occupation within the enclosure produced no Roman material, consistent with this conclusion. Where Roman occupation is clearly attested in close proximity, here as at Ewe Close or indeed at Levisham Moor, it seems reasonable to conclude that its absence may be as indicative of a pre-Roman (or conceivably post-Roman) date as its presence in primary contexts would be of contemporary occupation.

The Wolsty Hall roundhouse (Fig. 2.6, 5) was of a type that underlines the regional diversity of Iron Age roundhouse architecture. Its external wall, 13.5 metres in diameter, was based on a ring-groove, with two opposed entrances, each with a pair of post-holes marking the inner limit of a porch. Around the inner edge of the ring-groove the excavator detected traces of a turf wall or revetment, which in turn was defined on its inner edge by an arc of cobbled flooring. Whether the combination of timber and turf represents composite construction or a phase of rebuilding is unclear. A setting of four posts in the centre of the house, assuming that this is integral to its plan, is unusual, notwithstanding the example from West Brandon. Within the considerable diversity of roundhouse construction in the early Iron Age in northern England, there are, nevertheless, recurrent elements, including ring-groove construction and the use of double entrances. These features are also found in the roundhouses of the Borders and south-western Scotland, as we shall see in due course.

Chapter 3

The Borders and southern Scotland

Any re-evaluation of later prehistoric settlement in the Borders should begin with a review of the Hownam sequence (Fig. 3.1; Piggott, C. M. 1948). Hownam served as the type-site for Piggott's Tyne–Forth province (Piggott, S., 1966) and for nearly forty years provided the model for Iron Age settlement in south-east Scotland. Already by the early 1980s (Harding, 1982) the validity of the Hownam sequence as a regional model was being questioned, and today its limitations are widely acknowledged (Armit, 1999a). In essence the sequence was based upon an inferred structural progression from the simplest to the most complex, from palisaded enclosure through univallate enclosure to multivallate defences. A final phase or phases, assigned to the Roman period, was represented by an open settlement of stone-built houses on foundations scooped into and over the derelict defences. In broad outline there seems to be no compelling reason to dispute the validity of this sequence for Hownam itself, though the excavation report prompts questions regarding the correlation of earthworks around the western and southern circuits. The problem arose in its application more generally as a regional model, since more recent research has indicated that any supposed 'progression towards enclosure', even if locally valid, need not have been regionally uniform or synchronous. Still less would current opinion accept that hillforts appeared in southern Scotland as a result of cultural diffusion from the south.

Mercer's fieldwork of the mid-1980s in the adjacent Bowmont valley (Mercer, 1987) in fact suggested the possibility of parallel progression from palisaded enclosures to walled or embanked enclosures, at Camp Tops and Craik Moor, Morebattle, among other sites, which might imply similar social and economic conditions among neighbouring communities. Further afield, the classic site at Braidwood, Midlothian (Fig. 3.2, 3; Stevenson, 1949a), demonstrably had a palisaded or stockaded enclosure before the construction of earthwork defences. But elsewhere, most notably at Broxmouth, East Lothian (Hill, P., 1982b), the defensive sequence proved to be rather more complex, with ditched defences, univallate or bivallate, being maintained or neglected in a much more irregular sequence. Here too the final phase of occupation appeared to be post-defensive, and represented by roundhouses with stone-built foundations, though seemingly dating from the later pre-Roman period. Resurvey of the Braidwood settlement (Gannon, 1999) has likewise suggested a more complex sequence, in which periods of unenclosed occupation may have existed before, between and after the phases of enclosed settlement. Other excavations in East Lothian indicated a much greater diversity in settlement patterns. At St Germains, Tranent, the settlement sequence seemed to bear little similarity to the Hownam model (Harding, 1982: 189), though the published conclusion

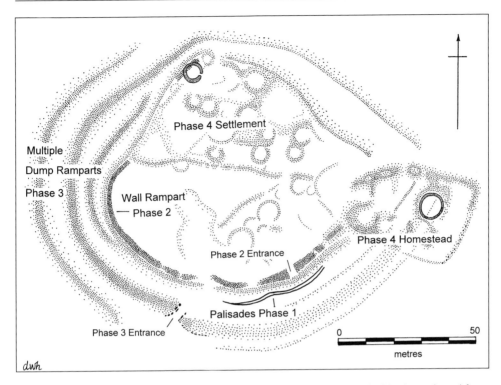

Figure 3.1 Hownam Rings, Roxburghshire, sequence plan. Drawing by D. W. Harding, adapted from Piggott, C. M. (1948).

still endorsed the general trend towards enclosure (Alexander and Watkins, 1998: 250). The twin enclosures at Fishers Road, Port Seton (Haselgrove and McCullagh, 2000), on the other hand, though incorporating both palisaded and ditched components, suggested a more complex system of complementary units within an integrated landscape pattern.

The predominance of field research in the post-war era in south-eastern Scotland has meant that the validity or otherwise of the concept of a 'progression towards enclosure' has generally been discussed in the context of the Tyne–Forth province. With some notable exceptions, such as Jobey's excavations at Burnswark and Boonies (1978a, 1974), south-western Scotland until recent years attracted less attention, an imbalance that has been redressed in some degree by Mercer's work in Eskdale and the Royal Commission's (1997) survey of Eastern Dumfriesshire. At the complex site at Gibb's Hill a sequence of palisaded enclosures is later than the earthworks around the north-western sector of the site, while unenclosed houses also overlie the earlier earthworks, and this pattern is likely to have been replicated widely through the Borders.

The fact is that palisading is simply a constructional technique, and cannot be regarded as chronologically or culturally diagnostic. Though requiring a substantial timber resource of suitable quality and convenient availability, it doubtless would have been less labour-intensive in construction than a stone-faced bank and ditch, and as such might well have been employed in the initial stages of establishing a settlement. Yet equally it could have been the simplest method of later renovation of a depleted earthwork. In

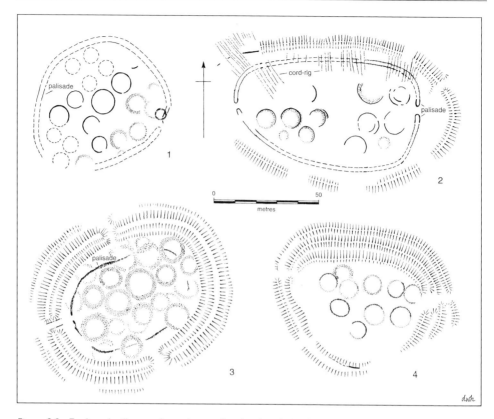

Figure 3.2 Enclosed villages of south-east Scotland and the Borders. 1, High Knowes B, Alnham, Northumberland, adapted from Jobey and Tait (1966); 2, Hayhope Knowe, Roxburghshire, adapted from Piggott, C. M. (1949) with additions from Mercer (1987) and DWH air-photographs; 3, Braidwood, Midlothian, adapted from Piggott, S. (1958b) with additions from Gannon (1999); 4, Camp Tops, Roxburghshire, adapted from RCAHMS (1956) with additions from Mercer (1987). Drawings by D. W. Harding.

some cases the palisades demonstrably cut across earlier earthworks, as at Corsehope Rings, Midlothian, and in other instances, like Blackbrough, Roxburghshire (Fig. 3.3), it seems improbable that the palisade within the earthwork would have survived had it pre-dated the more substantial enclosure. In any event, palisades and earthworks need not be regarded as mutually exclusive. The embanked palisade has been a recognised form of enclosure since Feachem's work at Harehope in Peeblesshire (Feachem, 1960), and a combination of bank and fence seems particularly appropriate where the shallow bedrock made excavation of a deep quarry-ditch impractical. Finally, it should be stressed that these techniques of defensive or protective enclosure were not necessarily restricted to the later prehistoric period. Similar techniques were employed in the post-Roman or Dark Age periods, and the paucity of diagnostic material remains from both pre-Roman and post-Roman contexts may make it hard to distinguish the two horizons.

What is commonly overlooked in contemporary reviews of the Hownam sequence is that Mrs Piggott's excavation at Hownam Rings was only one part of a more extensive campaign of field research into Borders hillforts and related settlements. Her two

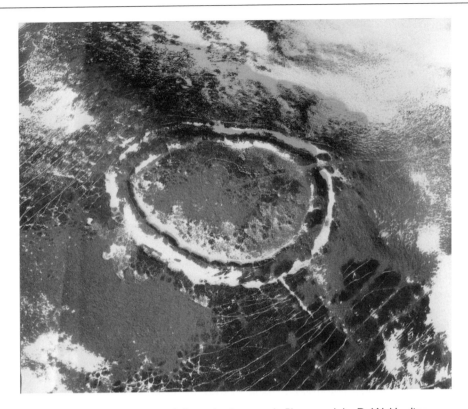

Figure 3.3 Blackbrough Hill, Roxburghshire, air-photograph. Photograph by D. W. Harding.

subsequent excavations, at Hayhope Knowe (Fig. 3.2, 2; Piggott, C. M., 1949) and at Bonchester Hill (Fig. 8.1, 1; Piggott, C. M., 1950) more than amply demonstrated the diversity of character of Iron Age settlements in the region. At Hayhope Knowe the double palisade was indeed followed by the construction, presumed incomplete, of an earthwork enclosure. But even this latter apparently incorporated an element of palisading in its revetment. Bonchester Hill showed no trace of a primary palisade, either from Curle's work at the beginning of the twentieth century (Curle, 1910) or from Mrs Piggott's more thorough investigation of 1950. It did, on the other hand, yield a sequence of earthwork enclosures displaying at least three major constructional phases, probably from the early Iron Age and continuing into the late Roman or post-Roman Iron Age. The older excavations within the enclosure had produced saddle-querns from two of the roundhouses together with a crook-headed pin, which certainly points to the possibility of occupation from the earlier Iron Age, though whether in an open or enclosed settlement must remain in question. A La Tène 1c brooch spring from a residual context equally argues an early Iron Age occupation, rather earlier than the conservative dating offered by the excavator at the time. In effect, Bonchester hardly conforms to the classic Hownam sequence, whilst the significance of its later occupation, clearly appreciated by Mrs Piggott, has been largely overlooked ever since.

During the late 1970s and 1980s, when air-photographic survey was greatly amplifying the number of known sites in the south-eastern Borders, especially those of the newly recognised cord-rig agriculture, criticism was expressed by some senior professional archaeologists of this concentration on areas already intensively documented, to the implied neglect of other areas that had been less well researched. Rational enough on the face of it, this criticism missed the point that air-photography was not simply about collecting new sites like postage stamps, but about increasing qualitatively our understanding of later prehistoric settlement. In areas like Hownam and Morebattle, intensive survey, from the air and on the ground, had resulted in a density of known sites that must approach very closely the most comprehensive that the archaeologist could expect to achieve, so that it should be possible to reconstruct the nature of the later prehistoric landscape more reliably here than in most other areas.

Hillforts and enclosure

The broad category of hillforts embraces a very wide range of sites, in terms of their enclosed area, and the scale and complexity of their earthwork defences. In southern Scotland very few hillforts attain the scale of earthworks of many southern hillforts. The largest were commonly referred to as *oppida* by analogy with their southern British counterparts, with the questionable implication that they served as tribal centres with proto-urban functions and character. Some, like Eildon Hill North and Traprain Law had been linked to known tribal entities like the Selgovae and Votadini, and assigned a late pre-Roman date accordingly. Most hillforts, certainly within the south-eastern Borders, are relatively small and hard to differentiate in terms of archaeological classifications from enclosed homesteads or small enclosed villages, though in some cases their enclosing earthworks, though not massive in absolute terms, may be disproportionately substantial relative to the area enclosed.

Before the widespread application of radiocarbon dating, dating of hillforts in the Borders was problematic in the face of a very meagre material assemblage. The diffusionist approach prevailing at the time of Mrs Piggott's excavations was integrally linked to the need to establish cross-dating with Southern Britain, with due allowance for 'time-lag'. Accordingly, most sites were cautiously assigned to the closing centuries of the pre-Roman Iron Age. On the Northumbrian side of the Cheviots, two adjacent sites in the Breamish valley were excavated by George Jobey (1971) with a view to obtaining radiocarbon dates for their construction. The single third century BC date (I-5315) for material from beneath the double-faced stone rampart at Brough Law is strictly no more than a *terminus post quem*, but the absence of Roman material from the rampart cutting, by contrast to that recovered earlier from the stone-built roundhouses within the fort, would be consistent with an earlier construction of the defences. Broadly contemporary, on the basis again of a single radiocarbon date (I-5316), was an embanked palisaded settlement on nearby Ingram Hill, which itself overlay an earlier palisaded settlement. More recently a fuller suite of radiocarbon dates from Wether Hill (Corbie Cleugh) has indicated occupation from the second half of the first millennium BC (Topping and McOmish, 2001).

The most comprehensive excavation yet undertaken of a hillfort in southern Scotland was the total examination in advance of destruction of the site at Broxmouth, East Lothian, in 1977 and 1978. Given the substantial revisions offered in successive interim statements (Hill, P., 1979, 1982), it would be unwise to endorse too positively the proposed sequence, but it is clear that the structural sequence does not conform to a simple progression along the lines of the Hownam model. The importance of the Broxmouth excavation lies first in its series of radiocarbon dates, which convincingly demonstrates occupation of the site and the presence of enclosing earthworks from the mid-first millennium BC. Second, it challenged the conventional belief that stone-built 'Votadinian' houses, as opposed to ring-ditch houses or those that were timber-built with postholes or ring-groove foundations, were by definition of the Roman period, as had long been inferred from Jobey's work in Northumberland. The evidence for this certainly needs to be examined carefully when the final report is available, but *a priori* there no longer appears to be good reason for assuming that stone-built houses, including those that belong to a post-defensive phase, were necessarily the result of the imposition of the *pax Romana*. Some activity at Broxmouth in the early Roman period is indicated by samian and glass bangle fragments in a post-defensive context, but there can be no doubt that the main occupation lay within the pre-Roman Iron Age.

The convention of late dating was similarly applied at Woden Law (Fig. 3.4), a site that was undoubtedly occupied in the pre-Roman period initially, and probably at a much earlier date than the selective excavations of Richmond and St Joseph (RCAHMS, 1956: 169–72) suggested. No clear dating evidence was recovered from the single section through the fort's eastern defences, and the late dating offered was based in part on analogy with Hownam Rings, and in part on the assumption that the reduction of the second period earthworks was related to the Roman use of the site as a practice ground for artillery operations. Whether or not this needs to be assumed, the original ditchless wall could have been significantly earlier.

Widely distributed in Atlantic Europe, and occasionally represented in Northern Britain, are *chevaux de frise*, swathes of stones set on edge in front of a defensive wall with a view, as is generally inferred, to impeding a direct attack by cavalry (Harbison, 1971). In the case of the spectacular *chevaux de frise* at Dun Aengus in the Aran Islands off Galway Bay, the close-set, jagged stones would also frustrate an attack on foot, had they completely screened the perimeter of the fort. But here, as so often, they were restricted in extent, so that they could easily have been circumvented, giving the impression of a token, if dramatic, rather than an effective military device. At nearby Dun Dubh Cathair the effect of the *chevaux de frise* might have been supplemented by the very fissured nature of the outcropping rock, whilst at Ballykinvarga in Co. Clare the swathe of stones was more extensive, showing more than one phase of construction. By contrast, the examples of *chevaux de frise* known from southern Scotland (Fig. 3.5), from Kaimes hillfort on the edge of the Pentlands and from Dreva in Peeblesshire, amount to little more than scatters of small edge-set stones that can hardly have offered more than a token gesture of protection. The slightly more impressive series from Cademuir 2, Peeblesshire, are still located only along one flank of the hillfort. In effect, we might question to what extent any of these supposedly defensive works were ever put to the test in practice, and how far they had become symbolic defences or status symbols of the social hierarchical infrastructure.

In the south-west, the distinction between defended homesteads and small hillforts is as indistinct as it is in the south-eastern Borders. Among the more prominent hillforts, Burnswark at six hectares with a topographical prominence that commands access to Annandale from the Solway Plain, may have some claim to having been a regional tribal centre. Limited excavation (Jobey, 1978a) yielded evidence of a structural sequence from an early palisade through two phases of timber and stone-faced wall ramparts, and whilst

(a)

(b)

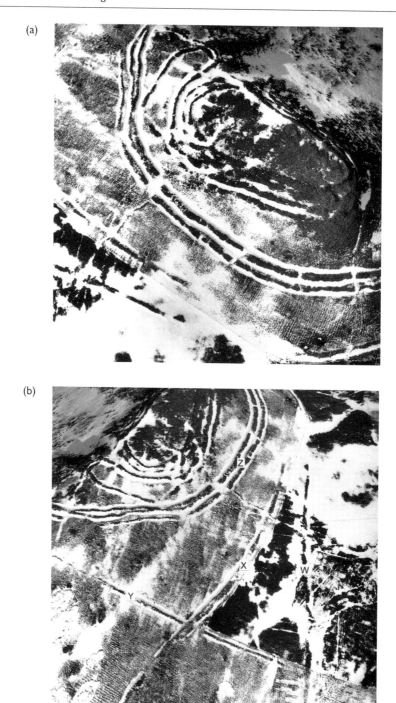

Figure 3.4 Woden Law, Roxburghshire, air-photographs. a, from the east showing cord-rig and siegeworks Z; b, from the south showing cord-rig and linear earthworks W, X, Y. Photographs by D. W. Harding.

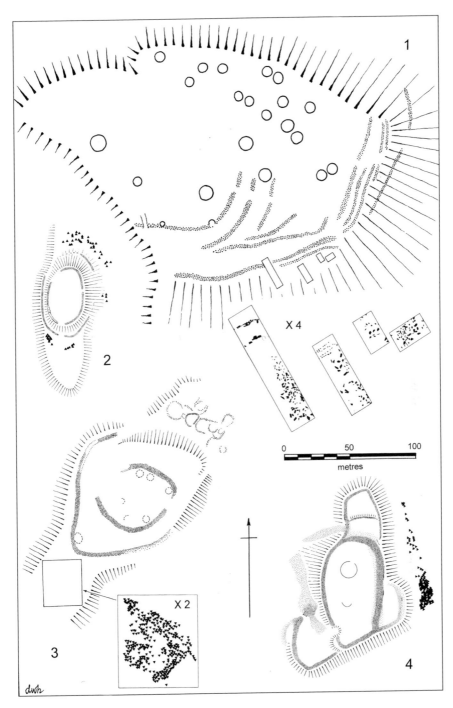

Figure 3.5 Hillforts with *chevaux de frise*. 1, Kaimes, Midlothian; 2, Fell of Barhullion, Wigtownshire; 3, Dreva, Peeblesshire; 4, Cademuir 2, Peeblesshire. Drawings by D. W. Harding, adapted from Simpson (1969), Harbison (1971) and RCAHMS (1967).

the radiocarbon dating was equivocal, there is every reason to suppose that the site's occupation began in the early Iron Age at least. Its role in the Roman period as a military training ground is well attested by the presence of two camps, the more southern of which displays prominent artillery emplacements along its north-western flank facing the hill-fort. Excavation had shown that the hillfort ramparts, at least at the northern end, were no longer actively defended by this time. Excavation nevertheless revealed a scatter of first and second century Roman material in proximity to a group of roundhouses at the south-western end of the hill, so that there may still have been some occupation of the site at this late stage.

Mercer's field survey and selective excavation in the 1980s in Eskdale and the Scottish Royal Commission's fieldwork in the 1990s in eastern Dumfriesshire (RCAHMS, 1997) have gone a long way to redress the imbalance of research in southern Scotland. Contrary to expectations, Castle O'er and Bailiehill, whatever their origins, were evidently still in use in the early centuries of the first millennium AD as centres of a thriving pastoral community. Accordingly these sites will be considered in the context of the establishment of the Roman northern frontier. Some activity into the Roman Iron Age is also implied at Rispain Camp, near Whithorn (Haggarty and Haggarty, 1983), by a fragment of enamelled bronze plate of late first or second century date found in topsoil, but otherwise Roman material is conspicuous by its absence. In fact, the origins and initial occupation of this site can be confidently attributed on the basis of radiocarbon dates to the later pre-Roman Iron Age. Though its rectilinear plan would not be out of keeping with Iron Age homesteads in parts of Northern Britain, this site is unusual for the formidable scale of its enclosure earthworks, with a ditch in excess of 4 metres in depth flanked by inner and outer banks, and with no sign of reduction or deliberate slighting. The two substantial timber-built roundhouses, one nearly 14 metres in diameter with opposed entrances (Fig. 2.6, 7), hardly endorse any suggestion of a diminution in house size on the eve of the Roman conquest.

For the great majority of enclosed sites in the south-west the problem, as in south-eastern Scotland, is to detect any meaningful sub-division at the morphological interface between small hillfort and protected homestead. Only a handful of sites exceed a hectare in extent, with rather more around 0.5 hectares, and the majority are smaller than that in enclosed area. In its survey of eastern Dumfriesshire the Royal Commission devised the term 'smaller robustly enclosed settlements' to describe the latter group. Despite their small size, there can be little doubt about the defensive character of sites like Brieryshaw Hill in Ewesdale, or of Beattock Hill in upper Annandale. Though the date of these sites remains unconfirmed, the proximity of an unenclosed settlement including ring-ditch houses, and the presence of a stone-built house within the fort at Beattock Hill suggests a protracted if intermittent occupation through the first millennium BC. In some instances, like Minsca in the valley of the Milk, the defensive enclosure demonstrably forms one element within a sequence of construction that included a palisaded enclosure and possibly an unenclosed settlement before that. Among the cropmark sites of lower Annandale several are remarkable for their multivallate defences, in some cases like Greenhillhead probably resulting from composite construction over several periods. The impressive fourfold ditches of the hill-slope fort on Archwood Hill may reflect similar concerns to Wheeler's concept of defence in depth (RCAHMS, 1997: 134; Wheeler, 1943); alternatively it may have been a mark of social status of the occupants or community that commissioned its construction.

One feature of the settlement pattern in eastern Dumfriesshire that is matched in the south-east is the occurrence of enclosed sites in close proximity to each other, in a manner which might seem to vitiate defensive effectiveness of both. Some distinction in function or in the identity of the communities that built and occupied them is presumably implied. In the case of Brieryshaw Hill, where a scooped settlement lies some 100 metres from the fort, there is no problem in regarding the two as belonging to different periods of occupation. But in the case of Newhall Hill two enclosures lying within a few metres of each other, even if constructed sequentially, can hardly have co-existed other than by design. Less extreme examples of the same phenomenon can be seen in the eastern Borders, for example, in the bivallate and multivallate cliff-edge enclosures at Ayton, Berwickshire (Fig. 3.6, 3). As we shall see in more extreme form north of the Forth, some of these promontory sites seem to be disproportionately elaborate in their defensive circuit relative to the area enclosed.

Relatively few of these smaller ditched or palisaded settlements in south-west Scotland have been excavated in modern times. At Hayknowes, west of the Annan on the

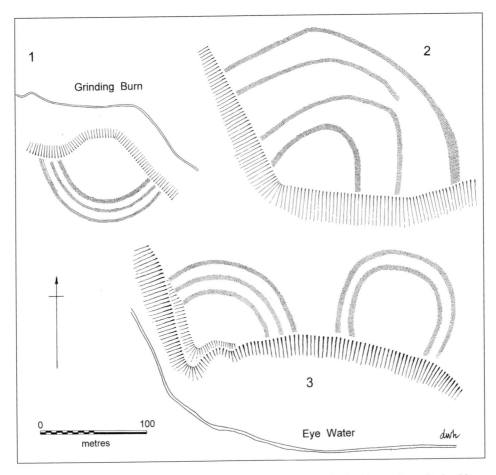

Figure 3.6 Multivallate cliff-edge forts in south-east Scotland. I, Hassendean Bank, Minto, Roxburghshire; 2, The Pleasance, East Lothian; 3, Ayton, Berwickshire. Drawings by D. W. Harding from DWH air-photographs with data from NMRS.

coastal plain, a concentric double-ditched enclosure defines a compound around 75 metres across, within which a small cluster of buildings could have been contained. One was excavated (Fig. 2.6, 6; Gregory, 2001), a ring-groove house 11 metres in diameter, again distinguished by having a second entrance opposite its more elaborate, south-east-facing porched entrance. More unusual, however, was its large setting of four posts in its interior, perhaps a constructional device used subsequently for supporting a mezzanine floor or internal fittings, as has been argued earlier, rather than for providing roof support directly. Radiocarbon samples from the gateway structures and enclosure ditch terminals indicate an occupation in the later first millennium BC.

Air-photography (Cowley and Brophy, 2001) has revealed a similar double-ditched enclosure with traces of at least one internal ring-groove roundhouse at East Galdenoch, whilst complex, multi-period settlements are indicated by the density of crop-marks at Garphar, where the ring-groove houses extend well beyond the circuit of a double-palisaded enclosure. The ring-groove, however, as has long been recognised, is only a constructional technique, and need not be indicative of any particular chronological or cultural horizon. In the south-west of Scotland, the site at Woodend, provides a salutary example of this lesson. Within its double-banked enclosure, a complex of intersecting ring-groove buildings argued for a prolonged occupation of the site, while the total absence of material remains of the Roman period seemed to endorse a dating through the second half of the first millennium BC. Radiocarbon dates, however, from structural contexts of the buildings consistently point to a Roman native occupation, though the earliest, possibly unenclosed settlement on the site, could still be somewhat earlier. The absence of Roman material from a site in close proximity to a Roman road and military establishments must, if they are genuinely contemporary, indicate positive rejection of accord between native and Roman.

The very fact that archaeological classification has difficulty in drawing a dividing line between small hillforts and enclosed homesteads perhaps suggests that this was not a distinction that reflected the social order of later prehistoric settlement in the Borders. Some small hillforts were surely located with defensive considerations in mind. Sundhope Kipp in Roxburghshire, occupying a steep-sided spur at 420 metres OD, and with triple ramparts barring access from its easiest northern approach, has all the hallmarks of a defensive site. The presence of ring-ditch houses within the enclosure suggests a relatively early date for the defensive enclosure. Likewise Huntfold Hill, a little to the west, also occupies a steep spur to which the easiest access is blocked by multiple earthworks and strengthened by secondary outworks. In other instances, however, like the Chesters at Drem in East Lothian, the hillfort is actually overlooked by higher ground to the south, giving an impression of almost wilful disregard for defensive advantage. Since considerations of defence seem not invariably to have been the dominant factor in choice of topographic location, it would be tempting to regard enclosure in these instances as reflecting other social factors of status or identity as much as the security of the community and its stock. Enclosure was evidently an aspect of later prehistoric settlement for the best part of a millennium before the Roman occupation, and it would be unwise to presume that throughout that period or across the whole of southern Scotland it signified the same thing or served the same purpose.

In south-eastern Scotland the older conventional view of the 'trend towards enclosure' through the Iron Age saw its culmination in the major *oppida*, Traprain Law in East Lothian (Fig. 3.7), Eildon Hill on the Tweed (Fig. 3.8), Hownam Law (Fig. 3.9) and

Figure 3.7 Traprain Law, East Lothian, general view. Photograph by D. W. Harding.

Yeavering Bell in the Roxburghshire and Northumberland Cheviots among other candidates. With enclosed areas variously between 8 and 16 hectares, and with evidence of house stances in great numbers within their walls, these were regarded as major community centres, and the culmination of the progression towards enclosure on the eve of the Roman conquest. Accordingly sites like Traprain and Eildon were inevitably linked with the tribal names of Votadini and Selgovae, and regarded as the native strongholds from which resistance to Rome might have been marshalled.

In fact the excavated evidence from Traprain Law had always indicated a hiatus in the occupational sequence in the Iron Age, with more abundant evidence for activity in the later Bronze Age and again in the Roman period. More recent excavations have endorsed that impression, with indications of significant occupation in the Roman period. Limited excavations in the 1980s at Eildon Hill North suggested a similar pattern of occupation (Rideout *et al.*, 1992). Later Bronze Age occupation was apparently represented by circular house foundations, and after an apparent lapse there was similar evidence of occupation in the Roman period. The date of the enclosing banks at Eildon remains uncertain, but there is no obvious reason why they should not have originated with the Bronze Age occupation. Mercer considered the possibility that the occupation of Hownam Law, at nearly 450 metres OD, might be re-assigned to the middle Bronze Age (Mercer and Tipping, 1994: 5), while Halliday (1985: 238) had already suggested that Hownam Law, together with Cademuir at nearly 400 metres and White Meldon at 425 metres were improbable sites to have been occupied as late as the later Iron Age. Alternatively, Halliday saw the nucleated settlement pattern of an earlier period fragmenting in the Iron Age in south-east Scotland into a pattern of dispersed smaller forts and settlements.

Figure 3.8 Eildon Hill, Roxburghshire, air-photograph. Photograph by D. W. Harding.

In so far as enclosure served a purpose not required or met by unenclosed settlement, we might suppose that both forms could co-exist, depending upon the needs of the communities that occupied them. There need be no assumption that the one is superior or more desirable than the other, or that there should be any expectation of progression from one to the other. For Hingley (1992) open settlement was the norm, from which enclosure was a 'temporary monumental elaboration'. If enclosed settlements are more in evidence at one period than another, this plainly requires explanation. But there need no longer be any expectation that this forms a regular, unilinear progression, culminating in multivallate hillforts or regional *oppida* on the eve of the Roman conquest. Above all, the reality is that unenclosed settlement is much more difficult to detect, even from air-photographic survey.

Settlements and domestic structures

The regular occurrence together of palisaded enclosures, ring-ditch houses and cord-rig agriculture, sufficiently often in the absence of visible settlement of other periods in the locality to assume that they were elements within a contemporary and planned settlement system, was convincingly demonstrated by field research in south-east Scotland in the early 1980s. Evidence from Broxmouth (Hill, P., 1982b), Dryburn Bridge (Triscott,

Figure 3.9
Hownam Law,
Roxburghshire,
air-photograph.
Photograph by
D. W. Harding.

1982), and Douglasmuir, Angus (Kendrick, 1982, 1995) confirmed that ring-ditch houses could be assigned to the mid-first millennium BC. Palisades may certainly be found from other, later periods, and cord-rigging too may have continued later, but the combination of the three, sometimes in association with additional unenclosed houses also, is now well established as a mid-first millennium phenomenon. In fact, ring-ditch houses occur in open settlements, not only north of the Forth, as at the excavated settlement at Douglasmuir, but also in the Borders at Stirkfield and Huskie Rig in Peeblesshire or in Roxburghshire at Hangingshaw Hill above the Kale Water. In Dumfriesshire several open settlements with ring-ditch houses have been located (RCAHMS, 1997: 118) in the uplands between the Annan and the Esk, and regularly in proximity to tracts of cord-rig agriculture and palisaded enclosures.

Palisaded enclosures take a variety of forms and sizes (Fig. 2.3). They commonly represent the first phase of defensive enclosure, not just of hillforts, but of protected homesteads like Braidwood in Midlothian or Hayhope Knowe, Roxburghshire. Several, like Hayhope Knowe or High Knowes, Alnham, Northumberland, or certain phases of the Gibb's Hill, Dumfriesshire, sequence, have a double palisade, joined at the entrance in a continuous loop. This would plainly form a more effective barrier against intruders, human or animal, than a single palisade, and guard dogs could be left unleashed to patrol the enclosed circuit. This form of double palisade is in plan not unlike the framework of a simple, timber-framed box-rampart, however, and the suggestion has been made (Halliday, 1995; RCAHMS, 1997: 126) that double palisades like those at Stanshiel Hill,

Roxburghshire, and perhaps at Gibb's Hill, might have supported a timber-framed wall with fighting platform and breastwork, effectively being a timber box-rampart in which the timber framework remained unfilled. Such a rampart would have been extremely vulnerable to firing, however, though as a stage in the development of a more permanent perimeter it might make sense. It also may have been adopted where bedrock inhibited construction of a ditch, and where material for the core filling was less readily available. In terms of internal settlement, some palisaded settlements like Hayhope Knowe (Fig. 3.2, 2) contain a number of houses in an ordered disposition along a central 'street', giving the appearance of a small village. Others, like Greenbrough, Roxburghshire (Fig. 2.3, 5), contain just one large, central roundhouse and one subsidiary house, and can have been no more than a single family homestead. At High Knowes (Fig. 3.10) two sites enclosed by double palisades both contain ring-ditch houses, and were probably in broadly contemporaneous occupation, notwithstanding the later Romano-British roundhouse overlying the palisade of High Knowes B. High Knowes A, however (Fig. 2.3, 3), contained just two principal roundhouses, each with subordinate lesser circular buildings. High Knowes B contained no less than sixteen houses, of which a number must have been occupied at any one time, and has the appearance of a small village community. The social distinction between homestead and hamlet, and the division of title to the surrounding landscape between the two communities, remains a matter of speculation.

Palisaded enclosures include rectilinear as well as the more common curvilinear variants. One group of rectilinear palisades in Northumberland, including Tower Knowe, Belling Law and Kennel Hall, is generally considered late, not because they have been independently dated, but because their plans are closely followed by later stone-built enclosures on the same site. On the other hand, as we have seen, there are good grounds for regarding the rectilinear, double-palisaded enclosure at West Brandon, Co. Durham, as relatively early, albeit largely on the grounds of the absence of later finds rather than the presence of diagnostically early associations. The fact remains that, as with recti-linear and curvilinear ditched enclosures in Northern Britain generally, there are no convincing grounds for ordering them into chronological sequence. The earliest, nevertheless, whether representing the first stage of defensive enclosure as at Fenton Hill, Northumberland, or as a free-standing stockade like Dryburn Bridge (Fig. 2.3, 7), must be assigned on the basis of radiocarbon dating to the first half of the first millennium BC.

Ring-ditch houses (Fig. 3.11), though regularly referred to as such in the literature, have never been explained entirely satisfactorily as domestic houses. When Stevenson excavated at Braidwood the assumption was that the house stood on the central platform, around which the ditch formed a sump for surface water and run-off from the eaves. Only with the realisation from excavation, first at High Knowes, where the outer wall was clearly bedded in a ring-groove foundation, and subsequently at Douglasmuir and Broxmouth, that the outer wall of the house enclosed the ring-ditch itself, came the necessity to explain exactly what was the purpose of the ditch within the building. The problem was compounded by the fact that the ring-ditch was often intermittent, effectively a series of scoops or twin scoops rather than a continuous ditch, and that these were generally filled with stony rubble. One viewpoint (Reynolds, D. M., 1982), developing a suggestion proposed by Jobey for High Knowes, argued persuasively that these buildings could have been used for stalling cattle tethered radially, with fodder provided centrally or stored in the roof space. Armit (1997a: 32) developed this idea

Figure 3.10 High Knowes, Alnham, Northumberland, air-photograph. Photograph by D. W. Harding.

into the concept of a 'byre-house' with more recent Highland analogies in mind. Stalling livestock need not have excluded human occupancy, particularly if an upper floor or mezzanine was provided. The absence of central hearths might be explained by this interpretation. Kendrick on the other hand (1995: 64) saw the deeper ring-ditches of the

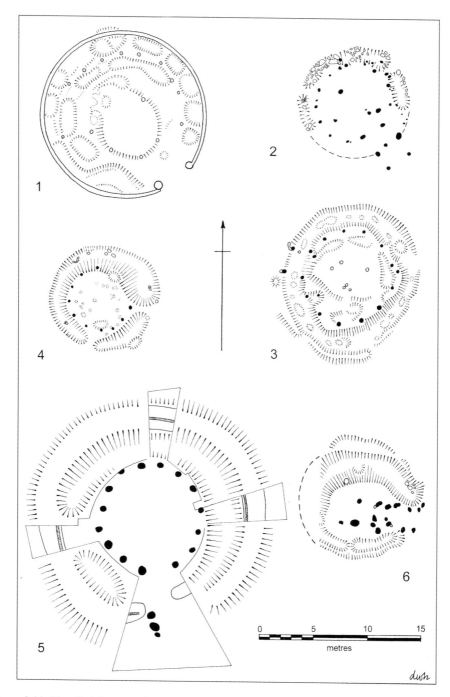

Figure 3.11 Ring-ditch houses, plans. 1, High Knowes, Alnham, Northumberland; 2, Dryburn Bridge, East Lothian; 3, Braidwood, Midlothian; 4, Douglasmuir, Angus, house 5; 5, Culhawk, Angus; 6, Ironshill, Angus, house 2. Drawings by D. W. Harding adapted from Jobey and Tait (1966), Triscott (1982), Stevenson (1949a), Rees (1998) and Pollock (1997).

Angus examples as related to the function of souterrains. As regards dating, Dryburn Bridge affords one of the earliest occurrences of the type. House 2 there yielded four dates: 2280+/–55 BP (GU-1283), 2450+/–50 BP (GU-1257), 2550+/–50 BP (GU-1287), and 2615+/–55 BP (GU-1284), all from structural contexts of the ring-ditch house. The houses from Douglasmuir produced an even more consistent series of dates, so that the origins of ring-ditch houses in the first half or middle of the first millennium BC can hardly be in doubt.

An important conclusion drawn from the Broxmouth evidence related to the introduction of stone-built houses, for many years in Northumberland and the Borders regarded as coincident with the Roman occupation. Reviewing the evidence for timber antecedents to stone-built roundhouses at Kennel Hall and Belling Law, Hill (Hill, P., 1982a: 9) preferred to stress continuity in architectural tradition. The key to this re-appraisal was House 4 at Broxmouth, which underwent a series of structural modifications in which the stone perimeter wall of the house, revetted into a scoop against the slope of ground, was successively refaced. The excavator particularly noted the absence of Roman material artefacts from the earlier levels of House 4, regarding the later introduction of a door sill with external paved porch as the first indication of the influence of Romano-British domestic architecture (Hill, P., 1982b: 175). The radiocarbon dates from House 4 would be consistent with this interpretation, though they do not place the issue beyond doubt. At Wether Hill, Northumberland (McOmish, 1999; Topping and McOmish, 2001), where surface survey indicated that at least one stone roundhouse had been built over the tail of the hillfort rampart, the excavators were surprised that radiocarbon dates suggested the possibility that stone houses and hillfort had been in contemporary use in the second half of the first millennium BC. In a long sequence within a relatively compact settlement there is always the risk, of course, that residual material from earlier occupation may have been incorporated in the construction of later stone houses, distorting the radiocarbon dates. Alternatively, the stone house settlement may indeed have originated in an earlier period, expanding later to encroach upon the line of the rampart when the defences were no longer being maintained.

To distinguish this class of stone-built house from those of the Roman period Hill coined the term *Votadinian* houses. Whether or not their introduction in south-east Scotland significantly preceded the Roman occupation, there are precedents enough elsewhere in northern England for believing that stone-built houses were current in the pre-Roman Iron Age. On the other hand, in Dumfriesshire and the south-west, the excavated evidence of Boonies and elsewhere suggested that timber construction continued to be the prevailing fashion into the Roman period. This was certainly also the case at Carronbridge, Dumfriesshire (Johnston, 1994), where both radiocarbon dates and artefacts indicate occupation from the late pre-Roman Iron Age into the later second century or beyond. Though the sequential square-within-a-square plan of the enclosure ditches is superficially comparable to Burradon and other Northumbrian settlements, there is no evidence for the adoption of stone building, nor convincingly of the internal layout of the Northumbrian farmsteads.

If recent research suggests that stone-built or Votadinian houses date from the later pre-Roman Iron Age, it might imply that scooped settlements, within which they frequently are found in the south-eastern Borders at any rate, similarly began at an earlier date than hitherto supposed. Even if the origins of these sites are detached from the Roman horizon, there is no doubt that in the south-east and in Dumfriesshire they are commonly located overlying the ramparts of abandoned hillforts, so that some significant disruption of the settlement pattern is implied. From the south-east, Romano-British material of the first and second centuries AD has been recovered from scooped settlements. In the south-west the evidence is more equivocal, and the sequence of structural super-imposition at Boonies could imply a much more protracted occupation. The probability is that scooped enclosures appeared in the later pre-Roman Iron Age, though they are still best documented as Roman native settlements. Their lower dating, whether they continued in occupation into the late Roman period, is equally uncertain.

Crannogs

The south-west of Scotland is one of the principal provinces in the crannog distribution (Henderson, Jon, 1998a), with Milton Loch 1 still a type-site for the early regional series (Fig. 3.12, 1). Excavated in 1953 (Piggott, C. M., 1953; Guido, M., 1974), before the widespread application of radiocarbon dating, it also illustrates the limitations of archaeological dating on the basis of casual artefacts alone. A dress-fastener of the second century AD was among the few dateable objects from the site, and on this basis the crannog was assigned to a Romano-British horizon. Subsequent radiocarbon dates for structural timbers indicated beyond doubt that the construction and initial occupation of the site was in the second or third quarters of the first millennium BC, though there is no reason on that account to dismiss the possibility of continuing or renewed occupation in the first or second centuries AD.

Reviewing Mrs Piggott's report we might well suspect that there were successive phases of construction, and the specific details of the ground plan might well be open to debate. Certainly timber was the predominant building material, with carefully laid horizontal floor timbers retained within an outer perimeter of uprights. From this platform, not much more than 10 metres in diameter, a timber causeway lead to the shore. At the back of the island, away from the shore and sheltered by the house from the prevailing south-westerlies, was a boat noost or small harbour. Subsequent research has confirmed the existence of at least two other crannogs in Milton Loch, one of late pre-Roman Iron Age date, the other certainly occupied in the early historic period, though not on present evidence earlier. Crannogs in Barean Loch and Loch Arthur have also yielded dates within the early Iron Age (Henderson, Jon, 1998a), confirming the longevity of loch-side settlement in south-western Scotland.

Agricultural economy

Identifying and dating with any degree of confidence field-systems and agricultural patterns can be a frustrating exercise. Not only are such features seldom associated with dateable artefacts from stratified horizons, many have been obscured or simply obliterated by later agricultural activity. In some instances agricultural landscapes are manifestly composite and multi-period, such that disaggregating Bronze Age or Iron Age from Mediaeval or later features may be complicated in the extreme. Whilst periods of woodland clearance or arable extensification may have triggered major changes in the agricultural landscape, in other periods little change need have occurred over protracted periods of time. Much of our information is necessarily derived from landscapes that survive above the zone of later agricultural destruction. Yet this does not mean that earlier communities did not exploit the lower-lying slopes or valley bottoms, merely that the

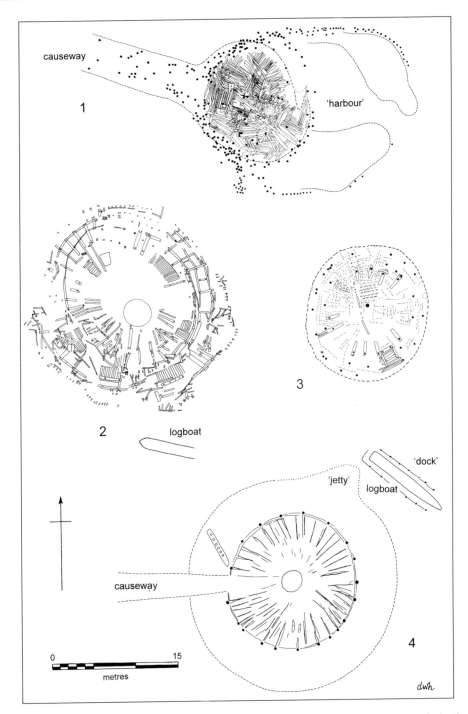

Figure 3.12 Crannogs, plans. 1, Milton Loch, Kirkcudbrightshire; 2, Buiston, Ayrshire; 3, Lochan Duighall, Clachan, Argyll; 4, Dumbuck, Dunbartonshire. Drawings by D. W. Harding, adapted from Piggott, C. M. (1953), Munro (1882), Munro (1893), Munro (1905).

activity of later generations has there obscured the evidence for earlier usage. Basing our conclusions upon upland, often increasingly marginal locations, therefore, may distort our understanding of the nature of Iron Age agriculture. One basic tenet is now generally accepted, however, namely that Iron Age communities were capable of efficient agricultural practices, both arable and pastoral, and that, subject as ever to the vagaries of climate and related environmental factors, they were capable of managing an economic regime above bare subsistence level.

In the course of the Royal Commission's Roxburghshire survey, several sites were investigated where settlement was associated with a system of cultivation plots or lynchets that were compared to the 'Celtic' fields of the southern British Iron Age. These were generally assigned to the Roman period, however, once again on the basis of Roman material found in the related settlements, and in the absence of diagnostically earlier associations. In the case of the Tamshiel Rig complex (Fig. 3.13), however, there are better grounds for suggesting that the field-system had its origins in the pre-Roman Iron Age (Halliday, 1982). The settlement sequence at the core of the complex comprised three elements, an early fort enclosure, a later settlement, and several stone-built houses, which from their disposition could well have been later still. It was from these last that the evidence of Romano-British occupation was derived. The field-system displays at least one major addition, and there is every reason to suppose that it underwent lesser modifications over time, so that the fact that sections of field-bank over-ride the original fort earthworks need not in itself preclude an early beginning of the basic system. Within the outer enclosing banks an area of 12.5 hectares was divided into parallel strips, within which air-photographs revealed smaller cultivation plots. The perimeter bank with external ditch was evidently designed to be stock-proof, but the fact that the internal banks were similar led Halliday to conclude that the system was designed to be internally stock-proof as well, that is, to permit manuring of fallow plots by grazing animals. The Tamshiel system, therefore, and others like it, suggests a mixed agricultural regime in which arable cultivation has in the past been an under-rated element. Even at Woden Law, where the hillfort is surrounded by cord-rig, it is possible that the outlying linear earthworks (W, X and Y; Fig. 3.4b) are related to the Iron Age agricultural system rather than to the Roman siegeworks, to which they seem entirely tangential.

Elsewhere in the Border uplands there are linear earthworks which doubtless formed estate or agricultural land divisions, and though their dating remains uncertain some may have their origins in later prehistory. On the low-lying plains of East Lothian and Berwickshire there are other instances of land boundaries, sometimes in quite extensive and complex networks, which may well date from the Iron Age on the basis of their proximity and apparent relationship to hillforts. A good example is the system around the hillforts at the Chesters, Drem and Kae Heughs by Barney Mains (Fig. 3.14). These linear boundaries may be made up variously of continuous ditches, pit alignments and double pit alignments, the first two on some air-photographs seeming to merge one into the other. Apart from the hillforts, other settlements of known Iron Age type, including several small ditched enclosures and at least one palisaded enclosure, are known in close proximity, but the idea that these, together with the land divisions and focal hillforts, might have formed an integrated landscape system is still a matter of inference rather than demonstrated fact. At Castlesteads and Newton, Midlothian, a similar system of single and double pit alignments forms a network of land divisions by the lower Esk, with several ditched enclosures in close proximity (Armit, 1997a: Fig. 42).

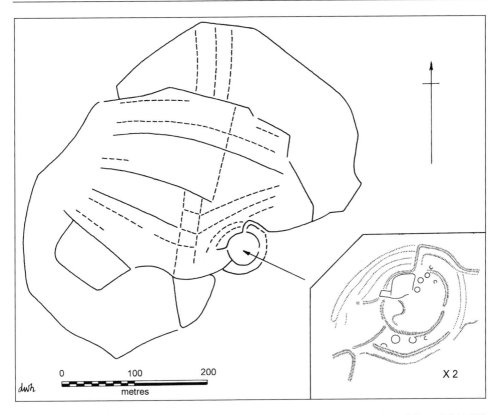

Figure 3.13 Tamshiel Rig, Roxburghshire, plan. Drawing by D. W. Harding, adapted from RCAHMS (1956).

That these pit alignments and ditches formed land divisions is hardly in doubt, though how exactly the pit alignments functioned in contrast to a continuous ditch is less obvious. From MacKay's (1980) excavations at Drem the individual pits were apparently relatively shallow, and showed no trace of having held posts or any other structural feature. As quarry pits for an upstanding bank they would have been less effective and not much less labour-intensive than a continuous ditch, unless the bank was topped by a fence or hedge of which no trace has survived. What dating evidence is available suggests the possibility that these systems of land enclosure and division belong to the later first millennium BC, though it must be recognised that pit alignments elsewhere have been dated from the Neolithic onwards. They may indeed represent a period of agricultural intensification and perhaps population growth towards the end of the Iron Age (Halliday, 1995: 35 and forthcoming).

A major breakthrough of the late 1970s and early 1980s in south-eastern Scotland was the recognition that cord-rig, much narrower and slighter than later rig-and-furrow, being less than 1.5 metres apart, could be assigned to the first millennium BC. First recognised as potentially early from its discovery beneath the Roman fort at Rudchester, it was subsequently traced by air survey over extensive tracts of the Roxburghshire Cheviots, and in Peeblesshire and Lanarkshire. Its proximity to sites at heights over 400 metres OD like Arbory Hill or Woden Law, in areas where there was no evidence to

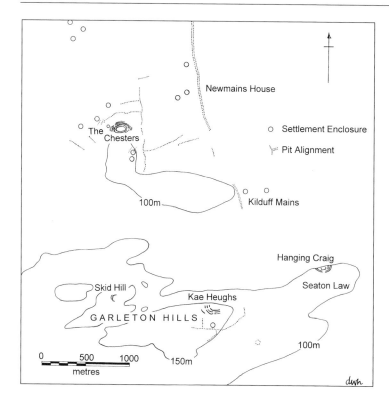

Figure 3.14
Settlements and land boundaries around Drem, East Lothian. Drawings by D. W. Harding, adapted from Cook (1999), data from NMRS, and DWH air-photographs.

associate it with later settlement, presented an *a priori* case for regarding it as Iron Age. Whilst archaeological association was hard to demonstrate beyond doubt, the regular occurrence of cord-rig in proximity to palisaded settlements with ring-ditch houses made inevitable the eventual acknowledgement that these constituted complementary elements in a later prehistoric landscape. The fact that the rigging respected the very slight boundary trenches of palisaded sites like that east of Woden Law (Fig. 3.15) would hardly be credible if it was the product of much later cultivation. Subsequent research has only qualified this conclusion by the recognition that cord-rig, like palisades and possibly ring-ditch houses, had a much longer currency, and is by no means exclusive to the early Iron Age. This is clear from the air-photographs themselves, for example at Hayhope Knowe, where the cord-rig apparently cuts across both palisade and subsequent earthwork enclosure. In other parts of Scotland, including Arran and Sutherland, radiocarbon dating has suggested that a similar form of cultivation may have continued in use until the Mediaeval period (Carter, 1994), but this should not detract from its later prehistoric origins in southern Scotland.

Much of the cord-rig in the Borders appears to be unenclosed, but in close proximity to either palisaded settlements, as at Gibb's Hill, Wauchopedale, or to earthwork enclosures as at Orchard Rig in Peeblesshire. Hut Knowe, Hownam (Fig. 3.16), is exceptional in its ordered system of field banks, though even here in its final form the rigs appear to spill over the edges of those fields. Elsewhere what might at first sight appear to be extensive swathes of rigging on closer examination prove to be much smaller plots, sometimes disposed in a patchwork of contrasting orientation and thus giving the

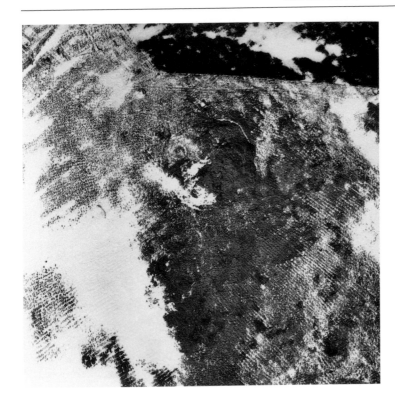

Figure 3.15 Woden
Law East,
Roxburghshire,
air-photograph.
Photograph by
D. W. Harding.

appearance of small-scale cultivation in shifting plots. This may be indicative of the
nature of cord-rig cultivation, or it may be a product of the fact that what survives for
the field archaeologist and air-photographer to record is necessarily what was left when
the system went into decline and was abandoned.

In the south-west examples of cord-rig have been located by field survey or from
air-photography in the upland zone of survival between Eskdale and Annandale, and
some instances are recorded in Nithsdale. Though in most cases the surviving patches
are relatively small, occasional tracts of rigging cover between 1 and 3 hectares, with the
exceptional case of Crawthat Hill, where it attains as much as 8 hectares. Significantly,
in Dumfriesshire cord-rig is not found regularly in proximity to scooped settlements,
which, with some qualifications regarding their beginnings, are commonly indicative
of a late Iron Age or Romano-British date.

There is still some debate whether cord-rig actually was the product of ploughing or
spade cultivation. Hill's (Hill, P., 1983) excavation of a section across the system at Hut
Knowe North (Fig. 3.16) revealed relatively steep-sided rigs, which the excavator
was inclined to attribute to spade digging. Halliday (1993: 72) subsequently proposed
a more complex practice, in which the initial tilth was created by ploughing ('sod busting'
in Peter Reynolds' graphic phrase), after which relatively small areas would have been
cultivated by hand. What was being grown is also subject to debate. It need not follow
that cereals or legumes for human consumption were the sole objective of cultivation;
growing foodstuffs for animals is also an option for communities engaged in stock-
rearing. In any event, given the presumed climatic deterioration around the turn of the

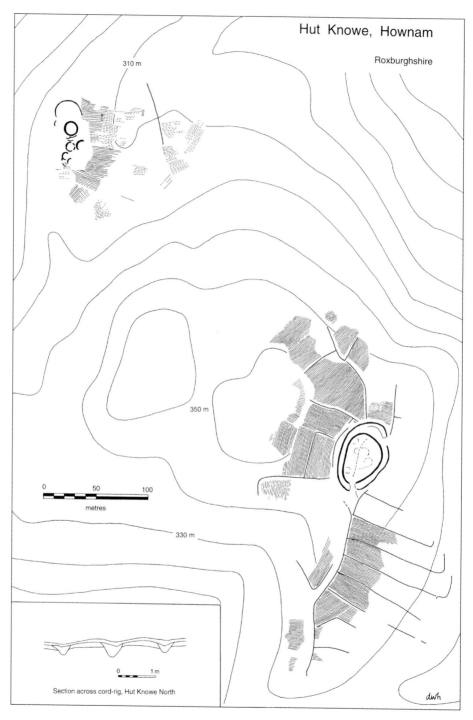

Figure 3.16 Hut Knowe, Roxburghshire, plan with cord-rig fields. Drawing by D. W. Harding, adapted from Hill, P. (1983), Halliday (1993) with additions from DWH air photographs.

first millennium, it is doubtful whether conditions at heights over 350 metres would have been conducive to cereal cultivation much after the middle Bronze Age.

Climatic deterioration would undoubtedly have had an impact on the land that was sustainable for occupation and cultivation, forcing down the upper limits of viable settlement. Jobey had presented this in the early 1980s as a series of progressively reducing contour ceilings, from the high-water mark of second millennium cairnfields and unenclosed platform settlements, to the intermediate contours favoured for palisaded enclosures and eventually to the lower-lying scooped settlements of the Romano-British period (Harding, 1982: 191). In reality of course we must assume that earlier settlement also exploited the lower contours, and that what survives is simply a series of progressively lowering high-tide marks. Hillforts and exceptional sites like Arbory Hill may be expected to transcend this contour model, which cannot therefore be applied too strictly as an indicator of a site's probable chronological horizon. Halliday (1999) subsequently developed the contour model with his concept of a dynamic 'hierarchy of environmental niches' in which settlement patterns were subject to dynamic change within their own core and periphery. In fact the environmental evidence strongly suggests that a process of agricultural intensification was under way by the end of the first millennium BC, which may have manifest itself in a significantly re-ordered landscape at this time.

Burial and ritual

Along with large parts of Britain in the early Iron Age, southern Scotland appears to be largely devoid of a regular and recurrent burial type. In the south-east there is a handful of cist burials, including those from Torwoodlee, Selkirkshire and Burnmouth, Berwickshire, where artefactual associations suggested a later pre-Roman Iron Age date (Whimster, 1981). The discovery of a small cemetery just outside the ramparts of the Broxmouth hillfort, therefore, together with the more scattered evidence of Iron Age burials from Dryburn Bridge, represented a significant advance in the data-base available for early Iron Age burial practices in the region. The radiocarbon dates from Broxmouth leave no doubt that the cemetery belonged to the second half of the first millennium BC. But the minimal number of burials – just nine graves in this group – compared with the scale of the site and the length of its occupation indicated by its structural sequence, points to highly selective use of the cemetery. Despite its small size, the cemetery showed considerable diversity in the structure of the graves, including circular or oval pits, with and without capstones or lining stones, and rectangular or polygonal graves with cist-like slabs and capstones. The rite was nevertheless consistently flexed inhumation, with a predominantly NNE–SSW or diametrically reciprocal orientation. There were no grave-goods, underlining the problems of dating in the absence of radiocarbon dating.

Whilst the location of these burials just beyond the limits of the outer enclosure ditch of the fort looks like a classic choice of a liminal location for the cemetery, there were in addition four further formal burials within the fort, in graves that reflected similar rites, but more randomly distributed. In addition there were fragments of human skeletal remains from middens, reflecting a pattern quite widely recorded in the British Iron Age. The inference from the Broxmouth evidence must be that formal disposal of the dead is not the primary purpose reflected by these burials, but some more selective ritual activity. Unless there remains to be discovered a class of cemetery which has so far eluded even chance discovery, or unless Iron Age burials have been consistently attributed by archaeologists mistakenly to other periods, we must conclude that disposal of the majority of the dead was by some means, such as cremation and scattering, which has left no permanent archaeological trace.

At Dryburn Bridge (Fig. 2.3, 7; Triscott, 1982) the ten burials that were contemporary with the later prehistoric occupation of the site were likewise too few in number and too spread out in date remotely to equate with more than a very small minority of the population. One group from the secondary phase of occupation was aligned along the former boundary of the palisaded enclosure. Another group in a line within the enclosed area may equally have reflected a former boundary of some sort, which has not left earth-fast traces. Flexed inhumation in pits was the normal rite.

A trawl of the literature can certainly yield isolated instances of burial for which an Iron Age date can reasonably be inferred. At Alnham, for example (Jobey and Tait, 1966), the inclusion with one burial of a diagnostically Iron Age artefact – a cast bronze ring-headed pin of Irish type – in a cairnfield that was otherwise apparently of regular Bronze Age type demonstrates our dependence upon artefactual associations. Though most cairnfields and barrows in southern Scotland are unquestionably of Bronze Age date, there are occasional examples, like Broughton Knowe and Langlaw Hill in Peeblesshire or Toftcombs in Lanarkshire that do not altogether accord with the standard Bronze Age pattern. Re-use of older burial grounds by Iron Age graves may also be witnessed at Cairnpapple (Piggott, S., 1948; Barclay, 1999) though whether these secondary graves belong to the pre-Roman Iron Age or early historic period is still open to debate.

One distinctive deposit is the chariot-burial from Newbridge, Midlothian (Carter and Hunter, 2003). Despite the poor condition of the assemblage, sufficient survived to identify the wheel-rims and fittings of a two-wheeled vehicle, prompting the suggestion that this could have been a northerly offshoot of the early and middle La Tène tradition of eastern Yorkshire. Closer examination of the Newbridge burial prompted doubts, however, regarding its cultural affinities. First of all, the vehicle had been buried intact, a practice not typical of the Yorkshire ritual, in which the chariot was normally dismantled for burial, but closer to Continental models from the Champagne or middle Rhine. Second, the sub-keyhole outline of the burial pit itself was more closely paralleled in Germany than in eastern Yorkshire. Accordingly, we might have to consider the Newbridge burial as a direct introduction from the Continent, rather than as an extension of the eastern English distribution. Unfortunately, excavation in the vicinity failed to yield any further burials to indicate that it was part of a more extensive cemetery. The Newbridge find therefore remains unique and anomalous, so that, beyond its intrinsic interest, it cannot cast much light upon the nature of Iron Age ritual or funerary practice in southern Scotland.

The fact that archaeologically some regions at certain periods display a dominant funerary rite need not lead to an expectation that there should have been a recurrent and regular form of disposal of the dead in all circumstances. Wait (1985: 121) suggested that there may have been several and variable mortuary practices in the British Iron Age, and warned against the assumption that any 'norm' should be archaeologically recognisable. The inference must be that, even where a distinctive mode of burial is archaeologically visible, we need not assume that it was the only rite being practised. In any event, the archaeological record only testifies to the final stage of deposition; two apparently contrasting cultural groups, one with a distinctive burial rite and the other with none, could in reality have followed much the same ritual formulae until that final act of deposition. The disposal of the dead in a dedicated cemetery may have been the exception rather than the rule, and the elusive burial ritual may have been much more closely integrated into the function of settlements.

Interpreting evidence for ritual was formerly regarded as being on the limits of archaeological inference (Hawkes, 1954). Currently, however, ritual has too often become an explanation of first, rather than last, resort, and what prehistoric societies believed or practised is presented as assertion rather than reasoned inference. For a society in which ritual and the mundane were doubtless inextricably interwoven, few sites can be regarded as expressly for ritual or ceremonial activities, though at a slightly later date the unusual 'amphitheatre' at Over Rig in Eskdale might lay claim as such (Mercer, 1985). Important ceremonials, like the inauguration of kings, on analogy with early historic models in the Celtic world, might have taken place at major regional foci, perhaps like Traprain Law and Eildon Hill, or at Ingleborough or Carrock Fell in northern England.

Hoards are sometimes regarded as ritual deposits, along with a range of other explanations for depositing a collection of valuables in the ground. Those that are found in watery locations, like the early Roman hoards with later Iron Age cauldrons from Carlingwark Moss, Kircudbrightshire, and Blackburn Mill, Berwickshire (Piggott, S., 1953a), are particularly thought of as votive deposits, in a tradition that is widespread across the Celtic world from Transylvania to Wales. At an earlier period, some late Bronze Age hoards, like the bronze shields from Yetholm, Roxburghshire, may equally have been from a votive deposit. The fact that these finely wrought sheet-bronze shields, unless backed with wood or leather, would have been impractical for other than ceremonial purposes endorses this view. The resurgence of the practice of ritual deposition in the Roman Iron Age, when communities felt under threat from an alien culture, would be entirely consistent with the underlining of local identity.

Material culture

As in the case of northern England, the Iron Age material culture of southern Scotland and the Borders is characterised by its comparative poverty, and by the absence of clearly diagnostic types. Pottery in particular, elsewhere the staple of archaeological classification, is sparse in quantity and poor in quality. Nevertheless, coarse ware jars with relatively thick walls and inward-curving rim-profiles are known from a series of sites – Broxmouth, Kaimes and Hownam Rings, for example – so that some uniformity of style and perhaps concurrency of use may be inferred. At Broxmouth, where the length of occupation and depth of midden deposits made possible an attempt at ordering the material remains into sequence (Cool, 1982), preliminary examination suggested the existence of early, middle and late Iron Age assemblages. Of these, the earliest was least well represented in terms of the ceramic assemblage, a situation which may be matched in more recent analyses of the material from the north-east of England (Willis, 1999). The principal early finds were saddle-querns, presumably indicating a pre-quern transition date, and undiagnostic stone tools such as pounders and rubbing-stones, together with some shale bracelets. A long-handled antler comb was also associated with the early defences. Among exotic finds, a putative bronze swan's neck pin might indicate a date in the mid-first millennium BC or earlier. Pottery was notable for its virtual absence. The middle period at Broxmouth, in radiocarbon years centring on the fourth century BC, saw the appearance of pottery and small stone balls in some numbers. Shale continued to be used for rings.

Particularly distinctive of the middle period at Broxmouth were a series of bone and antler pins, including a yoke-shafted form which the excavator (Hill, P., 1982b) thought were derived from metal prototypes. A ring-headed variant could be a rigid skeuomorph of a flat-bowed La Tène 1c brooch. Long-handled combs were also represented in this and the ensuing phase, but, together with bone or antler handles, do not appear to be chronologically diagnostic. The final phase at Broxmouth, from the second century BC, saw the appearance of bucket-shaped pottery in finer fabric, together with other bone and antler types. Rotary querns are in evidence, superseding the earlier saddle-quern technology. In the very last phases in the first or second centuries AD, samian ware and Roman glass bracelets were in circulation. The Broxmouth assemblage is undoubtedly one of the most instructive yet recovered. That it should not be more definitive for the earlier Iron Age is a measure of how limited is the range of surviving artefacts and how intractible they are to diagnostic classification.

High-status metalworking in southern Scotland for the most part is also more evident in the later pre-Roman Iron Age than in the earlier. Swords and scabbards of Piggott's (Piggott, S., 1950) Group III in the south-east probably dates from no earlier than the first century BC, whilst Group IV, like the example from Mortonhall, Edinburgh, belongs to the early first century AD. These are undoubtedly Brigantian types, and though conceivably introduced by refugees from further south, could equally have been diplomatic gifts or the product of social exchange. The production and display of conspicuous and portable symbols of identity is not surprisingly encouraged by the presence of an alien and threatening cultural force, so that in the years following the Roman invasion of Britain, some of the more spectacular items of Celtic art are to be found in the frontier regions of the north and west.

Stevenson's map of Scottish Iron Age metalwork (Stevenson, R. B. K., 1966, Fig. 2), was the product of a generation in which population movement was almost invariably regarded as the sole catalyst for cultural change or innovation. The model of diffusionism and the concept of time-lag, as we have seen, was also responsible for the retarded dating accorded to exotic imports into Northern Britain or to the local developments that they were assumed to have triggered. The southern affinities and even origins of some items of prestigious metalworking are undeniable. The gold torc terminal from Cairnmuir, Peeblesshire (Netherud), for example, is so close to the south-eastern style of the first century BC, most splendidly exemplified at Snettisham, Norfolk, that it might have been the product of an Icenian workshop.

Other products from southern Scotland, however, indicate other external influences, notably the existence of an Hiberno-Scottish connection well before the period of historically recorded settlement of Dál Riata. Among the earliest high-status metalwork, the Torrs pony-cap from Kirkcudbrightshire shows more obvious influence from the Irish La Tène school that produced the Loughnashade trumpet than it does from eastern Yorkshire or from the Witham-Wandworth tradition with which it has been inextricably linked for the past half-century (Atkinson and Piggott, 1955; Harding, 2002). Cross-channel connections between Northern Ireland and southern Scotland, and perhaps, despite the unwarranted red herring of Piggott's (Piggott, S., 1950) 'plantation of Ulster', with northern England too seem probable from at least the third century BC. At a rather later pre-Roman Iron Age date, the scabbard from Bargany House in Ayrshire has been recognised as an Irish type, if not actually of Irish manufacture, while the sword from Stevenston Sands (MacGregor, 1976: no. 139) is also of Irish type. In this context it is worth remarking that the pair of bronze spoons found in a cist burial at Burnmouth, Berwickshire, are of beaten bronze in the manner of Irish spoons, rather than cast like their southern British counterparts. We have already noted that the bronze cast ring-headed pin from High Knowes, Alnham, was of a distinctively Irish type. By the opening centuries AD, as we shall see, the cross-channel connection is maintained over a wide area in the distribution of door-knob spear-butts and their moulds, so that the Hiberno-Scottish connection is well attested archaeologically long before documented history.

Chapter 4

Central and eastern Scotland

In the generation following the Second World War, research into later prehistoric archaeology concentrated notably on south-eastern Scotland and the Atlantic north and west. Eastern and north-eastern Scotland did not benefit as did the south-east from being the focus of field survey and research by the Royal Commission on the Ancient and Historical Monuments of Scotland. For this reason in his scheme of provinces and regions (1966) Piggott's North-Eastern Province was perhaps the least well documented of the four. The only field monuments that rated serious consideration were hillforts, notably those with timber-framed or vitrified ramparts. The regions of Strathearn, Strathtay, Strathspey and Cromarty/Moray were largely ignored, and the crannogs of the central Highland lochs, whose distribution (Henderson, Jon, 2000) effectively corresponds to a fifth, central Highland province, were not included. In terms of material culture the only significant distributions to be discussed were the late massive armlets and Donside terrets, being major highlights in the archaeological data-base. In the present generation, eastern Scotland north of the Forth has seen a great resurgence of fieldwork, which is transforming our understanding of settlement in the later prehistoric and early historic periods and greatly diversifying the data-base of known field monument types.

Forts and earthwork enclosures

Hillforts are not nearly as numerous in central and north-eastern Scotland as they are in the Borders, but the distinction between hillfort and homestead is more obvious. Though hillforts are found around the Cromarty and Moray Firths, along the coast of Moray and Banff, on Donside and Deeside, and quite widely from Angus to the Forth, their distribution is not dense, and across quite extensive areas they are hardly represented. Radiocarbon dating has made it clear that hillforts not only had their origins in the later Bronze Age, but that many were re-occupied, or even built anew in the early historic period. The Hownam model, which envisaged a progressive elaboration of defences from palisaded enclosure to wall-ramparts, and from simple, univallate works to more complex, multivallate constructions, was never presumed to apply to central or eastern Scotland. A complex, multi-period plan like that recently excavated at Braehead, Govan (Ellis, 2001), might have prompted comparison with the settlements of the south-eastern Borders, with its palisade trenches, ditched earthworks and ring-groove houses, but its structural sequence hardly follows a unilinear progression from simplest to most complex. Indeed, some house foundations and palisade trenches apparently cut through ditch fillings, indicating a reversal of any such trend, so that any assessment of this important site sequence must await its full publication.

In 1935 Childe had identified two groups of hillforts, which would no longer be regarded as discrete and different types, but which were particularly represented in north-eastern Scotland, 'Gallic' forts and vitrified forts (Childe, 1935a). The former were characterised by timber-framed ramparts, then presumed to have been derived directly from the Continental tradition described by Caesar at Avaricum as a *murus gallicus*; Burghead in Morayshire, Castle Law, Abernethy and Forgandenny in Perthshire were cited as examples. For the vitrified series, Finavon in Angus, excavated by Childe himself between 1933 and 1935, served as the model (Childe, 1935b). The defences at Burghead were subsequently recognised as belonging to the mid-first millennium AD, as are the defences of several other coastal promontory forts in the north-east. On the other hand, Abernethy, where excavations in the late nineteenth century exposed a substantial wall-face through which gaps indicated the positions of stout horizontal beams (Fig. 4.1b), remains firmly accepted as early Iron Age on the strength of its material associations. Providing a wall-rampart with timber framing is a structural device for increased stability, bracing the front and rear facing walls or timber uprights into a rigid 'box'. It further enabled the builders to achieve a greater height-to-width ratio than would have been possible simply by heaping the rampart material into a dump, and allowing it to assume its natural angle of rest. If timbers of sufficient length were used in a systematic structure it could indeed have provided additional strength and stability to the wall, as Caesar reported during his Gallic campaigns. Various arrangements of internal timbers are known through Britain and Europe in the later prehistoric and early historic periods, which have inevitably been subject to archaeological classification. At Abernethy, section drawings also indicate the use of longitudinal timbers, creating a framework that was backed against the natural slope of the terrain (Fig. 4.1a). Whatever design was adopted, timber or timber and stone techniques of construction are not exclusive to any one period or region, and as such are not culturally or chronologically diagnostic. They certainly would no longer be widely regarded, as Childe presumed, as evidence for invasion or colonisation of Scotland, although the idea that timber-framed forts may have been introduced by Urnfield or later Hallstatt settlers has proved remarkably enduring (Cunliffe, 1991: 103; MacKie, 1995: 661).

Oblong enclosures

The oblong forts at Finavon and Forgandenny are representative of a class of enclosure (Fig. 4.2) that affords perhaps the best case for recognising a distinctive regional group in central and eastern Scotland. To these might be added the vitrified oblong fort on the summit of Tap o' Noth, Aberdeenshire, and the smaller elongated enclosure on Turin Hill, Angus, among others. A striking aspect of these sites is their apparent lack of an entrance, which would have inhibited easy access, especially for stock or wheeled vehicles, even allowing for the use of ladders or timber ramps to surmount the walls. Any breach in a hillfort's enclosing ditch and rampart, such as an entrance causeway and passage, is an obvious weak point in the defensive circuit, but defensive integrity is generally compromised in the interests of non-military functional utility. So the question arises, what was the function of oblong enclosures? At Finavon, despite Childe's claims, the domestic assemblage is actually quite limited, showing little evidence of the working of antler or bone, for example, despite the occurrence of animal bone in profusion. A defensive purpose, however, seems to be belied by the fact that its elongated, oblong

(a)

(b)

Figure 4.1 Abernethy, Perthshire, hillfort rampart. a, reconstruction drawing (D. W. Harding); b, wall-face exposed by excavation *c.* 1898 (copyright Royal Commission on the Ancient and Historical Monuments of Scotland, courtesy of the Society of Antiquaries of Scotland).

plan pays little heed to the natural contours, as a primarily defensive layout might have been expected to do. Furthermore, despite the existence of extensive quarry-pitting, there is no evidence that there was a formal defensive ditch. An alternative interpretation, therefore, might be to regard these oblong enclosures as ceremonial or otherwise special enclosures, on analogy with the Banqueting Hall at Tara or some of the later Bronze Age and Iron Age rectilinear cult enclosures of Central and Western Europe, without being as exclusively dedicated to a single ritual function as those sites may have been. Demonstrating cult activities archaeologically is notoriously difficult in the absence of formal temple plans, altars, ritual dedications or votive deposits, but at Finavon the fragments of human skull found within the filling of a dry, well-like shaft at the east end of the enclosure would not be inconsistent with evidence of ritual practices from Celtic Europe.

Finavon is also an example of a timber-framed fort with walls vitrified by firing. Once regarded as a peculiarly Scottish device for solidifying and strengthening the rampart, this is now regarded as destructive rather than constructive, and possibly the result of a deliberate and punitive act of destruction after capture of the fort. The practice was not restricted to central and eastern Scotland, as the example of Dunagoil, Bute, demonstrates, nor was it limited only to the later prehistoric period, as both radiocarbon dating

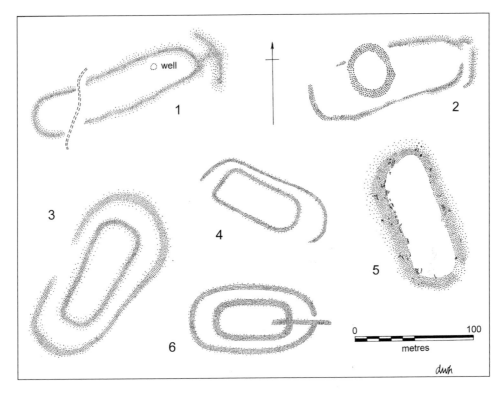

Figure 4.2 Oblong forts of eastern Scotland, plans. 1, Finavon, Angus; 2, Turin Hill, Angus; 3, Craig Phadrig, Inverness; 4, Dunnideer, Aberdeenshire; 5, Tap o' Noth, Aberdeenshire; 6, Castle Law, Fogandenny, Aberdeenshire. Drawings by D. W. Harding, adapted from Alexander (2002), Feachem (1955), Hogg (1975), MacDonald (1890).

and thermoluminescence have indicated. The key point, of course, arising from these conclusions is that vitrification cannot be regarded as culturally or chronologically diagnostic, the forts thus affected being simply timber-framed forts that were subjected to destructive firing, and whose stone core was amenable to vitrification. At Finavon Childe found considerable quantities of burnt timber, which may have resulted from the firing of timber structures integral to the walls but, as elsewhere, he noted particularly that virtually nowhere in his relatively extensive exposure of the walls at Finavon did he find the facing walls themselves as opposed to the core rubble to have been vitrified.

Despite the excavations of Childe (1935b) and MacKie (1976), the date of the construction and occupation of Finavon remains arguable. MacKie's radiocarbon dates certainly suggested construction of the fort in the early-middle first millennium BC, with occupation probably lasting over several centuries, but the error margin of the Gakushkin laboratory dates in particular at the time of excavation has been questioned (Ashmore, 1997: 240). A pre-Roman date, though much later in the first millennium BC, was also suggested by archaeomagnetic dating (Gentles, 1993). Thermoluminescent dates, on the other hand (Sanderson et al., 1988) yielded a range in the mid-first millennium AD, which led Ritchie (Ritchie, A., 1995) to argue for an important role of both Finavon and Turin Hill in the early historic period, located as they are on the ridge route linking the symbol-stones at Aberlemno to the ecclesiastical centre at Brechin. The idea that these sites were re-used in the later Iron Age need not be incompatible with construction and occupation in the later Bronze Age or early Iron Age. Sections through the ramparts at Finavon (Fig. 4.3) could suggest two periods of wall construction, the first represented by the stone-faced wall, the second by the dump of material above and behind it. The rear wall-face of 'box' ramparts was not invariably left exposed, but integral dumps, as reinforcement or for access to the wall-head, were seldom of these proportions. But either way, Childe's explanation of the dump material as collapse seems improbable, especially in sections where that collapse was apparently upslope rather than downslope. The suggestion advanced by MacKie (1976), and followed by Alexander (2002), that the crest of the rampart appearing to be behind the rear revetment was a product of later quarrying was not entirely convincing, being based upon a wish to establish the relative status of the radiocarbon samples from the underlying occupation level. In fact, this thick, dark deposit could still equate with the early Iron Age occupation, whether the overlying material was collapsed debris of the primary rampart or a dump rampart of a later episode of reconstruction and re-occupation. The firing of the walls that resulted in vitrification must nevertheless have marked the end of the primary phase. Whatever uncertainties persist regarding an early historic occupation of Finavon, the total absence of Roman material surely excludes its use during periods when the region was in contact with Roman influences.

The same programme of thermoluminescence dating which yielded unexpectedly late dates for Finavon also produced a consistent set of remarkably early dates for the vitrified fort at Tap o' Noth in Grampian region, centring on a mean age of 4140 BP. The idea that vitrification might occur at any date presents no problem, but the fact that the vitrified fort at Tap o' Noth is another apparently gateless oblong enclosure would lead to some expectation of concurrency with Finavon, Forgandenny and the other sites of this class. Below the summit is an outer wall, now recognisable as a line of substantial boulders (Feachem, 1963: 105–6), enclosing a massive 21 hectares. More than a hundred platforms, which may have been quarry scoops but some of which at around 10 metres

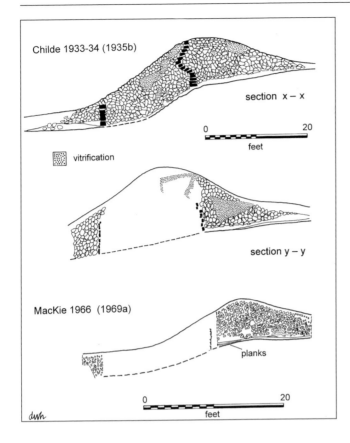

Childe 1933-34 (1935b)

section x – x

0   20

feet

vitrification

section y – y

MacKie 1966 (1969a)

planks

0   20

feet

dwh

Figure 4.3 Finavon, Angus, hillfort rampart sections. Drawings by D. W. Harding, adapted from Childe (1935b) and MacKie (1969a).

in diameter resemble house platforms, could be indicative of a much more extensive settlement. The summit of Tap o' Noth lies at 560 metres OD, still somewhat lower than Ben Griam Beg in Sutherland, which rises to 620 metres (Ralston and Smith, 1983). The high altitude of these sites has prompted the suggestion that their occupation, even if only seasonal, might have been more appropriate to a period preceding the climatic deterioration of the sub-Atlantic around the end of the second millennium BC. We have already seen, on the other hand, hillforts in northern England like Carrock Fell in Cumbria at similar heights, and most strikingly Ingleborough in west Yorkshire at over 700 metres. Eight miles to the east of Tap o' Noth, though at less extreme altitude, Dunnideer replicates its structural layout, with an outer, though intermittent and perhaps unfinished enclosure, within which are some possible scooped hut platforms. The summit enclosure, in which vitrified material occurs in profusion, is again an oblong in plan with no clear entrance.

Further north, at Craig Phadrig, Inverness (Small and Cottam, 1972), another oblong fort dominated a summit which evidently attracted occupation in later prehistoric and early historic times. Both outer and inner ramparts were timber-framed, stone con-structions, the inner much the more massive and showing signs of vitrification. Once again, no entrances are visible in the inner enclosure wall, so that the site appears to conform to type. Radiocarbon dating has indicated that these enclosure walls date from the mid-first millennium BC, but excavation within the interior yielded fragments of late Roman or sub-Roman pottery and a mould for a hanging-bowl escutcheon, which plainly testify not only to later occupation, but to the site having been a residence of high status in the early historic period. The impression is reinforced that, whilst many hillforts show evidence of prolonged, if intermittent, occupation, doubtless occasioned by their dominant landscape location, the massive-walled oblong 'forts' in particular seem to have retained their status for more than a millennium.

In the west, at Craigmarloch Wood in Renfrewshire (Nisbet, 1996), overlooking the Clyde, a small, sub-oblong fort, this time with one certainly original entrance, also displayed extensive traces of vitrification, combined within a rubble wall that included earth and turf within its exterior stone facings. From cavities within the wall core and impressions on the underside of the vitrified material the excavator inferred a framework of transverse, longitudinal and possibly vertical timbers. Here, as in the classic Hownam sequence, the fort was preceded by an earlier palisaded settlement, itself probably of more than one phase of construction. Its occupational material could be distinguished from that of the later fort by virtue of the fact that the palisaded enclosure extended beyond the limits of the vitrified fort, and was effectively sealed stratigraphically by its foundations. The material assemblage included basic utilitarian types such as spindle-whorl, pounders and whetstones, together with pottery with incurving, barrel-shaped profiles in coarse, Dunagoil-style fabrics. But like Dunagoil, it also included a number of shale ring fragments, and the presence of crucibles and a clay mould for a decorative boss indicates bronze-working for higher-status products. A single early radiocarbon date for the palisaded phase is entirely consistent with the dating of palisades elsewhere, but the fact that a single date from the vitrified wall is rather later than might have been expected prompts caution in placing too much weight upon either.

Vitrified forts

Vitrification is in essence what happens under extreme circumstances when a timber-framed rampart is fired. The technique of constructing wall-ramparts using an internal timber framework, with rubble core and internal timber lacing faced with dry-stone courses front and rear, is characteristic of many regions of Western Europe from the Bronze Age through to the early Mediaeval period. When a timber-framed wall is fired, the result will only be vitrification where the stone core is of appropriate rock; the effect on limestone, for example, as at Leckhampton in Gloucestershire, is not vitrification but reduction. Current opinion now discounts vitrification as a construction technique for several very good reasons (MacKie, 1976). First, the technique is not uniformly applied throughout the defensive circuit of any recorded site. Second, its effect is not to provide a consolidated and strengthened wall; instead it distorts and thus weakens the wall. Third, the evidence for vitrification at Finavon included burnt debris found resting on the latest occupation levels, rather than being in evidence from the primary deposits, suggesting that it was indeed a destructive rather than constructive process. Finally, there are numerous examples of timber-laced stone or rubble walls where there is no evidence whatsoever of vitrification, so that if we regard it as a constructional technique we must ask why it was not applied more consistently.

Experimental firing to simulate the creation of a vitrified wall has been attempted on more than one occasion, by Childe and Thorneycroft (1938b) at Plean Colliery, Stirlingshire and at Rahoy in Argyll, and at East Tullos, Aberdeenshire (Ralston, 1986).

These exercises have demonstrated empirically that setting fire to a timber-laced wall is a complicated task, requiring preparation and patience, and even then it is prone to frustration by the rigours of the Scottish weather. It seems improbable therefore that such a task could have been successfully accomplished in the heat of battle as a practical means of attacking a hillfort rampart, though this is not to say that fire would not have been deployed against timber gateways. In consequence, it seems more plausible to think of the firing that caused vitrification as part of punitive reprisals against a hillfort after capture, intended to send an unmistakable signal of submission to the surrounding communities. The presence of sites in some numbers which display vitrification, therefore, must be regarded as a measure of political instability, though whether it should be taken as a sign of a widespread series of broadly contemporary episodes, or simply as an indication of inherent unrest between neighbouring communities, perhaps over a protracted period of time, remains a matter of debate. Though constructive vitrification seems to be conclusively discredited, it is worth remarking that no single explanation needs to be imposed on all examples, particularly in view of their occurrence over a very long chronological span; the very varied character of vitrification could reflect a variety of causes, accidental and deliberate.

The fact that it is commonly the core, rather than the wall-faces, that is vitrified, as at Finavon and Dunagoil, still requires satisfactory explanation. It is sometimes suggested that this arises from the firing of timber structures along the wall parapet, encouraging the spread of burning to the internal timber framework of the wall from above. The possibility of casement construction in part of the walls encouraging internal firing has never been seriously investigated. But it is hard to imagine why the wall-faces should have been immune, except where the surviving courses were so low as to have been covered in accumulating occupational and vegetational deposits, as could have been the case at Dunagoil. Spontaneous internal burning, as in haystacks or coal-tips, though once proposed for Castle Hill, Almondbury, seems improbable.

Causewayed forts

The diversity of types of field monument hitherto grouped under the umbrella heading of hillforts is further demonstrated by sites with multiple entrances, of which an example at the Barmekin of Echt in Aberdeenshire has its number of entrances reduced from five to just two in its later phase. The most extreme example, however, is the multi-phased enclosures on the Brown Caterthun in Angus, which have up to nine entrances (Fig. 4.4). This number of breaches in the enclosing earthworks, reminiscent of Southern British causewayed camps of the Neolithic period, can hardly have been compatible with effective defence, and must have been designed to meet some other social or agricultural purpose. Systematic excavation of the Brown Caterthun in the mid-1990s not only revealed the character of these enclosing earthworks and their entrances, but also through radiocarbon dating afforded an indication of the chronological sequence, which broadly spanned the second half of the first millennium BC, with occupation potentially beginning as early as the second quarter of that millennium. The site thus belongs securely in the pre-Roman Iron Age, with no evidence at present of occupation thereafter. Excavation revealed a considerable diversity of enclosure construction, including palisades and various wall-building styles, ranging from the use of a simple rubble core faced with boulders front and back or the same with transverse timbers within the core, to a

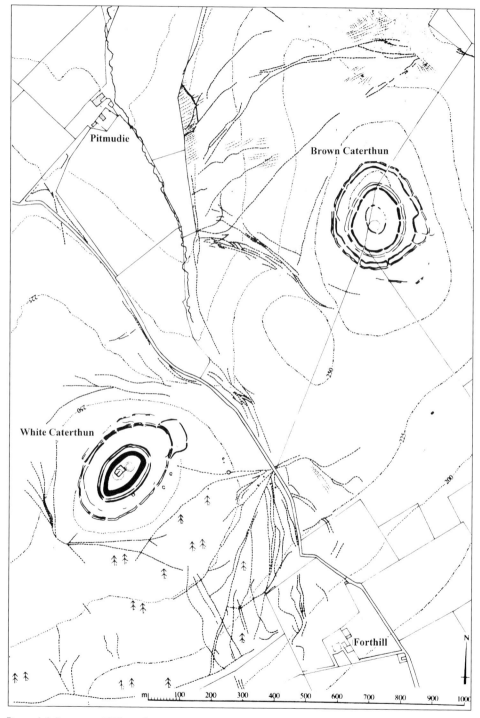

Figure 4.4 Brown and White Caterthuns, Angus, plans. Copyright Royal Commission on the Ancient and Historical Monuments of Scotland, reproduced by kind permission.

dump or *glacis* technique with external quarry-ditch. These differences seem to accord with distinct episodes within the constructional sequence. Unlike the Hownam model, however, the palisades appear to be among the latest elements in the sequence. Common to all phases is an apparent concern with 'rites of passage' into the enclosures, with each of the excavated entrances showing some structural evidence for the creation of a flanking passageway. Not all the entrances of each sub-concentric set of enclosures were aligned, though no less than six did permit direct access to the interior through the successive enclosures. Structural evidence for occupation within the site, on the other hand, was limited.

The White Caterthun, less than a kilometre to the south-west, has been less extensively investigated. It is dominated by the oval outline of a massive stone-built enclosure, of which possibly more than one wall and their entrances lie obscured in the rubble spread. Beyond this a further enclosure consists of bank with internal quarry ditch and palisades that need not be contemporary, whilst the outermost line of enclosure has been resurveyed to show multiple entrances comparable to those of the neighbouring site to the north-east. The massive stone fort, not matched at the Brown Caterthun, may be the latest in the structural sequence, probably obscuring the detailed complexity of the earlier enclosures. The existence of unenclosed ring-ditch houses and an extensive field-system in proximity to the White Caterthun would be consistent with settlement focused on the enclosure in the early to mid-first millennium BC. It is certainly hard to imagine that there was not significant overlap in the occupation or use of the adjacent enclosures in the Iron Age, even if the ruins of the stone enclosure at the White Caterthun conceal a secondary and possibly early historic re-use of the site.

Taken together, these complex and long-lived enclosures hardly appear to be primarily defensive in function. The multiple entrances in particular seem to connote social ordering of access for whatever communal activities took place within. There can be little doubt that such activities, seasonal or festive, legal, inaugural or ceremonial, could well have been an important aspect of the role of hillforts generally, but it is only when the structural elements of the site more obviously diverge from the expected character of a defensive stronghold that the archaeologist is disposed to consider alternative interpretations.

Promontory forts

The earliest of the coastal promontory forts of the north-eastern province is at Castle Point, Troup, otherwise known as Cullykhan (Greig, 1970, 1971, 1972). Here it appears that the earliest phase of fortification was represented by a palisade along the western, landward side of the promontory, which was subsequently replaced by a timber-framed wall with elaborate entrance passage. Radiocarbon dates based upon samples from structural timbers suggested a date in the mid-first millennium BC for these defences. Further east the remains of a vitrified wall, which was said to overlay the earlier occupation deposits, was thought to date to around the end of the millennium. Once again, however, there is some artefactual evidence, supported by a single radiocarbon date, to suggest that the site may have been re-occupied in the later Iron Age. The importance of Cullykhan, however, lies as much in its evidence for domestic and industrial occupation as for its defensive sequence. The assemblage included a handled crucible for bronze working, as well as waste from iron working. Domestic artefacts included beads, spindle-whorls and fragments of jet bracelets. Among the bronzes was a tanged chisel or leather-worker's knife of a widespread Atlantic late Bronze Age type (Roth, 1974), sometimes found, as at Staple Howe, in association with imported Hallstatt C types. Cullykhan might thus be seen as a northerly manifestation of Haselgrove's 'north-west European Hallstatt Interaction Zone', which was invoked in the context of the introduction of Hallstatt C elements along the North Sea coastal route.

The practice of fortifying coastal promontories, which in the later Iron Age saw the construction or re-occupation of a chain of sites along the Moray, Buchan and Aberdeenshire coastline, seems to have been less common in the early Iron Age than in some other regions of Britain where the necessary topographical conditions were also available. Often far from practical as settlement or even as defensive sites, it is arguable that these sites were expressly selected as prominent landmarks of maritime communities, intended to make a territorial statement to sea-borne traders and traffic. Inland promontories too, like the Lower Greenyards fort at Bannockburn, Stirlingshire (Rideout, 1996), have obvious topographical advantages, though not so precipitate as some of the coastal sites. Here as elsewhere it has been remarked that the multiple defences across the neck of the promontory are disproportionately elaborate relative to the area enclosed (Fig. 4.5, 1),

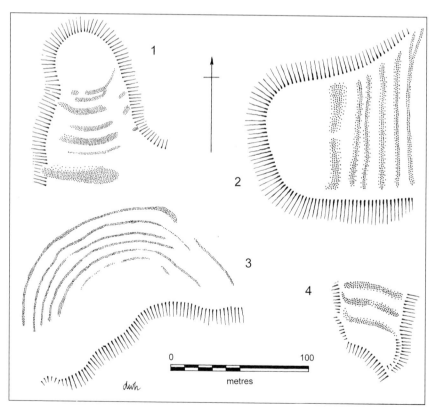

Figure 4.5 Small multivallate forts in central and eastern Scotland. 1, Bannockburn, Stirling; 2, Inchtuthill, Perthshire; 3, Rosemount, Perthshire; 4, Rait, Perthshire. Drawings by D. W. Harding, adapted from Rideout (1996) and RCAHMS (1994).

which might therefore be taken as an index of social status. On the other hand, it was impossible through excavation to resolve the complexity of the sequence of ditches and palisades, which quite evidently represented a long period of occupation, perhaps spanning a millennium or more from the late Bronze Age into the early historic period. Re-alignment of the entrance through one phase of ditch construction, together with external roundhouses indicative of an element of unenclosed settlement, combine to endorse a protracted occupation of the site. Despite current fashion, however, there is nothing in the Lower Greenyards site that requires its interpretation as a ritual or ceremonial site, rather than as a domestic settlement, assuming that it is necessary to draw a distinction between the two.

Defensive earthworks disproportionate to the scale of area enclosed have also been remarked at Inchtuthil (Fig. 4.5, 2), in the small, native promontory fort which lies at the west end of the plateau occupied by the Roman encampments. Once again the earthworks may not all have been in contemporary use, and the presence of ditch and palisade trench within the interior further argues a long structural sequence (Abercromby *et al.*, 1902). An even more exaggerated example, in a cliff-edge rather than promontory location, is afforded by the crop-mark fort at Rosemount, north-east of Scone (Fig. 4.5, 3), where no less than six lines of enclosure occupy a considerably greater area than the compound within. Notwithstanding arguments for defence in depth, it is improbable that this could have been a normal community settlement, and the possibility that multiple lines of enclosure were a measure of social status within a settlement hierarchy deserves consideration.

Homesteads and settlements

Until relatively recent years the domestic settlements of the Iron Age north of the Forth were not nearly so well documented archaeologically as those of southern, and more especially south-eastern Scotland. With modern field research has come the realisation that houses need not be represented in the archaeological record exclusively by post-hole or ring-groove plans, and that they are characterised by much greater structural diversity than was implied by archetypal sites like Little Woodbury on the Wessex chalk downs or like West Brandon in Co. Durham or Hayhope Knowe in the Roxburghshire Cheviots. Among older excavations, Steer's investigation at West Plean, south of Stirling (Steer, 1956), provided a regional type-site which nevertheless displayed much the same characteristics of an enclosed homestead containing a single large roundhouse, an *Einzelhof* in the tradition of Bersu's Little Woodbury. The enclosure was circular rather than sub-rectangular, and its shallow ditch had, in part of its circuit at least, an *external* bank, so that the enclosure was evidently not primarily defensive in function. The remains of a palisaded hornwork at its eastern entrance had been truncated by the ditch terminals, from which the excavator inferred that there had been an earlier, palisaded enclosure. This may have correlated broadly with the two principal phases of internal occupation, one represented by a simple post-ring house with central post, the other by a larger building based upon an external ring-groove with internal circle of roof-supporting post-holes (Fig. 2.5, 6). There was no stratigraphic basis for determining which was the earlier, and Steer's presumption that the smaller was replaced by the larger is not in principle or from experience above challenge. No radiocarbon dates were available at the time of excavation, but the material assemblage from West Plean, including notably a handled cup of sandstone, and several other artefacts of shale or stone, would be consistent with a date in the later Bronze Age or early Iron Age. A fragment of rotary quernstone from the cobbled 'yard', however, implies occupation at least into the post-quern transition phase.

Barely a mile from West Plean a circular, palisaded homestead adjacent to the Bannockburn promontory fort (Fig. 2.3, 8; Rideout, 1996) mirrored the form of the West Plean homestead. Significantly larger than the West Plean enclosure, its central round-house, the full extent of which was unfortunately not made available for investigation, was likewise substantially larger. Evidently two structural phases are represented in the two arcs of postholes and double arc of ring-groove construction. At 18.6 metres in diameter the outermost post-ring might be thought to be beyond the normal limits of roundhouse construction, unless as the basis for grounding rafters, and the ring-grooves at around 15 metres in diameter are perhaps more probable as the line of the external wall. The ring-groove of the complete house-plan recovered from within the area of the promontory fort, however, is around 14.5 metres in diameter, and if the rafters had been grounded on a circle aligned on the external posts of the projecting porch, as for example at Pimperne, Dorset, then this outermost ring would have been around 18.5 metres in diameter. From excavation it was impossible to be certain whether this large roundhouse stood in isolation within a palisaded enclosure, like its neighbour to the east, or whether it continued in use into the period of the presumptively later ditched promontory fort. In fact the large roundhouse at Bannockburn, though larger than the Pimperne or Little Woodbury houses, shares exactly their proportions between external and weight-bearing walls, the crucial ratio of 'roundhouse geometry', and, contrary to the notion of a 'special' function for the site, this itself suggests a normal domestic structure.

A key factor in the Bannockburn plan, however, is the presence of a smaller roundhouse, itself showing secondary rebuilding, not only outwith the defensive enclosures, but impeding or anticipating the line of access through its main entrance. This building was of a different scale and layout from the larger internal roundhouse. Its external ring-groove, 10 metres in diameter, contained a post-ring just 5.5 metres in diameter, and the entrance lacked the distinguishing projecting porch. Whether it was earlier or later than the fortified settlement, or whether it was contemporary with any of the neighbouring palisaded homesteads, is quite uncertain, but we certainly should not preclude the possibility of enclosed and unenclosed settlements of broadly the same chronological horizon. The material assemblage at Bannockburn was pretty meagre, in keeping with much of Northern Britain in the earlier Iron Age. Radiocarbon dates from the Lower Greenyards fort were hardly conclusive, but endorsed a dating broadly in the second half of the first millennium BC.

More obviously anomalous among the older settlements was that excavated by Bersu at Scotstarvit Covert, overlooking the river Eden in Fife (Bersu, 1948). Here a sub-circular ditched enclosure contained a single, large central building that had undergone reconstruction more than once (Fig. 2.5, 4). The plan comprised three concentric elements, at least in its first two phases. The outermost consisted of a continuous ring-groove in which no specific post emplacements were recognised, the intermediate ring-groove contained posts set at regular intervals, and the innermost element was a ring of individual postholes. An entrance hall-way extended from the innermost ring of posts to the outermost ring-groove, raising interesting questions regarding the order of access to internal space. The excavated traces of gullies suggested that, as with brochs, the peripheral areas of the house could not be accessed directly from the entrance passage, which led straight to the central area. As to the symmetry of plan, the outline of the ring-grooves was much less regular than in many Iron Age roundhouses. Furthermore, the rings were spaced at approximately equal distances from centre to perimeter, thus departing from the roundhouse geometry that is regularly associated with a conical roof with a pitch of 45 degrees. At its largest extent, the outermost ring-groove was around 18 metres in diameter, which would impose almost insuperable problems if such a roof were implied. The structure evidently also included an element of earthwork, surviving as surface traces of a low bank around an arc just within the outermost ring-groove, which Bersu interpreted as the basis of a raised platform for benches or beds.

Bersu's view of the site was evidently coloured by his experience in the Isle of Man (Bersu, 1977), where he had excavated multi-ringed houses that he believed were roofed in turf over much greater diameters than would be possible with a standard conical roof. It would be instructive to investigate experimentally the combination of turf roofing of the perimeter around a steeper central cone of thatch. In fact, phases 1 and 2 at Ballacagen site A might be better interpreted as freestanding roundhouses within an enclosed compound. Phase 1 in particular (Bersu, 1977: 12, Fig. 4) displays radial plank decking between the house and the perimeter wall, which might be compared to the radial trenches detected by Bersu projecting in several places from the house at Scotstarvit (1948: Fig. 4). In the matter of dating Bersu was almost certainly too conservative in opting for a late pre-Roman context for Scotstarvit, though this must remain a matter of opinion in the absence of a diagnostic material assemblage or radiometric dates. Equally the question of function must remain open, since the problems of roofing a building of this size preclude the automatic assumption that it was a domestic, residential building.

Houses of ring-ditch type are now known quite widely north of the Forth. The best-documented example from modern excavation is the open settlement at Douglasmuir in the Lunan valley in Angus (Kendrick, 1995). The fact that the Angus houses share structural characteristics in common with the ring-ditch houses of the Borders need not mean, of course, that they functioned in exactly the same way. Six houses were excavated, ranging in size from 10 to 13 metres in diameter, discounting the width of the external bank which must have been the product of their construction, and which in some cases probably served as the foundation for their roof-rafters. Internal post-settings did not always form regular patterns, but in Houses 3 and 5 (Fig. 3.11, 4) at least clear post-rings were detected around the inner lip of the ring-ditch on the edge of the central platform. In the case of House 3 alone, a further inner ring of posts may have been for furniture and fittings rather than being integral to the structure itself. In one instance, House 6, there was evidence for posts and paving in association with the entrance. Elsewhere, odd lengths of crescentic ditches and clusters of pits, possibly the truncated remains of further houses, suggest that the village could have had twice that number of houses in all. Differences from the Borders ring-ditch houses include the steeper profile of the ring-ditch at its external face, and the relative lack of stony filling of the ditches, both possibly pointers to a different function. A series of radiocarbon dates from contexts associated with the houses was consistent in confirming that they belonged to the middle of the first millennium BC.

At Douglasmuir it is impossible in the absence of preservation of animal bone to estimate the contribution, if any, of animal husbandry to the domestic economy. But the presence of more than fifty fragments of quernstone and significant samples of grain from the settlement is surely indicative of a significant component of cereal cultivation. Accordingly it would be reasonable to regard the ring-ditch houses as being adapted in some measure to the storage of cereal products, in contrast to interpretations of the Borders houses in which stalling of livestock has been argued as one probable function. The fact that the ring-ditches at Douglasmuir survived up to a depth of 1.8 metres encouraged Kendrick's view that this constituted a form of proto-souterrain, a storage vault contained beneath the floor of the house. The fact that there were other structures on the site, notably six-posters and related settings, at least one of which was associated with a cache of wheat grains, should not preclude the need for alternative storage for agricultural produce, matching the apparent use in Southern Britain of upstanding granaries in tandem with underground pit storage.

As regards the practical use of ring-ditch structures, the penannular ditch could have been simply a device to compensate for lack of headroom near the perimeter of the building, but if so this does not explain the frequently irregular, segmented character of the ditch, where a continuous ditch would have been more efficient. If achieving headroom without the need for high external walls was the objective, then lowering the entire floor area, as in subterranean wheelhouses, might have been easier and more effective. Much the same purpose was achieved in the sub-rectangular *Grubenhäuser* of later prehistoric and early historic European settlements. Yet even in these latter there is occasional evidence of suspended floors and therefore a capacity for under-floor storage, and this may well have been the practice in ring-ditch houses of the Northern British Iron Age. From this perspective, the penannular ring-ditch is simply another structural technique available to the Iron Age house-builder, and as such need not be culturally or chronologically diagnostic any more than are ring-grooves, scooped platforms or any other practical constructional device. The absence of hearths or domestic bric-à-brac still leaves open the question whether ring-ditch houses were indeed dwellings in the conventional sense rather than primarily agricultural buildings, or perhaps buildings in which human occupation, stock and storage were combined. Armit (1997a: 32), as we have seen, developed the idea of the ring-ditch house as an Iron Age 'byre-house', with human occupation of an upper storey above the stock and storage at ground-floor level. A 'barn-house' would make equally good sense, except perhaps that one might have expected produce to be stored in the cellars or in the loft in this instance.

The ring-ditch house excavated at Culhawk Hill, Kirriemuir, Angus (Fig. 3.11, 5; Rees, 1998) is seemingly one of the largest known, with a low external bank around 20 metres in diameter. Within this the ring-ditch itself was relatively slight, and around its inner lip a ring 9.5 metres in diameter of fifteen substantial posts provided the main support for the roof. A ring-groove around the outer edge of the ring-ditch was apparently a secondary feature, but must have accorded approximately to the position of the footings of the roof rafters of the main house. A building on this scale, whether its roof was pitched at 45 degrees or arguably somewhat lower, would have been a strikingly monumental structure on this exposed and open hillside, though there is no reason to suppose that the site was other than domestic. Radiocarbon dates suggested an occupation between the fourth century BC and the second century AD, so that the currency of the ring-ditch type was apparently longer north of the Forth than it appears to have been on present evidence in the Borders. The dates from the settlement at Auchlishie, Kirriemuir, Angus (*DES*, 1999: 111) might seem to endorse this conclusion. Both the ring-ditch house and the Dalladies-type souterrain have dates around the end of the first millennium BC, which would be consistent with the early first millennium AD dates and Roman material associations from the ensuing occupation.

Recognising the great diversity of house types and the likely ephemeral character of their truncated remains is a far cry from the expectation of regular post-plans in the Southern British chalk lands. Reconstructing the original layout of a settlement like Dalladies, Kincardine (Watkins, 1980a), therefore, must necessarily be speculative. Several circular concentrations of postholes or post-pits indicated the presence of 'conventional' post-built roundhouses, but it would also be possible to regard some of the short lengths of crescentic ditch as the truncated remains of ring-ditch houses. Most of the curvilinear ditches, however, including those that appeared to be associated with roundhouses or phases of roundhouses, had uniformly steep sides in which any timber revetment was evidently part of their souterrain function rather than structural components of a house. Nevertheless it would be possible to regard Dalladies as a stage in the development of 'barn-houses' from one in which the ditch was integral to the penannular plan to one in which the storage facility had developed as a fully independent souterrain.

The proximity between souterrains and surface structures had long since been recognised from stone-built settlements like Ardestie and Carlungie, Angus, but it was only with the excavation at Newmill in Perthshire (Watkins, 1980b) that the possibility that souterrains had been accessed from the interior of timber-built houses was first seriously advanced on the grounds of archaeological evidence. Air survey in south-east Perthshire in the early 1990s identified a number of sites, like the south-eastern cluster at Pitroddie (Fig. 4.6), where a complex of souterrains may have been grouped in proximity to domestic buildings. In retrospect, the particular reconstruction at Newmill looks less than convincing, but the idea holds good nevertheless and has gained widespread support from the evidence of air-photography, including the possible connection of a ring-ditch and souterrain close to Newmill itself (DES, 1992: 79). One of the earliest dated examples of the association of roundhouse and souterrain was at Cyderhall, near Dornoch in Sutherland (Pollock, R., 1992). Here a stone-walled souterrain and a smaller earth-cut 'gully', both with timber supports along their passages, led directly from the primary roundhouse, the foundations of which were likewise sunken into the ground. Carbonised grain and pits indicated barley storage on site, though not necessarily as the primary function of the souterrain. Radiocarbon dates for these structures indicate construction and use from the mid-first millennium BC.

Crop-marks, detected by air-photography, of later prehistoric and early historic settlements, including some potentially indicative of souterrains in proximity to domestic structures, were the focus of a field research programme in the Motray Water district of north-east Fife (Watkins and Selkirk, 1992). At North Straiton in 1987 three circular houses of an unenclosed settlement were investigated, including the largest, some 15 metres in overall diameter, from which led a curving ditch of the proto-souterrain type. In fact the ring-ditch of the air-photographic crop-mark concealed several phases of ring-groove construction, the deepest of which implied a foundation up to 75 cm deep. The souterrain too had been rebuilt on several occasions, and because of its relative lack of depth was assumed only ever to have been partially subterranean. Subsequent seasons of excavation on the Leuchars crop-mark complex revealed structures of related type dating from the later Bronze Age to the early historic period, of which the later variant included a subterranean structure over a metre deep, the walls of which had been revetted

Figure 4.6 Pitroddie, Perthshire, unenclosed settlements, ring-ditches and souterrains, air-photograph. Photograph: Royal Commission on the Ancient and Historical Monuments of Scotland, copyright reserved.

with substantial boulders. What sort of superstructure was sustained on this foundation, and whether the sub-structure was intended for habitation or for storage, remains a matter for speculation.

Souterrains or proto-souterrains were a distinctive element of the crop-mark settlements detected by air-photography in Strathmore (RCAHMS, 1994: 59–62). The interrupted ring-ditches of south-east Perth have yet to be excavated and dated reliably, but the smaller examples, up to 17 metres in diameter, could well be domestic structures analogous to North Straiton, and potentially of the pre-Roman Iron Age. Some, on the other hand, including the largest of the multi-period crop-marks at Mudhall and Grangemount (Fig. 4.7), are too large to have been roofed structures, and some are more likely to represent enclosures within which a roofed building may have stood. This has prompted comparison (RCAHMS, 1994: 62) between the interrupted ring-ditch enclosures and the upstanding, stone-built double-walled enclosures of north-east Perth (RCAHMS, 1990: 3–4), in some of which the outer wall quite clearly functioned as an enclosure wall rather than as a double wall over which a unitary roof was pitched. Each of these variants, in timber or stone, could indicate a close integration of domestic and storage capabilities.

The use of a hollow, or a scoop with its sides stone-revetted into the slope of ground, is characteristic of several Iron Age habitation sites that have been excavated in the Lunan valley of Angus in recent years. At Ironshill, Inverkeillor (Pollock, 1997), a house of rather irregular, post-built plan had been levelled into the slope, with a stone revetment built against the uphill side of the platform, in a manner reminiscent of some 'Votadinian'

Figure 4.7
Grangemount,
Perthshire,
unenclosed
settlement with
souterrains,
air-photograph.
Photograph:
Royal Commission
on the Ancient
and Historical
Monuments of
Scotland, copyright
reserved.

houses in the south-east. The Ironshill house yielded a radiocarbon date from one of the
postholes of its porched entrance which, together with a fragment of rotary quern,
indicated a date around the end of the first millennium BC. Significantly earlier, on the
evidence of a single radiocarbon date, was an adjacent house of ring-ditch construction (Fig. 3.11, 6), pointing to the possibility that the stone-revetted Ironshill house
type was a genuinely late development of the pre-Roman Iron Age. A second site at
Ironshill, a palisaded enclosure in which the large, central building was primarily post-
built, may also prove to belong to an earlier Iron Age horizon. Essentially of the same
class as the Ironshill stone-revetted roundhouse was the structure excavated in 1999
at nearby Hawkhill, where the revetment wall of an oval building some 10 by 12 metres
across still survived with up to five courses of boulders intact. Nearby was a stone-lined
souterrain, which from air-photographic evidence appeared to be related to another large
roundhouse.

Further north, in Morayshire, excavations since 1991 at Birnie have uncovered a
settlement of ring-ditch and ring-groove roundhouses, which, though unquestionably
in occupation in the first and second centuries AD, almost certainly had its origins
much earlier in the first millennium BC. Like many of the settlements detected by air-
photography along the coastal valleys, Birnie was an unenclosed settlement, yet from its
material assemblage was evidently a site of some importance locally during the Roman
Iron Age. Dating of enclosed and unenclosed sites in the region remains to be established,
and it may be premature to assume a progression from enclosure in the early Iron Age
to open settlements in the Roman Iron Age on the basis of Birnie alone.

Upland stone-built settlements

The upland regions of north-east Perthshire especially are characterised by stone settlements, the dating of which remains uncertain to a degree, in that they probably represent a long sequence of occupation from the later second millennium BC through the earlier Iron Age at least. They can occur up to the 450-metre contour and beyond, and though they occur in groups it is probable that this represents a succession of occupational episodes rather than social groupings of several family units. The great majority of hut-circles are simple plans with low stone foundations, but disproportionate attention has focused on the minority of double-walled houses (Fig. 4.8), and some more complex units in which two or three hut-circles are enclosed within a single conjoined compound. Typological studies were founded on Thorneycroft's (1933, 1946) pioneer research at Dalruzion, developed more recently by Harris (1984), but there is as yet no adequate basis for suggesting that the typology accords with any chronological order. Perhaps of significance is the occurrence of ring-ditches, apparently similar to those of the lowlands of eastern Scotland, in association with stone-built hut-circles, including half a dozen with double-walled and enclosed walled hut-circles. In terms of size, the Perthshire stone houses range from very small to a maximum of 15 metres in diameter, and even in the case of double-walled houses the presumption must be that the house roof was founded on the inner wall head, even if the outer yard was independently roofed for storage. In the case of paired houses, there is some evidence for one of the pair being secondary, but the basic idea of compound structures is known elsewhere, including in lowland contexts

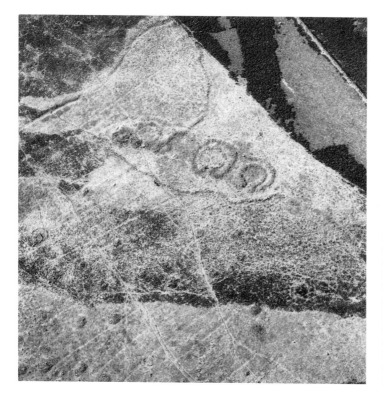

Figure 4.8 Upland settlement with double-ring stone houses, Hill of Kingseat, Perthshire, air-photograph. Photograph: Royal Commission on the Ancient and Historical Monuments of Scotland, copyright reserved.

of Southern and Midland Britain. Apart from hut-circles, clearance cairns and field banks are well preserved in upland Perthshire, and though it is hard to demonstrate contemporaneity, the exceptional relationship between fields, trackways and houses in the case of Drumturn Burn (RCAHMS, 1990: 124–10C) implies an integrated system, even if modified over time. In some instances moorland fire has exposed areas of cord-rig not unlike that now recognised as later prehistoric in the Borders.

Settlements with associated agricultural traces are also known from the later second millennium BC in Sutherland, though here the evidence for continued or renewed occupation in the Iron Age is attested by houses for which radiocarbon dating is available. At Lairg (McCullagh, 1992) there was a pattern of alternating settlement and agricultural horizons, ending with an Iron Age roundhouse. At Kilphedir in the Strath of Kildonan stone-walled houses of circular or oval plan appear to have been occupied from the mid-first millennium BC intermittently if not continuously for several centuries, again with evidence of cultivation in proximity.

Loch-side and estuarine crannogs

Crannogs are unquestionably a distinctive and important component of the Iron Age settlement distribution in Northern Britain, and it is therefore the more regrettable that they have too often been treated as a study separate from field research of terrestrial settlement landscapes in Scotland. Recent attempts at rehabilitating crannogs into Scottish Iron Age settlement studies (Henderson, Jon, 1998a; Harding, 2000a) have underlined the fact that Highland crannogs effectively constitute a fifth 'province' ignored by Piggott's 1966 scheme. One reason for the detachment of crannog research from Iron Age settlement studies has been the perception of crannogs as spanning a long chronology, from Neolithic to sixteenth century AD or later (Morrison, 1985), and therefore as having an existence detached from conventional period-based syntheses. That lochs were natural arteries of communication through the Highlands for water-borne traffic, and that loch margins were settled by local communities throughout prehistory and early historic times is as undeniable as it is unremarkable. Some of the better-preserved examples, like Ardanaiseig in Loch Awe (Fig. 4.9b), probably were occupied in early historic times. Others, like Ederline pier (Fig. 4.9a), for which a single radiocarbon date suggests early Iron Age occupation, survive only as largely submerged foundations. Crannogs were especially prevalent from the later Bronze Age and throughout the Iron Age, and an increasing number of radiocarbon determinations now endorse this fact.

Crannogs include a variety of structural types, in which the constructional components, and indeed function, may have differed or been modified over time. Those that have been investigated in Highland lochs like Loch Tay and Loch Awe nevertheless conform to expectations of a single domestic homestead, the lacustrine equivalent of the duns or rath-like enclosures that occupy the surrounding hillsides, and with which the crannogs may well have integrated as part of a contemporary settlement system. A distributional relationship between crannogs and agricultural land was proposed by Morrison (1985) for Loch Awe and by Henderson (Henderson, Jon, 1998b) for the lake of Menteith. A priority for research should be selective test excavation of land-based duns aimed at obtaining samples for dating of sites that, according to the Morrison model, should be broadly contemporary with the crannogs of Loch Awe and Loch Tay. Whether crannogs were necessarily pile-dwellings, as envisaged by the early investigators of the Swiss lakes

(a)

(b)

Figure 4.9 Crannogs of Loch Awe. a, Ederline Pier; b, Ardanaiseig. Photographs by D. W. Harding.

on the basis of ethnographic parallels, or as reconstructed at Kenmore on Loch Tay on the basis of excavations at Oakbank crannog, remains an issue of contention. That debate necessarily has to address the issue of fluctuating loch levels, in which the natural seasonal rise and fall can still be very substantial (setting aside the matter of modern water-level controls), and in which changes in mean level since prehistoric times are not easy to estimate with confidence.

Crannogs are generally sited in sheltered inlets, away from the full force of the prevailing wind and the fetch generated over exposed water. They are commonly located on a relatively shallow shelf at the furthest point before the loch bed drops away steeply, thereby affording a measure of protection from the shore, to which they may be linked by a timber walkway. Notwithstanding their secure location, there can be little doubt that sites like Oakbank were essentially domestic homesteads, occupied in the mid-first millennium BC, and engaged in a mixed agricultural economy in which the pastoral component, supplemented by the exploitation of hunting, fishing and wildfowling, would have been dominant. Individual crannogs doubtless housed a single, extended family unit, and there is no evidence of any significant clustering into village communities, though these dispersed sites were undoubtedly in visual contact along the shore line or across the loch. Occasionally, as at Dall Bay or Fearnan on Loch Tay, or in Cameron Bay (Fig. 4.10) on Loch Lomond, a couple of crannogs occur in close proximity, but the probability in these instances is that they are successive rather than contemporary neighbours. The dwellings are regularly assumed to have been circular, though the archaeological evidence is still far from sufficient to be certain that this was invariably the case. They generally occupied the greater part of the artificial island or raised platform, with perhaps an extension or annexe in some instances for ancillary structures or activities.

Figure 4.10 Crannogs in Cameron Bay, Loch Lomond, air-photograph. Photograph by D. W. Harding.

The probability must be that other buildings or wharves were located along the shore-line in proximity to the crannog itself. Log-boats of substantial proportions have been found in many locations, and may have been designed, constructed and used in different ways according to purpose (Mowat, 1996).

The study of crannogs in tidal estuaries or rivers, like that of inland lochs, dates from the pioneering days of underwater archaeology. Crannogs at Langbank and at Dumbuck on the Clyde were investigated at the end of the nineteenth century. At Dumbuck (Munro, 1905) the results were in part discredited by the discovery of a number of fake antiquities, which created great hostility between the local antiquarians and Robert Munro, the undisputed authority on Scottish and European crannogs. Nevertheless, the plan (Fig. 3.12, 4) of a circular timber structure some 15 metres in diameter and defined by 27 oak piles with a floor of radial timbers can be regarded as authentic. A log boat nearly 10 metres long was found nearby, in a boat-noost linked to the main crannog. Recent re-investigation has not only confirmed the basic reliability of the excavators' plans, but has established through radiocarbon dating that the site was occupied around the end of the first millennium BC (Hale, 2000; Sands and Hale, 2001). Langbank (Bruce, 1908) was excavated shortly afterwards, and was found to have similar structural remains. The finds, however, suggested a slightly later occupation, in the opening centuries of the first millennium AD, when its occupants must have been aware of and known to the Roman military presence in the area.

These inter-tidal crannogs certainly were sites of substantial structures. How they were affected by or coped with fluctuations in water level is once again hard to estimate in view of substantial modern controls over the water channels of the Clyde. Other estuarine crannogs, notably those investigated by Hale (2000) on the Beauly Firth, must have been even more susceptible to flooding, being nowadays accessible only for a few hours at low tide. Nevertheless, excavation at Redcastle revealed a number of structural timbers below the boulder capping of the crannog, with wattle-lined pits among the primary features. Radiocarbon dates point clearly to a later Bronze Age use of the site, which also yielded some quantities of butchered animal bones. It seems improbable that these sites were intended for permanent habitation, and thus their relationship to crannogs of inland lochs, or even those of the Clyde, seems limited beyond the circumstances of location and wetland preservation. Their location in proximity to low promontories or former shore-lines suggested to Hale that their purpose was to afford access to navigable channels for the surrounding communities rather than being independent domestic sites.

Material culture

As elsewhere in Northern Britain, the material culture of the early Iron Age in central and eastern Scotland is largely undiagnostic, comprising a range of utilitarian stone artefacts, hammer-stones, whetstones and polishers, spindle-whorls, and pottery that is sparse in quantity and undistinguished in character. Childe (1935a) identified three metal types that he associated with his Abernethy culture, and which he attributed to immigrants from the south in accordance with prevailing diffusionist models. The first was the safety-pin form of brooch, of which a La Tène 1 example was found at Abernethy itself. Even Childe had to acknowledge, however, that La Tène brooches were extremely rare in Northern Britain, as they are in Britain generally by comparison with the pro-fusion of finds from Continental Europe. The second distinctive type was the ring-headed pin, represented at Abernethy by a crook-headed variant that is generally regarded as early within the series. Though not found in substantial numbers, they are distinctively Scottish, and like the later Scottish projecting ring-headed pins should be regarded as northern variants on a wider theme, rather than derivative from Southern Britain. Finally, Childe cited the spiral bronze ring, represented in eastern Scotland at Abernethy and Laws of Monifieth, as a third component of the Abernethy culture assemblage. Unfortunately spiral bronze rings are so ubiquitous, from the middle Bronze Age to the early historic period, and from a wide European distribution zone, as to be at present of little value as a chronological or cultural indicator.

Plain glass beads almost certainly date from the early Iron Age, though reliable associations from this period are mostly lacking in Northern Britain. Whilst we may not in general subscribe to the 'reliquary theory', imagining that scraps of exotic artefacts were treasured as keepsakes long after the end of their usable currency, beads are perhaps the one type that might remain in circulation long after manufacture. Small, annular, opaque yellow beads of Guido's (1978) Class 8 date from the third century BC at Meare in Somerset, and there is no reason to suppose that examples from the west and north of Scotland are much later, though those from the vicinity of Hadrian's Wall may represent a later survival of the type. Culbin Sands in Morayshire yielded more than 250 beads of this class, and may well have been a production centre (Henderson, Julian, 1991). Chemical analysis suggests that beads or necklaces from Culbin Sands found their way to the Orkneys, Western Isles and south-west Scotland, but the principal concentration was local to the north-east. Small blue glass beads may likewise have a long currency, perhaps from the fourth century BC in Southern Britain, through to the later Iron Age. Their distribution again is widespread though not especially dense in the north. Types that have a distinctly north-eastern Scottish distribution are rather later, dating to the first and second centuries AD. These include Guido's Class 13 spiral-ornamented beads, and the rather amorphous Class 14, both of which are densely concentrated between the Dee and the Moray Firth. Their dating would therefore overlap that of the production of massive metalwork, including massive armlets and spiral snake armlets as well as massive terrets, all of which have a wider eastern Scottish distribution. In fact, Class 13 beads may conceivably have been in circulation by the first century BC, if the evidence from Dun Bharabhat in west Lewis is indicative, but the north-eastern associations, such as they are, appear to be later.

Bone and antler artefacts are occasionally in evidence in the early Iron Age, though pins and awls are of the simplest forms. Combs of the ubiquitous long-handled variety are found in eastern Scotland, but are more common in the Northern and Western Isles. Bracelets and rings of jet or lignite were in evidence at Finavon, and again almost certainly date from the early Iron Age, continuing into the early historic period. Finally, pottery is very seldom represented in the material assemblage, and then only in coarse, undecorated wares. Childe recovered a range of simple-rimmed and flat-bottomed jars from Finavon, but the ceramic assemblage from central and eastern Scotland remains very limited. In sum it represents the recurrent problem of the early Iron Age, that the material assemblage for the most part comprises basic utilitarian types that are not amenable to close characterisation and dating.

Chapter 5

Argyll and Atlantic Scotland

The early Iron Age in Atlantic Scotland is dominated by field monuments, essentially brochs, duns and island duns, and forts. Wheelhouses too may have been part of the range of settlement types in use by the end of the first millennium BC but, since they evidently continued to be constructed and occupied well into the first millennium AD, consideration of them will be deferred until a later chapter. This emphasis upon field monuments, as opposed to material culture, has sometimes been criticised as prejudicing a proper understanding of the social and economic aspects of early Iron Age society. The fact is, however, that the field monuments are quite exceptional in their surviving number and monumentality of construction, which rightly require attention and explanation. The potential for establishing regional sequences in material culture from long occupational sequences, however, has not been fully realised, and other aspects of artefact studies, not simply typology and chronology, but their social or cognitive aspects, have only very recently been addressed.

Atlantic roundhouses: context, classification and chronology

With around a thousand brochs and duns known in northern and western Scotland, their distribution is plainly indicative of a considerable population, even allowing for the fact that not all would have been in contemporary occupation. The distinction between brochs and duns, even if tenable in principle, is inevitably obscured in practice by the very small proportion of sites that has been excavated, and by their similarity as surviving mounds of tumbled masonry. Sites conventionally defined as brochs certainly predominate in Caithness and the Northern Isles, with significant numbers in Skye and the Western Isles; duns in variable forms are more characteristic of Argyll and the Inner Hebrides, with again a significant group of island-based duns in the Western Isles. These variant forms of monumental stone-built roundhouses should be seen as potentially contemporary regional manifestations of a widespread cultural continuum across Atlantic Scotland, with links to cognate building traditions in other parts of Atlantic Europe and the western seaways. For that reason, the term *Atlantic roundhouse* (Armit, 1990) has been widely adopted archaeologically to serve as an inclusive term for this overall class of Iron Age monument. The broch tower is simply a specific type of *complex Atlantic roundhouse*, but the term broch still remains a convenient shorthand for the class.

A broch or complex Atlantic roundhouse, like Carloway in Lewis (Fig. 5.1), is a circular or sub-circular, dry-stone building with cells or galleries contained within the thickness

Figure 5.1 Carloway, Lewis, complex Atlantic roundhouse. Photograph by D. W. Harding.

of the wall, giving the appearance of double-wall or cavity-wall construction. External windows are never in evidence. Access to the interior of the broch was through a single entrance, the low lintel and cap-stones of which, combined with long, low passage, implies a defensive purpose, or at least the physical and symbolic abaisance of anyone entering the building. The door was commonly supported against a rebate in the stone lining of the passage, and barred by timbers lodged in bar-holes on either side. Guard-chambers commonly flank one side of the entrance passage, though exactly how these functioned is not entirely clear: their opening on to the passage is again extremely constricted, and in most cases there is no alternative access from the guard-cell into the gallery or interior of the broch. The staircase to upper levels invariably rises clockwise within the wall cavity, perhaps indicative of a measure of conventional cosmology in the design of the building.

In addition to entrances at various levels from the interior into the intra-mural galleries, tall slots are found in the inner face of the inner wall, with their cross-ties resembling a stack of vertical pigeon-holes. The function of these is unclear, but they may have been stress-relieving rather than related to the use of the galleries. A key feature of brochs, depending upon their surviving height, is an interior ledge, or scarcement, around the inner face of the inner wall. This may be achieved by a single course of stonework projecting up to 30 cm from the face of the wall, or more substantially by offsetting the wall up to the required level of the scarcement. It is generally supposed that the purpose of the scarcement was to sustain an interior floor. It need not follow, however, that the floor was at the level of the scarcement, since it could have been sprung from a framework based on the scarcement ledge but supporting a floor at a higher level. In fact, the interior of the stone shell was probably lined with a framework of timber, to provide the basis for timber stairs and upper floors. Stone staircases commonly survive within the wall cavity at ground-floor level, and in some cases the flight of stairs continues up through the next floor level. But ultimately, with the sole exception among surviving examples of Mousa, Shetland (Fig. 5.2), the intra-mural gallery becomes too constricted to accommodate a stairway, as the walls converge with greater height, and at this point access to the wall-head must have been gained by means of internal stairs or ladders. That access to the wall-head was desirable must be assumed, not simply for defensive purposes, but also in order to service and maintain the building and its roof.

Internal fixtures and fittings are known within brochs, but the problem invariably arises whether these belong to the original internal design, or whether they are from secondary occupation. Early excavators generally did not appreciate the depth of secondary occupation, and may easily have conflated structures and material assemblages from successive phases of occupation. Hearths and stone-lined troughs, for example, are common to successive phases of occupation, though their design may change through time, but it is doubtful whether the hearth of a broch tower's primary occupation would have been on the ground floor. Radial divisions created by the use of upright slabs may indeed reflect the original social or functional division of space, but equally may be the product of secondary activity, perhaps influenced by the layout of wheelhouse or cellular building plans.

Controversy in the past has focused on whether brochs were completely roofed, and whether they had intermediate floor levels within the tower. Relatively few sites have produced evidence for internal upright supports (Fig. 5.3), and where these are recorded, as at Dun Troddan, Glenelg (Curle, 1921), there can be no assurance that they represent

Figure 5.2 Mousa, Shetland, complex Atlantic roundhouse. Photograph by D. W. Harding and I. M. Blake.

an original feature, rather than a secondary roundhouse built within the broch shell. On the other hand, the circle of timber posts at Dun an Ruigh Ruaidh in Ross-shire appears to have been part of the primary use of the site (MacKie, 1980). At Langwell in Sutherland (Nisbet, 1994) a circle of timber posts probably supported a conical roof, the burnt rafters from which were found collapsed in a radial pattern. Timber roundhouses required no additional roof support to span comparable internal diameters, so that internal supports would not have been essential. Setting aside the issue of timber supplies and the quantities required to build a multi-floored roofed building, there can hardly be any doubt as to the capability of Iron Age communities to achieve a comparable level of technical proficiency in timber to that which the broch structure itself manifestly demonstrates in stone. Pre-occupied with typological considerations, J. R. C. Hamilton in his early post-war investigations in Shetland advanced the theory that brochs had developed from stone-walled forts, taking the evidence from Clickhimin for timber ranges behind the stone 'ringwall' and imagining a model in which such a structure was compressed to the scale of a broch (Hamilton, 1968). The outcome was a broch in which a relatively low circle of timber-built, lean-to sheds was ranged around an open court in the centre of the broch, through which light might be admitted and smoke from the fire might be emitted. Studying the low entrance passages of brochs, and the case for assuming an internal hearth, Dr Peter Reynolds, the foremost exponent in recent years of experimental reconstruction of insular Iron Age buildings, pronounced this model to be akin to creating a blast-furnace. Lighting within a broch tower by means of a central light-well, even at the height of summer, would have been problematic, and archaeological evidence indicates the use of open-wick stone lamps. Furthermore, a

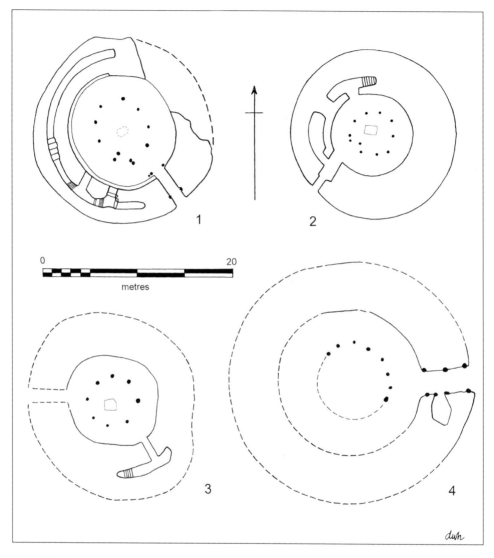

Figure 5.3 Atlantic roundhouses with internal post-rings. 1, Dun an Ruigh Ruaidh, Wester Ross; 2, Dun Troddan, Inverness-shire; 3, Leckie, Stirlingshire; 4, Langwell dun, Sutherland. Drawings by D. W. Harding, adapted from MacKie (1980), Curle (1921), MacKie (1982) and Nisbet (1994).

light-well would have allowed wind and rain to penetrate the fabric of the structure beyond probable levels of tolerability. A vent for the smoke from an internal fire is simply not necessary; smoke may hang in the roof, but otherwise filters naturally through it.

The principal objection to the lean-to shed theory, however, is simply that it is absurdly disproportionate to the grandeur and resource demonstrated by the stone structure itself. In consequence, most recent models of broch reconstruction have envisaged intermediate floors or mezzanine floors and a totally roofed apex to the building. How exactly this was achieved must remain a matter for speculation, though the feasibility of various methods could be tested experimentally. It is worth bearing in mind Fairhurst's (1984: 68) qualification, that not all brochs need have been roofed or internally equipped in exactly the same manner.

The shortage of suitable timber for roofing large roundhouses has been much emphasised, particularly in regions like the Western Isles where the absence of natural woodland is a feature of the modern landscape. Even allowing for environmental change, and for the depredations inflicted by the introduction of sheep, it is difficult to imagine that the landscape of the Western Isles in the Iron Age included more than limited areas of woodland, perhaps in some more sheltered locations along the eastern side of the islands, away from the prevailing westerly winds. There is certainly some evidence for the use of driftwood (Church, 2002), some of which may have attained sizeable proportions, and which could have been stockpiled to afford a useful supplement to local resources. We should certainly not underestimate the capacity of Iron Age communities to manage their limited resources, and indeed to initiate and control an effective system of timber regeneration. Such has long been inferred of prehistoric communities from the Neolithic onwards elsewhere in Britain, and there is no reason to suppose that the population of the Hebridean Iron Age was any more backward in husbanding such a basic resource. What needs could not be satisfied locally may have been acquired from the mainland. It is one of the ironies of the older diffusionist view of Scottish prehistory that settlers who were credited with overland or sea-going colonisation from Land's End to Sumburgh Head were not thought capable of importing timber across the Minch.

An aspect of broch construction that is seldom discussed is the question of the technical skills involved, and what archaeological evidence might be adduced for the builders' tool-kits. A specific question is the extent to which stonework was dressed. Occasionally the term 'roughly dressed' is used; dry-stone masons of course have an eye for which side of a stone will present the best face, and minimal striking off of unwanted nodes can simulate dressed stonework. The stone facing of the ground gallery containing the staircase at Dun Troddan, for example (Fig. 5.4), is much more regular than that in the gallery immediately above, where the cavity is too narrow for normal access, and where the sharply projecting stonework could have inflicted severe injury. Instances of deliberate embellishment include the massive triangular stones for the entrance lintels at Dun Dornadilla in Sutherland, or at Culswick in Shetland (Fig. 5.5). In the case of the recently uncovered example from Old Scatness, Shetland, the triangular stone is so thin relative to its size that it can have been no more than an ornamental façade (Fig. 5.5, c)

The methods deployed in construction are also instructive. The way in which out-cropping rock is straddled and incorporated into the structure, as at Carloway in Lewis, is a measure of the resourcefulness of Iron Age structural engineers. Even so, the number of cracked slabs on the same site, and the need for relieving gaps in the inner wall circuit, is indicative of the structural stresses of such massive buildings. Different techniques are used in raising the walls, some having their outer stones tilted back to create a continuous slope on the outer face, others having the courses marginally stepped inwards to achieve the progressive narrowing of the walls (Suddaby, 1995). Though not immediately apparent, the outer wall of the Carloway broch at its apex is vertically over the line of the inner wall's foundation, so that the whole construction must have been dependent upon its circular geometry being maintained in balance by the outward thrust of the roof. This alone is good reason for believing that the interior was of solid construction, and not just composed of peripheral ranges of lean-to sheds.

Figure 5.4 Dun Troddan, Glenelg, Inverness-shire, showing stonework of intra-mural gallery. Photograph by D. W. Harding.

(1)

(2)

(3)

Figure 5.5 (opposite and above) Complex Atlantic roundhouses with triangular entrance lintels. 1 (opposite), Culswick, Shetland; 2, Dun Dornadilla, Sutherland; 3, Old Scatness, Shetland. Photographs by D. W. Harding and I. M. Blake.

Sites like Carloway evidently stood in isolation, but others, including Mousa, were enclosed with evidence of external settlement in their secondary phases at least. The most conspicuous examples of brochs within a nuclear settlement are those of Orkney (Fig. 5.6), such as Gurness, Midhowe and Lingro, though even here the question of contemporaneity of broch and external settlement is much debated. Hedges (1987) argued that the nucleated layout at Gurness was essentially original; MacKie (1987) countered that the 'village' was manifestly secondary, following much the same view as had been advanced in the Royal Commission's *Inventory* of 1946. The crucial factor is surely the substantial enclosure, and the alignment of its main entrance towards the broch entrance, which implies a unitary layout. The surviving external buildings may be secondary, but the compound around the broch was evidently integral to the settlement concept from the start. The surviving structures at Midhowe may likewise be a secondary manifestation of an older local tradition. At the Howe, at least, there is some evidence for external structures within a rampart enclosure from a relatively early stage (Smith, B. B., 1994). In the Phase 7 enclosure they are well preserved, but the basic layout seems to have been established by Phase 5, which lacks the definitive criteria of a complex Atlantic roundhouse, but possibly only because it is so severely truncated by later occupation.

In the west, nucleated villages of the Orcadian variety are unknown, but outworks and possibly external occupation are certainly not (Fig. 5.7). At Dun Mor Vaul on Tiree (MacKie, 1974) the enclosure wall may well have been original, even if the ephemeral structures external to the broch were more probably secondary. Similar enclosed brochs are known on Skye. Closely related must be both simple and galleried duns on Tiree, Mull and Islay, which have enclosures surrounding or attached to them (Harding, 1997: 134–5), or, in some examples in mainland Argyll, cutting off access on either side of a narrow ridge (Fig. 5.8). In the Western Isles the extension of island dun sites to include an annexe behind the principal structure must imply some external activity, though not necessarily involving contemporary outbuildings, and in some cases, like Loch an Duna at Bragar in Lewis, an enclosure wall may be part of the original layout (Fig. 5.9). The walls flanking the entrance approach were evidently replaced more than once, and again may have been part of the original defensive design. At Beirgh, Lewis, (Harding and Gilmour, 2000) there were certainly external buildings close by the broch wall; though relatively early in the sequence, they cannot yet be shown to have been primary.

Island duns are a particular sub-group of Atlantic roundhouse found in the shallow lochs of the Western Isles. Apart from Dun Bharabhat, Cnip, in west Lewis, none has been excavated in modern times, but the probability is that their ruined stone heaps conceal similar structural complexities to the conventional brochs. Loch an Duin at Shader (Fig. 5.10) on the northern coastal belt of Lewis would be a strong candidate for excavation, now that the village has been connected to the main drainage system, so that visibility for underwater excavation has improved. Apart from the upstanding remains, an adjacent 'halo' is probably indicative of an immediately preceding structure, whilst to the west traces of stonework breaking the loch surface probably represents a still earlier island dun, perhaps dating from the early Iron Age. Some lochs were evidently re-used in Mediaeval times and later, as at Loch an Sticer in North Uist, where a network of causeways suggests a hierarchy of access to the focal dun.

The standard classification of brochs for much of the later twentieth century identified a fundamental distinction between *solid-based* brochs and *ground-galleried* brochs. The

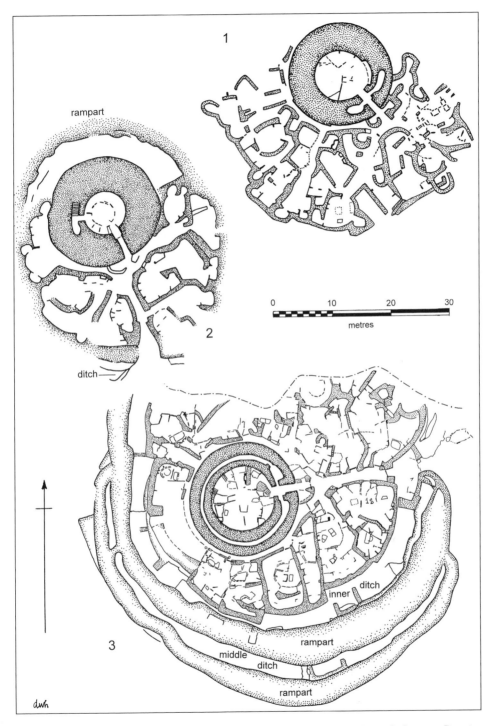

1

rampart

2

ditch

0   10   20   30

metres

3

inner   ditch

rampart

middle
ditch

rampart

dwh

Figure 5.6 Complex Atlantic roundhouse 'villages' in Orkney. 1, Lingro; 2, Howe; 3, Gurness. Drawings by D. W. Harding, adapted from RCAMS (1946) and Smith, B. B. ed. (1994).

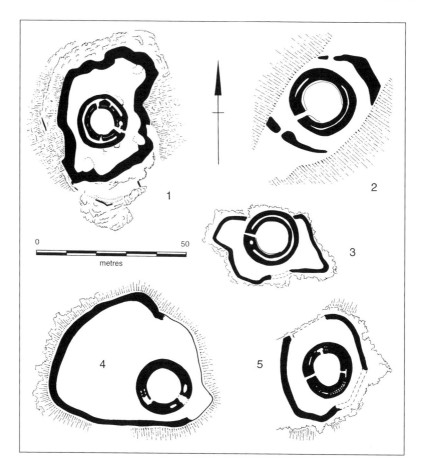

Figure 5.7 'Brochs' with outworks in the west. 1, Dun Mor, Vaul, Tiree; 2, Tirefour Castle, Lismore; 3, Dun Boreraig, Skye; 4, Dun Hallin, Skye; 5, Dun Colbost, Skye. Drawings by G. D. Thomas for the author, adapted from RCAHMS (1928), (1974), (1980).

solid-based type, as its name implied, had no intra-mural galleries or cells at ground-floor or foundation level, other than that which was necessary to contain the staircase. The ground-galleried brochs, by contrast, did display additional galleries or cells, in some cases like Beirgh up to six or seven. In general it was noted that the ground-galleried brochs were found in the west, whereas solid-based brochs were characteristic of Caithness and the Northern Isles. In fact, the distinction is not nearly as clear-cut as is sometimes implied, and its significance should therefore not be over-rated. Other aspects of the ground-plan of brochs showed contrasting regional traditions, including the position of the door rebate within the entrance passage, and the ratio of the wall thickness to the overall diameter of the broch (MacKie, 1975).

Making such comparative observations of broch typology, of course, depends crucially upon their state of preservation, and the availability of reliable plans. Apart from a few sites that survive to a sufficient height to allow examination of their structural details, the great majority of field monuments survive only as substantial heaps of stone, so that

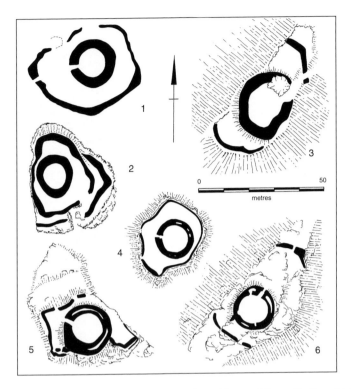

Figure 5.8 'Duns' with outworks in the west. 1, Dun Hanais, Tiree; 2, Dun Heanais, Tiree; 3, Camaslaich, Seil; 4, Dun Aisgain, Mull; 5, Dun Chroisprig, Islay; 6, Dun Rostan, Mid-Argyll. Drawings by G. D. Thomas for the author, adapted from RCAHMS (1974), (1980), (1984), (1988).

the recognition of key structural features, such as galleries, scarcements and rebates, is quite impossible. In some of the Orcadian structures, furthermore, galleries within which the staircase is located are themselves not always at foundation level, but as much as a metre above it, presumably having been accessible from ground level, either by three or four timber steps, or from a suspended timber ground floor. The recognition of galleries at ground level therefore is crucially dependent upon the height of the surviving remains, and the distinction between ground-galleried and solid-based brochs as a basis of classification becomes questionable.

The emphasis on broch typology was inevitably linked to a diffusionist view of the origin and development of broch culture. Some, like J. R. C. Hamilton, believed they originated in the north, where the distribution of brochs was certainly densest. Others, including MacKie (1965a), favoured an origin in the west, where brochs were believed to have developed from a local prototype termed a semi-broch. Both still adhered to a fundamental belief in the Southern and South-western British origins of the Atlantic Iron Age, as had Childe and Sir Lindsay Scott. The Glenelg brochs, typologically of the northern, solid-based form, were seen by MacKie as the product of a 'reflux movement' re-introducing the novel northern variant to the west. It is probable that there was a significant degree of inter-communication between the coastal communities of the Atlantic seaways. But to seek a single point of origin for archaeological types, whether

Figure 5.9 Island dun in Loch an Duna, Bragar, Lewis, air-photograph. Photograph by D. W. Harding.

structural or portable artefacts, seems to be an unwarranted simplification of what must have been a much more complex set of inter-relationships.

In the most specific version of the diffusionist model (MacKie, 1969, 1971) broch-building was attributed to refugees from Belgic invaders of south-eastern England, supposedly in the early first century BC, which in consequence imposed a totally artificial *terminus post quem* on the dating of brochs. Quite why a tradition of monumental building in stone should have been catalysed by colonisation of refugees from a region hardly noted archaeologically for its roundhouse building tradition, and certainly not in stone, remains an enigma. The only element of stone-building which the migrants seemingly acquired *en route* northwards was the use of guard-chambers, allegedly adopted from their observed use in hillfort entrances between Northamptonshire and North Wales in the earlier Iron Age. The cultural assemblage that this diffusionist process allegedly introduced into Atlantic Scotland prompted comparisons in various parts of Southern Britain dating from the later Bronze Age to later pre-Roman Iron Age. If these have any validity, they would argue for a diversity of trading contacts over several centuries, rather than a consistent and concerted introduction from one specific area in the first century BC.

In Atlantic Scotland the case for a western origin for brochs was based upon the belief that they developed from a prototype known as semi-brochs. The term was originally

Figure 5.10 Island duns in Loch an Duin, Shader, Lewis, air-photograph. Photograph by D. W. Harding.

used by Beveridge at the beginning of the twentieth century, but was developed (MacKie, 1965a, 1991) to embrace two rather distinct and divergent groups of field monument. 'Promontory semi-brochs', like Rubh' an Dunain on Skye, are variants on the widespread Atlantic tradition of promontory forts. Apart from their inclusion of intra-mural galleries and related structural features, which may or may not imply contemporaneity, they otherwise have no obvious relationship in size, plan or function with brochs, and are therefore hardly relevant as a typological antecedent. Cliff-edge or 'D-shaped semi-brochs', on the other hand, are of comparable size and plan to Atlantic roundhouses, and should be considered as part of that series. There really is no convincing basis, however, for regarding sites like Dun Ardtreck on Skye (MacKie, 2000) and Dun an Ruigh Ruaidh in Ross-shire (MacKie, 1980) as other than Atlantic roundhouses that have suffered cliff-edge erosion. The single radiocarbon date for Dun Ardtreck (GX-1120, 2005 +/– 105 BP), though capable at two sigma of sustaining an early origin for the site, no longer commands the chronological priority that may once have been claimed. The Ruigh Ruaidh dates hardly afford a consistent series (Harding, 1984a: 211), but we may agree with the excavator that 'a construction date at least as early as the third century BC seemed to be indicated, and perhaps as early as the sixth' (MacKie, 1991: 157). Ruigh Ruaidh therefore supports the contention that complex Atlantic roundhouses were being built in the second half of the first millennium BC. Its attribution to a hypothetical class of semi-broch only becomes necessary if a pre-condition is imposed that no broch was built before the first century BC.

Recent research in both Northern and Western Isles, as we shall see, increasingly supports a mid-first millennium BC date for the origins of complex Atlantic roundhouses. Parker Pearson and Sharples (1999) have defended the case for late dating on the basis of their work in the southern Hebrides, though their results could equally sustain the case for earlier origins. The fact is that once the diffusionist case is rejected, as it now almost universally is for broch origins, insistence on a first century BC date for the appearance of brochs has no logical basis, even in radiocarbon dating. The case against a longer sequence of development therefore reverts to the circular argument of typology. If a broch can be shown to have been built before the first century BC, then it cannot be a 'true broch', because by definition, true brochs date from the first century BC.

The structure at Bu in Orkney (Hedges, 1987), therefore, with radiocarbon dates assigning its occupation to the mid-first millennium BC or earlier, would not be accepted by traditionalists as a true broch, not only because it is too early, but also because it apparently lacked intra-mural galleries. In fact, the excavation of Bu was selective, with trenches disposed cross-wise over its circular outline, so that the full circuit of its enclosing walls was not uncovered. To argue that it might have contained a gallery within the unexcavated segments could of course be dismissed as special pleading. But if the ground-plan of its nearest neighbour at the Howe is superimposed upon the Bu plan,

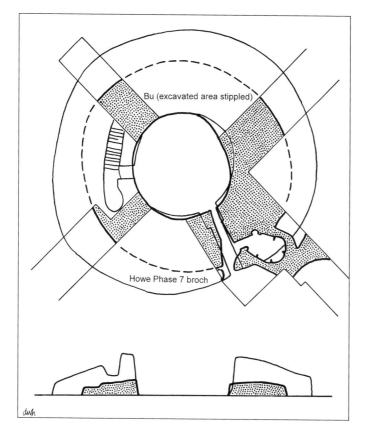

Figure 5.11 Bu and Howe, Orkney, comparative layout with entrances aligned. Drawing by D. W. Harding, adapted from Hedges (1987) and Smith, B. B. ed. (1994).

coinciding the alignment of their respective entrances, then the gallery falls exactly within one of Bu's unexcavated sectors (Fig. 5.11). It is also the case that the foundations at Bu did not survive to the height of the 'ground floor' galleries at the Howe, so that we cannot assert with absolute confidence that it had no similar features. Internally it displayed evidence for radial divisions of space, which is one of the characteristics of the Orcadian brochs, so that it certainly belongs within the tradition of monumental Atlantic roundhouse construction, even if it has to be classified as a proto-broch to satisfy typological pedantry.

The definition of a *complex* Atlantic roundhouse, of course, carries with it the implication that there should be a category of *simple* Atlantic roundhouse. This would effectively correspond to Feachem's earlier (1963) categories of galleried duns and simple duns. In the Armit model, Bu could be accommodated, without inferring complexities of construction that did not survive to be recovered by excavation, as a simple Atlantic roundhouse. More substantial than some of the early Orcadian roundhouses, like Quanterness, Pierowall Quarry or the Calf of Eday, it could certainly afford a mid-first millennium BC prototype from which complex Atlantic roundhouses might have developed, without the need for diffusionist explanations.

Caithness and the Northern Isles

Jarlshof on the southern tip of Shetland is quite exceptional in the longevity of its occupational sequence, extending over two millennia from Bronze Age to the Norse settlements. The site had been subject to a succession of exploratory excavations, notably by the landowner, John Bruce, at the end of the nineteenth century, and by Curle and Childe in the 1930s, before J. R. C. Hamilton attempted to clarify and consolidate the results of these investigations just after the Second World War (Hamilton, 1956). Hamilton took an essentially diffusionist view of broch culture, seeing it as the product ultimately of colonisation from Southern and Western Britain, but for the origins and development of brochs, he accorded priority to the northern series. His synthesis of Jarlshof was obviously constrained by the reliability of the earlier excavators' records, but in general his sequence seems sound. It begins with a later Bronze Age settlement (Fig. 5.12, 5), comprising courtyard houses, in which a central area with hearth was surrounded by a series of sub-circular cells. The dating of this phase is attested by fragments of moulds for casting bronzes, some of which could be identified as for socketed axes and for swords. This form of building has been shown by recent research to have a long ancestry in Shetland, with notable parallels at Sumburgh Airport and elsewhere (Fig. 5.12, 1–4). Hamilton's late Bronze Age village 2, however, is not necessarily so early. Apart from the accumulation of wind-blown sand and the apparently higher level at which they were built, these structures included truncated radial piers and souterrains, in one of which a fragment of iron slag proclaims its later date. The largest of these buildings could well belong to the simple Atlantic roundhouse class of the early Iron Age, broadly comparable to Calf of Eday.

Hamilton was able to establish at Jarlshof a sequence of structures following the demise of the broch, which will be discussed later. The broch itself has been severely eroded by the sea, but some important features survive. Within the wall thickness of its surviving segment are two cells. The sill of one is fully a metre above the floor of the interior, as at other sites in both Orkney and Shetland, so that its presence would have been undetected

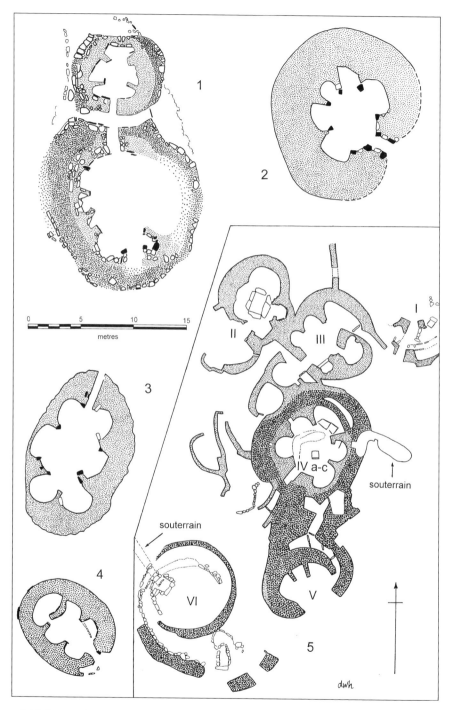

Figure 5.12 Bronze Age and Iron Age cellular structures in Shetland. 1, Sumburgh Airport; 2, Sulma Water; 3, Gravlaba; 4, Wiltrow; 5, Jarlshof. Drawings by D. W. Harding, adapted from Downes and Lamb (2000), Calder (1964), Curle (1936) and Hamilton (1956).

had the structural remains been more drastically reduced like Bu. The other principal feature of the broch is its well, dug 4 metres into the rock and accessed by a short flight of steps. Dating evidence for the construction of the broch is regrettably indeterminate beyond a broad assignment to the later first millennium BC (Fojut, 1998: 19).

The multi-period structural sequence of the settlement at Clickhimin, located in a loch separated from the sea by a narrow rocky isthmus in the suburbs of Lerwick, was investigated by Hamilton in the later 1950s as a sequel to his study of Jarlshof. The limitations of the published sequence (Hamilton, 1968) and an alternative interpretation have been outlined cogently by Fojut (1998), so that only the salient points need to be reviewed here. Unlike Jarlshof, further on-site examination is unlikely to yield clarification or resolution of the outstanding problems, since the site has been extensively conserved for public presentation. The principal differences between the interpretations of the excavator and the reviewer lie in the dating assigned to the earliest occupation, and the attribution within the sequence of the blockhouse, a monumental class of forework unique to Shetland. The earliest structures on the site were dated by Hamilton to the late Bronze Age, not on the basis of any definitive, associated artefacts, but evidently by analogy with the late Bronze Age 'courtyard' houses from Jarlshof. Fojut, who in any case regarded the Jarlshof examples as possibly Iron Age rather than late Bronze Age, is still less persuaded of the early date for Clickhimin. The blockhouse in Hamilton's sequence was an integral part of the early Iron Age defensive enclosure, and hence pre-broch; in Fojut's sequence it may have been subsequent to the broch construction rather than pre-broch. Unfortunately, however, in terms of absolute chronology, the Clickhimin sequence remains entirely speculative.

By far the most informative site sequence of broch and later occupation is that from Old Scatness (Dockrill, 1998, 2003), by the northern perimeter of Sumburgh Airport. Excavations initially concentrated on the post-broch settlement, including a range of circular, 'sub-wheelhouse' and cellular structures both within and clustered around the broch. Only recently has it been possible to examine the earlier structural evidence adjacent to the broch itself. From the application of several different dating techniques it is now clear that the broch was most likely constructed around the mid-first millennium BC or shortly thereafter, and that an aisled roundhouse had been added by the later centuries of the first millennium BC. The Scatness broch in effect is not far removed in date from the Bu roundhouse, but unlike Bu its credentials as a complex Atlantic roundhouse cannot be challenged. Not only has it a gallery containing the staircase adjacent to the entrance, but at least one other gallery has been identified within the wall core elsewhere on its circuit. The issue cannot therefore be avoided by semantic casuistry, by arguing that Old Scatness is not a 'true' broch. A full evaluation of the Old Scatness sequence must clearly await publication, but it is already abundantly clear that it will require a radical review of the belief that brochs belong only to a narrow middle Iron Age horizon.

For the dating of Orcadian brochs the significance of the radiocarbon dates from Bu has already been stressed. The Howe sequence is equally important, even though the earliest substantial building on the site (Phase 5) was so severely damaged by subsequent building that it can hardly be described as more than a thick-walled roundhouse. Nevertheless, the Phase 6 building, which should certainly qualify as a complex Atlantic roundhouse, was the immediate forerunner of an undisputed broch tower. Unfortunately the radiocarbon dates for the Howe sequence provide mainly a series of *terminus post quem* and *terminus ante quem* values for the various structural phases, rather than unequivocal dates for the construction and occupation of those structures. The excavator suggested on this basis a date span for Phases 5 and 6, including the development of the early broch, between the fourth century BC and the first century AD. The later broch, Phase 7, was attributed to a similar span from first to fourth centuries AD. A more recent review of the evidence (Gilmour, 2000) has suggested a slightly earlier beginning for the Atlantic roundhouses between the fifth and third centuries BC. A genuine problem in using the radiocarbon evidence is the 'flat spot' in the calibration graph, which falls substantially in the period around the mid-first millennium BC, where increasingly it seems likely that the complex Atlantic roundhouse tradition had its origins.

Recent research in Orkney has focused attention upon the anomalous role of wells within broch sites (Fig. 5.13). The well at Gurness, as Armit (2003) has argued, involved an extraordinary degree of elaboration for what must have been a very inadequate water

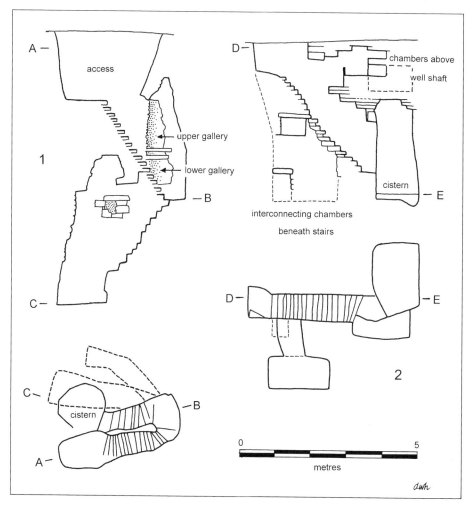

Figure 5.13 Wells at Mine Howe (1) and Gurness (2), Orkney. Drawings by D. W. Harding, adapted from RCAHMS (2000) and Hedges (1987).

supply. Much the same could be said of the Jarlshof broch in Shetland, like Gurness located so close to the sea that infiltration of salt water would surely have contaminated the supply. Recent re-opening of the unique site at Mine Howe (Card and Downes, 2003), however, has raised the possibility that such wells and underground cisterns were for cult activities akin to those inferred for ritual shafts and wells throughout the Celtic world. A long-standing tradition of ritual wells and springs might even be implied by the presence of similar remains on the later Iron Age site at Burghead in Morayshire.

On the north-east mainland, one of the first broch excavations to take advantage of radiocarbon dating was Crosskirk in Caithness (Fairhurst, 1984), where again a sequence of broch and post-broch occupation was distinguished through careful stratigraphic investigation. The broch itself was not the earliest structure on the site, and a sample centring on the mid-fifth century BC from immediately beneath its primary paving was cautiously regarded by the excavator as potentially residual from the earlier forti-fied phase. The remaining dates nevertheless would certainly allow the broch to have been constructed by 200 BC, as the excavator estimated, if not somewhat earlier. An even earlier date, in the fourth century BC, was obtained from another variant of complex Atlantic roundhouse in the northern mainland of Scotland, at the vitrified, galleried dun at Langwell in Sutherland (Nisbet, 1994). More recent re-examination of the brochs excavated in the nineteenth century by Sir Francis Tress-Barry (Heald and Jackson, 2001) promises new insights into a very important local distribution in coastal Caithness.

Recent research in the Western Isles

In the Western Isles the chronological debate centres principally upon the two modern excavation programmes conducted in west Lewis and the Uists respectively. In west Lewis the two key sites for the dating of complex Atlantic roundhouses are Dun Bharabhat, Cnip (Fig. 5.14; Harding and Dixon, 2000) and Beirgh, Riof (Harding and Gilmour, 2000) both on the Bhaltos peninsula. Bharabhat would be classified conventionally as an island dun. It has intra-mural cells and galleries, one with intra-mural staircase, together with door rebate and bar-holes. It did not survive to a sufficient height to show whether it had a scarcement, though this would be a reasonable corollary of the inference that the staircase led to an upper floor rather than simply to the wall-head. The overall diameter of the building, some 10 metres by 11 externally, was hardly of broch tower proportions, however, by comparison with the neighbouring site at Beirgh. The main occupation of Bharabhat may not have been very long, since it appears to have collapsed through the subsidence of its reinforced natural island foundations along one side of its circuit. It was, however, modified and rebuilt in more than one phase of secondary occupation. It was the burning of the roofing materials of the first of these *secondary* occupations that yielded radiocarbon dates centred on the first and second centuries BC. A single radiocarbon date from the foundations of the island dun, possibly from an immediately pre-dun occupational deposit, provided a *terminus post quem* centred on the sixth century BC. The primary or main occupation of the dun or complex Atlantic roundhouse is therefore provisionally assigned to the second half of the first millennium BC.

The primary levels of the Beirgh sequence have yet to be examined. Excavations came to an end in 1995 when funding for the project was exhausted, and despite the fact that the lowest, waterlogged deposits have the potential for revealing the most complete remains of primary broch occupation available anywhere in Atlantic Scotland, it seems

Figure 5.14 Dun
Bharabhat, Cnip,
Lewis, general
view of excavation.
Photograph by
D. W. Harding.

at present unlikely that the project can be resumed. The site was occupied from at least the earlier Iron Age through a succession of post-broch occupations down to the immediately pre-Norse period. Dating the origins of the broch therefore is tentative to the extent that it involves projecting backwards from the dates available for the post-broch occupation. These when calibrated at two sigma fall between the early third and end of the sixth centuries AD. Between this later occupation and the abandonment of the broch itself lies a succession of secondary roundhouses or possible wheelhouses, represented stratigraphically by up to a metre of archaeological deposits. By any reasonable reckoning, therefore, the very end of the use of the broch building itself might belong around the turn of the millennium or perhaps earlier, so that the origins of the broch should, like Bharabhat, lie in the second half of the first millennium BC. Admittedly the number of radiocarbon dates available for Bharabhat and Beirgh is fewer than would be desirable for absolute confidence. But if the radiocarbon evidence is as yet quantitatively insufficient to sustain an origin for complex Atlantic roundhouses in the Western Isles as early as the fourth or fifth centuries BC, it certainly no longer requires a belief in a universal first century BC horizon for the appearance of brochs.

That conclusion could be argued on the basis of the dates from Dun Vulan, South Uist, as easily as the later reading offered by the excavators. Like Beirgh, Dun Vulan contained within its circuit a figure-of-eight building in its later Iron Age re-occupation. Also like Beirgh it is difficult on a site so intensively re-occupied to isolate primary contexts uncontaminated by later intrusions. At Beirgh, even where a rising water-table had uniquely extended the vertical stratigraphy on the site, the broch galleries were still broken into for later re-use. The primary broch levels within the building at Dun Vulan, if they survived, were never examined, so that the radiocarbon dates on which the assessment of its construction was made were from secondary contexts, one within an intra-mural chamber, the other under a secondary revetment of the outer broch wall. The excavators inferred that this revetment was necessitated by subsidence shortly after the construction of the broch, and therefore should not be too far removed from it in time (Parker Pearson and Sharples, 1999: 39–40 and Fig. 5.2). Irrespective of whether this sample approximates to the construction horizon of the broch, which is certainly open to challenge, on its two sigma range it would still admit of a considerably earlier construction than the excavators were prepared to allow (Armit, 2000).

On this provisional assessment complex Atlantic roundhouses developed relatively early in the Iron Age with at present few signs of a simple Atlantic roundhouse antecedent or prototype. The surviving piles of stone that are all that commonly remain of brochs or duns could, of course, conceal solid-walled duns or simple Atlantic roundhouses. To surface survey Dun Bharabhat certainly so appeared, and was recorded as such in the Royal Commission's 1926 *Inventory*. In the event, Bharabhat proved within a few hours of boulder removal to be a galleried structure, and this experience seems likely to be repeated elsewhere, were selective investigation to be undertaken. Recent fieldwork and radiocarbon sampling has identified some sites that could fill the category of antecedent roundhouses, dating from the late Bronze Age and early Iron Age (Gilmour, 2002). An oval building at Coile a'Ghasgain on Skye may have been occupied in the early Iron Age (Armit, 1996: 104), while a substantial oval building at Eilean Olabhat in North Uist has been provisionally dated to a span around the fifth to third centuries BC. In the Uig district of west Lewis at An Dunan a possible ritual structure was dated to the second half of the first millennium BC, and domestic structures at Guinnerso nearby could have their origins in the early Iron Age beneath a long sequence of later occupation. Not all of these sites need have been for permanent occupation, and their marginal location in some instances may argue a seasonal, transhumance role, rather than as antecedents to, or lower order contemporaries of, Atlantic roundhouses. At Cladh Hallan in South Uist occupation is attested from the later Bronze Age by the presence of metal-working debris, as well as from absolute dating. The roundhouses themselves are unusual in their conjoined layout, with perhaps a chain of six or seven units flanking the principal building with its forecourt. Different functional areas within the building have been inferred, matching closely the model proposed for Thatcham in Berkshire (Fitzpatrick, 1994), but, equally important, both human and animal burials suggest that a highly complex set of cult practices was in vogue, perhaps indicating that the site's origins and function were not exclusively domestic.

Argyll and the Inner Hebrides

Among earlier broch excavations in the west, Dun Mor Vaul on Tiree (MacKie, 1974) was one of the first to yield radiocarbon dates, which themselves have prompted vexed debate. The stratigraphy within the broch occupation is complex, raising questions in matters of significant detail, but the main sequence seems reasonably clear. The earliest levels apparently produced some evidence of timber structures, together with pottery of the distinctive 'Vaul ware', which the excavator regarded as preceding the occupation of the broch itself. Dating of this phase derived from two radiocarbon dates (GaK 1092, 400+/–110 BC from context Epsilon 2 and GaK 1098, 445+/–90 BC from context Eta 2), which would be consistent with an initial occupation as early as the mid-first millennium BC. The construction of the broch itself was assigned by the excavator to the first century BC or AD on account of the associated material assemblage, which included pottery of Clettraval style, and by inference from radiocarbon dates derived from various contexts in the broch and post-broch sequence. In retrospect we might question whether the supposed pre-broch levels at Dun Mor Vaul were not in fact of the primary broch occupation, and subsequent levels, including the diagnostic three-sided hearth, were not instead part of the later broch and secondary occupation.

Dun Mor Vaul is one of the few brochs, conventionally defined, in Argyll and the Inner Hebrides. This region is characterised by a bewildering range of duns, doubtless including variants of quite disparate date and function. Those that warrant consideration within the Atlantic roundhouse series, like Rahoy (Childe and Thorneycroft, 1938a), conform broadly to the size and proportions which would permit their use as roofed dwellings (Fig. 5.15), and may display some architectural features analogous to brochs. On the evidence of Rahoy itself, some of these 'dun houses' should certainly be of early Iron Age date, though a number probably had secondary occupation too. Notwithstanding the occurrence of intra-mural features, such as medial wall-faces, many of these structures would be described as simple Atlantic roundhouses. Yet they cannot offer a direct antecedent for complex Atlantic roundhouses, even if their origins could be dated securely, because their distribution in the west is complementary to rather than coincident with that of brochs. Equally there is at present insufficient evidence to suggest a sequential relationship between simple and galleried duns in Argyll, parallel to the assumed progression in the Northern Isles from simple to complex Atlantic roundhouses.

In fact, the dating of duns in Argyll has excited as much controversy as broch studies, with one school of thought arguing an early historic, first millennium AD horizon for the majority of sites. Hence Alcock and Alcock (1987: 131) were adamant that of the dozen excavated dun sites, all but Rahoy were late, a view reiterated by Nieke (1990). There is no need to counter this statement, since the class of duns being considered is so diverse and heterogeneous that no one would reasonably expect some of the sites in question to have later prehistoric origins. At Kildonan in Kintyre both the site's sub-triangular plan and its location, overlooked by higher ground on the landward side, would hardly be typical of earlier Iron Age Atlantic roundhouses. Dun Fhinn, also in Kintyre, is a stack site of sub-rectangular plan, and as such stands in total contrast to the predominant circularity of building tradition which is the hallmark of later prehistoric settlement throughout the British Isles. The conventional inclusion of these sites confusingly into a single portmanteau class of duns has been the principal hindrance to progress in settlement studies in Argyll.

The Royal Commission's division between duns and forts, based upon the areal threshold of 4,000 square feet (375 square metres), was understandable as a simple expedient of classification for the purposes of the *Inventories*. It has nevertheless compounded the problem by including within the dun category enclosures that are self-evidently different from smaller, circular or sub-circular buildings that could have functioned as roofed dwellings analogous to brochs. Roofability is admittedly a subjective concept, and should probably not be used as the sole basis for classification; but in the initial stages

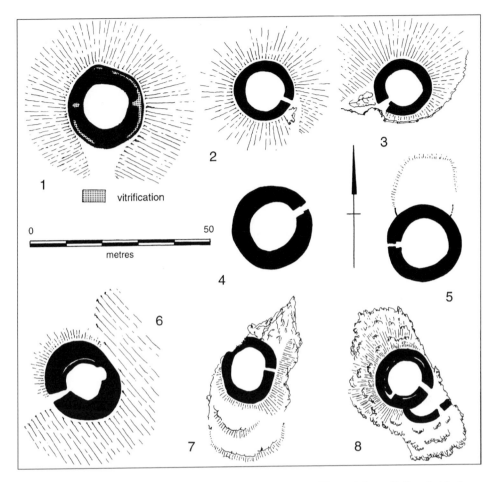

1

vitrification

0   50

metres

2

3

4

5

6

7

8

Figure 5.15 Dun houses in Argyll. 1, Rahoy, Morvern; 2, Tom a Chaisteil, Lorn; 3, Dun Leigh, Lorn; 4, Caisteal Suidhe, Cheannaidh; 5, Borgadel Water, Kintyre; 6, Dun Ballymeanoch, Mid-Argyll; 7, Cnoc a' Chaisteal, Lergychoniebeag, Mid-Argyll; 8, An Sean Dun, Mull. Drawings by G. D. Thomas for the author, adapted from RCAHMS (1971), (1974), (1980), (1988).

of sorting out structures of such manifest diversity it is one criterion among others that deserves consideration. Even within the more limited group of 'dun houses' (Harding, 1984a) there are examples with evidence of secondary occupation, in some cases into the early historic period.

For the present, Rahoy (Fig. 5.15, 1), enclosing an area some 12 metres in diameter with a wall 3 metres thick, remains the type-site for simple Atlantic roundhouses in Argyll. It was assigned to the early Iron Age, perhaps as early as the fourth century BC, on the basis of a La Tène 1c brooch and an iron socketed and looped axe of a type reckoned to be an early Iron Age imitation of a late Bronze Age model. It is significant that Childe did not apparently recover artefactual evidence of later occupation, since his description of internal features leaves little doubt that there were secondary structures, albeit of an ephemeral nature. A significant element at Rahoy was the vitrified character of the stonework, indicative of the fact that the wall originally had a timber framework.

Timber-lacing is, of course, more commonly associated with hillfort construction, and vitrification is the outcome of violent destruction of such sites. It cannot be regarded as diagnostically early Iron Age, since there are notable examples from the early historic period, but it was certainly widely practised in later prehistory, and would be entirely consistent with the generally acknowledged early date for Rahoy. We have already noted a similarly early example of a timber-laced, and vitrified, dun at Langwell in Sutherland. That site currently affords the best comparison with Rahoy in terms of chronology, if we can rely on the radiocarbon dates, though subsequent thermoluminescent and archaeo-magnetic dating has not yielded altogether compatible results (Gentles, 1993; Sanderson *et al.*, 1988).

The Argyll *Inventories* proposed a model of site development, exemplified by sites like Dun Skeig and Dun Mac Sniachan, Benderloch, in which there was a progressive con-traction in area, from larger enclosures to smaller, thick-walled duns. According to this model, the duns or Atlantic roundhouses would probably have been assigned a dating in the late first millennium BC or early first millennium AD. On the ground the evidence for sequence is sometimes extremely tenuous, and in any case it should not be assumed that any specific site sequence need constitute a regional model, any more than the Hownam sequence is generally applicable in the south-eastern Borders. Excavations at Balloch Hill (Peltenburg, 1982) demonstrated the limitations of the 'contraction' model, and Peltenburg concluded that 'no uniform evolution from one type of monument to another' should be assumed. The lack of more modern excavations is regrettable, and dating from older excavations has been hindered by the inherently undiagnostic character of the early Iron Age material assemblages.

Material assemblages of Atlantic roundhouses

Compared to the domestic assemblages of southern and eastern Scotland, and to mainland Argyll, excavation of settlements in the Atlantic north and west has yielded a more extensive material assemblage, notably in terms of pottery. Problems remain, however, in recognising the characteristic types of the early Iron Age, of the second half of the first millennium BC. Later Iron Age types, such as penannular brooches and composite bone combs, pin types in bronze or bone (Foster, 1990), and types of crucible, are suffi-ciently diagnostic to be confidently assigned to a mid–later first millennium AD horizons. Assemblages representative of broch-period occupation are more limited in their range of non-ceramic types, but include some that, whilst certainly current in the opening centuries of the first millennium AD, could have been in circulation much earlier. The lack of diagnostic types for the second half of the first millennium BC, however, and until recently the lack of radiocarbon dates, has constrained the dating of the material assemblages and of the longevity of broch occupation. The early Iron Age still has yet to be adequately defined in terms of its key material types, which consist very largely of such basic, utilitarian artefacts as spindle-whorls, hammer-stones, thatch- or net-weights, polishing stones and simple bone pins and needles. These types need not have changed significantly over hundreds of years, and therefore could easily be subsumed within a mixed assemblage resulting from long-term occupation of the same site, where the stratigraphic sequence is insufficiently distinct.

In marked contrast to western, central, southern and eastern Scotland, and northern England, in which the surviving pottery assemblages are minimal in quantity and extremely limited in range and quality (Harding, forthcoming, b), the ceramic assemblage of the earlier Iron Age in Atlantic Scotland is distinguished by a range of vessel forms and decorative styles, with some apparent similarities in detail to the Iron Age ceramics of Southern Britain. It is difficult to attempt an objective evaluation of these similarities without succumbing to the older, uncritical assumption of secondary derivation of the Northern British material from southern or south-western sources by a process of one-way cultural diffusion. Diffusionist processes should not be ruled out in principle, but they cannot be sustained on the strength of isolated parallels cited from widely different regions of Southern Britain, where they would be assigned to quite disparate dates and cultural horizons.

Perhaps the most striking similarity is the use of incised geometric ornament, with a combination of geometric rectilinear and simple curvilinear motifs, as exemplified in the pre-Cellular phases at Beirgh (Fig. 5.16) or from Dun Bharabhat (Fig. 5.17). These are certainly also characteristic of the latest Bronze Age or earliest Iron Age in Wessex, as exemplified at sites like All Cannings Cross and Longbridge Deverill in Wiltshire. There are important differences, notably in the absence from Atlantic Scotland of the white infilling of the decorative design and the use of a highly burnished haematite slip that distinguishes the finer Wessex wares. Plastic ornament in the form of applied cabled bands or finger-tip impressions also characterise both regions, though in Wessex the two styles are not combined on the same vessel as they are in Atlantic Scotland. If these two groups were in any way related, the implication would have to be that the Atlantic Scottish tradition had its origins somewhere in the later Bronze Age, from around the mid-first millennium BC at latest. As we have noted, an early ceramic horizon has long been recognised at Dun Mor Vaul (MacKie, 1974), which included not only the distinctive coarse 'Vaul ware' jars but also some examples of incised geometric ornament. The fact that this style of ornament apparently continues through the broch period in Atlantic Scotland, lasting much longer than its currency in Wessex, need occasion no surprise or concern. In fact, the pottery from early contexts at Dun Mor Vaul (Fig. 5.18) is not unlike some material from Dun Bharabhat, and may well be representative of the elusive early Iron Age styles of the Atlantic west.

The equally distinctive pottery of the middle Iron Age in the west, generally exemplified by the Clettraval style, with shallow-tooled or finger-impressed arcades, cannot at present be shown to have such early origins. But the short, everted-rim vessels on which that style is commonly applied may well prove to have a longer currency, with undecorated antecedents. Given the striking contrast between the pottery of Atlantic Scotland – more particularly of the Western Isles rather than of Caithness and the Northern Isles – and the remainder of Northern Britain or Ireland, it is certainly possible that maritime contacts via the western seaways provided a stimulus in its regional development. But the absence of any clear imports, by contrast to the imported Continental wares of the early historic period, for example, and the distinctively regional combinations of pottery forms and decorative motifs, make it unlikely that any significant population movement was involved.

The ceramic sequence in the Northern Isles is far from parallel to that in the west, but here too sites with a long sequence of occupation may be expected in due course to yield a type-sequence based upon stratigraphic and absolute dating. Recent research, based on excavations at Sumburgh Airport (Downes and Lamb, 2000) and at Old Scatness, may help to clarify the local Shetland sequence.

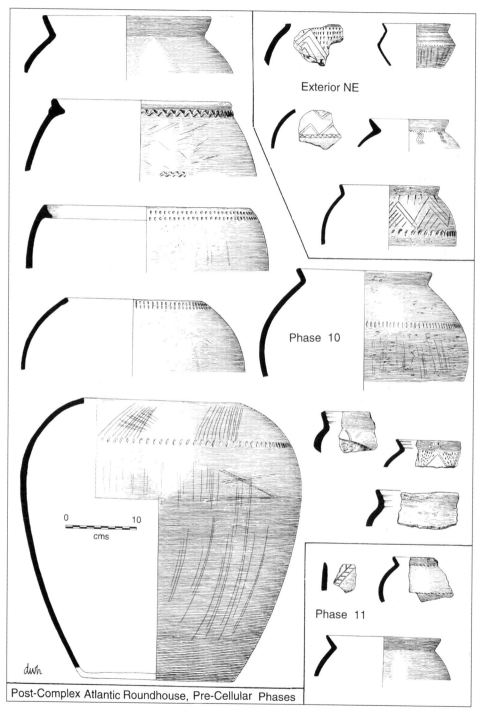

Exterior NE

Phase 10

0 ———— 10
cms

Phase 11

Post-Complex Atlantic Roundhouse, Pre-Cellular Phases

Figure 5.16 Beirgh, Riof, Lewis, pottery from post-complex Atlantic roundhouse, pre-cellular phases. Drawing by D. W. Harding.

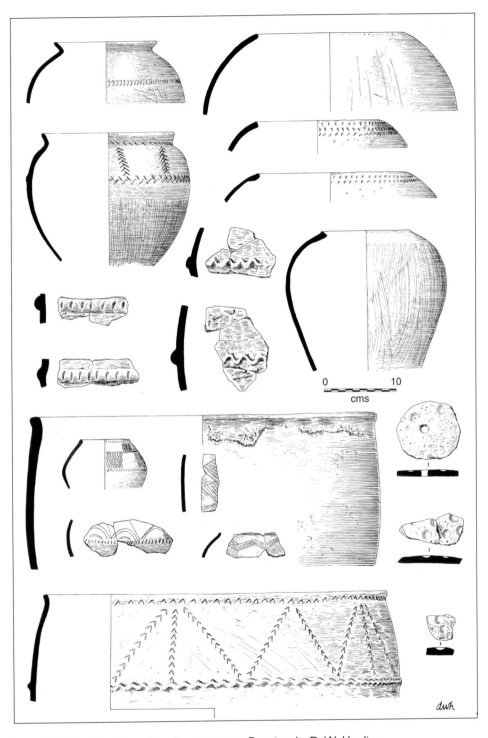

Figure 5.17 Dun Bharabhat, Cnip, Lewis, pottery. Drawings by D. W. Harding.

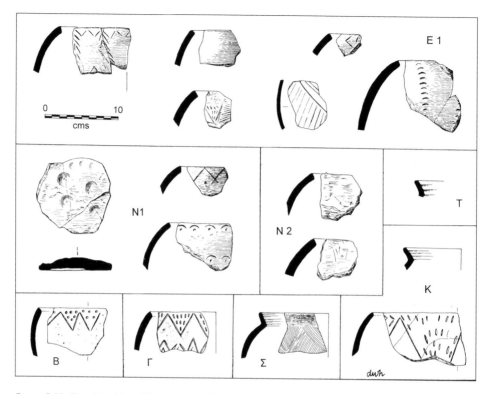

Figure 5.18 Dun Mor, Vaul, Tiree, pottery from early contexts. Drawings by D. W. Harding, courtesy of the Hunterian Museum, Glasgow.

Atlantic Scotland shares several non-ceramic types with other regions, but there is no reason to regard them as imports rather than local products (Clarke, 1971; Lane, 1987). *Ring-headed pins* are essentially an insular (British and Irish) type, not characteristic of La Tène Continental Europe. Atlantic Scottish examples are a distinctive group, characterised by having a projecting ring-head turned at 90 degrees from the stem. They form a distinct regional group, and are apparently much later than their Southern British counterparts, dating as yet no earlier than the first century AD. Earlier dating has been proposed on the basis of presumed impressions of such pins in pottery, but similar ornamental traits could have been the result of impressions using a bone tool. *Spiral finger-rings* have frequently been invoked as evidence of contact with Southern Britain in the early Iron Age. As we have seen, however, this is a type that has a wide distribution, and an even wider chronological currency from at least the middle Bronze Age until the mid-first millennium AD. *Glass beads* occur widely through the British Isles, as in Continental Europe, in a great variety of forms. Establishing a close chronology for individual types on the basis of site associations or a limited number of absolute dates has proved inconclusive, since some of the simpler basic types of translucent blue and yellow beads appear to have had a long life-span. More distinctive variants have inlaid spiral ornament, and may be amenable to closer dating. *Long-handled combs* are characteristic of the insular British Iron Age (Tuohy, 1999), though the Scottish examples again are noticeably distinct from, even if cognate to, their Southern British counterparts. Traditionally regarded as an adjunct to weaving (for compressing the strands in a loom), their true function still generates debate. *Querns* of the discoid rotary variety which characterises Atlantic Scotland are generally regarded as quite separate and distinct from the La Tène tradition of England or southern Scotland, having instead Atlantic connections with Ireland, Brittany and possibly the Iberian peninsula. Their chronology has yet to be clarified, but they evidently post-date the 'quern transition' (from saddle-quern to rotary), generally assigned to around the second century BC (Caulfield, 1978). As in the case of mainland crannogs, the island settlements of the Outer Hebrides have a considerable potential for the preservation of organic artefacts. From Dun Bharabhat in west Lewis, wooden vessels, a wicker peat creel and fragments of heather rope were preserved from the Iron Age occupation levels.

Forts in Argyll and the west

In Atlantic Scotland, forts and allied enclosures are primarily concentrated in Argyll and the Inner Hebrides, but they are by no means absent elsewhere. Promontory forts in particular have a wide distribution throughout the Atlantic north and west, wherever topography lends itself to their construction. In the north, in particular, distinctive forms of fort construction include 'blockhouses', the function of which remains far from clear, but which may have served a ceremonial as much as a defensive role. In considering later prehistoric and early historic forts, therefore, we should recognise that the term is used for a great diversity of sites without prejudice to the primary function or multiple functions that any of them may have served.

For the purpose of site classification in the *Inventories* of Argyll, the Royal Commission, as we have noted, distinguished between duns and forts, based on the threshold of 375 square metres or 4,000 square feet enclosed, a distinction that resulted in sites of the Atlantic roundhouse class being grouped together with less regular dun enclosures (Fig. 5.19; Harding, 1984a). It also meant that dun enclosures and forts of very similar plan might fall on either side of the areal threshold. The system nevertheless reflected the problems of classification where, as in the south-eastern Borders, small enclosures merge progressively with larger sites for which eventually the term fort would not be disputed. In fact the Commission's threshold, though artificial, was not entirely arbitrary, or without social implications. Duns thus defined 'would . . . normally hold only a single family group' (RCAHMS, 1971: 18; see also Maxwell, 1969), so that forts enclosing a larger area might be supposed to have been used as larger 'community' sites.

Unlike brochs, duns and crannogs, there has been general agreement among archaeologists regarding the early Iron Age dating of hillforts in Argyll and the west, based upon the material assemblages recovered from early excavation, such as the thirty-odd saddle-querns from Duntroon, and more recently upon radiocarbon dating, as at Balloch Hill. In some cases, notably at the Torr, Shielfoot, Dun Skeig and Dun Mac Sniachan, Benderloch, the larger enclosures were apparently the earliest, with smaller, stone-built sub-circular duns representing later occupation in the model of relative diminution.

Not surprisingly, the majority of later prehistoric and early historic sites in Argyll are located in the coastal lowlands, often on locally defensible or even precipitous sites, but seldom above the 200-metre contour. Whatever climatic variables may have affected the periods in question, the warmer, wet coastal lowlands would doubtless have been

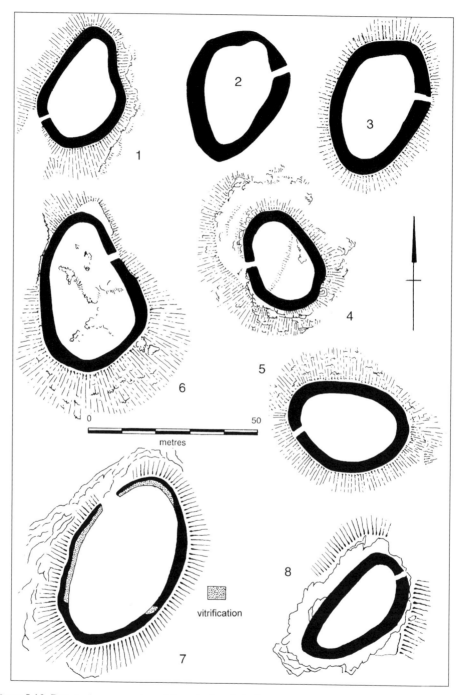

Figure 5.19 Dun enclosures and small forts in Argyll. 1, Dunan an t-Seasgain, Gigha, dun; 2, Barr Mor, Lorn, dun; 3, Ballycastle, Luing, dun; 4, Barr Iola, Cowal, dun; 5, Cnoc na Sroine, Mull, inner enclosure, dun; 6, Dun Breac, Ardvergnish, fort; 7, Duntroon, inner enclosure, fort; 8, Dunadd, summit citadel. Drawings by G. D. Thomas for the author, adapted from RCAHMS (1971), (1975), (1980), (1988).

preferable for settlement to the cooler, wet uplands, at the same time offering the benefits of proximity to better agricultural land and the resources of a marine environment. Nevertheless, contrasting the distributions of forts and duns in Kintyre, no less than 30 per cent of the forts are located at heights above the highest of the duns. These include those very few forts that occupy locations above the 200-metre contour, such as Knock Scalbert, Ballywilline and Ranachan Hill, which dominate a series of summits on the north side of the Laggan in Kintyre. It may seem surprising that Knock Scalbert, and Largiemore in the same chain of Laggan forts, are among those few sites in Argyll in which there is any surface trace of hut emplacements, though it need not follow that these were for permanent, rather than seasonal occupation. The absence of surface traces elsewhere may indicate the use of timber rather than stone for internal buildings.

In terms of area enclosed, all these sites are of very modest proportions in comparison with hillforts of Southern Britain, or even some of those in the Borders. Dun Ormidale in Lorn and Cnoc Araich in Kintyre rank among the largest at 3 and 2.5 hectares respectively, whilst the majority measure less than 100 metres across, with even multivallate examples seldom exceeding 150 metres in their maximum axis. In such circumstances, and without other evidence of function, use of the term 'minor *oppidum*' (strictly meaning a town, but widely applied archaeologically for community sites of presumed proto-urban character) seems a trifle extravagant. There are, however, sites like Beinn a Chaistel in which short lengths of walling are deployed across a wider topographical area to effect a measure of territorial enclosure, on a much smaller scale comparable to the territorial *oppida* of the later pre-Roman Iron Age in Southern Britain.

In their wall-construction, the stone-walled forts are relatively simple, with little evidence for intra-mural features, entrance guard-chambers or other complexities. The walls themselves are either of simple, drystone construction, or they may include an interior framework of timbers, which provided strength and stability that would be lacking in stone-faced walls with uncoursed, rubble filling. 'Medial walls' are known, which in some cases may be the residual traces of intra-mural galleries or cells, where the wall thickness was sufficient to accommodate such features. But for the most part this is not the case, and more probably the 'medial walls' too are a device for internal strengthening of the wall. This technique is also found in the 'dun houses' of Argyll, some of which, notably those on the islands of the Inner Hebrides, certainly had intra-mural chambers comparable to those of complex Atlantic roundhouses. Distinguishing the two kinds of medial wall might be problematic from surface inspection alone, but where there are double revetments an internal cell might be suspected, except where both wall-faces are outward-facing, as at Allt Cill Chriosd, Mull, in which case internal strengthening was surely the intention. At Dun Mhadaidh, Mull, an outward-facing revetment appears to have been included to stabilise the wall on a steep slope, whereas other medial walls on dun houses on Mull and Tiree are more probably indicative of intra-mural cells.

The fact that there were two distinct wall-construction traditions, the solid drystone technique and the timber-framed, is implied by the occurrence of vitrification on Argyll forts and duns, since firing walls would only have been feasible where there was a timber framework. It is significant therefore that there is no evidence of medial walls on sites that display vitrification. Without a timber framework to provide stability, some other technique would have been needed to counter the stress that a rubble core would exert upon the front and rear faces of the wall. This problem may have been addressed by the concentric laying of stones through the wall, as at Ballymeanoch, Mid-Argyll (RCAHMS, 1988: no. 273). Medial walls, dividing the wall into sections or boxes, would be a less labour-intensive solution. They could at the same time be used to create a stable, tiered rampart, comparable to the *murus duplex* technique of rampart construction. Occasionally elsewhere quasi-casemate construction, in which a stone box-construction, filled with rubble rather than left open as an intra-mural magazine, provided sectional solidity to the wall. Sectional construction, perhaps involving separate gangs of builders, has some-times been suggested in hillfort construction. In some cases the appearance of medial walls may also result from secondary refacing or buttressing, but this seems an inadequate explanation for such a recurrent feature of the Argyll forts.

Hillfort entrances in Argyll and the west are often relatively simple in design, and seldom show features such as guard-chambers or even a rebate within the passage for a door. Exceptionally Knock Scalbert has a door-check in the entrance passage, and at Dun na Maraig in Mid-Argyll the entrance included bar-holes. Portable barriers could have been inserted into the entrance passage, as Peltenburg suggested for Balloch Hill, particularly as many are built with their walls converging slightly towards one end. The width of the entrance passage seldom averages more than 1.5 metres, however, and hardly ever exceeds 2 metres. Access therefore would have been severely constrained by comparison with Southern British or Continental hillforts, in which wide carriage-ways through the entrance permitted wheeled traffic and livestock to enter the enclosure. Given the small size and topographical inaccessibility of some of these small forts, this underlines the fact that the function of such sites must have been very different from the proto-urban hillforts of Southern Britain or Europe.

Apart from some limited rescue excavation, Balloch Hill remains the only hillfort in Argyll to have been subject to a programme of modern research excavation (Peltenburg, 1982). It demonstrated archaeologically that the Feachem model (1966: 87–8) that regarded smaller duns as later than larger hillforts, was not universally applicable. The *Inventory* (RCAHMS, 1971: no. 158) had argued that the inner dun wall was 'patently of later date' since it lay within the larger enclosure and was better preserved. Peltenburg believed that the differential state of preservation was misleading, and resulted from the soil mechanics of the steeper slope on which the outer wall was built. He thus regarded the two as part of a contemporary, bivallate enclosure, in which the inner wall, seemingly lacking a gate in its entrance, was a monumental statement rather than a defensive work. Given the number of sites of similar character and proportions in Kintyre, he did not regard it as of particularly high status, notwithstanding evidence for bronze working, which some have regarded as evidence of social status. In the site's final phase of occupation, the inner wall was reduced or fell into disrepair, and three sub-circular stone houses overlying the debris represented a period of open or undefended settlement.

The occupation of the bivallate fort at Balloch Hill was assigned on the basis of radio-carbon dates to the second half of the first millennium BC, and the open settlement, the house foundations of which stood directly upon earlier timber roundhouses, need not have been later than the opening centuries of the first millennium AD. This assessment would be consistent with the material remains from the site, notably an elaborate bronze brooch with elements of Plastic Style ornament, which should date from around the third century BC. The opaque blue glass beads need not be later than the turn of the millennium, and could easily be earlier, while the presence of only saddle-querns likewise argues for an earlier Iron Age occupation of the site.

A significant number of forts in Argyll and the west show traces of vitrification of their walls, sometimes as at Carradale Point and Dunagoil, Bute, along extensive lengths of walling, but by no means all of the enclosing circuit. Dunagoil (Fig. 5.20) is one of the most important site complexes in the west. At its centre is a small fort of somewhat irregular, rectangular plan, the timber-framed walls of which in substantial sections had been destroyed by fire, resulting in vitrification. From this site in the early twentieth century a wealth of material finds was recovered. The findings have been reviewed in detail elsewhere (Harding, forthcoming, c). There is evidence on the site for bronze working, in the shape of crucibles, moulds and slag, and possibly for the working of iron, according to the report of the early excavators. Lignite, whether local or imported, was also manufactured into bracelets in quantity, and there is evidence too for the more usual Iron Age industries of bone and antler working. Pottery, by contrast, was crude in the extreme, represented by thick-walled vessels of poorly fired fabric that stands in marked contrast to the highly developed bronze working or lignite industries. Mainland Argyll is effectively aceramic during the Iron Age, however, with the more sophisticated styles of the Western Isles manifesting themselves only on sites in the Inner Hebrides such as Dun Mor Vaul on Tiree or Dun Cul Bhuirg on Iona (Topping, 1985). We may conclude, therefore, that other media, such as leather and wood, were used for normal domestic vessels and implements, and that the few coarse sherds recovered from Dunagoil served some other industrial or agricultural purpose.

The principal outcome of surveys of Dunagoil in 1994, however, has been the recognition that the vitrified fort may have been just the citadel within a much larger territorial enclosure. The citadel fort, though well defended both by precipitous cliffs to north and east and by its enclosing rampart, probably originally around its entire circuit, is nevertheless screened from the east by a parallel ridge, which would have afforded cover for any assailant approaching the site from the landward side. It therefore makes sense to include this prominent feature, itself naturally defended by a steep cliff-face on its eastern side, within the defensive perimeter. This would also effectively control the lesser inlet from the sea, Port Dubh, which would have provided a landing when the prevailing winds were against the use of the principal anchorage of Dunagoil Bay. Between the citadel fort and the parallel ridge to the east is a lower-lying and more sheltered 'bailey', in which later agriculture has unfortunately obliterated most of the area where Iron Age settlements might have been located. At the northern and southern limits of the 'bailey' lengths of walling link steeper natural defences, effectively enclosing the two ridges into a single unit. The north-western sector of walling included evidence of vitrification of the outcropping rock itself, which must therefore represent *in situ* firing rather than the spread or re-use of vitrified debris from earlier occupation of the citadel fort. Between the citadel and the sea similar evidence suggested that this area was probably also part of the original defensive network. Whether Little Dunagoil, which was shown by excavations of the late 1950s (Marshall, 1964) to have been occupied in the later Iron Age, was also part of the later prehistoric defensive circuit is certainly arguable, not least because of the discovery during that excavation of fragments of a late Bronze Age axe mould under the later walls.

It seems possible that from the late Bronze Age or early Iron Age Dunagoil was effectively a 'terrain fort' or 'terrain *oppidum*', not limited to the defended enclosure of the citadel fort alone, but including all the prominent topographical features of the area, controlling the anchorage and access routes from the sea, and from the landward

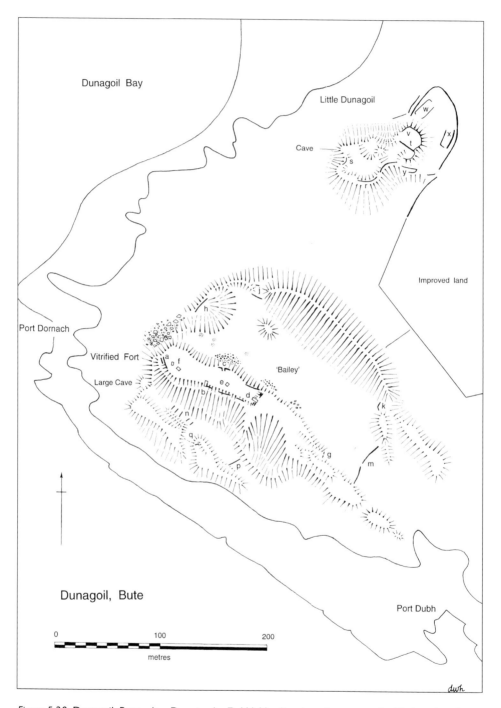

Figure 5.20 Dunagoil, Bute, plan. Drawing by D. W. Harding, based on survey by Christopher Burgess and Jon Henderson.

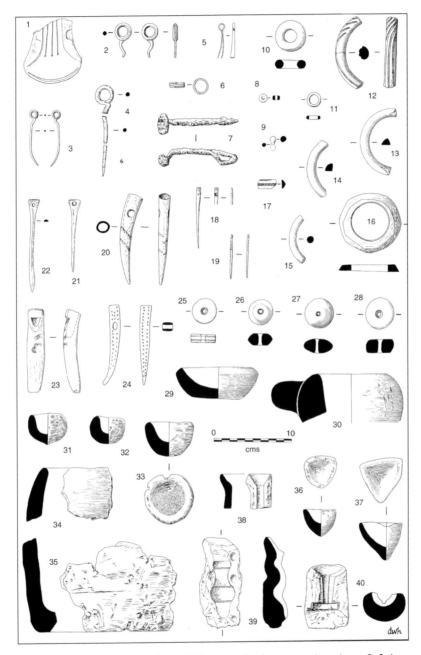

Figure 5.21 Dunagoil, Bute, artefacts. 1, mould fragment for bronze socketed axe; 2–3, bronze ring-headed pins; 4, iron ring-headed pin; 5, bronze tweezers; 6, bronze spiral ring; 7, iron La Tène 1c brooch; 8, blue glass bead; 9, dumb-bell bead; 10–11, rings; 12–16, lignite bracelets; 17, fragment of glass bangle; 18, 20, 21, bone needles; 19, bone pin; 20, 24, antler 'cheek-pieces'; 23, bone whistle; 25–28, spindle whorls; 29–30, stone cups; 31–33, miniature pots; 34–35 fragments of 'Dunagoil' ware; 36–37, crucibles; 38–40, clay moulds. Drawings by D. W. Harding, courtesy of the Bute Museum, Rothesay.

side protected in some measure by marshy ground that evidently has been subject to improvement in modern times. It must therefore have been an important regional centre from the outset, perhaps maintaining that role into the early historic period. That role is reflected in the wealth of its material culture (Fig. 5.21), and the evidence for industrial activities on the site. How the timber-framed structures came to be fired, whether by accident following an industrial disaster, or as a result of systematic and punitive destruction as a result of conflict, remains uncertain, as does the date of this episode in the site's long history.

Terrain forts of this kind are known elsewhere in Argyll, where access to the citadel is controlled by a series of intermittent outworks blocking the approaches between rocky outcrops, or where terraces and plateaux that could have served a variety of domestic or agricultural functions are brought within the overall defended circuit. At Dun Chonallaigh north of Kilmartin a small citadel dominated a much larger area enclosed by intermittent outworks, while Dun na Cleite on Tiree shows a similar pattern of citadel and outworks. Even the vitrified fort at Carradale in Kintyre has half a dozen short lengths of walling controlling access to the citadel. Apart from the expedient use of intermittent walls between rocky outcrop or naturally defended cliff faces, the concept of the terrain fort is not so different from multivallate enclosures such as Ranachan Hill, except in so far as the irregular terrain afforded natural divisions into separately segregated areas. Multivallation itself, of course, could have been devised as a means of segregation, functional or hierarchical, rather than simply as a means of doubling or trebling the defensive barriers, and where multivallation is widely spaced, there is every reason to suppose that this was the case. At all these sites, the question remains whether they were for permanent, seasonal or special occasional occupation. Even if the terrain forts housed a small, permanent community, it seems possible that this was supplemented seasonally or at times of communal activities or festivals. Aside from these terrain settlements, the conventional focus upon hillfort enclosures has almost certainly been to the neglect of fugitive traces of surrounding fields, unenclosed house-platforms and related features that could have been part of the settlement system. Future landscape survey in Argyll, as in other regions of Atlantic Scotland, may be expected to amplify substantially our understanding of the role of these focal sites in the wider communities they served.

Coastal promontory and related forts

The layout of promontory forts and of allied types of field monument such as cliff-edge forts and stack forts is self-evidently determined by the topography in which they are located, taking advantage of a steep, coastal situation in which sheer cliffs minimise the need for artificial defences. Sometimes their locations are so exposed and precipitous that we might question their utility as sites for regular occupation. Because promontory forts are topographically determined, it follows that they cannot be regarded as culturally diagnostic, nor even as necessarily contemporaneous. They are nevertheless especially characteristic of certain regions in certain periods, as for example, in the Iron Age of south-western England or Brittany. It was the use by the Veneti of the Breton peninsula of promontory forts in the late pre-Roman Iron Age, inferred from Caesar's accounts (*dBG*, III: 12), that encouraged archaeologists for many years to regard the occurrence of similar sites in Atlantic Scotland as evidence for Iron Age migrations along the western seaways from Brittany and south-western England. Simplistic equations between archaeological and historical evidence are generally hard to sustain on closer examination, and this is no exception. Caesar's description of Venetic strongholds plainly refers to lower-lying tongues of land, which might be approached on foot when the tide was out, or evacuated by ship when the defenders were hard pressed. This hardly fits the craggy and sheer-sided cliff-castles of Brittany or the coastal promontory forts of Atlantic Britain and Ireland, as has long been recognised (Hogg, 1972: 22). Furthermore, though some Breton cliff-castles may have been used or re-used in the late pre-Roman Iron Age, archaeological evidence increasingly shows that their principal period of construction and occupation was rather earlier. So to suppose a direct derivation of the promontory forts of Atlantic Scotland, even of those particularly distinguished by the use of multivallation (Lamb, 1980: 62), is hardly warranted. Naturally defended coastal promontories offered an obvious opportunity for reinforcement with minimal effort, whether by a single or multiple barrier according to need or status.

Discussion of promontory forts cannot be divorced entirely from consideration of Atlantic roundhouses, not least because a broch with outworks located on a promontory might well be indistinguishable on the ground from a promontory fort within which a broch had at some stage been built. Dun Mara, Lewis might be a case in point in the west, or in the north the Broch of Burland, Lerwick, Shetland. There are additionally sites in the Hebrides where the defensive wall cutting off the promontory itself displays architectural characteristics similar to those of complex Atlantic roundhouses. The most dramatically situated of these is at Sròn an Duin, by Barra Head lighthouse, Berneray, situated 600 feet above the Atlantic on the southernmost point of the Western Isles. Cutting off an area some 40 metres by 12 are the remains of a massive wall, one section of which had superimposed intra-mural galleries. The entrance itself displays broch-like features in its door check and bar-hole, though it has been subject to secondary modification. Almost identical in layout, though smaller in area now enclosed, is the promontory dun at Rubh' an Dunain, Bracadale, Skye, which likewise has a rebated entrance passage and an intra-mural gallery in the longer length of its wall. Rubh' an Dunain also has a scarcement, low down on its inner wall-face, which has generally been supposed to have supported a lean-to structure (MacSween, 1985: 20). Why it should be so low for this purpose is unclear, and an alternative might have been support for a bench or tier of benches in the manner of a grandstand. The position of the entrance in both instances is to one side of the promontory, allowing a longer intra-mural gallery, and the layout of these features relative to the headland is identical. Whether convenience, convention or some more compelling reason determined this plan is a matter of conjecture, and depends in some measure upon whether we regard these sites as primarily defensive or ceremonial. Another site that appears to be comparable is Dun Vlarveg, Skye, which is also said to have had a galleried wall. In all three instances the wall presents a wide front across a converging headland, rather than the narrow neck of a promontory, so that the term 'headland fort' may be preferred to 'promontory fort' in this instance. The point is not just semantic: given the availability of narrow-necked promontories in the topography, the choice of presenting a wider façade may have been deliberate, for monumental ostentation, or for privacy of whatever activities took place beyond the barrier. In any event, there seems to be no good reason for treating small promontory forts or headland forts with galleried drystone walls as fundamentally different from other promontory or headland sites in which the transecting walls were of less complex construction.

Until relatively recently the number of promontory sites in the Western Isles was limited by the lack of archaeological field survey. One of the largest, at Rubha na Beirgh, Shawbost, Lewis, was reported by Captain Thomas (Thomas, F. W. L., 1890) as having a 'mural passage' within its wall core, no trace of which is now visible. Dating is uncertain without excavation, but if the cellular structures in the collapsed debris of the principal wall are indicative of later Iron Age occupation, then the promontory fort itself could easily have later prehistoric origins. Coastal erosion survey of north Lewis (Burgess and Church, 1997) has greatly enhanced the known data-base of promontory sites. Not all are necessarily presumed to be prehistoric or even early historic, but some may well date from the Iron Age or even from the later Bronze Age. North of Garenin, Lewis, a promontory known by the common Gaelic name of Beirgh contains several house platforms, and test excavation suggested the existence of timber structures beneath the extant stone foundations. A headland of similar name two miles to the south-west, Beirgh on the Aird Laimishader, was possibly once a promontory but now is virtually detached from the mainland by erosion of the cliffs. Here, excavations conducted in the 1960s and early 1970s also yielded a complex settlement of cellular structures that included the use of edge-set slabbing, a technique of construction familiar in the post-broch Iron Age of the region.

In west Lewis the small promontory at Gob Eirer, Crowlista, was investigated following coastal survey (Burgess *et al.*, 1998). Now linked to the shore only by a shingle ridge, the site was protected by a single, low wall, behind which excavation exposed a pair of rectilinear buildings that were tentatively considered as Norse on the evidence of associated pottery. The site's location, flanking the Camas Uig and access to the bay where the Lewis chessmen were found, revived the notion of Norse sea-raiders establishing a foothold from which they could launch their piratical expeditions (Lamb, 1980: Appendix 2, for a critical evaluation). Whatever was the secondary history of the site, however, radiocarbon dates now suggest an older, possibly late Bronze Age date for its establishment.

There is also a significant distribution of promontory forts on the Isle of Man, among which some were re-occupied in the Norse period. The fort at Close ny chollagh (Gelling, 1958) was certainly occupied until the first century AD, but may have been built considerably earlier.

Cliff-edge forts, that is, enclosures which incorporate a significant length of cliff face as part of their circuit, as opposed to the much smaller Atlantic roundhouses which have been subject to erosion, are relatively rare in Atlantic Scotland. An archetypal example in the Atlantic west would be Dun Aengus on Inishmore, Co. Galway, where multivallate defences of a cumulative sequence define a D-shaped precinct of which the seaward edge is a sheer cliff dropping 300 feet into the Atlantic. The site was doubtless an important focus of the island communities, and a special function, for ritual or inauguration ceremonies, has been postulated (Rynne, 1991, 1992). There is nothing in Atlantic Scotland quite comparable, though Sròn Uamha in Kintyre might have approximated to this form. Nevertheless, if we are right in believing that Dun Aengus could have been a site of special, ritual significance, then equally the location of some Atlantic Scottish promontory or headland forts, precipitate to the point of impracticality, could be regarded in the same light.

Few regions of Atlantic Scotland are better suited topographically for the construction of promontory forts than Shetland. As in the west, some sites, such as the Broch of

Burland, Brindister, cut off a small promontory with multiple banks and ditches behind which are the remains of a complex Atlantic roundhouse. The broch at Houbie on Fetlar is similarly enclosed on a cliff-edge site. The multivallate promontory fort on Hog Island, Nesting, on the other hand, the narrow isthmus of which has been completed eroded by the sea to leave the headland as an island, must originally have confined nearly a hectare of land (Fig. 5.22). Multivallation, as has been suggested, may have been a measure of status, hierarchically superior by degrees to bivallation and univallation. But in some instances, as perhaps at Burland, the banks may have been the product of cumulative episodes of construction (Carter *et al.*, 1995). Origins in south-western Britain and Brittany have already been discounted. The size, morphology, location and dating of sites with multivallate defences throughout Britain and Western Europe are far too variable to assume a single purpose or a single point of origin for them all.

The term 'blockhouse' was introduced by J. R. C. Hamilton (1968) in his discussion of Clickhimin; 'gatehouse' fort is sometimes now used for the same class of monument (Fig. 5.23). This unusual form of drystone construction, apparently built either as a free-standing forework or intended as a monumental façade to an enclosing wall or ring-work, is characterised by the presence of architectural traits normally associated with complex Atlantic roundhouses. These include intra-mural chambers within their flanking walls, door rebate and bar-holes in the entrance passage. The Clickhimin blockhouse also had a scarcement (Fig. 5.24b), which Hamilton thought supported an adjacent timber range against the rear wall. Upper storeys have been proposed for Clickhimin on the basis of its intra-mural staircase, and the same may be inferred from early accounts of the remains at the Loch of Huxter. At Scatness a possible flight of steps up the inner wall-face,

Figure 5.22 Hog Island, Shetland, air-photograph. Photograph by D. W. Harding.

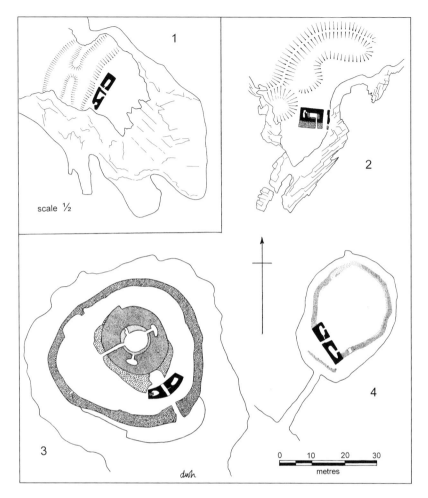

Figure 5.23 'Gatehouses' in Shetland. 1, Ness of Burgi; 2, Scatness; 3, Clickhimin; 4, Loch of Huxter. Drawings by D. W. Harding, adapted from RCAMS (1946), Carter *et al.* (1995), Hamilton (1968).

obscured by the secondary buttressing of the walls, together with secondary internal revetment of the gallery walls, was taken as evidence for an upper storey (Carter *et al.*, 1995).

The four certain examples of blockhouses are the promontory sites of Scatness and nearby Ness of Burgi, and the two loch-forts of Clickhimin and Loch of Huxter. There can be little doubt that the similarities between these examples is such that they must surely be broadly contemporary constructions by culturally related communities. In the light of problems that have accrued from the imposition of too rigid a typology on the study of Atlantic roundhouses, however, we may prefer to include other cognate structures within the general class of blockhouses. Lamb (1980) also included Burgi Geos, Yell, among the Shetland group, despite its singular layout and uniquely perilous location. Allied structures have since been claimed elsewhere, including Caithness and the Western Isles, and certainly at one level the Shetland blockhouses could be seen as monumental

(a)

(b)

Figure 5.24 Clickhimin, Shetland, views of 'gatehouse'. a, from the enclosing fort wall; b, from within, showing scarcement. Photographs by D. W. Harding and I. M. Blake.

barriers to promontory sites for much the same purpose as the headland sites of Skye and the Western Isles. The coincidence of scarcements at Clickhimin and at Rubh' an Dunain, Skye, in particular, prompts the idea that these galleried foreworks could have served a similar function.

The unique and apparently baffling aspect of the Shetland blockhouses, however, is the fact that they are free-standing, with their wall-ends properly faced, showing that they were never intended to extend further. Even where the blockhouse forms an integral part of the ring-work, as at the Loch of Huxter, Whalsay, it is not actually bonded into the enclosure wall. In the case of Ness of Burgi, the walls stop well short of the cliff edge, not apparently as a result of collapse, robbing or erosion, but again by design. Hence it has been inferred that the blockhouse could never have served as a defensive barrier, except in a symbolic sense in which any act of warfare followed a strictly ritualised pattern (Hingley, 1992: 19). Of course, had they been intended as a practical defensive barrier, their builders would surely have recognised the problems posed by constant erosion of the wall-ends, a hazard which nowadays would be met by the use of barbed wire, every bit as effective, if less monumentally imposing than a stone wall. Whether a framework of timber stakes and thorn branches could have been used without leaving earth-fast archaeological traces we can only guess. In the case of the Ness of Burgi, however, it should be noted that access along the neck of the promontory is in places so narrow and perilous that defence need not have focused on the gatehouse site alone. Inaccessibility could also have been an attraction if these sites fulfilled a ritual or ceremonial function. Though positive demonstration is lacking for most sites, Anna Ritchie (2003) has argued that the Clickhimin gatehouse led directly to a building for which a ritual purpose might be suggested.

Even if defence did constitute a conscious element in the design of blockhouses, it is difficult to see how the site at Burgi Geos could be explained this way. The site is located on a remote promontory, accessible only across a hinterland of deep peat, now up to 10 metres deep and presumably therefore already dominating the landscape by the Iron Age. The site occupies a sinuous isthmus between the North and South Burgi Geos, commanding the approach to the headland (Fig. 5.25). The possible blockhouse, if such it is, is situated on the north flank of the approach path; it has no entrance passage, and there is no evidence that any structures on the southern flank have eroded away. On the landward side of the isthmus, the approach passes between a line of boulders, which may once have revetted an embankment, and an elongated mound into which are set the boulders of *chevaux de frise*. But these features present no obstacle to access; rather they channel traffic towards the promontory. The conclusion must be that this was not a fortified site in the normal sense. Its location, remote from arable land, its inaccessibility from the sea, and its perilously precipitate topography make it an unlikely candidate for settlement or even as a practical refuge. Accordingly current opinion once again favours a ceremonial or even ritualistic purpose for the site.

Finally, there remains the question of chronology of the Shetland blockhouses. Their use of 'broch architecture' has generally been taken to affirm an Iron Age date, though radiocarbon dates from Scatness indicated that the blockhouse there was still intact into the second half of the first millennium AD. Despite the deficiencies of the Clickhimin sequence, the balance of probabilities favours an early Iron Age construction. One conclusion seems apparent, however, that 'broch architecture' need not have been restricted to the horizon of occupation of complex Atlantic roundhouses. Though it is undoubtedly a distinctive feature of the monumental buildings, whether forts or roundhouses, of the earlier Iron Age, the lasting visibility of these structures alone could account for the survival of some of these architectural traits into later periods.

Figure 5.25 Burgi Geos, Shetland, air-photograph. Photograph by D. W. Harding.

Part 3

The Roman Iron Age and its impact

Chapter 6

Romanisation to the northern frontier

Definition of Romanisation

Most accounts of the Iron Age in Northern Britain agree that the impact of Romanisation upon the native population was minimal. The fact that villas and urban settlements are comparatively rare in the north, to the point of non-existence in the forward frontier zone, and the fact that rural settlements, of a type indistinguishable from their pre-Roman precursors, seldom yield more than the odd scrap of Roman pottery, endorse this conclusion. Yet few commentators until recent years have tried even to define the concept of Romanisation or to ask what impact upon the native communities Roman annexation might have been expected to make. In the last decade, particularly prompted by the publication by Martin Millett of his *The Romanization of Britain* (1990), a younger generation of archaeologists, and not exclusively those whose principal concern is the archaeology of Roman Britain, has begun to examine the concept of Romanisation more critically in the context of theoretical concerns with the concept of identity, and how it might be expressed or identified archaeologically.

Measuring degrees of Romanisation depends crucially upon our yardstick of *Romanitas*, which itself is not a constant or unified concept across the Empire or throughout its duration. Ethnicity and identity are not absolutes that can be recognised like a samian bowl form; equally the extent to which individuals felt more or less assimilated to the Roman way of life will have varied within and between communities. The principles of citizenship or the legal and administrative structure may have had universal application, but the manifestations of Roman culture that impact upon the archaeological record have a much greater diversity across the Empire. Thus a villa in the Mediterranean was altogether a different entity from a villa in provincial Britain, both in architectural plan and social use, and the Mediterranean concept of urbanisation translates in Britain into a range of settlements whose structural layout and function, political and economic, were not the same as the models upon which they were based. The role of these settlements and the social order that they embodied changed considerably between the Principate and the later Empire. Even between Britain and Gaul the impact of Roman institutions appears to have differed quite substantially (Woolf, 1998). Furthermore, in the nature of empire, and through the recruitment policy of the Roman army in particular, there would have been an element drawn from other parts of the Roman world that progressively integrated with the indigenous communities of Britain. Establishing any kind of independent model of Romanisation is therefore a highly subjective exercise in itself. What we can be sure of is that a Mediterranean Roman would have found Britain as alien as a Victorian Englishman would have found India or the African colonies, which is not to say that British institutions or fashions of living did not make a profound effect upon those countries.

To articulate our expectations of Romanisation in such circumstances would plainly be to risk simplistic caricature, not least because the most critical qualities of Roman-isation may be those which archaeology is least well equipped to recognise. On the basis of documented examples from elsewhere in the Empire we may assume that the local aristocracies in Iron Age Britain retained a substantial measure of delegated authority, at least where they had not met the colonial power with outright or sustained resistance. It has been suggested (Millett, 1990: 65–6) that they constituted a significant element in the decurial class of landowning élite that made up the *curiae* or councils of the *civitates*. Some of these will doubtless have acquired at least a pragmatic literacy for the exercise of their functions, and doubtless chose to emulate Roman fashions in personal dress and habits. Archaeologically, however, recognition of their Romanisation is more likely to derive from the excavation of their country houses, with evidence of accumulated wealth displayed in the form of stone and tiled buildings with hypocausted heating systems and tesselated floors, or from the recovery of imported table ware and domestic goods, all of which stand as proxy evidence of Romanisation. As Taylor (2001) has implied, however, the equation of a villa with Romanisation is not implicit in the description of its furnishings and fittings, though the building or acquisition of a villa may have been a Roman means of expressing wealth and status. Conversely the absence of evidence for Roman forms of wealth accumulation is not necessarily indicative of poverty, particularly in the northern territories of Roman Britain.

To an older generation of classically trained scholars it was axiomatic that Romanisation meant bringing civilisation to replace savagery, much as it would have justified its own government's colonial ambitions. In this perspective Iron Age communities in Britain were primitive barbarians as the classical authors portrayed them, head-hunters who practised human sacrifice and spent their wretched lives in a state of drunkenness or boastful combat. By the 1940s serious scholars had progressed beyond the notion that Iron Age communities in southern England were pit-dwellers, though the idea was surprisingly durable (Wheeler, 1943: 52). Its counterpart in the north was the idea that souterrains were earth-houses where a family could cower like Eskimaux to endure the severe winter storms (Childe, 1935a: 187). The fact that Iron Age communities had the capacity to marshal resources for the construction of hillforts or to create technical works of outstanding craftsmanship like parade armour and personal ornaments, was increasingly recognised as incompatible with the view of Celts as savages, however noble.

Yet despite the evidence, archaeological as well as documentary, for an increasing population in the Iron Age becoming progressively more hierarchical, and probably already with distinctive tribal identities, it is still possible for scholars to characterise societies as 'fairly small-scale and . . . in a continuous state of warfare and conflict' on to which 'the Roman Empire imposed a new order . . . integrated into tribal groupings, each based upon a single *civitas* (tribal) capital' (Hingley, 1989: 10). Before we can consider the extent of Romanisation, it is evidently necessary first to identify the key characteristics of the culture that was about to be exposed to Romanisation. In particular we need to consider to what extent Iron Age communities were already involved in market economy and external trade in order to assess the extent to which these were indeed catalysed by a Roman monetary system and integrated marketing structure.

An aspect of the process of Romanisation that has engendered considerable debate in recent years is the extent to which it was imposed by the Roman administration through coercion, and to what extent it was adopted and adapted by local élites to their own advantage, polarised viewpoints that have been characterised as the 'interventionist' and 'non-interventionist' models. Millett (1990) believed that it was Roman policy in its own self-interest as far as was practicable to assimilate local political rulers into their own administration, and challenged the idea that annexation of Britain to the Empire was a decision prompted solely by systematic economic imperialism. It is not at all clear that the invasion under Claudius came as an unexpected or even in some quarters unwelcome intervention. Even during Caesar's raids of the mid-first century BC some tribal leaders had evidently been more pro-Roman than others, and in the century between Caesar and Claudius there is documentary evidence for the continuation of some diplomatic alliances between Rome and insular dynastic rulers. To what extent this was fostered by kinship relationships with Gaulish tribes that were already integrated into the Empire is uncertain. Likewise it has been argued (Creighton, 2001) that there could already have been trading settlements and even auxiliary forces in Britain by invitation to bolster the political authority of local rulers: the fact that no such activity is directly recorded in the surviving texts is no reason for assuming that such liaisons were not taking place. Equally it is possible that the presence of *obsides* (not, as Creighton has rightly observed, best translated as 'hostages', but parties to an institution intended to strengthen bonds of mutual benefit) from ruling houses of the British tribes in Roman political households could have contributed to a climate in which annexation was not resisted universally.

The current debate has further highlighted the fact that the effects of Romanisation in Britain, however measured, seem to have been less enduring than in other parts of the Empire. For the most part, for example, place-names of Roman settlements and the *civitas* structure itself do not seem to have survived much beyond the fifth century, by contrast, for example, with Gaul, where it continued to form the basic territorial divisions into the Middle Ages. Hill (Hill, J. D., 2001) rightly rejects the simplistic notion that Romanisation is thus shown to have been no more than a veneer, and that native communities in Britain thereafter reverted to their Iron Age customs and beliefs. The reality must be more complex, that the communities that faced a new process of 'Germanicisation' had transformed their own identities as a result of dynamic interaction with the cosmopolitan world of the Roman Empire. Identifying native from invader in the archaeological record of the post-Roman period presents many of the same dilemmas, in theory and in practice, as it had for the period of Romanisation.

Britain on the eve of the Conquest

It is a common bias in British Iron Age archaeology to characterise settlements, funerary practices and economy on the eve of the Conquest predominantly in terms of the south-east of England, that region flanking the Thames estuary where innovations of the so-called Aylesford-Swarling culture were once attributed to settlers of the first century BC from Belgic Gaul. The region north of the Thames is particularly distinguished by its wealthy burials of the classic Welwyn series, in which wine-amphorae and high-status drinking or serving vessels testify to trade or diplomatic exchange with the Roman world. Furthermore, the appearance of imported pottery of Arretine, Gaulish or Gallo-Belgic wares, together with the production of locally made pottery which is wheel-thrown for the first time, indicates the development of new markets and a new kind of economy. Coinage had been introduced into south-eastern England probably already before 100 BC, but its adoption as currency as opposed to its various possible uses in diplomatic, political or social contexts at the level of tribal élites is less easy to establish. Though in absolute terms the quantities of imports recorded archaeologically may not be large, relative to other parts of the Roman world, there can be little doubt that they do reflect a highly developed dynastic society in the south-east in which status was measured by the capacity to control resources, including imported goods, and conspicuously to dispose of such wealth in the tombs of their tribal aristocracy.

To the west of this region was another territory in which cross-channel trade was active in the later pre-Roman Iron Age, focused on the port of Hengistbury Head, but doubtless exploiting several natural landing points from Chichester to Poole harbour and beyond. Here the distribution of Dressel 1 amphorae is apparently less impressive in quantity, though this may be a factor of discovery, since finds derive not from cemeteries but from settlements. Bradley (1984) drawing upon Haselgrove (1982b) envisaged a south-eastern 'core' area, extending from the Thames estuary to the Chilterns, that through its coastal centres was in contact with Continental traders, which in turn exploited the resources and agricultural production of the 'peripheral' zones to the north and west. Cunliffe (1991) extended his core to include the whole of south-eastern England as far west as the Isle of Wight, and to the north-west the middle Thames and the Ouse. Beyond this was a peripheral zone, including the coin-issuing territories from Dorset to Lincolnshire. Beyond that still were non-coin-using tribes of the remote north and west, whose prospects for Romanisation in any sense other than through military coercion thus appear predetermined to be minimal.

In terms of settlements, a distinctive innovation of the later Iron Age in south-eastern Britain was the territorial *oppidum*, not apparently an urban settlement in any sense that would be recognised by a Roman, despite Caesar's ironic use of the term, but nevertheless tribal centres of power that in several instances, like Colchester or Silchester, became important centres under Roman occupation. With the sole and important exception of Stanwick in north Yorkshire, which incorporates more continuous earthworks in its largest enclosure than its south-eastern counterparts, these territorial *oppida* are confined to Cunliffe's 'core' area of the south-east of England and its margins. How long conventional hillforts lasted in use in this core area is uncertain. Oldbury in Kent certainly was occupied in the first century BC, but by the early first century AD the shift towards territorial *oppida* may well have resulted in the abandonment of hillforts. In the peripheral zone there is ample evidence of hillforts being defended on the eve of Conquest, from Maiden Castle, Hod Hill and Spettisbury in Dorset through to South Cadbury in Somerset, Bredon Hill, Gloucestershire and Sutton Walls, Herefordshire, though it is by no means certain that the Romans were responsible for the carnage in evidence at all these sites in the initial stages of the Conquest. In the territory of the Durotriges especially the existence of numerous multivallate hillforts suggests a local social structure rather different from that of the south-east of England, though whether this is indicative of a more fragmented society, in which local chiefdoms were loosely united in federation, as has sometimes been suggested, is open to question. It is reasonable to suppose that the Durotriges were one of the two 'strongest' tribes to whom Suetonius referred, which hardly implies a fragmented society, and the fact that no less than twenty *oppida* had to be taken by force actually suggests a degree of solidarity in the resistance that is more likely the result of unified political control. In fact, the Dorset hillforts, if Hod Hill is a model, were densely occupied on the eve of the Conquest, and may have approximated more closely to urban settlements than the territorial *oppida* of the south-east. As Richmond rightly underlined (1968: 6), Hod Hill at 55 acres enclosed was considerably larger than Maiden Castle, and together with Hambledon Hill might justifiably be regarded as a more important focal centre of the Durotriges.

Other categories of late Iron Age settlement are more difficult to classify. For the most part the Little Woodbury type of homestead, with its large roundhouse, was obsolete by the first century BC, and there is some evidence in Wessex for the fragmentation of settlements into smaller units around this time. Small circular huts survive in some numbers at Hod Hill, where Richmond believed that the chieftain's hut was demarcated by its isolation within an individual compound. It would certainly not be easy to sustain the view that the roundhouse was the universal domestic unit in the immediately pre-Roman Iron Age, however, and there is some evidence from south-eastern England (Rodwell, 1978) for the use of rectangular buildings already before the Conquest. Any suggestion therefore that rectangularity in domestic building plans might be a measure of Romanisation needs to be qualified to take into account the possibility of its currency in Britain already in the later Iron Age, if not earlier. Part of the problem may rest in the fact that rectangular buildings may be constructed using techniques other than the earth-fast post-hole, so that a pre-occupation with houses of the Little Woodbury kind may have militated against the recognition of different types of building.

In northern England, within those regions that subsequently came within the Roman frontiers, Iron Age society appears to have been based upon dispersed rural settlements of which enclosed homesteads, either rectilinear or circular in plan, and containing one or more circular house, were a widespread element over much of the first millennium BC. Occasional hillforts may still have been in use, but were never as numerous as in parts of southern England. The number of permanent settlements and extensive linear earth-works and field-systems may indicate an ordered division of the landscape into territorial and agricultural units, so that we should be wary of misty visions of Celtic cowboys and shepherds drifting aimlessly across the upland hills. The Brigantes, as we have seen, were probably at most a federation of local groupings, so that their reported schism into pro-Roman and anti-Roman factions was probably no more than a reflection of their lack of political coherence.

The establishment of Roman control in southern England

Roman domination of southern and south-eastern England will evidently have come about as a result of a combination of military conquest and negotiated annexation. The documentary sources, fragmentary and therefore possibly misleading, indicate that political liaisons were being negotiated before the Conquest, probably linked to internal hostilities between native rivals. Some tribal groupings may have negotiated client status with Rome, and internal political dissent between pro-Roman and anti-Roman factions among the tribal aristocracies may well have resulted in some territorial realignments in the decades before the Conquest.

In consequence, Millett has plausibly argued that the Conquest proceeded on a tribe-by-tribe basis, so that where a single paramount authority controlled a substantial tribe or tribal federation, progress would have been more rapid than in regions where a more fragmented structure prevailed. As well as being a natural geographical axis the Fosse Way frontier quite probably corresponded to the borders of the tribes of the 'peripheral' zone, the Durotriges, the Dobunni and the Corieltauvi. To the south and east of this frontier the tribal territories duly acquired *civitas* capitals, generally located at or near former tribal centres. It remains a matter of debate how far the *civitates* themselves represented political realities of the pre-Roman period, and how far they were really constructs of the Roman administration. Archaeologists have conventionally assigned tribal names to several of the pre-Roman coin distributions, in the expectation that these reflect tribal groupings, or at least the distribution area within which a tribal élite's authority was recognised. These distributions may be a truer reflection of such units than the distribution of pottery styles, which could easily have an inter-community circulation. In any event the political map of later pre-Roman Iron Age Britain was most probably in a state of dynamic change, which would make any such identifications more difficult.

Older studies of Roman Britain generally treated towns and the countryside as two entities, related but distinct. With the social and economic emphasis of contemporary archaeology they should probably be regarded as mutually dependent parts of a single system. Urbanised settlements under the Roman occupation are conventionally classed in Roman terminology either as *civitas* capitals, as *municipia*, or *colonia* (colonies initially established by the commandeering of land for army veterans). Less clearly defined is the category of 'small town', while *vici*, or civilian settlements, grew up in the immediate vicinity of forts. Even the major settlements did not always conform to the classical model; their *fora* frequently did not include temples, for example, which in British towns were often clustered elsewhere in the urban plan. Should this be regarded as a departure from a Romanised norm, and thereby a measure of qualified Romanisation, or simply as a rational adaptation to local circumstances? The status of the lesser 'urban' settlements is still more equivocal if measured against a rigid norm. Small towns could seemingly grew up around rural temples, as at Frilford, Oxon. In the northern zone the *vicus* at Piercebridge, located on either side of the river crossing over the Tees on the main route of Dere Street northwards, has sometimes been thought of as a small town (Millett, 1990: Fig. 64). More recent finds suggest another contender at Sedgefield in Co. Durham. In terms of understanding the political, social and economic functioning of the Roman province, it is clear that applying strict definitions based upon formalised expectations of size or plan is not a particularly helpful exercise.

Likewise, rural settlement in Romanised Britain hardly accords to a Mediterranean model of estates focused around country house or mansion, either in architectural plan or social ownership and use. Conventionally Roman archaeologists have classified villas in Romanised Britain into categories by ground-plan, aisled and halled villas, corridor and winged-corridor villas, or courtyard villas, with a sub-text of progressive social sophistication. Even some of the earlier establishments may have been stone-built with tiled roofs, and furnished with hypocausted heating systems and tesselated or mosaic floors. But some of the earliest were of wood and daub construction with thatched roofs, and might be seen as evidence of native occupants translating their timber roundhouses into the more acceptable Roman mode of rectangular building. Actual site continuity is not unknown. At Gorhambury, Herts (Neal, 1978; Neal and Selkirk, 1983), located in close proximity to the tribal *oppidum* at St Albans, the late pre-Roman phase included an

Iron Age, timber-built aisled house which underlay a subsequent aisled house of the Romano-British phase of occupation. These structures were interpreted as the estate workers' quarters of the villa that came to dominate the settlement's principal enclosure, which by around AD 100 was a stone-built house of simple plan, with separate adjacent bath building. Its predecessors, however, were built of timber in the first century AD, and the relative social hierarchy between the two enclosures would have been far less obvious. Woodhouse Hill, Studland (Field, 1965), overlooking Poole Harbour, represents a lower social order altogether. Here the occupants of late Iron Age sub-circular huts in the first century AD acquired samian tableware and Roman coins. By the third century they were living in two-roomed 'cottages', which, though their stone foundations remained unmortared, their floors of earth and their roofs of thatch rather than tiled, nevertheless represent the lowest order of aisled longhouse.

The simple aisled house and its more developed variant, the hall-house, are of particular interest in that their social design appears to place a greater emphasis on a communal central hall, around which smaller rooms are clustered, by comparison with the linear suites of broadly equal-sized rooms that characterise other villa types. In some instances the peripheral space created by the aisled structure was reinforced by partitions; in the hall-house this function is formalised in a series of clearly separate adjacent rooms. In its basic form this layout has been compared with the design of larger Iron Age round-houses of the Little Woodbury or Pimperne class in which there is an implied division between central, public space and peripheral, private or functionally specific space (Millett, 1990: 201), but translated into rectilinear geometry. The origins of the aisled plan in Britain are obscure, perhaps through lack of excavated evidence, though, as we have seen, its presence has been recorded in the later pre-Roman Iron Age in south-eastern England. Most though not all examples of the Roman period are of late date, and were conventionally assigned to the poorer and more primitive elements in Romano-British rural society (Collingwood and Richmond, 1969: 147). There seems no reason to assume any direct input from the Northern European Iron Age tradition of aisled longhouses, itself a developed manifestation of a long-standing tradition of rectangular domestic architecture east of the Rhine, from which Britain in the earlier Iron Age need not have been totally isolated or immune. Its occurrence therefore at Gorhambury in the later pre-Roman Iron Age and in close proximity to the dyke-system of the regional *oppidum* is of particular importance in establishing an insular pedigree for the type.

An important contribution (though the idea goes back to Haverfield originally) was the recognition that villas may have been in joint or even multiple ownership and occupancy. A significant number of villa sites in Britain conform to a pattern which has been termed the unit system (Smith, J. T., 1978), in which two separate buildings were apparently occupied contemporaneously by social groups of approximately the same size and social standing. Richmond assumed that the second building was for occupation by estate workers or socially subordinate groups, but increasingly evidence suggests that this is not the only plausible explanation. Beadlam in Yorkshire is a good northern example, but the distribution covers most of the lowland zone south and east of the Jurassic Way. Much the same principle seems to be at work in the remarkable plan of the second-century winged corridor villa at Gadebridge (Neal, 1974), literally semi-detached in plan to the point of having duplicated porches. The implications of dual or multiple occupation in terms of property-owning and land-holding are self-evident, and prompt questions as to whether Roman or local legal conventions were in play. The suggestion that twin buildings were the product of native Celtic practices in inheritance cannot be dismissed simply because it should have manifested itself in progressive sub-division into ever smaller entities. The fact that land may have been sub-divided on this principle does not mean that the houses should follow suit beyond the inheriting generation. The existence of conjoined circular houses or house-plots has been widely remarked in the pre-Roman Iron Age, from Pilsdon Pen in Dorset (Gelling, 1977) to the uplands of Perthshire (RCAHMS, 1990).

Stanwick and north-eastern England

Excavations and re-assessment of the Stanwick fortification in the 1980s has resulted in a major review of Wheeler's conclusions of the 1950s. The threefold progressive enlargement of the enclosure from a primary hillfort located on the Tofts field to a terrain enclosure of 300 hectares had already been questioned by Dobson and others in the 1970s. Even a superficial inspection of the extant earthworks indicated that they are of much greater complexity than Wheeler's survey indicated, with many features excluded, presumably on the grounds that they were considered more recent and therefore of no relevance to his first century AD historical focus. The inclusion within the overall circuit of a semi-circular cemetery enclosure around Stanwick church, and the close proximity of Forcett church with its Norse hogbacks, both argue for an important Norse and early Mediaeval presence in the area, so that any archaeological investigation might have been expected to take a longer chronological perspective. The structural sequence itself was inferred from surface inspection rather than demonstrated by selective excavation. Crucial relationships at the junctions between the earthworks were not strati-graphically tested or testable. Furthermore, the ramparts of Phase 2 petering out across the Tofts enclosure towards the Mary Wild Beck, and the dog-leg round Henah Hill, always looked implausible and made very little tactical sense as a defensive enclosure. The status of Henah Hill, and the unexplained earthworks leading east from the area of Site C, perhaps to follow the line taken later by the road around its foot, were never adequately investigated, being set aside with tactical arguments that can only be regarded as spurious.

Excavations in the 1980s concluded that Wheeler's view of Stanwick as the stronghold of an anti-Roman faction in the first century AD was totally misplaced, and that more probably the Stanwick aristocracy was in treaty relationship with Rome, enjoying the benefits of Roman imports from the south. From the open settlement of the first century BC, the site was expanded on a massive scale in the mid-first century AD by the construction of the major earthwork enclosures, not as an expanding sequence, but as a unitary concept in which a smaller, northern compound formed the focus of habitation, while the larger, southern compound enclosed areas set aside for arable and pastoral activities (Haselgrove *et al.* 1990). Though not remotely on the same massive scale as the southern or south-eastern *oppida* exemplified at Chichester or Colchester, Stanwick could certainly have been designed as a terrain-enclosing site of a similar general class. Evidence of the material assemblage from Stanwick, and from the contemporary occupation of the nearby site at Melsonby, indicates high-status occupation. Spanish amphorae used for importing olive oil and Rhodian wine-amphorae, samian ware and flagons of the Neronian and early Flavian periods, all signify Roman imports before the conquest of northern England. The unusually wide range of samian types represented on both sites and the high proportion of decorated vessels indicate that this ware was especially valued (Fitts *et al.*, 1999). Both Stanwick and Melsonby also yielded quantities of briquetage from their late pre-Roman occupation, evidence with finds from other local sites of an extensive regional network of salt production and distribution, probably based upon sources around the mouth of the Tees.

Recent research on the Melsonby hoard (Fitts *et al.*, 1999) has also prompted radical reinterpretation of its possible context. Previous opinion had considered the possibility that it was a votive hoard, or a founder's hoard buried in the political emergency of the Roman advance north. Wheeler had suggested that it might have been a chariot burial, not least because of the reported proximity of several 'large iron hoops', which could have signaled tyres from chariot wheels, notwithstanding the fact that Melsonby lay well beyond the main distribution of Arras culture vehicle burials. As regards the dating of the hoard, analyses have confirmed that, with one important exception, the majority of pieces are in fact a zinc alloy or brass, and hence unlikely to be earlier than the first century AD, and entirely consistent with its conventional dating (MacGregor, 1962) around the middle of that century.

As to a possible burial context, re-examination of the hoops has indicated several technical reasons why they cannot have been tyres, but might plausibly have been iron binding-hoops for a stave-built wooden bucket of the kind known from Marlborough in Wiltshire and sites of the late pre-Roman Iron Age in south-eastern England. These, and their counterparts in north-eastern Gaul, were not infrequently used to contain cremation burials, raising the prospect that the Melsonby hoard could have been from an aristocratic burial of the mid-first century AD. Heat damage to several of the items in the hoard would be consistent with their exposure to a funeral pyre. The wooden frame of the bucket would have decayed long since, and the few calcined remains of a cremation could easily have been overlooked by the hoard's nineteenth-century finders. This tentative proposal would certainly reinforce the idea of an élite group at Stanwick that was in regular exchange with peers in south-eastern England.

The current view, therefore, that the occupants of Stanwick were engaged in positive trading activities with the Romanised south in the decades before military annexation, possibly through a treaty relationship, now makes better sense than Wheeler's belief that it was the headquarters of an anti-Roman faction among the Brigantes. What remains puzzling, nevertheless, is the apparent abandonment of Stanwick around the end of the first century. A clue to the reason may be provided by the relative proximity of the villa settlement at Holme House, Piercebridge the character of which suggests a Romanised native estate rather than one imposed by the military or civil authorities.

In discussing the Romanisation of northern England it is important not to assume that the entire province from the Trent to Hadrian's Wall was uniformly responsive or hostile to annexation and acculturation. The distribution of villas and related settlements in comparison to military establishments, without regard specifically to the question of date and duration of occupation (Fig. 6.1), makes clear that Romanisation made a greater impact on the east than it did west of the Pennines (Branigan, 1980: 18). The reason for this is doubtless in part related to geography, and to the pattern of the military advance; but it may also be in part a question of the responsiveness to change of the eastern tribal groupings, and the extent to which they had already been in contact with imported fashions from south-eastern England in the years before the Conquest. The evidence from Stanwick, as currently re-interpreted, is pivotal in this regard.

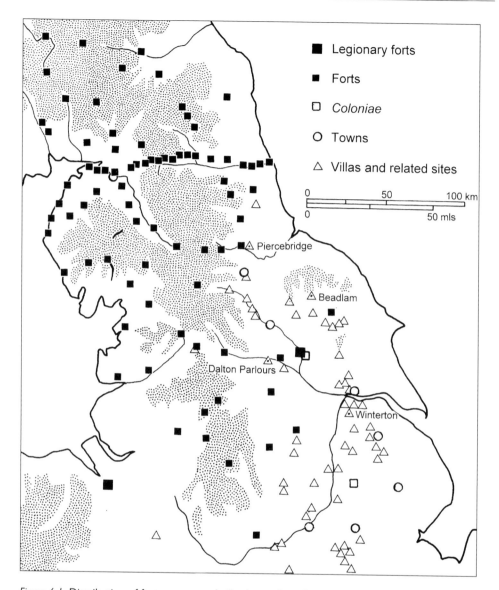

Figure 6.1 Distribution of forts, towns and villas in northern England. Drawing by D. W. Harding.

The distribution of villa settlements in the north, of course, may not just reflect the amenability of the local population; we need first to consider who owned the land on which they were built and who occupied them, together with potential constraints upon Romanisation that the political or military character of the frontier zone might have imposed. Branigan isolated the unusual plans of buildings at Drax and Snape as possible villas built by army veterans on land that had presumably been acquired from former native control. The sites of Langton and Gargrave, on the other hand, displayed a greater integration of 'native' and 'Romanising' elements, which would be consistent with the progressive adoption of Roman building styles by local élites. The extent of Romanisation evinced by northern villas should not, however, be over-stated. Not only are they few in number, but they are of modest proportions, and even in the third and fourth century their mosaics must have appeared extremely provincial and even crude by southern English standards.

Most northerly of the recognised unit villas is Beadlam on the northern edge of the Vale of Pickering (Fig. 6.2, 2). Here two distinctly separated corridor buildings are disposed at right angles to each other, in a manner that certainly implies two units rather than one integrated villa. The fourth-century occupation at Dalton Parlours (Wrathmell and Nicholson, 1990) also apparently had two residential buildings (Fig. 6.2, 1), one a small winged corridor villa in which the eastern rooms were hypocausted and the western boasted mosaic floors. The basic layout of this building, with central oblong room and flanking square rooms, has been compared to similar buildings on villa sites at Langton and Beadlam to the north-east. The second major structure was an aisled building, the dating of which was less secure, but which probably overlapped the winged corridor villa in occupation rather than being its precursor or successor. In at least one phase of use it was certainly residential. Both buildings may have had use of separate, external bath-houses, one of which at least was embellished with elaborately painted walls and ceiling. Ancillary buildings, kilns and ovens have been interpreted in the context of an agricultural economy, and estate workers or slaves were probably housed in native buildings external to the main residential quarters. This pairing of principal buildings would certainly be consistent with joint proprietorship (ibid.: 283), but in this instance the lapse in occupation since its earlier Iron Age phase, and the silted-up state of its ditches, argues against the progressive Romanisation of a native family and community. In fact, the presence of some items of military equipment among the excavated metal-work, and the previously reported existence of tiles with stamps of the sixth legion from the site, suggests instead that the site may have been within the military jurisdiction of the legionary headquarters at York. It is quite possible that it was one of the farming estates that supplied the army, and even that it was under the control of a retired legionary veteran or veterans.

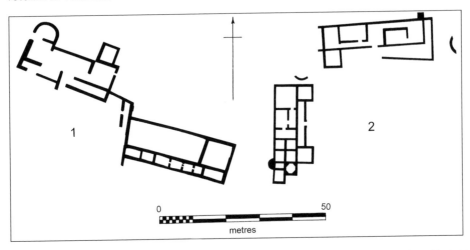

Figure 6.2 Unit villas in northern England, plans. I, Dalton Parlours, Yorkshire; 2, Beadlam, Yorkshire. Drawings by D. W. Harding, adapted from Wrathmell and Nicholson (1990) Stead (1972), Wilson (1966).

Among the most northerly known villas, and one of the earliest, Holme House, Piercebridge (Fig. 6.3; Harding, 1984b) is strategically located on the southern bank of the Tees, close by the main northern route of Dere Street, but still within 5 miles of the former territorial *oppidum* of Stanwick. That its security was assured by proximity to an early fort at Piercebridge remains probable but unconfirmed. But the expansion of the civilian settlement on the south side of the river to something approximating to a significant small town in the second century may well have provided a social and economic context that could explain the aggrandising of an existing native homestead.

If the unit principle was in play in the north-east, then the layout in the second century at Holme House is especially intriguing. Here the principal structures comprised initially a simple cottage-style rectangular house (to which more elaborately furnished dining-suite and bath-suite were subsequently added) and a large, circular house of Little Woodbury proportions, the foundations of which were likewise built of stone, though its earliest form may have been of timber. At first sight, this appeared to be a textbook

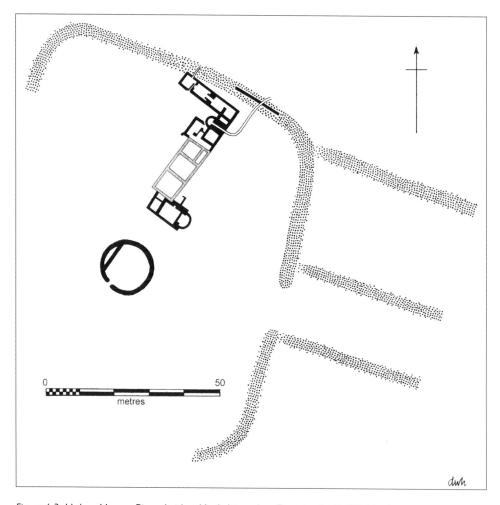

Figure 6.3 Holme House, Piercebridge, Yorkshire, plan. Drawing by D. W. Harding.

case of a native occupant abandoning the traditional Celtic roundhouse in favour of a progressively more Romanised villa. In fact, dating evidence points unequivocally to the contemporary occupation of both buildings, the floor areas of which in the villa's primary, simple layout would have been very similar. Here, therefore, we may have a particularly eloquent example of unit occupation, where one party to the shared occupancy is under-lining its native allegiances. Richmond would doubtless have regarded the roundhouse as for occupation by the estate workers, alongside their more Romanised masters, but in its initial phase of construction the rectangular 'villa' was still, like the roundhouse, a simple clay-and-wattle building with thatched roof, and of no greater pretensions than its traditional neighbour.

The Holme House roundhouse may nevertheless have been the original building on the site in the late pre-Roman Iron Age. It was centrally located within the sub-rectangular ditched enclosure, presenting a plan which is matched by innumerable 'native' settlements in the north-east of England, some of which undoubtedly date from

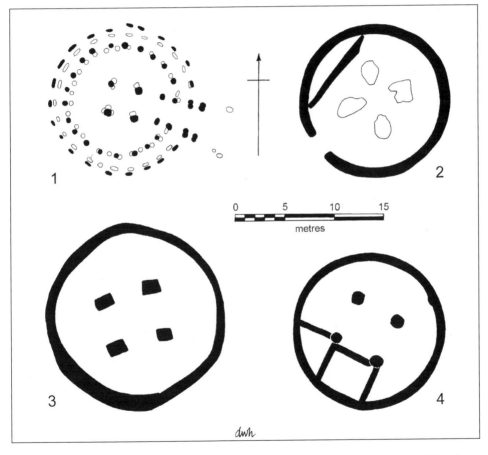

Figure 6.4 Iron Age and Romano-British roundhouses with four-post settings. 1, Little Woodbury, Wiltshire; 2, Holme House, N. Yorkshire; 3, Winterton, Lincolnshire; Bozeat, Northamptonshire. Drawings by D. W. Harding, adapted from Bersu (1940), Harding (1984b), Stead (1976) and Wilson (1966).

the earlier Iron Age. Beneath the stone foundations and within the building was a mass of postholes and pits, which were almost certainly indicative of a long sequence of earlier roundhouses on the same site. There is every probability that these buildings were established well before the Roman occupation, and that the site therefore represents in its initial layout a later pre-Roman Iron Age homestead. The roundhouse itself notably retains the central four-post arrangement of the Little Woodbury model, as do several circular stone buildings of the Roman period in eastern England (Fig. 6.4, above). The Romanised rectangular building is then introduced between the dominant roundhouse and the enclosure boundary and, significantly, in its extended second century layout expands across the partially infilled boundary ditch, itself almost a metaphor for the process of Romanisation.

After the abandonment of the Holme House settlement at the end of the second century, almost certainly as a result of persistent flooding of the Tees encroaching upon the villa precincts, and equally surely not, as older received wisdom insisted, a result of historically documented unrest among the frontier tribes, the focus of settlement shifted. There is some evidence of later Roman activity at Holme House, but if the villa itself was rebuilt, as its systematic dismantling may imply, then its alternative location was most probably on a higher terrace immediately to the south.

An important aspect of the Piercebridge complex is the relationship of the villa to the *vicus* on the one hand and to several native settlements in the locality, known principally from air-photography, on the other. The *vicus* was already extensive by around AD 100, straddling both banks of the Tees and attaining the proportions of a small town. The

Figure 6.5 The Tofts, Piercebridge, Co. Durham, air-photograph. Photograph by D. W. Harding.

early fort itself still eludes discovery, though air-photographs of the Tofts field (Fig. 6.5) suggest an earlier street alignment that could have led to a fort now concealed or lost beneath the modern village. Clack (1982: 393) has suggested that the Holme House villa was the centre of a small estate that included several local native settlements as subordinate communities, the produce from which would have supplied the local garrison, and with surpluses marketed in the *vicus* or exchanged for consumer goods. That such a system could have been in operation in the second century no doubt provides the context in which the older order, represented at Stanwick, fell into decline. Nevertheless, it seems improbable that such a system could have been sustained much further north, and the identification of other villas in Co. Durham remains tenuous. There was certainly a site of some importance in the fourth century at Old Durham, which boasted a bath-house at that time. The two circular stone buildings of second-century date (Wright and Gillam, 1951), though sometimes described as threshing-floors, on the Holme House analogy could have been circular, stone-built houses of a native farmstead that had yet to adopt rectangular villa-style buildings.

Lancashire and Cumbria

Though the frontier works themselves affected native communities on east and west in equal measure, it was undoubtedly the west that from the archaeological record appears to have been least Romanised. The absence of villas west of the Pennines or north of Cheshire is surely significant, and cannot be accounted for as a product of inadequate archaeological research. In Cumbria quite explicitly air-photographic survey was directed at the detection of villas or related settlements in the Solway-Eden regions without success (Higham, 1989: 161). The few instances of the adoption of rectangular building plans on native sites in Cumbria by the Severan period, such as Risehow (Blake, 1959) was more probably influenced by familiarity with buildings in the military *vici* than by the villas of the east and south. The distribution of forts and military establishments of the early second century (Breeze and Dobson, 2000: Fig. 11) shows such an overwhelming concentration in the west, from the southern Pennines, through the Cumbrian Pennines and the Lake District to the Cumbrian coast, in contrast to the distribution of villas through the Vale of York to the Tees and into Co. Durham, that the northern half of the province appears to have been divided fundamentally on an east–west axis.

It has been argued (Higham, 1982: 117) that native sites in Cumbria have yielded a richer assemblage of Roman material than native sites in Northumberland, including samian and black-burnished ware, presumably acquired through the local *vici*. Even if this proved to be the case – and the number of excavated sites in Cumbria is limited – it need hardly occasion surprise that settlements within the frontier had more regular access to such material than sites that were for much of the period beyond the frontier. On the German *limes* the distribution of Roman material fades dramatically beyond the frontier (Fulford, 1989), and the economic importance of any 'buffer zone' and the consequential impact upon it of Romanisation by proximity should not be exaggerated. The problem remains that dating of native sites is not sufficiently fine-tuned to make possible valid comparisons between communities within and beyond the frontier. That frontier itself is known from historical and epigraphic sources to have shifted within periods of too short a span to be dated definitively in the native archaeological assemblage.

Figure 6.6 Whitley Castle, Alston, Cumbria, Roman fort, air-photograph. Photograph by D. W. Harding.

It is hard to see what benefit the Roman presence could have brought to native communities in the north-west. Basic supplies of timber and stone for building purposes would have been commandeered, while pottery and other everyday goods would have been imported. It is generally argued that the Roman army was provisioned as far as possible from local supplies, but in the north-west this was likely to have been less than sufficient, and requisitioning would have left the native population under-provided. Further extensification of agriculture might have been practicable in the north-east in response to military demands, but in Cumbria agricultural potential was more limited, thus further enhancing the east–west divide. The army of course would also have made substantial demands upon the local population for meat and hides, possibly through purchase, but doubtless also through taxation in kind or simple extortion. Local mineral resources were evidently exploited by the Romans, like lead from the South Tyne valley, where the multiple ditches of Whitley Castle (Fig. 6.6) indicate that defence in this region was no mere formality.

The frontier zone

The negative impact of Romanisation must inevitably have been more enduring in the immediate frontier zones than in regions further south. The establishment of the frontier works themselves, and the network of forts and depots in the hinterland, would have entailed the confiscation of native land, the displacement of local communities and considerable restrictions upon native mobility to seasonal pastures or traditional sources of supply. Almost certainly the linear frontier of Hadrian's Wall would have cut across traditional tribal territories, dividing kin from kin, and, like the Berlin Wall of more recent times, imposing restrictions on movement that must have been deeply resented. This, together with the burden of taxation, together with the risk of enslavement or conscription, would have generated a degree of hostility to the Roman military presence which, even when not actively expressed in resistance, would have inhibited the process of Romanisation.

This apart, the environment and opportunity for the local population to feel the benefits of Romanisation that were available to their cousins in the south were plainly not applicable in the frontier zone. The lack of acculturation could in principle be accounted for in one of three ways. The Roman military regime may not have permitted it, the native population may actively have rejected it, or the economic and social infrastructure of the native communities may not have been conducive to it. The first two in essence involve political decisions, while the third might have resulted from more complex factors. It has sometimes been argued that control of external contacts, resulting in the import of exotic goods, presumably in exchange for local products such as mineral ores, cattle, hides and even slaves, was an important element in sustaining the hierarchical structure of Celtic society. In effect, the tribal élites controlled a prestige goods economy and the distribution or redistribution of economic production among their clients in the social order. Something approximating to this system may have obtained into the second century AD in lowland Scotland, with lowland brochs acting in the role of élite centres (Macinnes, 1984). Within the borders of Empire, however, the Romans were dealing not with friendly kings but with a subjugated population, so that there was no need to indulge in such diplomatic niceties. Furthermore, in northern England there were not even the rudiments of a native market economy system that might have been adapted to mutual advantage under Roman occupation. In Gaul on the eve of conquest, and in south-eastern England too, there is evidence for the beginnings of a market economy with the specialist production of pottery and personal bronzes like brooches, together with the use of smaller denomination currency. All of these were alien to Northern Britain, so that there were neither the economic infrastructure nor the market centres where such activities could be encouraged. In fact, archaeologically there is no clear evidence for the existence of a tribal aristocracy in north-western Brigantia, no dominant sites within the dispersed settlement pattern, and no evidence for their presence within the military *vici*. In fact, we may question whether the social structure of Brigantia at large was at all like that inferred for Southern Britain or even north-eastern England in the later pre-Roman Iron Age and under the Roman occupation.

In the south of England, as in Gaul, the former tribal aristocracies would have been encouraged to assume a role of responsibility within the Romanised *civitates*. This inevitably would have entailed a breakdown of the social bond between native élites and their client dependants, doubtless to the disadvantage of the dependants, and a shift in the basis of élite authority from social bonds to Roman patronage. But in the frontier zone of northern England it is not clear what opportunities there were for such acculturation into the Roman system, even had tribal aristocracies wished to opt for them.

A measure of the inherent insecurity of the northern frontier is the creation of the Vallum, unique among all the frontiers of the Roman Empire, and in its sheer scale indicative of a problem that was far from token. Evidently included in the design of the frontier works at the time of, or very shortly after the construction of the Wall itself, the immediate effect of the Vallum was to reduce the number of points at which the frontier could be crossed, mainly to those manned by the frontier garrisons. As Breeze and Dobson recognised (2000: 57–9), the Vallum was designed to reinforce the security of the frontier from its rear, and presupposes a threat to it from the south. At the same time, its dual ramparts flanking a medial ditch do not conform to any logical defensive layout, since the outer bank would afford cover to hostile forces, and the alignment of the Vallum in any case does not follow the best tactically defensive course (Jones and Woolliscroft, 2001: 81). The conclusion must be that the Vallum was designed to inhibit traffic rather than unencumbered armed bands; in effect that it was intended to prevent cattle-raiding, or movement of stock and wagons other than that which was strictly controlled through army checkpoints. The implication of the entire frontier network must be that the native communities were far from passive and still less persuaded of the attractions of Romanisation.

Unlike southern England, where the *civitas* capitals and network of lesser urban centres provided a framework of local administration and economic integration in which the former native élite and entrepreneurs could flourish, in the frontier zone there was no such urban infrastructure. The two most obvious urban centres, Corbridge and Carlisle, were nevertheless unique establishments, substantially dependent upon the frontier garrisons for their *raison d'être*. Corbridge developed into a walled town of 12 hectares, but remained essentially under military authority. Carlisle may have been the centre of a regional territory in north Cumbria which, on the basis of epigraphic evidence, appears to have acquired in the mid-third century the status of a *civitas* of the Carvetii, perhaps a sub-group of the Brigantian confederacy.

Among the *vici*, most if not all were totally dependent upon their parent garrisons for their economic existence, though Piercebridge in the south-east came closest to acquiring the economic independence of a small town. Within the hinterland of the Wall the *vicus* at Vindolanda (Fig. 6.7) has been extensively excavated, revealing numerous simple rectangular 'strip houses', the foundations of which were of stone with tiled roofs over upper levels of timber and clay. Functionally it is assumed that the ground floors served as shops or workshops, with living accommodation above. The *vicus* also had a *mansio* or inn and other residential buildings. At Vindolanda the *vicus* extends directly out of the fort along the main road, whereas at Old Carlisle (Fig. 6.8) it is noticeably aligned along the road from Papcastle to Carlisle as if its location was determined as much by its regional connections as by its immediate dependency upon the fort. This impression is reinforced by the apparent concentration of native settlements in the vicinity (Higham and Jones, 1975).

The *vici* undoubtedly served as the markets for the wider distribution to rural settlements of those Roman products that did reach native households, of which there is widespread but hardly prolific evidence. Samian and Roman coarse wares, together with occasional glass ornaments, are found on Romano-British settlements in the frontier zone, but the quality of these products is relatively low grade by comparison with what was circulating in the forts and *vici* themselves. The rural settlements must have been producing basic agricultural products in some quantity for the frontier army and its dependants, but the almost total absence of coins from native sites suggests that this was extracted as taxation or by exchange in kind. There is little evidence that the local

Figure 6.7 Vindolanda, Northumberland, Roman fort and *vicus*, air-photograph. Photograph by D. W. Harding.

Figure 6.8 Old Carlisle, Cumbria, Roman fort and *vicus*, air-photograph. Photograph by D. W. Harding.

economy was boosted by the opening up of new markets, or that the agricultural economy itself was revitalised and re-organised for greater productivity, as is implied elsewhere. In consequence, the *vici* in turn were vulnerable to political and economic fluctuations, and seldom achieved economic independence of the garrisons from which they had developed.

Romanisation and insular Celtic art

The impact of Romanisation and the native response to it is nowhere better illustrated than in high-status metalwork. The century following Caesar's raids of 55 and 54 BC on south-eastern England saw a substantial increase in the import of wine and oil and a range of Roman provincial goods from the Continent into south-eastern and central southern England. This in itself should hardly be taken as a measure of insular Romanisation, merely that aristocratic society in late pre-Roman Iron Age Southern Britain was quite prepared to adopt Continental fashions to enhance its status and political influence. Until the Conquest native craftsmen maintained nevertheless a considerable degree of stylistic independence in the production of warrior and equestrian equipment, in personal ornaments, including lavish gold torcs in a variety of forms, and vessels for drinking at the aristocratic feast. With the Conquest the infrastructure of production and supply was evidently disrupted, and craftsmen who had formerly produced weaponry and armour under aristocratic patronage were displaced by makers of mass-produced brooches and trinkets for what Megaw and Megaw have caricatured as the tourist market (2001: 230). Presumably some ruling groups chose exile beyond the subjugation of Rome, and it is therefore perhaps hardly surprising that some of the more striking examples of Celtic art of the period following the Conquest and into the second century come from the fringes of the advancing Roman frontier, from Wales and the west, from northern England and then Scotland.

The distribution of metalwork types (Fig. 6.9), especially items of horse-trappings like bridle bits, strap junctions and terrets, shows a spread of usage from southern England to the north which would be consistent with refugee movements, but at the same time there developed, in northern England and beyond, distinctive variants that plainly originated in the north. The so-called 'derivative' three-link horse-bits (Palk's (1984) 'straight-bar snaffles'), characterised by having their side-rings cast in one piece with the outer links of the bit, are plausibly derived from a type of three-link bit in which side-rings are loose and independent of the links which is found widely to the south and east of the Jurassic ridge. The derivative variant itself, however, is found only from Brigantia through into southern Scotland, with notable collections in the Melsonby (Stanwick), Yorks, and Middlebie, Dumfriesshire, hoards. Platform terrets, so named from the three or four raised, flattened knobs or platforms which decorated their outer edges, are also concentrated between the Humber and the Forth, though examples from Essex and East Anglia indicate continuing links with the south-east. One of the most striking examples of a north–south connection is the distribution of Piggott's Group IV swords and scabbards (MacGregor, 1976: Map 13), with its preponderance in Brigantia and lowland Scotland, and with a small but surely significant group in Dorset. These latter come from Durotrigian sites that would have been among those captured by Vespasian in the early years of the Conquest, and their form would be consistent with an earlier first century AD date. Those from the north date from the Flavian period into the early second century.

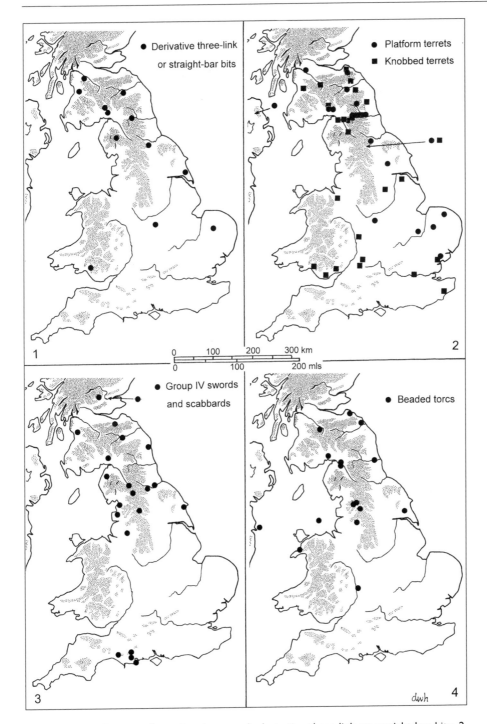

Figure 6.9 Distributions of metalwork types. 1, derivative three-link or straight-bar bits; 2, platform terrets and knobbed terrets; 3, group IV swords and scabbards; 4, beaded torcs. Drawings by D. W. Harding, adapted from MacGregor (1976).

Notwithstanding the dangers of simplistic equations with recorded historical episodes, the dating of the series would not be inconsistent with MacGregor's suggestion (ibid.: 83) that the type was introduced to Brigantia by Durotrigian refugees in the wake of their defeat by the advancing legions.

Characteristic metalwork types of the first and early second centuries AD that are exclusive to the north of Britain, or nearly so, include beaded torcs, among which there are variants in which the beads are threaded on to the rod and others in which the simulated beads are cast in one with the torc. Commonly made of bronze, the rods may nevertheless be of iron, and in at least one instance there is evidence of gilding. The torcs are annular, being opened by mortice and tenon joints. The torc is, of course, a widespread Celtic type of probable regal or ritual significance, and the use of beading as ornament has a long ancestry in Hallstatt and La Tène Europe. Within Southern Britain from the first century BC there are several variants, notably of penannular types, of which occasional examples found their way north.

One of the finest products of a native workshop of the first century AD is the Stichill collar from Roxburghshire (Fig. 6.10). It shows technical affinities to Irish metalwork of the same period in the use of background tooling to create a relief effect, like the Bann disc, Cork horns and Petrie crown. At the same time it displays typological affinities with south-western British and wider artistic fashions. The hinge mechanism of the collar allies it to a group of collars from south-western Britain, of which the finest example is that from Wraxall in Somerset. Located on the fringes of the expanding province, these collars display a conservative use of La Tène motifs undiluted by Roman provincial fashion. The combination on the Stichill collar of distinctive technical traits from different

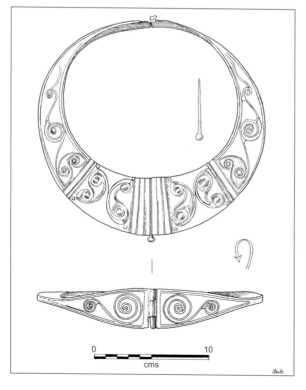

Figure 6.10 The Stichill, Roxburghshire, collar. Drawing by D. W. Harding, adapted from MacGregor (1976) and Jope and Jacobsthal (2000).

regions, and the development of the ornamental theme to its climax at the front of the collar is hardly the work of some provincial hack, but of a master craftsman familiar with the skills and artistic fashions of the northern and western Celtic schools. As to date and origin, the suggestion that it was the product of a Hiberno-Scottish workshop of the first century AD in the Solway–Clyde region (RCAHMS, 1956: 22) still seems reasonable.

Roman influence in the ornamental metalwork of the first century AD is perhaps best exemplified in the bronze mounts which are conventionally interpreted as embellishments for wooden caskets, not themselves for containing the remains of the dead, though commonly found in graves, but probably for jewellery or personal items. The Elmswell, Yorkshire, mount (Corder and Hawkes, 1940) has as its central motif an omega-lyre which conceals a cartoon-like zoomorphic face, of which the 'ears' are formed by trumpets and the 'eyes' by berried rosettes. A more explicit version of the same motif figures in *repoussé* on a bronze strip from Great Tower Street, London. Berried rosettes abound, and may be attributed to Roman influence, though Celtic art had earlier adopted this motif from Mediterranean originals. Certainly Roman is the inspiration for the vine-scroll with *champlevé* enamel that forms the attached strip of the Elmswell mount, for which parallels on decorated samian vessels were cited by Hawkes. A related piece is the bronze strip from the Santon, Norfolk, hoard, which likewise abounds in berried rosettes in a rather uninspired and repetitive design.

A fusion of Celtic and Roman provincial styles or types is well exemplified among personal ornaments by brooches. The dragonesque brooch takes essentially the basic S-motif and embellishes its terminals typically to form the head of a sea-horse, at the same time elaborating the central portion of the brooch with polychrome enamel inlay. The British distribution lies entirely south of the Forth, though not especially concentrated in Brigantia and southern Scotland as often claimed, but with hardly any in Wales or the west of England. Dating of dragonesque brooches extends from the first century AD and throughout the second. The form also is found quite widely through north-Alpine Europe from France to Hungary. Trumpet brooches, likewise a distinctively Roman provincial British type but probably derived from Continental late Iron Age types, have a widespread distribution in the Roman military zone, continuing into the second century with a variety of forms including some with polychrome enamelling. Finally there are fan-tail brooches of which the finest example is undoubtedly the massive silver-gilt Aesica brooch (Fig. 6.11) from the Roman fort at Great Chesters in Northumberland, part of a later third or fourth century hoard but itself undoubtedly of later first century AD manufacture. The design on the brooch defies simple or even consensual description. Its relief ornament consists of trumpets, peltae, S-scrolls and even suggestions of comma-leaf motifs, combined so skilfully as to suggest zoomorphic or ornithomorphic images. MacGregor (1976: 119–23) saw an equine face and muzzle between spring-cover and bow; Jope convincingly argued for an opposed pair of birds with swan-like necks but whale-like bodies and tail-fins on the fan-foot (Jope and Jacobsthal, 2000).

Toynbee (1964) seemingly was disposed to see masterpieces like the Aesica brooch as evidence for the stimulating effect of the Roman Conquest, rather than seeing Roman-isation as an agency directly or indirectly for the suppression of insular Celtic art. It is significant, however, that a number of the finest examples are from the northern or western fringes of the expanding military zone. Though commentators in the past have been only too ready to regard these as products of more southerly workshops, there is

Figure 6.11 The Aesica brooch. Photograph copyright the Museum of Antiquities of Newcastle upon Tyne, University of Newcastle upon Tyne and the Society of Antiquaries of Newcastle upon Tyne.

really no reason for regarding the north and west as cultural backwaters incapable of independent production, particularly if they were reinforced by displaced élites and their entourages from further south. Much of what is produced under the Roman occupation is pedestrian and uninspired, but the finest pieces would seem to suggest that the continuing manufacture of high-quality and high-status products in the pre-Roman artistic tradition, even evoking deliberately the memory of styles of a long-past era, was a potent means of re-asserting the independence and identity of the native aristocracy.

Chapter 7

Romanisation between and beyond the frontiers

The northern frontier: nature and purpose

Most studies of the nature and purpose of the Roman frontiers of Northern Britain begin from the premise that there was a consistent policy in the establishment and maintenance of the frontiers of the Roman Empire, whether in Germany, North Africa or Britain, and that frontier policy was determined by some governing principle, generally perceived as rational, just and paternalistically benign, in the way that was once assumed in the minds of the enforcers of British imperial administration. The extent to which subjugated native populations adopted a Romanised way of life was seen as a measure of their innate receptivity to civilisation or the capacity of their primitive social and economic infrastructure to adapt to such improvement. Until relatively recently, the possibility that native communities may have exercised positive choice in the matter, and actively rejected Romanisation, was not seriously entertained. In the case of the northern frontier of Britain, it is also possible that the option of Romanisation was limited from the outset, and that the impact of the Roman presence was one of cynical exploitation with little pretence of colonial altruism.

It is generally acknowledged that Roman frontier policy would have been modified pragmatically between the early years of colonial expansion and the period of consolidation in the later Empire. The northern frontier of Britain, in any event, was unique in its circumstances and problems, and inherently unstable from the beginning. The advance from Hadrian's Wall to the Forth–Clyde line in the Antonine period, with phases of withdrawal and re-advance, is indicative of that instability, and has resulted in the commonplace observation that the Romans only actually occupied Scotland at most for sixty or seventy years. As Whittaker has argued (1989), however, the concept of the Roman frontier may have entailed the exercise of indirect or negotiated control over territory beyond the line of the formal *limes*, over a 'buffer zone' between those communities that lay within the legal jurisdiction of the subjugated Empire and those tribes that occupied territory wholly beyond the immediate range of Roman influence. The apparent occupation of a limited number only of forts along the Antonine Wall in its second period of use, together with the contemporary occupation of some of the forts between the Tyne–Solway and Forth–Clyde lines, would be consistent with this notion of frontier in depth.

The archaeological evidence for Roman and native on the northern frontier is very unequally informative. On the one hand archaeolological evidence for Roman military dispositions in the Borders and southern Scotland can be amplified from historical sources to provide a closely dated narrative of events on the northern frontier in a period in which the political impact of the Roman advance upon native communities must have been profound. More particularly Hadrian's Wall itself and its military history has been studied in great detail, to the point where books can be written on its forts and milecastles, their plans and histories, and the detachments, commanders and ranks that occupied them, almost as if they occupied a vacant landscape. It is as if recent historians were to study the Berlin Wall on the basis of its construction and design, its checkpoints and watchtowers, without reference to the daily trials of a divided community or the personal tragedies of those who vainly tried to escape. On the other hand, archaeological evidence for the effects of the Roman presence upon native settlement is remarkably sparse, but this is in no small measure a product of past priorities of archaeological research. A major inhibition has been our inability to fine-tune dating of the occupation of native sites to the same level as historically recorded episodes or horizons of Roman military activity. This problem of close dating also impedes any attempt to compare the impact of Romanisation on settlements beyond the frontier with its effect on settlements within the frontier, since episodes of advance and withdrawal in the second century make it impossible to know on the basis of archaeological data with which phase native occupation of sites between the Tyne–Solway line and the Forth–Clyde line coincided.

In terms of Millett's (1990: 100) model of Roman impact upon native societies, communities in Northern Britain would doubtless be regarded as 'decentralized and egalitarian'. Accordingly we might expect that the nature of the Roman impact would have been substantially negative through military occupation, and the opportunities for towns and villas to develop extremely limited. In the frontier zone, however, the situation is more complicated, and more especially so in the case of communities that lived beyond the frontier, whether periodically or permanently. An intriguing question is whether inducement to liaison with communities beyond the formal frontier might not have resulted archaeologically in greater apparent evidence of 'Romanisation' than among those whose territory had already been subject to military annexation.

The fact that the Roman occupation made so little impact upon Scotland really should occasion little surprise, for the simple reason, though seldom acknowledged overtly, that it was both politically and militarily a failure. According to textbooks of Roman archaeology, the tribes north of the Tyne–Solway line were 'conquered' on innumerable occasions following the celebrated victory at Mons Graupius. Yet repeated 'withdrawals' were necessary and punitive attempts at reconquest were frustrated before the final tactical retreat to Hadrian's Wall. Yet even then, according to Roman documentary sources, barbarian incursions occurred on more than one occasion on a scale that could not be concealed. For Northern Britain behind the Tyne–Forth line the concept of 'Romanisation' might have some relevance. For Scotland beyond the Forth–Clyde line, particularly after the effective defeat and expulsion of Roman forces at the end of the second and beginning of the third centuries, the question is largely irrelevant.

Rural settlement in Northumberland and the Cheviots

Whilst there may be little evidence of direct Roman intervention to trigger a widespread re-organisation of the rural landscape, the sheer density of native settlements in the frontier zone and beyond the line of Hadrian's Wall does not suggest any major depopulation of the 'buffer zone', and in fact would not be inconsistent with a population expansion during the years of occupation. Native settlements in Northumberland (Jobey,

1960) show considerable regularity in plan and layout and, on the basis of limited finds of Roman pottery, and in the absence of any definitive evidence of earlier (or later) occupation, have been dated to the late first and second centuries AD. Many in the regions immediately north of the Wall are broadly sub-rectilinear in their enclosure outline, sometimes with an external ditch, or even with slight counterscarp as at Riding Wood. The circular, stone-built houses, commonly three to five in number and around 7 or 8 metres in diameter, are located on the leading edge of an upper terrace at the back of the enclosure, and are generally approached by means of a causeway across two flanking cobbled yards. Towards the Cheviot foothills curvilinear enclosures predominate, in which up to half a dozen stone-built circular houses, each some 7 or 8 metres in diameter, are ranged around the back of the enclosure with a scooped yard in front of them where livestock doubtless could be corralled. Their distribution is not uniform, but for the most part reflects the availability of better agricultural land or pasture. A concentration of sites in the north Tyne valley is so close to Hadrian's Wall that they cannot have been occupied other than by negotiated agreement with the military authorities. In fact, the seeming regularity of distribution even suggested to Jobey (1966b: 6–8) the deliberate ordering of settlement for the purposes of agricultural development. Further north in the Cheviots some degree of regulation was also probably in force, the more so presumably when the northern Antonine frontier was operational.

These stone-built homesteads seldom contain just a single house, and they must represent an extended family or kin group. None of the houses is in any way distinguished from the others to indicate social differentiation. Larger settlements are also known, however, among which Greaves Ash in the Cheviot foothills (Fig. 7.1) is the largest of the series. Here as many as forty stone-built houses survive in two adjacent groups, though these were almost certainly not all in contemporaneous occupation. At Hetha Burn (Burgess, C. B., 1970) the Roman Iron Age sequence began with a pair of stone-built roundhouses within a sub-rectangular stone-walled enclosure, then progressing through two further stages of structural development, in which the number of houses was increased. In its final stage the enclosure was extended so that no less than ten stone-built houses could be accommodated in what amounts to a small village. In contrast, on the coastal plain of Northumberland the site at Burradon (Jobey, 1970), in its pre-Roman phase characterised by a succession of ring-groove houses, is replaced in the Roman period by a single house within its inner, rectilinear enclosure. Perhaps surprisingly the uncharacteristic plan of this building is seldom remarked. Set within a penannular ditch some 15 metres in diameter, its two post-circles, emanating from two pairs of porch posts, are unusually closely spaced, leaving an area up to 10 metres across, within which there was a mass of features forming no coherent plan. If nothing more, Burradon provides a salutary reminder of the diversity of house-plans in the Northern British Iron Age, assuming that its function was indeed domestic.

Stone-built roundhouses also characterised sites like Hownam Rings, Roxburghshire, in its final phase of occupation (Fig. 3.1), in which the earlier defences had been sup-planted by an undefended settlement dated by material associations to the Roman period. These so-called scooped settlements have features in common with the Cheviot and Northumberland Romano-British settlements, so that the distinction between these classes should not be too strongly emphasised (Burgess, C. B., 1984: 166). For many years, as we have seen, the switch from timber to stone construction was implicitly seen as a direct result of Romanisation. There were numerous examples recorded by Jobey and

Figure 7.1 Greaves Ash, Northumberland, native settlement, air-photograph. Photograph by D. W. Harding.

Feachem where stone-built settlements overlay the reduced or abandoned defences of earlier hillforts, from which it was inferred, not unreasonably, that such sequences might represent the resettlement of a local community under the *pax Romana*.

One site that stands apart from the general pattern is the enclosed settlement that replaced the earlier Iron Age multivallate fort at Edgerston, Roxburghshire (RCAHMS, 1956: no. 457). Here were several stone-built roundhouses, averaging 12 metres in overall diameter with stone walls nearly 2 metres thick, the inner faces of which were revetted by a timber framework bedded in a circular trench. These houses lay within an enclosure wall constructed in similar technique, though the exact structural sequence was not resolved by excavation in the 1930s. Finds were relatively prolific, including horse-harness and a range of personal ornaments, suggesting occupation of relatively high status in the first and second centuries AD. Perhaps this site served as a centre for the redistribution of prestige goods in much the same way as has been suggested (Macinnes, 1984) for the lowland brochs north of the Tweed.

It was Jobey's own work on a group of sites in the north Tyne region, notably at Tower Knowe (Jobey, 1973), Belling Law (Jobey, 1977) and Kennel Hall Knowe (Jobey, 1978b), that qualified the conventional view of stone building by demonstrating not only that some stone-built settlements were not constructed until the mid-second century, but also that they had a much longer antecedent sequence of timber roundhouses and enclosing palisades going back to the second century BC or earlier. The pattern of settlement was thus not established directly by the *pax Romana* but was part of a longer sequence of development. Dating evidence from native settlements, however, overwhelmingly points to their use in the later first and second century, reflecting perhaps more on the nature of the evidence than the span of the sites' occupation. At Crock Cleugh in Roxburghshire excavations (Steer and Keeney, 1947) suggested the possibility of occupation continuing into the late Roman or even sub-Roman periods, while the latest stone houses at Hownam Rings were also assigned to the later Roman or even post-Roman periods. Evidence of later occupation in general, however, is remarkably sparse, to the point that Hill was moved to talk about 'tableaux of desertion which may be compared with . . . the Highland clearances' (Hill, P., 1982a: 10). Without allowing the documentary record of Roman withdrawal from the Antonine Wall and late second century political upheavals on the northern frontier to pre-judge the issue, it is not unreasonable to infer that the fortunes of native settlement between and beyond the walls would have fluctuated with the political stability of the Roman frontier.

South-west Scotland

Among the hillforts of the south-west, Castle O'er in upper Eskdale (Fig. 7.2), together with its neighbour on Bailiehill (Fig.7.3), has yielded evidence of a thriving occupation in the early centuries of the first millennium AD (RCAHMS, 1997), broadly contemporary with the Roman advance into Scotland and the establishment of the permanent northern frontier on the Tyne–Solway line. The date of occupation is of particular interest because it raises challenging questions regarding the native relationship with the occupied territories. Situated some 10 miles from the fort at Birrens and the Annandale route into Scotland it is scarcely credible that Castle O'er could have been occupied without the diplomatic agreement of the Roman authorities, perhaps involving the supply of cattle and hides for the Roman army.

Though small in its enclosed core area, Castle O'er appears to have been an important nuclear centre of a predominantly pastoral community, controlling a landscape divided by a complex system of linear earthworks. The fort displays two principal phases of construction, an earlier undated enclosure comprising double banks and medial ditch that may well have had its origins in the earlier Iron Age, and a later stone-walled enclosure within it, which on the basis of radiocarbon dates appears to have been occupied in the early centuries AD. This later enclosure was itself modified in a secondary phase of construction that saw the addition of a double horn-work around the south-west entrance. The whole nucleus is extended by an annexe that was evidently secondary to the primary hillfort, the outer wall of which it over-rides at the north end. Radiocarbon samples from the annexe ditch again suggested activity in the opening centuries AD. The buildings within the interior of the fort reflect its defensive complexity. At first sight a series of roundhouses would appear to flank a central street extending from the fort's northern to southern entrances. In fact these represent cumulative construction over a period of time, and one group of roundhouses at the north end over-lies and therefore post-dates the dereliction of the fort defences. These houses were evidently timber-built, in some instances with ring-groove foundations, and with diameters up to 16 metres, certainly qualifying as 'substantial roundhouses' (Hingley, 1992). In striking contrast to south-eastern Scotland, these houses show no sign of stone construction, either in the later pre-Roman Iron Age or in the period of Roman occupation. The relationship between the fort and the surrounding linear earthworks is hard to demonstrate definitively because of damage by afforestation, but the case for regarding some significant part of the system

Figure 7.2 Castle O'er, Dumfriesshire, hillfort, air-photograph. Photograph by D. W. Harding.

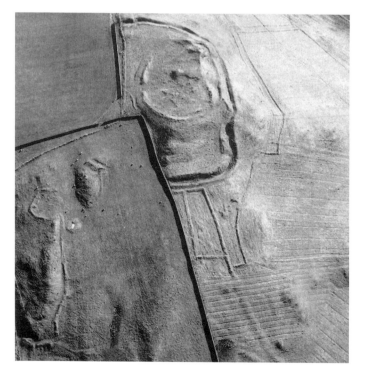

Figure 7.3 Bailiehill, Dumfriesshire, hillfort, air-photograph. Photograph by D. W. Harding.

as originating in a later pre-Roman Iron Age pastoral landscape has been convincingly argued (RCAHMS, 1997).

South of the confluence of the White and Black Esks the hillfort on Baliehill shows a parallel sequence of structural development, again with intensive occupation of the core fort by circular, timber-built houses, and with an enclosing annexe in which there are no traces of domestic occupation. It is hard to resist the conclusion that these two forts must have been broadly contemporary centres of territorial units associated with the pastoral communities of the Iron Age in upper Eskdale.

Within the Castle O'er complex, in a low-lying natural amphitheatre by a bend in the river White Esk, lies the enigmatic Over Rig enclosure. Its triple ditches describe a C-shaped enclosure, with an outlying earthwork on the higher slopes to the north and west. Notwithstanding its timber palisade and a pair of circular buildings of concentric ring-groove construction, the layout of the site and its location did not suggest a normal domestic function. In particular, a trapezoidal stone setting some 4 metres across formed the principal structure within the surviving area. Finds from the waterlogged ditches included two wooden 'daggers', the purpose of which is more likely to have been ceremonial than practical. The site conforms to no known class of settlement or ritual monument, but the excavator's inference that it was a place of ceremonial assembly seems not unreasonable (Mercer, 1985). Radiocarbon dates do not preclude the site's earlier origins, but the balance of probabilities favours its use in the opening centuries AD, contemporary with the occupation of the nearby forts.

A question of interest is how long this network of sites continued in occupation. Radiocarbon dates from the annexe outworks of Castle O'er could well indicate a prolonged use of the earthwork complex through the Roman period, while the timber roundhouses overlying the hillfort earthworks at its north-east end, as we have remarked, evidently represent occupation after those defences themselves had fallen into decline. As ever, the lack of definitive or diagnostic material associations makes it difficult to demonstrate later Roman or even post-Roman occupation, but the environmental record from the locality suggests continuing activity until the mid-first millennium AD.

Stone-built houses were also conspicuous by their absence in the Roman Iron Age occupation of the settlement at Boonies, Dumfriesshire (Jobey, 1974). This small enclosure corresponds to what in the south-east would have been a scooped settlement, though its relatively level situation resulted in only the yard being noticeably sunken. The occupation of the interior at Boonies demonstrated at least seven phases of construction, almost certainly from the pre-Roman Iron Age, though the enclosure itself was probably a late addition. The latest settlement was represented by five roundhouses in a group at the back of the yard. Each was defined by a ring-groove between 5 and 8 metres in diameter, and each had an area of paving leading to its entrance. These buildings were smaller than the ring-groove houses of earlier phases, in which seldom more than one was occupied simultaneously. This change in house size and number must indicate a change in social organisation, but it is difficult to match it to any widespread pattern of social change. It may therefore reflect local circumstances, such as the impact of a form of partitive inheritance on the kin group. A single radiocarbon date, from a wood sample sealed by the bank, centred on the turn of the first and second centuries AD, while the material assemblage, including Roman pottery, a fragment of glass bracelet and a penannular brooch, together with less diagnostic native pottery and stone artefacts, was broadly consistent with the same chronological horizon.

Despite the evidence of radiocarbon dates, which somewhat erratically endorse a pre-Roman dating for the site at Long Knowe in Eskdale (Mercer, 1981b), it is worth recalling that here too the excavator believed that the final phase of occupation was represented by a shift in the domestic pattern from a pair of ring-groove houses to a group of five roundhouses of reduced diameter. The presence of paving within these buildings or leading to their entrances affords a further parallel with Boonies. Given the recognition of at least seven successive phases of construction of these buildings, it is possible that the site's occupation reflects a similar pattern of progressive social change, represented by the phenomenon of size reduction and increase of unit number of domestic houses.

Roman period artefacts were also found at Carronbridge within the area of the main ditched settlement (Enclosure A), including a melon bead, a fragment of glass armlet and a fine trumpet brooch (Johnston, 1994). On the basis of radiocarbon dates, this site evidently continued from probable pre-Roman origins through the second century AD and perhaps later, with metalwork finds of the ninth or tenth centuries indicating later activity in the area still. The parallel in plan between Carronbridge Enclosure A and Burradon, Northumberland, is deceptive. In both cases the double ditches are composite; at Burradon the early occupation comprised the larger enclosure, which was replaced by the smaller, inner enclosure, whereas at Carronbridge the sequence was apparently reversed, the larger being the later. The principal structure of the later occupation was apparently a ring-groove building with two, opposed entrances (Fig. 2.6, 8), a feature already noted in later pre-Roman Iron Age settlements in northern England and the Borders. The very close proximity of a Roman temporary camp argues for a break in the sequence of native occupation, which might have coincided with the change in enclosure plan.

The more recently excavated enclosure at Woodend in Annandale (Banks, 2000) also showed a pattern of superimposed ring-groove structures, ranging in size from 5 to 10 metres in diameter, with some structures underlying the bank and others external to the enclosure altogether. The largest building, 12 metres in diameter, was interpreted on the basis of phosphate analysis and soil micromorphology as a stock pen, though a 'byre-house' of the kind discussed earlier might leave similar evidence. Otherwise the remainder were all considered to have been domestic in function. Radiocarbon dates did not exclude the possibility of a pre-Roman origin for the site, but they clearly indicated that its occupation must have extended well into the Roman period. In view of this, the total absence of Roman finds, on a site that lay barely half a mile across the river Annan from the Roman road, is surprising and not easily explained. This, together with the poverty of the material assemblage, which comprised exclusively coarse stone artefacts, is hardly indicative of a high-status settlement. Despite the absence of preservation of animal bones, the excavator nevertheless assumed that pastoralism would have been dominant in the local economy, and we may wonder whether the site might not have served a seasonal purpose rather than as a permanent settlement.

In sum, the evidence from south-western Scotland, not yet as abundant as for the south-eastern Borders, indicates a considerable diversity of settlement continuing into the Roman period, with some notable regional differences in building fashions from those that have come to typify the Roman Iron Age on the basis of the south-eastern evidence. Major hillforts are not in evidence, allowing for the fact that Burnswark was apparently no longer in native occupation, and the evidence of field monuments might suggest a fragmented and less obviously hierarchical society than elsewhere. The continuing occupation of the hillforts at Castle O'er and Bailliehill, therefore, though not themselves major sites in terms of area enclosed, assumes greater importance. The number and quantity of finds of Roman material is limited, and distributed principally along the southern coastal settlements.

Lowland brochs

A distinctive element in the Roman Iron Age landscape of southern and south-eastern Scotland, and one that in many respects appears anomalous in a regional environment of small, enclosed homesteads, are the lowland brochs and duns. They appear even more anomalous in the light of recent research in the Atlantic north and west, where complex Atlantic roundhouses can now be dated from the second half of the first millennium BC, since the lowland examples were evidently occupied in the first and second centuries AD, on the basis of Roman material found in their domestic assemblages. How these monumental structures relate to the local settlement pattern is not at all clear. Whether they represent an influx of élite groups from the north and west, or whether they are a demonstration of native monumentality by already established local élites in the face of the threat from an alien Roman culture, is a matter of debate. At Edin's Hall, Berwickshire (Dunwell, 1999), the broch seemingly did integrate within a larger settlement, or at least one phase of that larger settlement (Fig. 7.4), and the same could be argued for Torwoodlee, Selkirkshire (Piggott, S., 1951). Structurally the Edin's Hall broch poses problems of reconstruction, having an internal diameter that exceeds that of the largest of the complex Atlantic roundhouses, so that roofing in a single span might be regarded as impractical, even in a region where supplies of suitable timber might have been more plentiful than in the broch's native environment. Whilst it may appear to conform to the archaeological typology, therefore, it is by no means clear that in this context it fulfilled the same role as a complex Atlantic roundhouse.

Site continuity from early Iron Age antecedents is not in dispute. At both Leckie, Stirlingshire (MacKie, 1982) and Fairy Knowe (Main, 1998) there was evidence of antecedent occupation, though this in itself does not minimise the radical nature of the structural innovation. Macinnes adopted a somewhat equivocal view: 'drystone architecture, of which brochs are perhaps the finest expression, was being adopted in southern Scotland independent of the brochs themselves'; but at the same time 'the various mural features characteristic of brochs were not duplicated in the local settlement record and the idea of these could indeed have derived from northern Scotland' (1984: 239). We are thus left with the tantalising question, was this an independent local development, or was the idea consciously borrowed from the Atlantic roundhouse cultural tradition? Stone building technology was certainly well established in lowland Scotland and the Borders both for the construction of hillfort defences and of the foundations of domestic roundhouses, but the scale of the brochs brings with it attendant technical complications that would have been unfamiliar to local engineers, as well as social implications for the use of the building.

Macinnes (1984) argued persuasively that, before the construction of the Antonine Wall, high-status sites including most conspicuously the lowland brochs and duns would have been the focus of a prestige goods economy, effectively monopolising the acquisition and redistribution of Roman goods in the buffer zone north of Hadrian's Wall. Their role would therefore have been not as fortified centres of native resistance to Romanisation

Figure 7.4 Edin's Hall, Berwickshire, broch and native settlement, air-photograph. Photograph from the John Dewar Collection, Royal Commission on the Ancient and Historical Monuments of Scotland, copyright reserved, reproduced by kind permission.

but as the primary points of contact with emissaries of the imperial power. This need not be considered incompatible with a chauvinistic display of monumental identity in the broch itself, since much the same combination of extravagant display of native identity and willingness to adopt the luxury goods of the foreign power characterised the native dynasties of south-eastern England on the eve of the Conquest. On the other hand, the total lack of Roman goods at Edin's Hall would seem to be at odds with this model, though the site otherwise is not lacking in material evidence for its high status. With the establishment of the northern frontier on the Forth–Clyde line, of course, this role of advantage would have been ceded, as the native population came into regular contact with the Roman military and civilian apparatus at first hand, without need of élite intermediaries.

The Antonine frontier

The Antonine Wall was occupied for a relatively short period in the mid-second century, so that a substantial impact on the rural landscape is hardly to be expected. In any event archaeological dating techniques would be hard pressed to identify sites or phases of native settlements that could be attributed quite so precisely to this short interlude. Once again, however, a civilian presence is attested in the immediate environs of forts, notably at Inveresk, which occupied an important strategic site by the shores of the Firth of Forth. Early excavations revealed structures of some sophistication, which could have been town houses or a *mansio*; more recent excavations (Thomas, G. D., 1988) uncovered a succession of simple timber-built rectangular structures of the Antonine period. Not far distant the site at Cramond has also yielded evidence of extensive extra-mural settlement. The presence of the military garrisons undoubtedly produced a demand for grain and other produce, though whether field-systems located by air-photography in close proximity to forts at Inveresk, Croy and Carriden, for example, are evidence of agricultural intensification at this time must be wholly speculative.

The Forth–Clyde line at the time of the construction of the Antonine Wall has some-times been regarded as a political, cultural and possibly even linguistic boundary among the native tribes (Maxwell, 1976). Stevenson (Stevenson, R. B. K., 1966: 28) certainly saw 'a real difference in population north and south of the Forth' on the basis of the distributions of glass bangles, dragonesque brooches and dress-fasteners. Nevertheless we cannot simply equate the occurrence of Roman-style artefacts in the archaeological record with 'Romanisation' without closer analysis of the nature of those exotic imports. For the ruling élite of the Maeatae control of Roman goods in the second century in the buffer zone beyond the frontier may have sustained a selective prestige goods economy in much the same way as has been proposed for the first-century lowland brochs. With the added factor of possible protectorate status providing security against potential aggression from Caledonian neighbours, they may have been replicating the policy of appeasement which some of the tribal élites of south-eastern England had adopted in the initial stages of the Conquest. But this is not to suppose that native identities were subsumed by Romanisation, or that traditional practices were abandoned. As Hunter has shown (Hunter, F., 1997) hoard deposition in the north-east proclaimed a distinctly native regional tradition, and Roman imports were not used except in a handful of graves. Presence or absence of artefacts from the record therefore depends not just upon their availability, but on what communities chose to do with them.

The fact that Roman policy reputedly preferred the creation of its frontiers along natural geographical or cultural and tribal boundaries need not mean that this was actually achieved in the case of either of the northern frontiers in Britain. The debate has even been refined to consider whether the Tay–Clyde line was closer to a meaningful cultural division between the native populations, and might thus have commended itself even from the time of Agricola (Maxwell, 1989: 125). Macinnes (1982) saw a distinction between the settlement patterns north and south of the Tay, and wondered whether the population of the Fife peninsula might not have had some Roman sympathies or alliance. Roman sources certainly speak of the hostile populations north of the Antonine frontier, first as Caledonians and Maeatae, thereafter as 'Caledonians and other Picti', though it is doubtful whether they were reliably informed on the actual tribal groupings within these populations. Identifying such groups archaeologically is likely to prove difficult in practice and questionable in principle, and is in any case bound up with the question of Pictish origins, to which we shall return later.

Traprain Law

In an era when hillforts were archetypally regarded as early Iron Age, Traprain Law (Fig. 3.7; Jobey, 1976) was regarded as the tribal capital of the Votadini of East Lothian, and, together with Eildon Hill North, its counterpart among the Selgovae of the Borders, was assumed to have been in occupation up to the eve of the Roman Conquest. As we have seen earlier, this view has been cast into doubt by modern excavation, which has indicated a sequence of occupation on both sites from the later Bronze Age through to the end of the Roman period at least, but with limited evidence for activity on either site in the pre-Roman Iron Age.

In the case of Traprain Law, recent excavations (Armit *et al.*, 1999a, 2000) have further undermined the older conventional progression of its defensive enclosures from a summit enclosure of around 10 acres, first to a 20-acre enclosure, then to 40 acres before reduction again in its final stage to a 30-acre enclosure (Feachem, 1963; Hogg, 1975). Only the rampart of the last phase, named the Cruden Wall after an earlier excavator and dated to the late Roman or sub-Roman period, survives as a significant bank, so that the proposed sequence was always tentative to a degree. In the event, the summit earthwork apparently never demarcated more than its northern side, being an addition in all probability of the later Roman period. Its faint extant alignment concealed a stone-founded wall, though scarcely one of defensive proportions, which in its incorporation of some stone of roughly dressed appearance and upright orthostats was not unlike the Cruden Wall, in construction if not in scale. The rampart of the 20-acre enclosure, sectioned in two places west of the summit, had evidently been a coursed, stone wall with rubble core, but had been reduced and levelled for the foundations of a succession of structures of the Roman Iron Age. Overlying levels included a fragment of second century samian ware, providing a *terminus ante quem* for the demise of the rampart, which thus could have been constructed and in use in the earlier Iron Age.

The recent campaign of excavation was directed only at the summit of the site, and did not in consequence investigate further the western plateau on which Curle and Cree in the early years of the twentieth century had discovered evidence of intensive late Bronze Age occupation and industrial activity. The importance of the recent work, however, is its demonstration of the fact that the summit of Traprain was extensively occupied, possibly from the late pre-Roman Iron Age, but certainly through the second and third centuries AD. The nature of the buildings, which may have included both circular and rectangular plans, was only sampled, but there is every probability that Traprain was occupied as an influential native centre in the Roman period, perhaps approximating most closely among such sites to an urbanised model.

We have already reviewed Macinnes' (1984) case for regarding lowland brochs like Torwoodlee, Fairey Knowe and Hurley Hawkin as centres of regional élites that in the later first and early second centuries AD controlled the import of prestige goods from the Romanised south in order to sustain their social status and political authority. Much the same role may have sustained the special status of Traprain Law. Macinnes (1989) detected contrasting patterns of distribution of Roman imports in the Antonine period from preceding and subsequent periods. Whereas earlier Roman imports had been geographically restricted to the south and east of Scotland, and apparently channeled through high-status sites, including Traprain itself, the Antonine distribution was much more extensive geographically, with finds occurring on a wider range of sites. At the same time, the artefacts in question tended to be of more everyday and mundane types. Traprain in this period nevertheless remained exceptional in the range, quantity and quality of types represented. In fact, Traprain continues to be exceptional into the later Roman period, when Roman products once again elsewhere became limited in their distribution. Macinnes' conclusion was that the currency of Roman finds in Scotland was greatest, and their distribution most extensive, in the limited periods of actual Roman occupation.

This would certainly accord with Fulford's view (1989: 87), based on coin evidence from the German frontier, that the *limes* there did indeed act as a significant barrier to trade or exchange with the 'buffer' zone or regions beyond.

A recent analysis has suggested a 'strong correlation between the typological spectra of the samian vessels from Traprain Law and several Roman military sites' (Erdrich *et al.*, 2000: 453). Yet taking the ceramic assemblage more generally it seems that Traprain, in common with most native sites, was attracted particularly to samian ware, rather than to other kinds of Roman pottery, a fact which tends to endorse the belief that samian was regarded as a prestigious acquisition. A similar correlation has been remarked for Traprain Law in the types of brooches present here and at military sites in Scotland (Hunter, F., 1996: 121–3), which, if sustainable, could certainly be regarded as an index of Romanisation, since it bucks the trend of native sites elsewhere. In general it seems that native communities favoured those brooches, like the trumpet, headstud and dragonesque types, which accorded more closely to their own taste in personal ornament and display (Hunter, F., 2001a: 300–1). One inference to be drawn from the analysis was that the army was instrumental in the supply of samian pottery to Traprain, most probably through markets based on the *vicus* at Inveresk. Whether or not the relative percentages of forms (Erdrich *et al.*, 2000: Table 1) absolutely demand this interpretation, the role of the local *vicus* in the supply of goods is probably more plausible than direct contact between the native centre and Roman *mercatores* or *negotiatores*. It is interesting in any case that the dining service of the native élite of Traprain Law had the same range of bowls, dishes and cups as their Roman suppliers in broadly the same proportions, since eating habits might be regarded as one of the more distinctive of cultural traditions. In sum, Traprain Law evidently enjoyed a status that was uniquely privileged in Roman Scotland in the Antonine period, and it was one which, from the continuing presence of Roman goods into the third century, would appear to have been maintained, albeit more remotely, after the Roman withdrawal to the Tyne–Forth frontier. Whether this resulted from a formal alliance of a quisling native aristocracy with the Roman authorities or from a mutual pact of co-existence, it evidently allowed Traprain Law to emerge at the end of the Roman occupation as a site of pre-eminence in south-east Scotland.

A final episode in the Roman Iron Age occupation of Traprain Law was the deposit in the early years of the fifth century of the famous hoard of late Roman silver plate (Curle, 1923). Among over a hundred pieces was a flagon embellished with *repoussé* ornament depicting biblical scenes, a pair of spoons bearing the *chi-rho* monogram and a wine-strainer with *chi-rho* and the name of Christ outlined in its perforations. These were plainly prestigious pieces, though their presence in the hoard need not imply commitment to Christianity on the part of the Traprain aristocracy. The assortment of flagons, bowls and miscellaneous fragments could have originated in various parts of the Empire, arriving in Northern Britain by a variety of different routes. Much of the silver had been cut up or folded ready for reprocessing, in a manner also noted in the later Norrie's Law hoard. It could represent loot from Roman sites in the political turmoil of the early fifth century. Equally it could have been an attempt to buy peace and neutrality from the tribal community based around Traprain, or even payment in kind for mercenary services. A votive deposit seems less probable, but should not be excluded (Hunter, F., 1997: 123, footnote 5).

Material culture: native and Roman

The evidence from native settlements, the role of lowland brochs in the distribution of prestigious Roman goods, and the special status of Traprain Law may all suggest that Roman goods were not uniformly available and were selectively received among native communities in Northern Britain. North of Hadrian's Wall the majority of Roman imports was evidently acquired by native communities during the period of Roman occupation, though this is more readily demonstrated in the case of samian ware and coins than for finds such as brooches, which are not so amenable to close dating. The presence of odd sherds of samian on native settlements, of course, is in itself hardly a meaningful measure of Romanisation. Hunter was surely right (Hunter, F., 2001a) to distinguish between occasional finds of a *single* type and those sites that yielded a greater *range* of types. Occasional finds may be no more than exotic curiosities or trophies, whereas the range of material displayed by Traprain Law, or the lowland brochs at Fairy Knowe, Leckie and Hurley Hawkin, suggests the adoption of new methods of food preparation and consumption, which may well signify a shift towards a 'Romanised' way of life.

The material types in question themselves display a degree of selectivity, being principally those associated with feasting and drinking or personal ornament, that is, the traditional obsessions of Iron Age Celtic societies in north-Alpine Europe that dictated the pattern of Greek, Etruscan and finally Roman imports. The third area of traditional interest, the warrior panoply and equestrian gear, is not directly implicated, though a degree of Romanisation might be attributed to the stylistic developments of native metalworking. The relative poverty of Roman goods from Scotland beyond the Roman frontier is commonly contrasted with the wealth of material in Denmark, a key difference being that the Danish material is largely derived from burial contexts in contrast to the surviving domestic debris of settlement sites in Northern Britain. The impact of Roman glass in Scotland, for example, is almost certainly underestimated in consequence by comparison with the lavish vessels known from Danish graves.

In fact, the distribution of Roman finds beyond the Antonine Wall is really quite extensive, especially on the east coast of Scotland. In the Inner Hebrides and Western Isles finds are fewer, despite an intensification of research in recent years. In these areas, Roman imports must have been exceptional and exotic, whether brought by Roman entrepreneurs or through down-the-line native exchange. There are fragments of Spanish amphorae from the Gurness broch, apparently attributable to the broch occupation (Hedges, 1987: II, 82) which suggests that even Orkney may have been directly or indirectly a recipient of Roman trading goods. The mechanisms whereby Roman material found its way into native contexts, therefore, were doubtless variable in different regions of Northern Britain, as indeed were the uses to which this material was put, and the relative esteem in which it was held. There can certainly be no automatic assumption that Roman products were held in awe by a native population that was technologically less advanced than the intrusive Roman culture.

The output and distribution of high-status native products at this time is instructive. Whereas much of the equestrian equipment of the first century AD, such as bridle-bits and terrets, appears to have been of southern derivation, and has for many years been regarded as evidence of the displacement of aristocratic refugees and their retinues in the face of Roman military annexation, two distinctive types of the later first and second centuries AD stand out as having an eastern Scottish distribution, with few outliers south of the Forth–Clyde line. These are the massive armlets and snake armlets (Fig. 7.5; MacGregor, 1976), ornaments whose sheer weight would have rendered them an uncomfortable extravagance for practical use, but which may well have satisfied the demands of chauvinistic ceremonial display. Massive armlets have been found between the Tweed and the Moray Firth, with just one outlier in Co. Down, which could easily be the product of diplomatic exchange. The snake bracelets are likewise concentrated in the east, between the Tay and the Moray Firth, with an outlier on Skye. A single example from a burial at Snailwell in Cambridgeshire, dating within the first half of the first century AD, has conventionally been regarded as the earliest, and therefore again indicative of an ultimate origin for the series in the south-east of Britain. Seeking stylistic antecedents, however, should not distract from the distinctive and markedly regional character of both types. Their distributions accord quite closely with the distribution of souterrains; indeed two of the massive armlets were found in souterrains. Yet other types, such as massive terrets, which are broadly contemporary, have on the one hand a more localised concentration in north-east Scotland and on the other a wider distribution extending through northern England with examples in the south-east and outliers in north Wales. It may be worth remarking that bridle bits are not found north of the Forth, almost certainly not because horses or horse teams were not harnessed, but because bridles of perishable material – leather or rope with wooden, bone or antler accessories – were used instead.

The distribution of Roman coins from native contexts north of Hadrian's Wall broadly conforms to the distribution of Roman finds in general. Nevertheless, we should question whether the distribution entirely represents an authentic product of antiquity. Casey (1984) showed, on the basis of fourth-century issues that can be assigned to specific mints, that the profile of coins from native sites other than Traprain Law was at total variance from the profile of mints of coins from military contexts, raising serious doubts regarding the reliability of many of the native finds. Robertson (1975) had already noted that the denominations represented on native sites were consistently too high to be explained as the product of market activity, that is, there was insufficient small change.

Notable hoards are found in native contexts, as at Falkirk, not far from the Antonine Wall, where 2,000 silver *denarii* spanning the first to early third century were discovered sealed in a coarse ware pot (Robertson, 1978). They may have represented the accumulated wealth of a native trader, or they may have been payments made to the native population as part of a non-aggression pact, in effect a political bribe like the later *danegeld*. According to Roman historians, the late second and early third centuries saw a good deal of turmoil on the northern frontier, and Cassius Dio (LXXV. 5) in a celebrated passage recorded the governor of Britain Lupus buying peace from the Maeatae for a great price. In fact there are over forty *denarius* hoards from Scotland dating from the Antonine period to the early third century, which may stand testimony to the Romans' desperate attempts to buy off trouble. One of the more northerly and most striking recent finds are the two hoards from Birnie, south of Elgin in Morayshire, actually buried within the precincts of a native settlement (Hunter, F., 2002). Here a settlement of timber roundhouses, probably dating from the early Iron Age, was occupied through the para-Roman period at least into the third century. The coin hoards, each containing just over three hundred *denarii*, were not the only evidence of 'Romanisation': Roman brooches included examples with silver and enamel inlay. Items of horse-gear suggested stylistic connections with southern Scotland. Attractive though the notion may be of payments for peace, we may wonder why natives from so far north were being bought

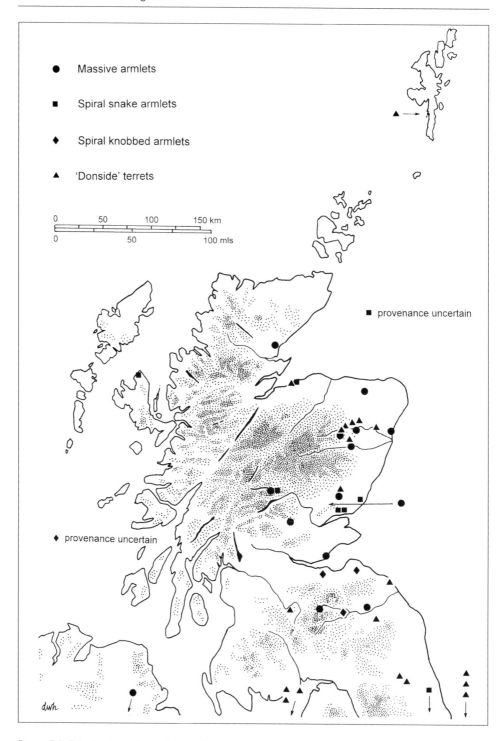

Figure 7.5 Distribution of massive armlets, snake-armlets, knobbed armlets and Donside terrets. Drawings by D. W. Harding, adapted from MacGregor (1976).

off with such relatively small sums, paid in coin that they had no monetary use for as currency or bullion. Was this simply their small share, passed down the line, of the peace dividend? Or was it brought by auxiliary veterans or deserters returning to exile in free Caledonia? Or could the hoards and personal ornaments have been acquired from maritime traders reaching the Moray coast? Would we have considered the idea of payments for peace, had not Cassius Dio sown the seed of that idea? By whatever agency it came, here was plunder or wealth to be extorted from the hapless custodians of the provincial frontier that would strengthen the fabric of native society and greatly enhance the status of its chieftains.

Some hoards of exotic material continue to defy simple explanation. The Helmsdale bowls (Spearman, 1990), from the coast of Sutherland, are of various probable dates and origin, in Britain or Continental Europe. Their date of manufacture probably lies within the second century, but several have been repaired and show signs of use over many generations, and it is probable that they were not finally deposited in the ground until the fourth century. They were evidently prestigious pieces, vessels, including strainers, associated with drinking and feasting, and would therefore have been attractive items for the chieftain's table. Whether he acquired them, directly or indirectly from southern neighbours, as booty or as a share in the price of peace, or whether diplomatic traders from the south still intermittently made direct seaborne contact with the tribes of the far north, remains a matter of speculation. That the Romans were familiar with northern waters from an early date is not in dispute, and there is every reason to suppose that any political tactic would have been exploited to secure the northern frontier from harassment.

Burial and ritual

We have already noted that cemeteries or individual burial sites are extremely rare in the pre-Roman Iron Age, and in the Roman period they remain equally scarce. Among those sites that may be positively or tentatively assigned to this period are a limited number of burials in stone-lined cists (Whimster, 1981: Appendix I, 2). Whether these represent the origins of a cist-burial tradition that became the dominant rite in eastern Scotland north and south of the Forth in the later Iron Age, ultimately in early Christian cemeteries, is arguable. In some of these burials Roman artefacts are found, though not necessarily as a result of a single or uniform set of circumstances. The burial at Merlsford in Fife (Hunter, F., 1996) contained, together with a fragmentary iron spearhead, a Langton Down brooch, the currency of which in Southern Britain was in the first half of the first century AD. It should therefore pre-date the Roman advance into Scotland, though it could have been several generations old when buried. The burials with Roman artefacts in the Hallow Hill cemetery in Fife (Proudfoot, 1996), on the other hand, though pre-Christian, plainly belong to the post-Roman period. Roman artefacts or, more especially, high-quality Roman artefacts may have been conserved in native contexts for generations after their original manufacture and currency, which is not to imagine that broken fragments of samian or Roman glass, as opposed to the intact vessels, were consciously cherished in the same way by gullible natives.

Other non-Roman sites from which Roman artefacts have been recovered include the Fife caves at Kinkell, St Andrews and Constantine's Cave at Crail, both investigated in the early years of the twentieth century. Both also produced evidence of industrial activity, iron working and antler working at Constantine's Cave and bone working at Kinkell.

A variety of Roman material spanning the second to fourth centuries was also recovered from the Sculptor's Cave at Covesea in Morayshire (Benton, 1931; Shepherd and Shepherd, 1995), where a long sequence of activity from at least the Bronze Age to the early historic period is attested. In all three rock carvings stand testimony to later use, small inscribed crosses at Kinkell and Constantine's Cave being indicative of early Christian activity, while the late Bronze Age ossuary and early historic symbol carvings at the Sculptor's Cave equally attest its long-lasting special status. Whether Roman objects had any symbolic or magical role in these contexts can only be guessed, but for societies in which domestic routines, industrial crafts and ritual activities were doubtless closely integrated these portable symbols of an alien identity may well have been seen as more than mere baubles.

The Celtic fascination with votive deposits in watery locations – lakes, rivers, marshes or wells – is widely attested archaeologically and in the documentary sources. Accordingly Piggott (Piggott, S., 1953a) was surely right in seeing a votive context for the deposits in Carlingwark Loch, Kirkcudbrightshire, at Blackburn Mill in Berwickshire and at Eckford in Roxburghshire, all attributed to the later first or second centuries AD. What distinguishes all three hoards is their combination of plainly Roman products with native Iron Age types, together with a number that are not definitively attributable to one rather than the other tradition, being common Romano-British types. Manning regarded Northern Britain in the Iron Age as technologically retarded (1972, 1981: 55–6), and cited the similarity between the contents of the hoards and assemblages from Roman forts on the frontier as evidence that the hoards were in some way related to the Roman military presence, perhaps as deposits by Celtic auxiliaries. Hunter (Hunter, F., 1997: 116–17), however, has pointed to recent metallographic and radiographic analyses that demonstrate clear differences between the hoards and military material, so that native deposit, albeit with exotic Roman items, seems confirmed.

What does perhaps warrant further consideration is the presumed unity of contents and character of the three hoards. Piggott's conclusion that all three were indicative of 'farmers, shepherds, peasants and the village blacksmith' (Piggott, S., 1953a: 8) seems unduly influenced by the substantial quantities of tools and domestic equipment in the hoards. Harness gear or vehicle fittings are present in all three hoards, and elsewhere would be accepted as high-status equipment rather than for farm carts and peaceable country pursuits. Certainly personal ornaments are decidedly absent, but cauldrons and cauldron chains, gridiron and tripod, would all normally be regarded as trappings for the aristocratic feast rather than for the use of shepherds and peasants. Finally, the presence of no less than eight tips of sword-blades from Carlingwark, together with a sizeable remnant of chain mail, must represent a martial component with very specific implications. Certainly Carlingwark, in the south-west, where Roman finds are less densely represented, stands apart in this respect from the other two hoards, which perhaps should not therefore be assumed uncritically to have been deposited in identical circumstances.

Souterrains

The study of souterrains in eastern Scotland in modern times owes its foundations to the fieldwork and publications of F. T. Wainwright, based particularly on his work at Ardestie and Carlungie in Angus and synthesised by him in a now seminal study (Wainwright, 1963). Though souterrains are conventionally thought of as coinciding in their distribution with the territory of southern Picts, Wainwright (1955: 91) was quite clear that chronologically their main period of use preceded the historical identification of Picts, and that they had probably fallen out of use by the third century. Furthermore, he understood from his own fieldwork that souterrains were essentially part of settlements. Whilst he no longer subscribed to the view that they served as dwellings, his conclusion that they were closely associated with habitation sites would still command general accord.

The souterrains of Fife, Perthshire and Angus are characterised by their curving plan, sometimes with side annexes, ranging between 15 and 25 metres in length, Carlungie 1 being exceptional at nearly 40 metres. The width of their passages varied from 1.5 to 3 metres, and whilst walls were sometimes partially corbelled inwards, as at Carlungie and Ardestie, or in the well-preserved example at Pitcur, Perthshire, it is unlikely that all could have been spanned with single, massive stone slabs. In the case of more complex examples, souterrains must have been the outcome of more than one episode of construction, and in the case of Pitcur (RCAHMS, 1994: 63) the principal annexe itself accords to the plan and proportions of many standard souterrains. Internal architectural details, such as door rebates and aumbreys in the walls at Pitcur and elsewhere, echo the techniques recognised in monumental stone buildings of Atlantic Scotland. The floor of the souterrain was frequently paved, and sometimes, as at Ardestie, a drain extended along its length. The passage could be up to 2 metres below the ground, but others were much shallower, and despite their name, it is clear that the roofs of many souterrains would have been visible above the ground. This factor is important since, together with their integral proximity to dwellings, it renders improbable the idea that souterrains could have served as defensive shelters, as Wainwright certainly recognised. Nevertheless, Warner (1980) made a cogent case for regarding Irish souterrains as refuges, so that purpose should not be discounted for some Scottish examples. Wainwright saw the classic souterrain as a stone structure, with stone walls and slabbed roof; where the latter was not in evidence archaeologically it was assumed they had been robbed in antiquity or early modern times. In fact, even without the evidence of the 'proto-souterrains' discussed earlier, the evidence from Newmill and elsewhere suggests that some roofs were of timber, in the case of those souterrains like Ardestie where the passage is less deeply founded, possibly being pitched rather than flat for extra headroom. Some souterrains had more than one entrance, perhaps, as Watkins (1980b) argued for Newmill, to permit access from within the integral dwelling as well as from outside.

Contrary to the popular equation with southern Pictland, souterrains are distributed quite widely in Scotland (Fig. 7.6), with significant local distributions in Deeside, Donside and the north-east, Caithness and Sutherland, the Northern Isles and in Skye and the Western Isles. The particular concentration in Angus and eastern Perthshire coincides broadly with the territory of the Maeatae, the tribe against whom Severus and Caracalla are reported as conducting punitive campaigns in the early third century. The coincidence of distribution between souterrains and Severan marching camps (Armit, 1999b: Illus. 4) is striking, but Armit adduced evidence to show that in fact souterrains appear to have gone out of use by the end of the second century, even if the settlements to which they were attached continued to be occupied. On the assumption that souterrains were storehouses for agricultural produce, he saw their increase in numbers in the second century as a native response to the need for provisions of the Antonine garrisons. Conversely, with the withdrawal of the army from the Antonine Wall in the

160s the market for agricultural surpluses disappeared, and with it the reciprocal source of prestige imports, with a consequent destabilisation of the native social order. Gillam (1958: 75) believed that the Maeatae in Antonine times had been in treaty relationship with the Romans, prompting Dio's claim (LXXV. 5. 4) that treaties had been broken by the insurrections of the late second and early third centuries. As for the idea of a souterrain abandonment horizon, several excavators have remarked that souterrains appear to have been deliberately infilled in a single episode of activity, rather than being allowed to silt up with natural weathering. This need not of course imply that this was a coterminous event occasioned by wider political or economic factors, and there is no direct evidence of Roman involvement in their abandonment. Close dating is perhaps more problematic, not so much because of the 'heirloom factor', which has possibly been over-rated, but because the lack of third and fourth century Roman material from settlement sites generally makes it more difficult to establish a close chronology for occupation of native sites of this period.

Armit's case for the particular use and abandonment of souterrains in Angus and eastern Perthshire should not obscure the fact that their distribution in Scotland is wider than that concentration, and their use, as indicated by radiocarbon dates from Cyderhall, Sutherland (Pollock, R., 1992) could begin significantly earlier than the Roman occupation. Analogous structures are known in south-western England and in Brittany, where they date from the early La Tène Iron Age, and from Ireland where most are assigned to the Early Christian period. There is no reason to suppose a single explanation for the function of souterrains, and there is certainly no reason to restrict their existence and use to the Roman horizon alone.

If the idea that souterrains were primitive dwellings is consigned to the realms of archaeological mythology, the most probable interpretation of their function is for storage, a northern counterpart to the pit-silos of southern England, which also were fancifully regarded as subterranean dwellings in an earlier age. Wainwright's belief that they provided shelter for livestock can hardly be sustained for any but the largest souterrains, and the current fashion for ritual interpretations is no more amenable to archaeological demonstration than are other possible functions. Storage itself implies a seasonal ritual, and the opening or closing of a souterrain would doubtless have been accompanied by special dedicatory or imprecatory ceremonies. Watkins favoured the idea of cereal storage, pointing to the broad coincidence between the distribution of souterrains and good-quality arable land in eastern Scotland. Barclay (1980: 206) argued that the cool environment of these underground cellars would have been especially suitable for the storage of dairy produce, to which might be added meat storage, or indeed related processes like the smoking and curing of meat or fish. The significant point, however, is that the capacity of the larger souterrains would have exceeded considerably the domestic requirements of the associated family household, and that some wider communal role is therefore implied. Whatever their function, it was evidently fulfilled by other means in the later Roman period, and even on the classic souterrain sites investigated by Wainwright evidence for occupation outlasts the use of the souterrains themselves, extending into the later Iron Age.

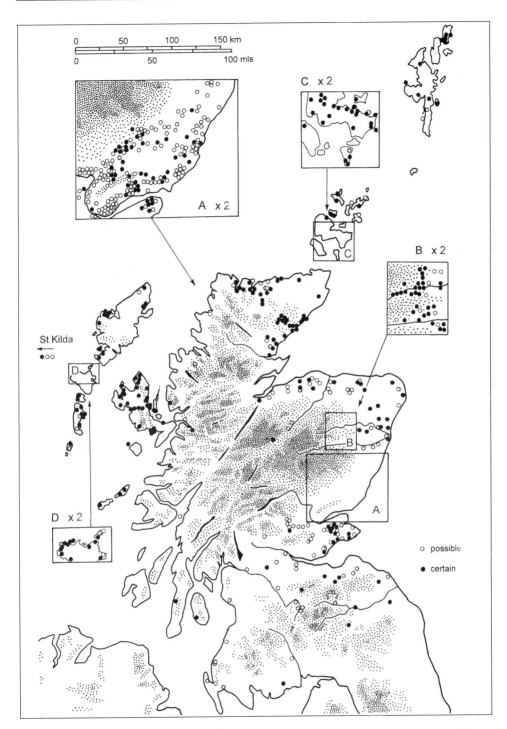

Figure 7.6 Distribution of souterrains in Northern Britain. Drawing by D. W. Harding, adapted from Armit (1999b), Miket (2002) and from NMRS.

Part 4

The later Iron Age

Chapter 8

The Borders and southern Scotland

Hillforts and homesteads in south-east Scotland

Whatever impact the relatively brief Roman occupation made upon native communities, it is unlikely to have changed radically the distribution of settlement or obliterated all memory of the importance of traditional centres, as the distribution of native sites in south-eastern Scotland and the Northumberland Cheviots shows. Where continuity is disrupted, it is more likely to have been the consequence of a shift in the focus of settlement well before the Roman advance, rather than the lasting consequence of short-term Roman repression. Tracing settlement continuity into the sub-Roman or post-Roman periods, however, is much more difficult, principally because of the lack of diagnostic assemblages in the period between the Roman occupation and the period of Anglian settlement.

As a starting point, we may revisit the classic sites of Hownam Rings and Bonchester Hill. At Hownam (Fig. 3.1) a stone-built house within the enclosure produced Roman material on its floor indicative of occupation in the later third and possibly fourth centuries. It was not clear whether this building was contemporary with the occupation of the homestead that straddled the former defences on the south-east side of the site, for which the dating evidence was more equivocal. Mrs Piggott nevertheless considered the possibility that occupation at Hownam extended into the post-Roman period. At Bonchester Hill (Fig. 8.1, 1) the intermediate circuit of enclosing ramparts, which unlike the earlier defences does not follow the contours of the hilltop, included a distinctive method of revetment of the front face of the rampart, using edge-set boulders with horizontal coursing above (Piggott, C. M., 1950: cutting X, Fig. 8). The excavator rightly observed that in Northern Britain this was a construction technique characteristic of post-Roman defences, and it closely resembles the method employed in cellular build-ings in Atlantic Scotland in the mid-first millennium AD. Whilst material evidence for later occupation at Bonchester was sparse, and the blue glass bead claimed as Dark Age would no longer be regarded as diagnostically post-Roman, a later re-use of the hilltop should certainly not be discounted.

At Woden Law (Fig. 8.1, 2) rampart 3, which again incorporated substantial boulders in its facing, is evidently not of the same design concept as enclosures 1 and 2, since its circuit ignores and blocks the entrance through the earlier three lines of defence. The apparently deliberate slighting of the Phase 2 earthworks having been equated with the Roman use of the site, the possibility of post-Roman activity represented by Phase 3 should not be discounted. At least one stone roundhouse was built into the inner face of this latest rampart. An even more radical redesign in plan and wall construction is evident

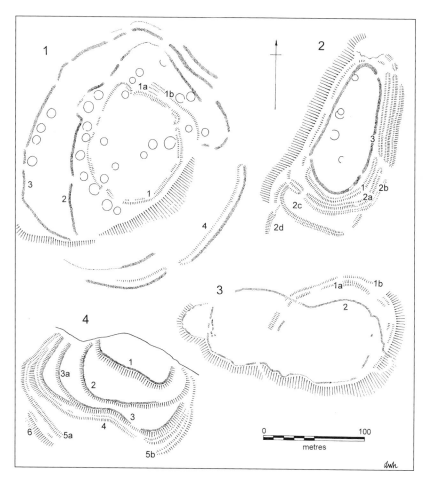

Figure 8.1 Hillforts with later Iron Age defences. 1, Bonchester Hill, Roxburghshire; 2, Woden Law, Roxburghshire; 3, Peniel Heugh, Roxburghshire; 4, Clatchard Craig, Fife. Drawings by D. W. Harding, adapted from RCAHMS (1956) and Close-Brooks (1986).

at Peniel Heugh, Crailing (Fig. 8.1, 3). Here the early Iron Age hillfort is succeeded on a markedly different orientation by a wall comprising an outer face of large orthostats with smaller masonry between, which, though exaggerated by some modern recon-struction, is plainly a different technique from that which characterises early Iron Age defences. There is little trace of occupation of either early or later enclosures, and in consequence no artefactual evidence of dating. On the basis of the wall structure alone, however, a post-Roman context would not be impossible. In fact, a good case could be made for selective test excavation aimed at retrieving samples for absolute dating in cases like Bonchester Hill and Woden Law, where discontinuity of plan suggests a different period of construction.

There are few instances in the Borders where artefactual evidence might support late occupation. At Crock Cleuch, Roxburghshire (Steer and Keeney, 1947), the ribbed annular brooch found on the floor of the principal house with sherds of 'native' pottery could well be from a post-Roman phase of occupation. The construction of the houses, with paved floor and central post, is distinctive, as are the massive orthostats incorporated into the outer face of the enclosure wall, and it is possible that the superficial evidence for Roman native occupation belies the longevity of re-use of such homesteads. At Huckhoe in Northumberland the rectangular buildings that represented the latest occupation on the site appear to have been successive to stone-built roundhouses of the Roman native occupation (Jobey, 1959). Apart from some scraps of fourth-century pottery, the site also yielded wheel-thrown wares that were assigned to the fifth or sixth centuries and compared to pottery from Dunadd, suggesting that occupation may have continued here uninterrupted into the post-Roman period.

The technique of boulder revetment noted at Bonchester Hill is also used in the construction of a pair of sub-rectangular enclosures linked by a trackway on Fasset Hill, Morebattle. One (RCAHMS, 1956: no. 678) has at least two periods of enclosure, the later extension embracing a building of rectangular plan. The neighbouring homestead likewise suggests structural modification, its surviving buildings being a sub-oval house and a smaller, probably secondary rectangular building. The trackway, and the cultivation terraces on the hill slopes beneath, are similarly revetted on their uphill side, and once again could represent a settlement pattern which continued from native Roman times into the early Mediaeval period. The settlement at Shank End, overlooking the Kale Water in Roxburghshire (ibid.: no. 310), likewise displays a combination of circular and rectangular house foundations, two adjacent to the enclosure wall and one more obviously overlying it within a secondary extension. The probability is therefore that rectangular plans were being adopted in the later Roman period on some native settlements, even if the tradition of circular building persisted among more conservative communities rather later into the sub-Roman period. Whether the two types of building were indeed in contemporaneous occupation on sites like Shank End, and if so, whether rectangular buildings served any different functions from their circular counterparts, is an issue that only research excavation can resolve.

The possibility that other forms of building characterised the sub-Roman or post-Roman phases in the region, as elsewhere in Scotland, is suggested by the secondary occupation at Park Law, Morebattle. Two sets of conjoined roundhouses in particular, in one group amounting to little more than small, oval outbuildings, suggest units akin to the cellular buildings of Atlantic Scotland in the early–mid-first millennium AD. At Staney Knowe, Morebattle (ibid.: no. 666), some stone-walled circular buildings likewise were conjoined, and Stevens noted in one a secondary structure, which he believed may have had a beehive roof. The presumed transition from round to rectangular, therefore, should not be allowed to obscure the possibility of other classes of domestic structure in the early historic period.

South-west Scotland and the kingdom of Rheged

Archaeological evidence for post-Roman settlement in south-western Scotland and Cumbria, in terms of sites that can be shown to have been occupied in that period, is minimal. In Cumbria the dearth of known settlements is probably owing to much the same reasons as impede the confident identification of non-fortified settlements of the earlier, pre-Roman Iron Age, principally the lack of diagnostic material assemblages. The alternative, that the region was largely depopulated in the early Iron Age, and again in the early historic period after a period of settlement intensification in the Roman period, is hardly credible. On the other hand the political disruption caused by the withdrawal of Roman authority, and episodes of raiding, and perhaps famine or plague, may have resulted in patterns of transient settlement that not surprisingly are hard to detect archaeologically. Major centres of settlement like Corbridge and Carlisle might be expected to have sustained some continuing occupation into the post-Roman period, but what evidence there is for this does not suggest a significant presence for very long, though doubtless the more substantial Roman buildings would have remained extant for some time. As in Northumberland and south-eastern Scotland, we might expect that some earlier Iron Age sites would have been re-occupied, though there are many fewer hillforts in the region that might have become the focus for local communities. There is some palynological evidence for woodland regeneration in the mid-first millennium AD, but the pattern does not consistently attest a decline in agricultural production, and it is probable that pastoralism continued to be an important and dominant element in the economy.

The regions flanking the Solway Firth are traditionally ascribed for the early post-Roman period to the kingdom of Rheged, ruled over in the later sixth century by the warlord Urien and his sons until the region was absorbed by the Anglian settlement of Cumbria and Dumfriesshire in the seventh century. The documentary evidence for Rheged is based upon Welsh genealogies and court poetry ascribed to Taliesin; other major sources such as Bede, the *Gododdin* or the *Anglo-Saxon Chronicle* make no reference to Rheged. Its existence, therefore, remains tentative and its location even more so. Smyth (1984: 20–21) included the Eden Valley, coastal Cumbria and Dumfriesshire in Urien's realm, extending Rheged's dominion as far as Catterick in the early post-Roman period. This was essentially the view of A. H. A. Hogg (1965), who saw Rheged as the early historic successor to the territory of the Brigantes, minus that region in its south-eastern quarter that was absorbed into the kingdom of Elmet. He even suggested that Burwens, one of the Westmorland series of 'native' sites, might have been the location of Urien's 'palace'. A more minimal view is taken by McCarthy, who points out that twenty-five years of careful, selective excavation in Carlisle has failed to produce any evidence of occupation there in the sixth century in the form of Mediterranean or Gaulish imports of the kind represented at Whithorn. Accordingly he places Rheged in the Rhinns of Galloway, whilst acknowledging that there is currently no archaeological evidence to support the linguistic identification of Dunragit, between Glenluce and Stranraer, as a stronghold of an early post-Roman kingdom of Rheged.

The one outstanding centre of early post-Roman occupation is the Mote of Mark, on the north side of the Solway Firth in Kirkcudbrightshire (Laing, 1973a, 1973b). Occupying a rocky knoll overlooking the Urr estuary, the Mote of Mark was evidently a site of importance disproportionate to its small size. Sub-trapezoidal in plan, it measures some 60 metres by 30. It was enclosed by a timber-laced rampart, now much denuded, which was destroyed by fire, resulting in traces of vitrification, and dismantled in the late sixth or seventh century AD. Within the interior Alexander Curle in 1913 had uncovered a rich assemblage of metalworking debris, including moulds for penannular brooches and for a mount decorated with interlace. This material could not be directly associated with the timber-laced defences, but it was argued that production was unlikely to have continued after the site's abandonment. Sherds of imported D-ware and E-ware, and Rhenish glass indicate long-distance connections with Continental Europe. The later occupation of the site apparently yielded Anglian finds, including two runic inscriptions. The metalworking assemblage uncovered in 1913 was not stratigraphically linked to the defences, but Laing's excavation of 1973 demonstrated that metalworking was contemporary with the early occupation, which, on the basis of a single radiocarbon date he assigned to the late sixth or early seventh centuries. The possibility of interlace ornament at this date was disputed by Graham-Campbell (Laing, 1975b; Graham-Campbell *et al*., 1976), but the early construction of the timber-laced rampart received endorsement from a very consistent set of dates resulting from further excavation in 1979 (Longley, 1982). The dilemma in part hinges on the assumption that the destruction of the defences must have been at the hands of intrusive Anglians, expanding westwards around AD 638, according to documentary sources. The possibility that this expansion took place at an earlier date, or that the destruction was through some undocumented agency at a later date, or indeed that metalworking continued on the site after its defences had been slighted, would all relieve the apparent conflict between archaeological and historical evidence, neither of which in this instance seems to be beyond debate.

Nuclear and citadel forts

The concept of the nuclear fort was first advanced by R. B. K. Stevenson (1949b), and has become synonymous with princely centres of the early historic period. The defining characteristic of the nuclear fort, as represented by the type-site at Dalmahoy, Midlothian (Fig. 8.2, 4), was its summit citadel, from which a series of subordinate enclosures looped out around lower plateaux to create a hierarchy of enclosures, determined largely by the naturally craggy topography of the site. The choice of site was evidently dictated by the requirement for this hierarchical relationship between citadel and subordinate enclosures. Since this was not a determining criterion in the location of earlier Iron Age fortifications, it is hardly surprising that some of the more distinctively precipitate sites, like Dundurn and Dumbarton Rock, appear to have had minimal if any previous history of occupation in the later prehistoric period. Though the concept of a nuclear fort could have been a unitary one from the outset, achievement of the concept in tangible circuits of enclosure may have come about progressively over time. This was demonstrated archaeologically by Alcock at Dundurn, and apparently was also the case at Dunadd (Fig. 8.2, 3; Lane and Campbell, 2000).

In his study of Pictish fortifications Feachem (1955) added a related category of 'citadel forts', in which the citadel is surrounded by outer ramparts, generally at a lower contour, but not linked together in the spider's web of the nuclear forts. This form was less obviously distinguished from earlier Iron Age hillforts with outworks; indeed, Feachem examined several sites where a citadel had seemingly been built within the derelict remains of early Iron Age forts, the walls of which he supposed were either re-used or served as a quarry for building materials.

Almost certainly of post-Roman date, on account of its extensive use of robbed Roman masonry, is the citadel and adjacent outworks on Rubers Law, Cavers, Roxburghshire (Fig. 8.2, 2). Here both the citadel wall and the wall surrounding the plateau to the south were of substantial proportions, incorporating the use of large boulders in their facing, and together with lengths of wall flanking the main approach to the summit from the north-east may be regarded as part of a unitary construction. The outermost wall (E), on the other hand, enclosing nearly 3 hectares around the contours of the hill, shows no sign

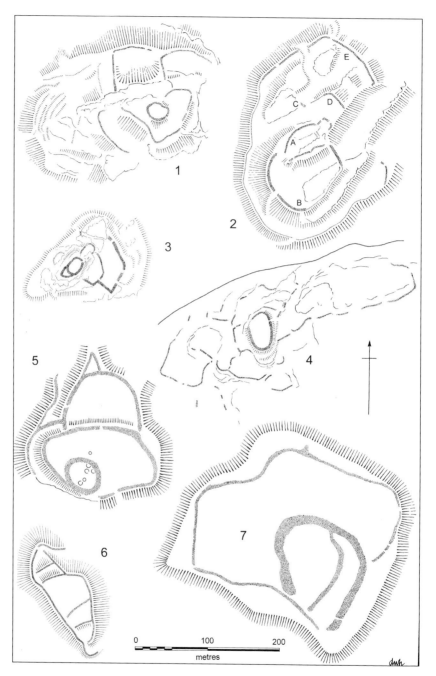

Figure 8.2 Nuclear and related forts, plans. I, Dundurn, Perthshire; 2, Rubers Law, Roxburghshire; 3, Dunadd, Argyll; 4, Dalmahoy, Midlothian; 5, Moncrieffe Hill, Perthshire; 6, Moat Knowe, Buchtrig, Roxburghshire; 7, Humbleton Hill, Northumberland. Drawings by D. W. Harding, adapted from Alcock *et al.* (1989), RCAHMS (1956), Lane and Campbell (2000), Stevenson (1949b), Wainwright (1955) and Waddington (1998).

of re-used Roman stonework, and may date from the earlier Iron Age. The presence of a Roman signal station on the site has been inferred not only from the re-used Roman masonry, but from the discovery of Roman finds on the site, notably the hoard of bronze vessels found in 1863. At Moat Knowe, Buchtrig (Fig. 8.2, 6; Fig. 8.3), by contrast, an early historic dating is based solely on the similarities in plan to the nuclear prototype, the central summit having two lower plateaux enclosed on its north and south sides. Again the walls of both summit citadel and lower courts are sufficiently substantial to suggest that they were part of a contemporary and unitary design. In the summit enclosure the use of edge-set slabs could certainly be matched in building techniques of the early historic period elsewhere. The fort on the summit of Chatto Craig, also in Hownam parish, is closer in plan to a citadel fort than a nuclear fort, but on the basis of its layout and use of outcropping terrain has been identified as potentially of the post-Roman period (RCAHMS, 1956: no. 305). In Northumberland Humbleton Hill (Fig. 8.2, 7) likewise has the prospective appearance of a citadel fort, though its date has yet to be confirmed by excavation, and Jobey (1965) was far from convinced of its candidature as a post-Roman site.

In the south-west of Scotland a possible contender for a small, nuclear fort, or perhaps an early Iron Age citadel around which outworks were added during an early historic re-occupation, is the site at Trusty's Hill, Anwoth (Thomas, A. C., 1960). Traces of vitrification in the citadel wall encouraged a belief that it was early Iron Age, but that could equally be later. Dating evidence from excavation was sparse, but activity in the sixth or seventh centuries AD is indicated by the carving on outcropping rock beside the southern entrance to the citadel of Class I symbols, a rare example in southern Scotland. In Nithsdale the prominent defences on Tynron Doon, a site occupied from the early Iron Age and through the Mediaeval period to the sixteenth century, almost certainly conceal an early historic phase of settlement. The summit citadel is flanked to north-east and south-west by natural plateaux that have been reinforced with ramparts of stone and earth. The evidence for early historic occupation includes part of a gold filigree bracteate of sixth–eighth century date, indicative of Anglian contacts.

Outside Scotland, forts with similar layout to the 'nuclear' type have been identified in North Wales and the Isle of Man. At Cronk Sumark, Man, the inner of two ramparts that loop around the summit citadel has yielded vitrified material, though the construction and occupation of the site remain undated (Champion, S., 1995).

A salutary lesson on the dangers inherent in interpreting field monuments on the basis of surface morphology, however, was provided by excavations in the 1960s and again in the 1980s at the Dunion, Roxburghshire, a site that was assigned on the basis of surface survey to a Dark Age date (RCAHMS, 1956: no. 33; Rideout et al., 1992). Neither campaign yielded any evidence whatsoever for construction or occupation in the early historic period, but they did demonstrate fairly conclusively, on the basis of radiocarbon and thermoluminescence dating as well as artefactual evidence, that the site was occupied in the closing centuries of the pre-Roman Iron Age, perhaps extending into the early Roman period. The description of one of its sections of rampart certainly accords with the technique of construction that we have identified potentially as post-Roman elsewhere. The use of massive boulders, up to a metre in height at one point (Rideout et al., 1992: 82), on top of which horizontal coursing could well have been added, might well have encouraged this view. If this is no longer tenable in the face of excavated evidence, then the case for regarding the site as an important local centre in the earlier Iron Age is

(a)

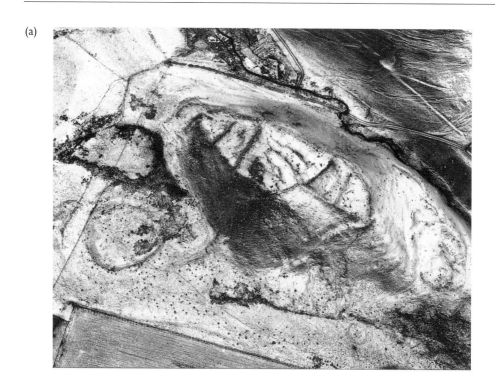

(b)

Figure 8.3 Later Iron Age hillforts in southern Scotland. a, Moat Knowe, Buchtrig, Roxburghshire, air-photograph; b, Mote of Mark, Kirkcudbrightshire. Photographs by D. W. Harding.

correspondingly enhanced, along with the possibility that the hierarchical arrangement of enclosures, exemplified most notably in the nuclear forts of the early historic period, may too have had its origins in an earlier social order.

Crannogs

Crannogs have been recognised in the lochs of south-western Scotland since the pioneer days of lake-dwelling research, among which Buiston and Lochlee in Ayrshire, extensively reported by Robert Munro (1882), are conventionally regarded as classic examples of early historic settlement in the region. These, together with a concentration of sites in the lochs of Dumfries and Galloway, fall within Jon Henderson's (1998a) South-Western or Solway–Clyde distribution. Some, like Milton Loch I and II and Loch Arthur have radiocarbon dates indicating occupation in the later prehistoric period. Others, like Milton Loch III and perhaps Barean Loch on the basis of radiocarbon dates might be assigned to the early historic period (Crone, 1993). Of those reported by Munro, the Black Loch at Inch (formerly Loch Inch Cryndil), yielded a composite bone comb with ring-and-dot ornament, suggesting occupation in the later first millennium AD. Though commonly attributed to the early historic period, Lochlee produced little evidence of occupation between the Roman Iron Age and the ninth century AD. Buiston crannog (Crone, 2000) is unique in having both radiocarbon dates and an abundance of artefactual evidence supporting its attribution to an early historic horizon.

In fact, Buiston also has the benefit of dendrochronological dating, which not only qualifies the evidence of radiocarbon values within a problematic range on the calibration graph, but also permits much greater precision in the assessment of the duration and structural episodes of its principal buildings. The initial construction of the artificial mound at Buiston evidently took place in the first or second centuries AD, but virtually nothing, structural or artefactual, survived from this period of use. The subsequent occupation may now be assigned to a relatively short occupational sequence between the later sixth and mid-seventh centuries, though the removal of 'thirteen cart-loads' of material from the site when the loch was reclaimed in the late nineteenth century (Munro, 1882: 190) may have destroyed the latest occupation levels. Unlike some crannogs that artificially reinforce a natural rocky outcrop on the loch bed, Buiston had been built on an island of stony rubble, timber, brushwood and turf on the loch sediments, so that its foundations were inherently unstable from the outset. Nevertheless, the successive surrounding fence-lines of substantial stakes of the later occupation were not intended to buttress the mound, but served as a stockaded perimeter for the compound. The technique of tying the external stockade with radial timbers into the crannog mound and the construction of the perimeter walkway are closely paralleled at Lochlee, some 10 miles distant from Buiston, leading Crone to suggest that the two settlements may have been the work of related, contemporary communities (Crone, 2000: 106). Tempting though this idea might be, the artefactual remains from Lochlee, with the exception of the much later ring-pin, provide little encouragement for believing that its construction was later than the first or second centuries AD. As regards access, there was no causeway at Buiston leading from the shore to the crannog, which must therefore have been approached by boat. Log-boats were recovered both from Munro's and the more recent excavations.

A further important outcome of the 1989–90 excavations was the reappraisal of the evidence for a principal oval house occupying with its walkway the entire island (Munro,

1882: Pl. iv, and reproduced in most subsequent studies, Fig. 3.12, 2). Crone argued that the outer wall of this structure was in fact one of the succession of perimeter stockades, and that the internal roundhouse was therefore not nearly as large as formerly inferred, being in its developed plan no more than 8 metres in diameter. The house itself was of stake-wall construction with no surviving evidence of daub, so that organic cladding of the wattle walls is inferred. An internal hearth of rectangular or trapezoidal plan, securely founded in a clay floor, was rebuilt on several occasions. Evidence for joinery was well preserved in the sodden conditions of the crannog, including sill-beams into which panels of wattling for internal partitions were jointed. Closest in technique of construction to the Buiston houses are those from Northern Irish sites like Moynagh Lough, but the much greater size of the broadly contemporary Irish sites is such as to suggest their use by a rather different social unit. On the basis of Munro's plan, Bersu (1977) had pointed to Buiston and Locklee as the closest analogies for his multi-ringed houses at Ballacagen and Ballanorris in the Isle of Man, dated by him to the early centuries AD, but possibly still in occupation somewhat later. In detail, however, the Manx sites are singular, and any relationship is hardly close.

Evidence for the economic basis of the Buiston community included barley, oats and flax, though it was not possible in the case of the latter to determine whether it was grown for oil or for textile fibre. The presence of rotary querns indicates the processing of grain, and the discovery of two ards endorses the probability that the occupants were engaged in cereal cultivation. The faunal evidence was limited, but includes cattle, sheep and pigs; two wooden churn lids and items of equipment ancillary to weaving indicated a range of secondary products. Natural resources like nuts, fruits and berries were exploited. Metalworking was carried out on a limited scale, witnessed by stone ingot moulds and three crucibles, but in quantities that scarcely match those of major centres of production like Dunadd or the Mote of Mark. External contacts are nevertheless testified by a range of imported goods, including E-ware vessels, in which it is possible that exotic spices and other goods may have arrived. One contained traces of dyer's madder, a prized source of purple dye not then native to Britain. Several other items, notably the hanging-bowl, annular brooch and coin (an ancient forgery) all derive from an Anglo-Saxon source. Other prestigious goods from Munro's investigations included two gold spiral finger-rings.

What all this amounts to in terms of the status of the Buiston crannog settlement, or by inference of others of comparable size and date, remains equivocal. Evidence for metalworking and the quality of the material assemblage argue for a high-status community, but there is little in the structural remains or in the evidence for food-producing economy, to suggest that this was more than the homestead of a wealthy farming family, assuming that the site was occupied permanently rather than seasonally. The scale of the site does not equate with the major Irish crannogs, such as Lagore or Moynagh Lough, which are nearly four times the size of Buiston, or Ballinderry 2, which is ten times larger in area (Crone, 2000: 164). Neither does the range and wealth of its material assemblage match the Irish royal crannogs like Lagore and Ballinderry. In a hierarchy of settlement, Buiston, therefore, might rank in a second tier, and as the homestead of a family of some status rather than as a community settlement.

Long-distance trade

There can be little doubt that, with the final breakdown of Roman administration in Britain, the political geography of Northern Britain would have been in a state of dynamic change, with rival kingdoms vying to assert their authority. One means of asserting that authority was through the control of imports and external communications, and there is considerable archaeological evidence for such external trade and exchange along the western seaways between the fifth and seventh centuries, in the form of imports of pottery, glass and other exotic items. The nature of these imports has been much debated, whether the product of mercantile trade, of cabotage along the western seaways, of imports controlled by and thence redistributed from key centres, or simply the scattered outcome of a handful of merchant venturers. The products themselves are almost as much an issue of debate as are the goods offered in reciprocation. It is, however, on the pottery and glass containers that archaeological attention has conventionally focused.

Imported pottery of the post-Roman period was classified many years ago as a series A–F (Thomas, A. C., 1959). Two groups of imports have been identified, overlapping and successive in their chronological currency, the first deriving from the eastern Mediterranean or north Africa, the second from sources in western Continental Europe (Lane, 1994; Campbell, 1996a, 1996b). A major component among the imports are amphorae, classified as B-ware with particular sub-groups resulting from various centres in the eastern Mediterranean over a considerable span of time. Their association with a class of tableware known as Phocaean Red Slipware allows the dating of these imports to south-western Britain to be assigned to a bracket from the later fifth to the mid-sixth centuries AD. The overall distribution of these wares, with concentrations in southern Spain and in south-western Britain, rather than a gradual fall-off in density of distribution with distance from the Mediterranean source, looks like targeted trade. This has prompted the suggestion that Mediterranean products – wine, olive oil and perhaps more exotic items such as perfumes, spices and silks – were being introduced in exchange for tin, and perhaps lead and silver, from south-western Britain. In this model, any examples from Ireland or western Britain, such as the amphorae sherds from Whithorn or Dumbarton Rock, would thus be the result of secondary distribution from south-western Britain.

In Northern Britain it was the Continental imports (Fig. 8.4) that appear in greater quantities, though in absolute terms these remain fairly modest. E-ware, comprising coarse-gritted white or grey ware jars, bowls, beakers and occasionally jugs, has a much denser distribution across Ireland and south-west Scotland, with some secondary transmission to east coast sites between the Forth and the Tay. There is a marked absence of instances of E-ware in North Wales, Lancashire and Cheshire or in Cumbria, suggesting that the Dee, Mersey or Morecambe Bay were not significant ports of entry at this time. Its Continental source is much debated, but must have been in west-central France around the Loire or the Charente regions. E-ware was conventionally regarded as kitchenware, but more recent analysis has shown little evidence of its use in cooking (Campbell, 1996a). Instead, it was evidently used for the import of exotic goods, such as plants used for dyes, and possibly also for exotic spices and herbs like coriander and dill.

Glass too, principally conical beakers but occasionally bowls, was imported from production centres in western France or the Rhineland. A distinctive element of the high-quality beakers is the decoration with opaque white trailed ornament. These glass vessels are sometimes associated with late sixth century D-ware, which is very rare in Britain,

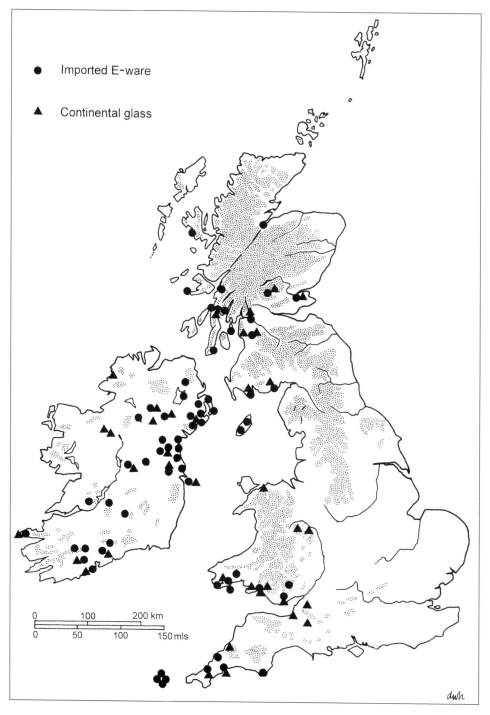

Figure 8.4 Distribution of E-ware and Continental glass in Britain and Ireland. Drawing by D. W. Harding, adapted from Alcock (2003), Lane and Campbell (2000), Campbell (1996a).

and in Britain was more probably introduced together with the majority of E-ware imports in the seventh century. Whether glass was imported as whole vessels, or as cullet for recycling in other ornaments, has been much debated, but recent research supports the belief that some at least arrived as intact vessels (Campbell, 1996a: 93; 2000).

We should of course consider these imports in the context of early historic trading and exchange patterns. Unlike the Anglo-Saxon world, there is no evidence in the Celtic north and west for trading emporia or a money-based market economy. Imports would therefore most probably have been controlled by major centres under royal patronage, or possibly by monastic communities with their own long-distance connections. Campbell (1996b) has shown how sites whose royal status is attested by documentary sources appear to have exercised some control not only over imports, but also over the production of personal jewellery or glass and other precious or prestigious goods. Other sites, not affirmed as royal in documentary sources, may nevertheless have enjoyed proximate status in a hierarchy of control over production and exchange. Sites like Dunadd, the Mote of Mark and Whithorn would evidently fall into the category of high-status centres in this model, with sites like Buiston crannog perhaps ranking in a second order. Changes nevertheless are evident from the sixth into the seventh centuries, with the Anglian expansion and the advent of monasticism doubtless among other factors. The redistribution process, as Mytum (1992: 266) has underlined, may serve to endorse relationships with social peers, or may affirm asymmetrical relationships with a system of clientship. The role of ecclesiastical foundations in this network is still not altogether clear, though the sacramental need for wine is self-evident. The influence of abstract ideas or artistic styles from both Mediterranean and Continental sources is also archaeologically difficult to estimate. What was being exported in exchange for imported goods is again hard to assess, though it is easy to fall back on the staples of the pre-Roman Iron Age, reported by Strabo and others, raw materials, hides and furs, and slaves. The traditional story of St Patrick, a Romanised Briton who was transported to Ireland by slave-traders before escaping captivity to begin his mission, is doubtless just one enduring image of the widespread practice of slave-trading in the centuries following the collapse of Roman rule.

The archaeology of early Christianity

The earliest archaeological evidence for Christianity in southern Scotland pre-dates the Columban mission by more than a century. It was in fact an extension or survival of Roman Christianity, and is conventionally associated with the establishment of Ninian from Carlisle as bishop at Whithorn. The so-named Latinus stone from Whithorn (Fig. 8.5), dating to the mid-fifth century, has been conventionally regarded as a memorial stone, though Charles Thomas has argued that it commemorated the establishment here of a *sinus*, 'a place of refuge, care or shelter', and thus figuratively a church. He insisted, however, that there was no implication of the establishment of a monastic settlement here in the fifth century (Thomas, A. C., 1992). The more recent suggestion (Craig, 1997) that the *si(g)nus* refers to the *chi-rho* symbol at the head of the inscription is ingenious, but takes liberties with the Latin spelling. Slightly later are the inscriptions from Kirkmadrine, one of which commemorates *sacerdotes*, priests or bishops, who may have had links with the Gaulish tradition of St Martin of Tours, or who may even have been monastic missionaries. The archaeological evidence for an early monastic centre at

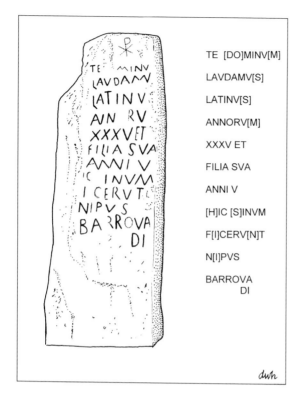

TE [DO]MINV[M]

LAVDAMV[S]

LATINV[S]

ANNORV[M]

XXXV ET

FILIA SVA

ANNI V

[H]IC [S]INVM

F[I]CERV[N]T

N[I]PVS

BARROVA
DI

dwh

Figure 8.5 The Latinus stone, Whithorn, Wigtownshire. Drawing by D. W. Harding.

Whithorn is still highly speculative, though the quantity of imported pottery and glass, together with evidence for metalworking and agriculture, plainly points to a community of some importance on the site from the early sixth century. Hill's excavations (Hill, P., 1997) certainly located sections of enclosure ditch, and the progressive expansion of the site to include secular buildings and cemetery seems plausible, though the fundamental premise, that the *monasterium* itself was on the crest of the hill, and inaccessible or destroyed beneath the later church buildings, is archaeologically undemonstrable. The rectangular or sub-rectangular buildings left minimal traces of their foundations, and were identified from the hollows and platforms on which they were built. Averaging around 8 metres by 5, their walls were of wattling based variously on stake-holes or narrow sill-beams, some with internal divisions and hearths. Two distinct forms of interment characterised the earlier cemetery at Whithorn, lintel-graves, in which the grave is lined and capped with stone or timber, effectively using the same technique as the long-cist cemeteries north and south of the Firth of Forth, and log-coffin burials, in which massive split tree trunks were used to contain the extended inhumation. The transition from the former to the latter rite, it was suggested (ibid.: 70), may have corresponded to a significant change in status of the communities concerned.

Long-cist cemeteries (Fig. 8.6) are widely distributed in south-eastern Scotland, predominantly south of the Forth but with a significant number in coastal Fife, and are broadly assigned to the middle or later first millennium AD. The form of burial, an extended inhumation in a long, stone-built cist, however, is itself hardly diagnostic; indeed Stevenson's verdict was that 'long cist graves seem to be part of a wider

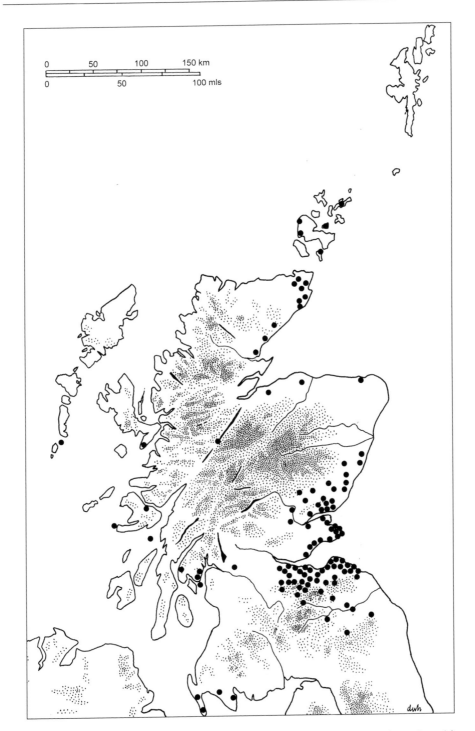

Figure 8.6 Distribution of long-cist cemeteries in Scotland. Drawing by D. W. Harding, adapted from Proudfoot (1996).

phenomenon over much of late Roman and sub-Roman Europe' (Stevenson, R. B. K., 1952: 110). The construction of the graves showed little variation, though some were marginally wedge-shaped or expanded around the shoulders to a conventional coffin shape. In some instances the floor of the cist was paved, in others not; likewise the form of covering slab has sometimes been suggested as a basis for sub-division. The graves were sometimes seemingly grouped into clusters, or more strikingly ordered into rows or alignments, which seems to indicate social or community affiliations. Almost invariably the graves lack grave-goods, which has generally been taken as an indication that they were Christian, though burials of the preceding Iron Age, like those at Broxmouth, East Lothian, generally lack grave-goods too. Their orientation was commonly east–west or veering from north-east to south-east, with the head at the west end. Most commentators have emphasised that this is no guarantee that they were Christian interments, since pagan cemeteries not infrequently adopted the same orientation. Nevertheless, it is generally assumed that long-cist cemeteries were predominantly Christian, and in some later instances are patently so from their site associations.

For the early discoveries like Parkburn, Midlothian (Henshall, 1956), dating evidence was minimal, though the excavator's assessment of use from the fifth to eighth or perhaps ninth centuries AD hardly requires revision in the light of subsequent research. The cemetery near the Catstane at Edinburgh Airport, first discovered in the 1860s and further excavated in 1977 (Cowie, 1978), produced several radiocarbon dates, indicating that it may have been among the earliest of the long-cist cemeteries, beginning perhaps as early as the later fifth century, but more probably in the sixth. The calibrated range at two sigma spans the later fifth to mid-seventh centuries (Dalland, 1992: 203–4; Greig *et al.*, 2000: 610). The dedicatory inscription on the Catstane itself has been assigned on epigraphic grounds to the late fifth or sixth centuries AD (Rutherford and Ritchie, 1974), so that in this instance archaeological and epigraphic evidence appears to converge. Three radiocarbon dates from a smaller long-cist cemetery at Longniddry, East Lothian, yielded a calibrated span almost identical to the Catstane cemetery.

Most recent of the long-cist cemeteries in the Lothians to be investigated is that from Thornybank, Dalkeith (Rees, A., 1997, 1999, 2002). The majority of stone-lined, long-cist burials were arranged in orderly rows in the northern half of the cemetery, whereas some thirty-eight simple graves, some of which produced positive traces of wooden or leather coffins, were discovered in irregular, small groups in the southern sector. Unfortunately the great majority of the thirty radiocarbon dates from the site, which span the fourth to seventh centuries AD, came from stone-lined cist graves, so that the chronological relationship between the two rites of deposition remains unclear. Two of the simple graves, however, were enclosed by shallow square ditches, in one case with a low cairn over the burial. Another simple grave had four postholes at its corners, suggesting uniquely in Britain some form of mortuary structure over the grave. The possibility that the simple burials and square-ditched enclosures derive from an earlier tradition, perhaps ultimately from earlier Iron Age practices, might be suggested by the presence on the site of a ring-groove house, a pit-alignment and a length of palisade, but necessarily remains unproven.

During the seventh century the so-called Petrus stone, commemorating a church dedicated to St Peter at Whithorn, combines a local tradition of cross carving with a dedication probably attributable to Northumbrian influence (Hill, P., 1997: 38), and by the eighth century, as implied by Bede, Whithorn had been taken over as a Northumbrian bishopric. Excavations revealed a sequence of structures, probably not the only group within the redesigned complex, the focus of which was a pair of timber oratories, subsequently combined to form a single, bicameral timber church. Adjacent to it was a burial chapel which boasted stone foundations and window glass of the kind employed in the Northumbrian monastic sites of Monkwearmouth and Jarrow. Parallel to these buildings beyond the inner enclosure wall was a line of timber halls, which the excavator interpreted as guest quarters. Beyond these again were smaller rectangular buildings that displayed close structural parallels with timber buildings from Church Close, Hartlepool (Daniels, 1988). The presence of Anglo-Saxon coins at Whithorn reinforces the Northumbrian connection in the eighth and ninth centuries.

Another important Anglian monastic settlement at Hoddom in Dumfriesshire may also have had earlier ecclesiastical associations. This extensive site, enclosing 8 hectares in a bend of the river Annan with bank, palisade and ditch, also encloses the old parish church, the origins of which may be traced to the eighth century. Fragments of monumental sculpture, recorded locally over many years, included some pieces that were compared to material from Hexham and Dacre of the eighth century (Cramp, 1960). Rescue excavation in advance of gravel quarrying in 1991 (Lowe, 1991, 1993) investigated a series of stone and timber buildings around the perimeter of the enclosure, including a bake-house, a smoke-house, a corn-dryer or malt-house, in effect the service area for the monastic settlement. Timber post-built structures up to 15 metres in length, some with their long walls markedly bowed in plan, were interpreted as possible barns. The most remarkable of the structures, however, was a semi-sunken rectangular building that incorporated re-used Roman stone in its fabric, including two fragmentary inscribed slabs, which could have come from the Roman fort at Birrens not far distant. A single radiocarbon date, calibrating around AD 600, together with the re-use of Roman masonry, suggests that this building may have been part of an earlier ecclesiastical settlement. Whether or not we endorse the suggestion that it was a baptistry, which doubtless is triggered in part by the site's traditional associations with Kentigern, the probability of an earlier religious centre at Hoddom confirms the belief that pre-existing sites may have been taken over in the Northumbrian expansion.

Timber halls and rectangular buildings

Like circular buildings, rectangular timber structures can be built using a variety of different foundations, each leaving its distinctive pattern in the archaeological record. Whether any of these is characteristic or diagnostic of any particular cultural or historically recorded group is arguable, just as it would be for any prehistoric style of vernacular architecture. The two most readily recognised structural techniques, wall-trenches, in which upright posts are bedded at intervals, and earth-fast postholes, are both in evidence and are no more than the equivalent in rectangular plans to ring-groove and post-ring construction of circular houses. Whether other types of foundation, of a kind such as sill-beams that may leave no archaeological trace, were employed, in isolation or in combination with either of these, remains uncertain. But the curiously open-ended plan of one of the Phase 7 buildings at Dunbar (Perry, 2000) certainly suggests that this may have been the case, since otherwise, as the excavator observed, the building would have been improbably exposed and vulnerable to the north-easterly winds. If this was the case, the question arises why a single building should incorporate two different foundation techniques? The answer may lie in the uses to which the building was put. If livestock were stalled at one end, as in the early Welsh long-houses, then a construction technique may have been employed which allowed that end of the building effectively to be dismantled for the purposes of periodic mucking-out (Geraint Coles, *pers. comm.*).

Wall-trench, earth-fast postholes, sill-beam construction and sunken foundations should all be regarded as constructional techniques rather than diagnostic of any one cultural group. Communities in time and space may exercise a preference for one or other technique for a variety of reasons, perhaps related to function, or to the nature of the topography or terrain in which they were used. Despite the growing number of rectangular buildings of Neolithic date from Britain and Ireland, it is still tempting to see certain specialised techniques like the so-called 'open book' wall-trenches at the gable ends of long, rectangular buildings, together with annexes and buttressing, as characteristic of Anglian settlements in Northumbria and southern Scotland. Buttressing evidently was an Anglian trait, and presumably implies an upper storey or colonnade along the long wall of buildings in which the entrances were almost invariably located.

Any analysis of rectangular 'halls' and houses (Fig. 8.7) must begin with the site of Yeavering, Northumberland (Hope-Taylor, 1977). Though the standard of the 1950s excavation was high, radiometric dating was not applied and the site's dating was based as much upon historical as on archaeological criteria. There remains therefore considerable debate as to the nature of the earliest post-Roman occupation at Yeavering, and whether it preceded the documented Anglian settlement of Northumbria (Scull, 1991; Frodsham, 1999). Acknowledging the tentative nature of the evidence (Alcock, 1988: 7–8), it seems likely that the earliest phases of occupation were British rather than Anglian. Yeavering has been identified as the seventh-century royal centre *ad Gefrin* named in Bede's *Ecclesiastical History*, and its archaeological remains, especially the unusual timber grandstand, certainly suggests that it was an important place of assembly. The twin-palisaded enclosure, with its distinctive rounded entrance terminals, is unlike the simple hairpin terminals of earlier Iron Age twin-palisaded enclosures, and the apparent absence of evidence for activity internally makes the Yeavering enclosure unique and enigmatic. Its function could have been for corralling cattle or perhaps horses, perhaps during major seasonal gatherings. The Yeavering rectangular timber buildings (Fig. 8.7, 1–3) have become archetypes for halls of putatively high status. Their plank-built construction, opposed entrances in the long walls of the building, and annexes are certainly distinctive. Unfortunately the truncated stratigraphy and absence of domestic debris make it difficult to reconstruct the function of individual buildings or the economic basis of the settlement as a whole. The site displays several periods of structural modification, apparently being destroyed by fire and rebuilt on at least one occasion, before abandonment at some time towards the end of the seventh century.

The very location of Yeavering on the Milfield plain is suggestive of the site's special importance. Overlooked by the 5 hectare Iron Age hillfort on Yeavering Bell, the plain was evidently a ceremonial centre from Neolithic times, as witnessed by a concentration of henge monuments and related sites (Harding, A. F., 1981). Whilst the issue of continuity is contentious, Bradley (1987) was doubtless right in believing that the site of the Yeavering 'palace' was deliberately chosen in the early historic period to invoke this tradition in order to legitimise its status. Recent survey indicates that the small ditched enclosure at the eastern summit of Yeavering Bell post-dates the occupation of the hill-

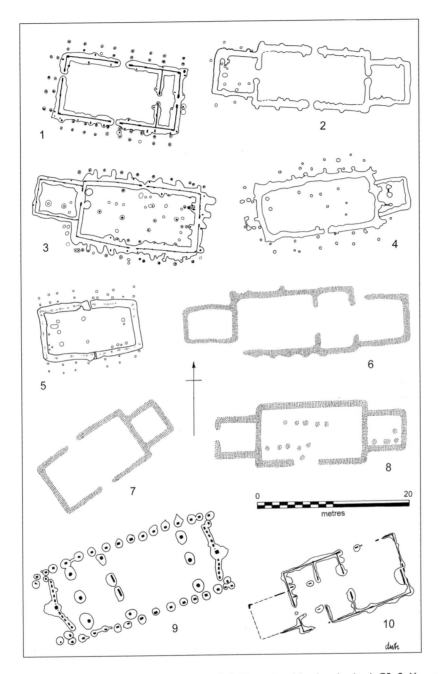

Figure 8.7 Halls and houses of the Anglian period. 1, Yeavering, Northumberland, C3; 2, Yeavering, Northumberland, A1b; 3, Yeavering, Northumberland, C4b; 4, Thirlings, Northumberland, C; 5, Thirlings, Northumberland, A; 6, Milfield, Northumberland; 7, Sprouston, Roxburghshire, E2; 8, Sprouston, Roxburghshire, F; 9, Doon Hill, East Lothian, A; 10, Doon Hill, East Lothian, B. Drawings by D. W. Harding, adapted from Hope-Taylor (1977), O'Brien and Miket (1991), Gates and O'Brien (1988), Smith, I. (1991), Reynolds, N. (1980).

fort, and could conceivably belong to an early historic re-use of the hillfort site itself (Frodsham, 1999: 198).

Within 2 miles of Yeavering, to the north-east and north-north-east, lie two more important settlements of the period, at Thirlings and at Milfield. Milfield, equated historically with Bede's royal site *Maelmin*, was evidently a settlement of some importance in view of its massive, polygonal, double palisade enclosing 12 hectares, within which air-photographs have revealed a suite of 'buttressed' timber halls (e.g. Fig. 8.7, 6; Gates and O'Brien, 1988). Earlier than this major enclosure is a fainter crop-mark indicating a palisaded enclosure that could well precede the Anglian phase of settlement on the site. A cemetery outwith the major twin-palisaded enclosure may nevertheless be broadly contemporary with its occupation. At Thirlings (O'Brien, 1982; O'Brien and Miket, 1991) there was no major enclosure, so that the site is presumed to be of subordinate status to its neighbours, though one rectangular house was located within a rectilinear timber stockade. The largest of the buildings (Fig. 8.7, 4), at 15 metres by 5, with a wall-trench a metre deep, was of 'hall' proportions; it also had a small annexe at one end, and 'buttress' posts flanking both its long walls. Five other wall-trench buildings and several rectangular, post-built structures were generally smaller and less elaborate, though some displayed evidence of buttresses and internal divisions (Fig. 8.7, 5). Radiocarbon dates indicated an early occupation of the site, perhaps from the late fifth to the seventh centuries.

Elements of the Yeavering model are, however, evident elsewhere, notably at the complex and doubtless multi-period site of Sprouston on the southern banks of the Tweed (Smith, 1991). Here too a major component is a double-palisaded enclosure, of comparable size but lacking on air-photographs the distinctive entrance terminals of the Yeavering model. At Sprouston, however, there appears to have been a smaller palisaded enclosure in a preceding phase, with palisades more widely spaced and less regularly twinned, which nevertheless implies a measure of site continuity, possibly from the earlier post-Roman period in view of the layout of the field-system with which it is apparently associated. As at Yeavering the concentration of rectilinear timber buildings lies outwith the palisaded enclosure and to its south-west, within what appears to have been an ordered landscape, divided by a system of trackways radiating from the palisaded enclosure. To the south of the settlement lies a cemetery of several hundred graves, aligned in multiple rows and grouped around a structure which has been tentatively interpreted as an early Christian church or oratory. Apart from the major halls (Fig. 8.7, 7–8), both trench-built and post-built, there are at Sprouston numerous lesser rectangular buildings, as well as what appear from crop-marks to be at least two groups of *Grubenhäuser*. Even allowing for multiple phases of occupation resulting in an air-photographic palimpsest, Sprouston was evidently an important site with a range of activities represented in the diversity of its physical remains. The palisaded enclosure, as at Yeavering, appears to be indicative of the site's status, though it does not enclose the focus of settlement as such.

At Doon Hill, East Lothian, the palisade does enclose the principal buildings, so that if this site too is deemed to be of high status, it is nevertheless different from Sprouston and Yeavering. There was also evidence of a small inhumation cemetery immediately beyond the enclosure boundary beside its main gate. Here the palisade is single, and polygonal in its outline, a plan which distinguishes it from the normal pre-Roman pattern, but which is by no means unique in the post-Roman period. Within the enclosure two successive rectangular halls were recognised, the earlier post-built and the later founded in wall-trenches (Fig. 8.7, 9–10). The later building had an annexe at one end in the manner of the Yeavering and Sprouston halls, but with more evidence for internal division of space. The earlier hall was post-built for the most part, with wall-trenching used only in the gable-end walls, which in plan formed an obtuse angle about a central posthole. A similar feature was detected on a crop-mark at Sprouston, but detached by some distance from the main focus of settlement. Hall B at Doon Hill has never been in doubt as Anglian, but the dating of Hall A was thrown into question by its apparent similarities to the rectangular hall at Balbridie, Aberdeenshire, which proved on excavation to be Neolithic. Arguments (Smith, 1991; Dark, 2000: 206) that Hall A, directly underlying its Anglian successor, might nevertheless be Neolithic, though ingenious, stretch credibility. In the light of more recent discoveries of rectangular Neolithic buildings the similarities between Doon Hill A and Balbridie seem now to have been over-emphasised, and important constructional differences have been understated (Walker, 2003). Hope-Taylor (1980) had argued vigorously for an early historic date for both buildings, and it has been suggested more recently (Lowe, 1999: 35) that abraded Roman pottery providing a clear *terminus post quem* for its construction was recovered from the postholes of the earlier as well as the later hall. Hence the balance of probabilities still points to the Doon Hill halls as closely successive, with Hall A being founded by the local Gododdin and Hall B representing the take-over of that native site by an intrusive Anglian élite (Ralston and Armit, 1997: 227).

The existence of palisaded enclosures with rectangular halls raises the possibility that other palisaded enclosures, where rectangular buildings are not evident on air-photographs, and assigned in consequence to the earlier Iron Age series, could in fact have been occupied in the post-Roman Iron Age. Only where the outline is polygonal, or comprises a close-set triple alignment, as at Hogbridge, Peeblesshire, does the plan depart sufficiently from the stereotypical early Iron Age form to alert us to the possibility of a later date.

Among more tentative examples, the crop-mark site at Whitekirk, East Lothian (Brown, 1983), includes rectangular buildings which may be considered analogous to early historic timber halls. Their size – the larger is around 23 metres by 11 – is at the top end of the range of those hitherto considered, but their slightly bowing walls is certainly not without precedent at Sprouston and Yeavering. Their plans appear to include an internal division towards one end, rather than an annexe of lesser width than the main hall. The buildings lie adjacent to a series of rectilinear enclosures, one corner of which straddles the larger of the two buildings, with which they are evidently not contemporary. Two smaller rectilinear buildings lie within the area of the enclosures. These, and other air-photographic sites, including some north of the Forth, may well be of the early historic period, but there is at present no sound archaeological basis for linking them to any particular period or historical horizon.

Sunken buildings (*Grubenhäuser*)

The use of semi-subterranean foundations, exemplified in various forms of domestic architecture of the early Iron Age, especially in eastern Scotland as we have seen, have their counterparts in the post-Roman period in rectangular or sub-rectangular structures, notably in southern Scotland and north-eastern England. Some of these (Fig. 8.8), particularly those in which numbers of loom-weights have been discovered, bear obvious

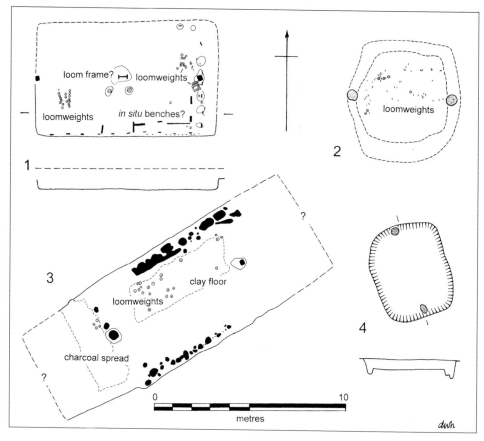

Figure 8.8 'Grubenhäuser', comparative plans. 1, Upton, Northants; 2, Ratho, Midlothian; 3, Dunbar, East Lothian; 4, New Bewick, Northumberland. Drawings by D. W. Harding, adapted from Jackson *et al.* (1969), Smith, A. (1995), Perry (2000), Gates and O'Brien (1998).

comparison with the *Grubenhäuser* of Anglo-Saxon England, first recognised by Leeds in his pioneering excavations at Sutton Courtenay in Berkshire, though the sub-rectangular form is not an exclusively Anglo-Saxon phenomenon. There is, furthermore, quite a wide range of size in the buildings in question, so that their classification as a single group may need to be re-examined.

Several buildings approximating to the *Grubenhaus* model have been excavated or identified by air-photography in south-eastern Scotland and the Borders. An example excavated at New Bewick in Northumberland (Fig. 8.8, 4; Gates and O'Brien, 1988), just south of the Milfield complex, was one of a dozen such features revealed by air-photography in close proximity to a ditched enclosure of uncertain date. It proved to be of standard size and construction at nearly 5 metres by 4, with postholes at each gable end. It also yielded fragments of two dozen or more clay loom-weights, indicative of weaving as one of the principal functions of the building. A similar function can be inferred for the nearly square building of similar proportions from Ratho, Edinburgh (Fig. 8.8, 2; Smith, A., 1995), in close proximity to two small, rectangular, wall-trench buildings. In the case of the Ratho *Grubenhaus* the main roof-supporting posts appear to have been midway along the marginally longer wall. The function of the building was again indicated by fragments of no less than sixty-eight clay loomweights. Significantly, the floor of the weaving-shed had been extensively reinforced with small pebbles, indicating that the base of the pit was indeed the floor, rather than simply a cavity beneath a suspended floor. Though this issue may still be open to debate in some instances, it does appear likely that the purpose of sunken foundations of *Grubenhäuser* was to provide greater headroom with minimal upstanding walls, an objective that would plainly be vitiated by introducing a suspended floor. If on the other hand under-floor storage was the objective, as has been implied for some of the earlier Iron Age roundhouses with sunken foundations, then substantial walls would still be required. Radiocarbon dates from Ratho point to the use of the weaving-shed in the seventh century: lengths of palisade trench, assumed by the excavator to be contemporary, could equally belong to an earlier phase of occupation.

The function of *Grubenhäuser* was discussed some years ago by Nowell Myres in the context of the building from Upton, Northants (Fig. 8.8, 1; Jackson *et al.*, 1969). Upton not only produced a set of loom-weights that had evidently fallen from an *in situ* loom, but also yielded the carbonised planks of *in situ* furniture. At 9 metres by 5 the Upton building was among the larger *Grubenhäuser*, but is by no means unusual in this regard. At Castle Park, Dunbar, a rectangular, sunken building, nearly 6 metres in width and more than 13 metres in length, appears to have had its roof supported on a ridge beam, either with gabled or hipped ends (Fig. 8.8, 3). Loom-weights again are indicative of weaving, but in a building of this size these activities were evidently being conducted on a significant scale. The dating of the building to Phase 7, from which other rectangular, trench-walled houses are dated on the basis of radiocarbon samples from mid-sixth to early seventh centuries, seems equivocal. A single radiocarbon date from what appears to have been structural timber from the *Grubenhaus* points to a calibrated span between the third and sixth centuries. On the other hand, it was recorded as cutting through structures that are assigned to two successive phases, though the excavator acknowledges problems with stratigraphy (Perry, 2000: 47–8). Plainly the early presence of these structures at Dunbar is crucial to a proper understanding of the early post-Roman archaeology of the region, and again indicates the importance of evaluation that is not predetermined by historical imperatives.

Similar structures may be indicated by amorphous blobs on air-photographs, as at Thirlings, Milfield and Sprouston, among an increasing number of sites. A similar building with sunken foundations at Hoddom, Dumfriesshire, as we have seen, was interpreted as a smoke-house for curing meat. The excavated evidence seems to indicate their use as workshops or ancillary buildings, rather than as domestic dwellings. But there was evidently a good deal of variation in their size and construction, and they could well have been used for a variety of different purposes over a wider geographical distribution and a longer period of time than was formerly imagined.

Archaeology and Anglian expansion

Evidence for the Anglian or Northumbrian expansion into lowland Scotland is based primarily on documentary rather than archaeological sources, annals, genealogies, historical and quasi-historical sources such as Bede's *Historia Ecclesiastica* and Nennius'

Historia Brittonum, biographies like Eddius Stephanus' *Life of St Wilfred*, and the epic poem *Y Gododdin*. The historical value of these is plainly highly variable and in some cases questionable, but the authenticity of the principal events, places and protagonists that they record need not be seriously challenged. Any reconstruction of the period based solely on the archaeological record by comparison would be sparse on episodic detail and *dramatis personae*, but perhaps more informative of settlements, burials and material culture. A crucial contribution to the inter-disciplinary tapestry is that of place-names (Fig. 8.9), which attest the Anglian expansion northwards into East Lothian and to a lesser degree in Cumbria (Nicolaisen, 1976). Had the period not been text-aided, or without the evidence of place-names, the Anglian expansion and conflict with their northern neighbours, predicated upon the evidence of archaeology alone, would doubtless have been dismissed as diffusionist invention.

Archaeologically, the appearance of large timber halls and some *Grubenhaüser* would not unreasonably be attributed to Anglian settlers, though some rectangular buildings may have pre-dated their advent, and others may be found well beyond any plausible extent of Anglian settlement. The correlation, therefore, is not absolute, and the structural types in consequence hardly diagnostic. The distribution of burials and cemeteries might be regarded as a more reliable indication of Anglian settlement. Burials of probable Anglian attribution of the sixth or early seventh centuries occur quite widely in north-eastern England, though most are relatively poorly furnished and few in number of graves in any one group. The group at Milfield North actually re-used the site of a Neolithic henge (Scull and Harding, 1990). More extensive cemeteries are known at Norton in Teesside, and at Yeavering itself, though in the case of the latter there is some ambiguity over the identification of Anglian and native British burials. Weapons and brooches from the cemetery at Greenbank, Darlington (Pococke and Miket, 1976), were unequivocally Anglian, and the extended inhumation from Castle Eden in Co. Durham included one of the most northerly examples of a glass claw beaker. Further north and west there are possible Anglian burials in the north Tyne valley and in the upper Eden valley, but north of the Tweed such distinctive burials are hardly known. It is generally assumed that the reason for this is that only pagan Anglian burials contain diagnostic grave-goods, and that the further expansion of Anglian settlement into southern Scotland post-dated the conversion to Christianity.

Occasional finds may signal an Anglian presence. The small gold pyramid finial set with garnets from Dalmeny, Midlothian, is sometimes assumed to have been from a warrior-burial, and the more recent gold stud with garnets set in *cloisonné* from Prestonkirk, East Lothian, is likewise probably from a rich sword assembly, in this case perhaps dating rather earlier in the seventh century. Among important finds of the early Christian period, probably of later seventh-century date, is the tiny fragment of a pectoral cross, made of gold leaf with red garnet settings, from an unstratified context in the excavations at Castle Park, Dunbar. Stylistically it resembles examples from Anglo-Saxon contexts, and its closest parallel is the pectoral cross of St Cuthbert in the Durham Cathedral Museum.

Among field monuments once attributed to the Anglian expansion into southern Scotland are cultivation terraces (RCAHMS, 1967: 38–9). Subsequent research (RCAHMS, 1997) has emphasised that the character of these terraces is largely a factor of cultivation practice and angle of slope, so that it would be unwise to assign date on the basis of surface morphology. Absolute dating or dating by artefactual association is unlikely, and stratigraphic relationships in the developing landscape sequence are not

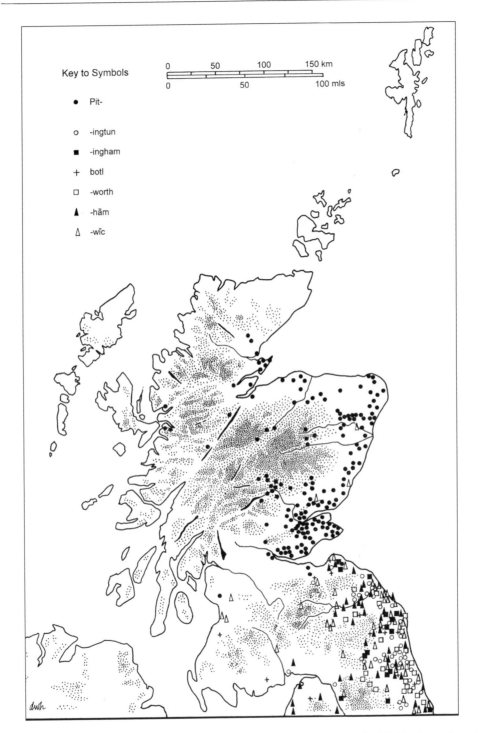

Figure 8.9 Distribution of Anglian place-names and Pit-names. Drawing by D. W. Harding, adapted from Jackson (1955) and Nicolaisen (1976).

always clear. It now seems probable that the earliest cultivation terraces date from the later prehistoric period, in some cases remaining in use through Roman and post-Roman times. Striking examples with steep risers and narrow treads, like those at Romanno Bridge, Peeblesshire, have almost certainly been exaggerated by Mediaeval agriculture. Cultivation terraces, therefore, were doubtless in use in the later Iron Age in southern Scotland, but any close correlation with Anglian colonisation should now be disregarded.

In south-west Scotland the appearance of Anglian crosses and sculpture, and the establishment of monastic settlements, is doubtless evidence of Northumbrian political influence. But these changes could have been brought about by the conversion of the ruling élite or by intermarriage between ruling dynasties, without signifying any major influx of settlers. By the eighth century the influence of Northumbrian Christianity extended far beyond the confines of the political kingdom within which it was based, acting also as an agent of innovation from Continental Europe. The development of the Hiberno-Saxon art style, with its residual Celtic elements combining with Germanic interlace and more exotic Mediterranean influences, and the vexed question of its origins, lies beyond the scope of the present study.

Chapter 9

Central and eastern Scotland

Burials: long cists, cairns and ditched-barrow cemeteries

Long-cist cemeteries have already been introduced in the context of early Christianity in southern Scotland. More recent publications of long-cist cemeteries, however, with radiocarbon dates, have come from sites north of the Forth estuary. A major cemetery, excavated in the 1970s, at Hallowhill, St Andrews (Proudfoot, 1996), produced some twenty radiocarbon dates spanning the sixth to ninth centuries AD. Of 145 burials the majority were long cists, but with some in graves outlined by boulders rather than sand-stone slabs, and with a small group of simple 'dug' graves that may have contained wooden coffins, of which all trace had gone. The cemetery was not enclosed, and its full limit could not be established, but the burials could have totalled several hundred in all. Among burials uncovered in the vicinity in the nineteenth century was a child's cist with at least one glass vessel and other fragmentary artefacts, whilst the more recent excavations included a two-tiered burial, the lower of which was that of a child with Roman artefacts among the grave-goods. The items included a seal-box decorated in *millefiori*, an object intended for official use rather than as a personal trinket. A Roman finger-ring and silver bracelet were both broken fragments, and together with a complete brooch could have been treasured over many generations before being finally deposited in the grave. Contrary perhaps to expectations of an earlier, pre-Christian, post-Roman date, the radiocarbon dates for the composite tiered cist are not significantly different from the rest of the graves in the cemetery. The excavator nevertheless argued for an older tradition of sanctity on the site, perhaps represented by a rectangular post-built structure of uncertain date and function, and one pit in particular which yielded a radiocarbon date around the end of the first millennium BC. In principle it seems possible that the early Christian long-cist cemeteries of south-eastern Scotland did develop out of an older, less clearly formalised tradition from the pre-Christian era.

The cemetery at Lundin Links (Greig *et al.*, 2000) has likewise a long history of discoveries since the nineteenth century. The most recent work, which exposed more than a dozen long-cist burials, produced radiocarbon dates between the fourth and late fifth centuries AD, indicating its chronological priority in the series. Yet excavations in the 1960s had uncovered a variety of different burial rites, including extended inhumations in long cists that had been covered with low cairns, some round and some oblong, defined by boulder kerbs. Round barrows or cairns have a long and widespread currency in prehistory, but rectangular or rectilinear cairns are more unusual, though not unknown in eastern Scotland. Two groups of burials at Lundin Links were of particular interest.

The so-called 'horned cairn complex' contained no less than eight skeletons, all certainly or probably female, and some apparently displaying congenital abnormalities, which suggested familial relationships. A second complex burial, described as the 'dumb-bell' but effectively being two round cairns conjoined by a rectangular cairn, contained a female burial beneath the rectangular element and male burials in the round cairns at either end. Evidently some selectivity was taking place in the choice of funerary monument, perhaps reflecting social status or role within the community. Notwithstanding limitations regarding the earlier radiocarbon dates from the site, the sequence obtained in 1999 would be consistent with the site's use between the early fifth and seventh centuries AD.

The distribution of long-cist cemeteries, as we have noted (Fig. 8.6), was formerly centred on the Lothians (Henshall, 1956: Fig. 6), but now with increasing numbers extending into coastal Fife and Tayside as a result of research since the 1970s. Individual examples of similar burials, or small groups, have been recorded elsewhere, notably in the Northern and Western Isles, but though these may be broadly of the same date, they need not be linked directly to the south-eastern group. The markedly estuarine distribution around the Forth and the Tay is a clear demonstration of the principle of geography uniting rather than dividing coastal communities. Most cemeteries appear not to have been enclosed, though the very partial examination of many sites must make this a qualified assertion. In Fife the probable associations with early ecclesiastical foundations may warrant the consideration of some cemeteries as *developed* in Thomas' classification (Thomas, A. C., 1971: 51). Radiocarbon dates certainly 'suggest a distinct possibility that burial in long graves and cists was prevalent throughout much of Scotland from some time between the second and fourth centuries AD' (Greig *et al.*, 2000: 608). Finding convincing antecedents in the earlier Iron Age is hampered by the fact that burial does not appear to have made a substantial impact on the archaeological record, despite the discovery of occasional small cemeteries like those at Broxmouth or Dryburn Bridge. The practice of long-cist cemeteries may indeed have spread from the Lothians north of the Forth over time, thus approximating to Thomas' model of the northward advance of Christianity (Thomas, A. C., 1968: 107–8; Burt, 1997: 65).

A distinctive form of burial in parts of eastern Scotland, notably around the Lunan valley in Angus, but also known further north in the Moray Firth region, is the square-ditched barrow, recognised extensively by air-photographic survey since the 1970s. Initially assumed to have been an extension of the early-mid La Tène mode of burial known from its concentrated distribution in eastern Yorkshire, with presumed Continental antecedents of the fourth century BC or thereabouts (see Stead, 1979, who actually altered the framework of his Fig. 10 to accommodate the new discoveries), the square-ditched barrows of eastern Scotland are now more generally assigned to the later Iron Age. One significant feature of the Angus square-ditched barrows is their use of corner causeways, a feature that is not characteristic of the major Yorkshire cemeteries, nor of their Continental early–mid-La Tène antecedents. Unfortunately, the burials under the Angus barrows have so far yielded little artefactual evidence for dating. At Boysack Mills (Murray and Ralston, 1997) the radiocarbon dates were not conclusive, but the square-ditched-barrow burial no. 1 did include an iron projecting ring-headed pin, which might indicate a dating in the opening centuries of the first millennium AD. Potentially more informative is the barrow cemetery at Redcastle, overlooking Lunan Bay (Fig. 9.1; *DES*, 1997, 1998, 2001), not least because of its close proximity to a souterrain. The cemetery comprised at

Figure 9.1 Excavated cemetery with square-ditched barrows, Redcastle, Angus. Photograph Royal Commission on the Ancient and Historical Monuments of Scotland. Copyright reserved. Reproduced by kind permission.

least five square-ditched barrows, each with causeways between the ditches at their corners, and each with a central burial. In addition, however, there were two round barrows, and two unenclosed burials. All the burials were extended inhumations, the majority set within long cists of local sandstone aligned approximately south-west to north-east. None of the burials contained grave-goods. Radiocarbon dates for the square-ditched barrows spanned the fourth to sixth centuries, while single dates for the round barrows lay in the second and sixth centuries, leaving their chronology more uncertain. Long cists without visible covering seemingly were fashionable throughout the use of the site. The adjacent souterrain proved to have no stone lining, capstones or paving, and was therefore of the Dalladies type; postholes indicated the probability of wooden construction. Within its entrance were found fragments of a Roman glass vessel. Proximity of course need not imply contemporaneous use, but there seems every possibility that the burials could have been contemporary with whatever settlement the souterrain served, even if the souterrain itself went out of use before the settlement and cemetery.

A combination of circular and rectilinear plans characterises two extant barrow cemeteries in Inverness-shire, at Garbeg and Whitebridge (Stevenson, J. B., 1984; Ashmore, 1980). The square barrows all feature causeways across their ditches at the corners, and one notably has large stones set upright at the corners. In effect, had the Garbeg barrows been ploughed level, they could well have appeared from air-survey very much like the barrow cemetery at Redcastle. Within one of the excavated square-ditched barrows was uncovered a rectangular setting of boulders, itself overlying an extended grave pit

(Wedderburn and Grime, 1984) in a manner which has prompted comparison with the timber 'mortuary structure' at Thornybank, Dalkeith. A similar elongated pit underlay one of the circular barrows, in the top of which the remains of a Class 1 symbol-stone were recovered. Among northern outliers of the square and circular barrow group are older finds from Ackergill in Caithness. Here seven rectangular cairns in alignment were retained within slabbed kerbs, with occasional uprights along their sides or at their corners. The burial rite was, like the south-eastern cemeteries, extended inhumation in long cists, among which were also examples of a double cist and a tiered cist. The cemetery also included a circular barrow, and two simple cist graves on the same alignment, and hence perhaps contemporary with the barrow cemetery, one of which was associated with a Class 1 symbol-stone with an ogham inscription.

In sum, later Iron Age burials in central and eastern Scotland included more than one distinctive mode of deposition. The burial rite itself is predominantly extended inhumation, either within a simple grave, possibly within a coffin made of perishable materials, or within a stone-lined long cist, of which there can be variant forms. North of the Forth, and especially in Angus, these may be covered by a low barrow mound or cairn, with a surrounding ditch of circular or more distinctively square or rectilinear plan. The long-cist cemeteries regularly contained graves arranged in orderly rows, closely adjacent but seldom if ever intersecting, which must signify some above-ground marker, most probably of wood. There can be little doubt that the later burials at any rate were Christian interments. Furthermore, the numbers of graves, running into several hundreds, implies that by the mid-first millennium AD this had become a standard method of disposal of the dead, rather than the selective burial of a limited social group.

Hitherto scholars working within an historical paradigm have set out to identify Pictish burials, and have found difficulties in identifying an archaeological type which matched the presumed date and distribution area of an inferred Pictish heartland. Long-cist cemeteries are concentrated too much south of the Forth; square-ditched barrows and cairns have localised but disparate distributions, and their dating remains equivocal. While so many questions regarding the basic data remain unanswered, and as new evidence continues to be uncovered, it may be better not to presuppose historical attributions until we have sorted out that data.

Hillforts and citadels

In southern and south-eastern Scotland we have already seen that earlier Iron Age hillforts were in several cases re-occupied in the post-Roman period. Even more so may occupation of traditional community centres have persisted in regions north of the Forth. At Craig Phadrig, Inverness (Small and Cottam, 1972), the presence of imported pottery and a fragment of mould for a hanging-bowl escutcheon implies high-status re-occupation of the site. Stevenson dated the mould to around AD 600, and suggested the presence of a workshop, though there was no direct evidence of metalworking. Finavon, as we have seen, may conceivably have had an early historic phase of re-occupation, and casual finds from East Lomond Hill in Fife (RCAHMS, 1933: no. 244) could well indicate early historic occupation. There is every reason to suppose that earlier sites would have been attractive for later use, both on account of their natural topographical advantages and because of their traditional significance as centres of authority. Equally, however, sites may have been newly fortified in the early historic period.

From surface survey the hillfort on Clatchard Craig, Fife (Fig. 8.1, 4; Close-Brooks, 1986) had all the appearances of being an early Iron Age hillfort, its citadel resembling an oblong fort of that period. Excavations in the 1950s in advance of destruction by quarrying in fact proved that its defensive ramparts, involving at least four lines of enclosure, some of which almost certainly embodied sub-phases of structural modification, belonged principally to the early historic period. No ditches were recognisable on the rocky terrain, and no entrance was ever satisfactorily identified. Differences in construction techniques, involving stone facing and timber-lacing, with burnt timbers conspicuous in the core of rampart 3, implies a long sequence of occupation. Rampart 2 significantly did not follow the contours of the hill, which appeared to indicate that it was not part of the same design as any of the other earthworks. Yet the radiocarbon dates for the innermost, second and third circuits are indistinguishable around the sixth and seventh centuries AD. Samples from the innermost and third ramparts were almost certainly from structural timbers. From the second, material like the Roman mortared stone and sherd of samian incorporated into the rampart core may have been residual from earlier occupation, so that it affords no more than a *terminus post quem* for the rampart's construction and use. The conclusion was thus that the innermost and third enclosures were contemporary, even though more widely spaced than is usual. They were also regarded as the earliest on the site, whilst the second rampart was assumed to be later. In the absence of radiocarbon samples, the dating of the outermost defences depended upon interpretation of the stratigraphic relationship in section between ramparts 3 and 4, which was far from definitive. Close-Brooks favoured the view that the outer ramparts were contemporary with or later than enclosures 1 and 3, but the relationship is between episodes of collapse, which need not be a reliable guide to the sequence of construction. Furthermore, as the report observed, rampart 3 in two of the excavated sections could well be interpreted as representing more than one phase of construction. In consequence, a case might still be made for the existence of an early Iron Age phase of enclosure, which would certainly be consistent with the material assemblage from the site.

Coarse wares from Clatchard Craig might be compared to the pottery from the Broxmouth hillfort. Fragments of saddle-quern would likewise argue for activity on the site before the second century BC or thereabouts, and fragments of shale bracelet and several spindle-whorls could as easily be early Iron Age as later. A cast bronze ornament in the form of openwork trumpets, together with the sherd of samian, could indicate activity on the site in the second century AD. Thereafter early historic occupation was well attested by imported E-ware and a number of diagnostic artefacts, including fragments of moulds for the manufacture of pins and penannular brooches, a silver ingot, and a bronze disc decorated with interlocking peltae 'in hanging bowl style' (Close-Brooks, 1986: 146). A final phase of occupation on the summit plateau was represented by the only surviving structural evidence from the site, a rectangular hearth, some intermittent paving and a pivot-stone that the excavators believed to have been *in situ*, which could have been the only surviving evidence of a rectangular building. If an early Iron Age phase of occupation had been demonstrated, then the site might well have fallen within Feachem's class of citadel forts, re-used in the early historic period.

Other hillforts in which a sequence of constructional phases is evident from ground survey may likewise have been occupied or re-occupied into early historic times. For Norman's Law in Fife (RCAHMS, 1933: no. 193) conventional wisdom regards the small oval 'citadel' on the summit as the latest defensive phase on the site, dating to the early historic period. The larger enclosure of the hilltop, with the still larger annexe which takes in the southern and south-western flanks of the hill, are generally assigned to the earlier Iron Age, though it remains unclear whether these are part of a contemporary system. Several house-circles are visible, including some within the citadel, where they are hardly likely to have survived had they been residual from an earlier phase of occupation. At Dunsinane, Perthshire (RCAHMS, 1994: 56), house foundations are visible in the lower annexe, but would hardly be expected to have survived nineteenth-century investigations in the summit citadel. Again the fortifications are apparently multi-period, the latest phase being represented by a massive wall up to 9 metres in thickness, enclosing little more than 50 metres by 25. On its north side the citadel earthworks appear to block an earlier trackway, which lower down the hill to the north-west leads through the outer enclosure. It is therefore reasonable to argue that the outermost enclosure was earlier than the citadel in its final form, and that its walls may even have been robbed in the construction of the summit enclosures. The citadel itself could nevertheless be the product of cumulative construction, and 'almost certainly occupies the site of an earlier fort' (RCAHMS, 1994: 55).

In some instances the final 'citadel' enclosure on these cumulative sites resembles a stone-walled dun in the Atlantic tradition, as in the case of Dumyat, Stirlingshire, one of Feachem's (1955) original 'citadel' forts, linked conventionally through its name (Watson, 1926) with the historical Maeatae. A similar sequence, with a stone-built dun or 'ring-fort' as the latest element, may be represented at Turin Hill in Angus (Feachem, 1955: 74–5; Alexander and Ralston, 1999). The concept of the ring-fort, borrowed from Irish terminology, where it is applied to innumerable small enclosures spanning a broad chronological range from later prehistory to the Mediaeval period, should not, however, imply any direct cultural connections.

What is needed to confirm or refute the tentative attribution of the latest phases of these fortifications to an early historic horizon is a programme of selective and limited test excavation, expressly targeted at obtaining samples for dating, along the lines of Alcock's research into historically recorded sites, an exercise which need not be unduly expensive or intrusive. The idea of early historic citadels being located inside older Iron Age fortified enclosures raises the question how novel was the hierarchical structure implied by the more celebrated nuclear forts? The fact that the earlier earthworks may have fallen into disrepair as defensive barriers does not preclude their continuing use as spatial boundaries in a hierarchical social system. Viewed in this light, the nuclear forts would then be the culmination of a process of social development, rather than a radical innovation of the early historic period.

Nuclear forts

We have already noted that the concept of the nuclear fort, first advanced by Stevenson (1949b) in the context of Dalmahoy, Midlothian, has become central to any study of fortifications of the early historic period. Excavation by Alcock at Dundurn (Fig. 9.2) and re-appraisal of Dunadd has challenged the view that the outworks of nuclear forts were necessarily constructed at the same time as the initial occupation of the citadel; the outer enclosures could instead have been cumulative over time. Assuming that such outworks were intended to reinforce the natural hierarchy of plateaux around the summit, this need not imply that the nuclear concept was not integral to the site from the outset,

Figure 9.2 Dundurn, Perthshire, nuclear fort, air-photograph. Photograph by D. W. Harding.

since non-defensive divisions could have been demarcated without leaving any earth-fast traces archaeologically.

In some cases, as we have seen, earlier Iron Age fortifications may have been re-occupied in early historic times; they may even have lent themselves to re-use as nuclear forts. Feachem's injudicious assertion, however, that Dunadd and Dundurn were most probably early Iron Age hillforts 'possibly repaired or improved by undiscriminating or desperate persons until as late as the seventh century' (Feachem, 1966: 85) prompted indignant repudiation by Alcock, not just for the two sites in question (Alcock *et al.*, 1989: 209), but for all the major early historic fortifications that he identified from documentary sources (Alcock, 1981: 178). Subsequent research at Dunadd (Lane and Campbell, 2000) has pointed to Iron Age activity and even a walled enclosure on the site, so that earlier occupation of these prominent locations should not be discounted. But Alcock's essential premise, that these early historic 'royal' sites were selected expressly to satisfy a purpose that had progressed beyond the role of earlier Iron Age hillforts, still seems to be a reasonable inference. The evidence of imported pottery and metalwork production, for example, endorses the inference drawn from historical sources that nuclear forts were important political and administrative centres, even under royal control. In terms of area they are small by comparison with major hillforts of the later prehistoric period in some regions, especially those in southern and south-eastern Scotland. North of the Forth, however, early Iron Age hillforts do not attain anything like the same size, in terms of area enclosed at any rate, and Feachem's 'minor *oppida*' of 6 acres or more are relatively few and far between. Nevertheless, these sites have a capacity for community occupation, which seems to be deliberately eschewed by the craggy topography of the early historic nuclear forts. Though defended by palisades or enclosure walls as well as by natural topography, nuclear forts are generally regarded as strongholds between which kings progressed in order to secure their territory and exact their dues from a subordinate aristocracy. Some like Dunadd may indeed have functioned as capitals, but this can only have been true of the paramount centres.

Alcock's excavations of 1976–77 at Dundurn (Alcock *et al.* 1989), though very limited in scale (and sometimes at the time, when larger area excavation was fashionable, deprecated as 'key-holing') in fact yielded a disproportionate wealth of information regarding the status and external connections of its occupants. Two imported pottery sherds, minimal in themselves, were identified, one as E-ware, the other as probably Rhenish. Two small fragments of glass were likewise recognised as imports, one probably from a beaker from the Rhineland or southern Gaul. Whilst Dundurn's location in Strathearn and its eastern access to the Firth of Tay might suggest trading contacts via the North Sea with the Continent, the distribution of E-ware (Fig. 8.4) makes clear the primacy of the western route into Atlantic Scotland and Ireland, so that secondary trade or exchange from Strathclyde is perhaps a more probable alternative. Two other high-status artefacts from Dundurn, however, suggest other cultural contacts. An ornamental pendant in silvered bronze depicts a beast biting its forepaw, for which the excavator cited stylistic comparisons with the *Book of Durrow* and the Sutton Hoo gold buckle. Second, a fragment of mould had traces of two animals in ribbon style, apparently to be rendered in filigree or a cast imitation of it. The archaeological contexts of these items indicate that they date from the seventh century at Dundurn, a surprisingly early period for this Germanic style to appear north of the Forth, and well before the conventional introduction of animals and interlace on cross slabs of Class II (Alcock *et al.*, 1989: 216–17). Finally, a decorative glass boss with inlaid discs and spirals, of eighth- or ninth-century date, prompted comparison with the early boss style on stone crosses, though whether implying Pictish or Scottish influence was left open.

As regards its basic economy, cattle were predominant at Dundurn, over pig, with sheep evidently a minor component of the pastoral regime. Cereal cultivation was practised in some degree, though the evidence from excavation was minimal. An outstanding problem of Dundurn and allied sites, however, is the nature of their occupation, as it may be deduced from the archaeological evidence rather than from documentary sources. There is little direct evidence for structures within either citadel or lesser enclosures, though there is certainly abundant evidence of activity in terms of artefacts and occupational deposits. Explaining their absence as a result of the use of timber and turf in surface-built rather than earth-fast methods of construction seems scarcely consistent with the case for the high status of nuclear forts, unless the site was only in use periodically. Nor is it consistent with the increasingly substantial body of evidence for early historic buildings in the Atlantic north and west, or from southern and south-eastern Scotland. R. B. K. Stevenson (1949b: 197–8) regarded the outer enclosures in particular as suitable for gathering stock for protection, and presumably for other seasonal gatherings, but such a functional explanation might undermine the concept of a hierarchy of enclosures, in which the subordinate enclosures were presumably assigned to lesser ranks and their retinues. Despite the briefest historical references to sieges of Dunadd and Dundurn, it is not even clear how permanent the occupation of such sites was; if their principal role was for periodic assemblies during a royal progression, then the number of permanent structures might well be minimal. Major issues regarding the archaeological evidence of nuclear forts remain to be addressed, in no small part because they have been subordinated to an agenda determined by the historical evidence.

Promontory forts

Along the north-eastern coast of Moray, Banff and Buchan, promontories were favoured as defensive locations in the early historic period, perhaps indicative of the importance of seaborne communications at this time. Pre-eminent among these sites was Burghead in Moray, at 3 hectares one of the larger enclosed sites in the region. It was defended on its landward side by three banks and ditches that were destroyed in the early nineteenth century with the creation of the modern village and harbour. The date of these defences is thus uncertain; they could have originated in the earlier Iron Age, or could have been built or adapted in the later Iron Age. Within the area thus cut off the natural topography divides into a lower and upper compound, each enclosed by further walls to create an upper citadel and lower annexe. From the rubble of these walls apparently came the celebrated plaques with images of bulls (Fig. 9.3) in various moods from quiescence to aggression, which presumably had once endowed the defences or an adjacent shrine with ritual or symbolic significance. In the lower compound was a rock-cut cistern or well, approached by a flight of steps, and despite later modifications probably originating from the early historic occupation of the site. Regrettably the buildings reportedly uncovered in the lower compound in the late nineteenth century were not properly recorded.

In the later 1960s Small (1969) opened sections through the western defences of the upper compound at Burghead. Here the wall on the cliff-edge was more than 8 metres thick at its base, faced with large boulders externally and with a neat, coursed drystone wall internally, which still survived to a height of 3 metres. The revetment wall was tied into the rubble core with a framework of longitudinal and transverse timbers that seemingly did not extend through the wall's full width, and which, in contrast to the recorded evidence of the boundary wall of the lower compound, used no iron nails in its construction. The major contribution of this limited research programme, however, was the establishment through radiocarbon dating of the early historic date of the rampart. This was probably built between the fourth and sixth centuries AD, an assessment that

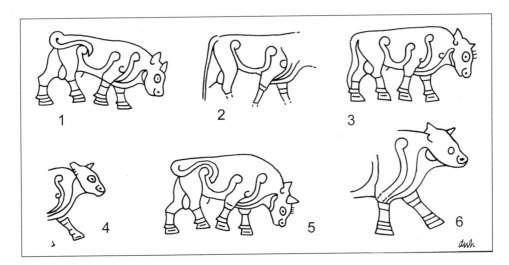

Figure 9.3 Carvings of bulls from Burghead, Morayshire. Drawings by D. W. Harding, adapted from Allen and Anderson (1903).

is broadly supported by subsequent dating and environmental analysis (Edwards and Ralston, 1978). Some disquiet has been generated by the fact that the latest of the radiocarbon dates for the Burghead rampart suggests an improbably long period of maintenance (Alcock, 1984: 21), but this anomaly could perhaps be accounted for by a later episode of repair, after an interval of abandonment, of the original wall. The rampart was evidently destroyed around the ninth century by fire, an event generally attributed to Norse agency, though archaeological evidence for this is lacking.

The bull carvings are plainly in the symbol-stone style, and the site is therefore conventionally regarded as a Pictish royal centre, though it is not identified as such in any documentary record. Though only six plaques survive, the antiquarian records suggest that there could have been thirty or more, symbols of power suggesting that the site was of high social and political status. Evidence for an early Christian site in close proximity, including fragments from a slab-built shrine, would be consistent with Burghead's importance as a major political and ritual centre in the later Iron Age.

Eastward along the coast at Portknockie excavations in the late 1970s (Ralston, 1987) examined the much smaller promontory fort at Green Castle, again demonstrating that its principal timber-laced rampart was of early historic date. This wall extended along the edge of the promontory, presumably originally enclosing a considerable part of it, rather than simply cutting off access across its neck. The burnt timbers, longitudinal as well as transverse, were well preserved, with some evidence for vertical timbers, though not bedded in postholes. Most of the timbers were roughly squared, and there was abundant evidence for mortise joints, suggesting even that some timbers had been re-used. Later prehistoric activity on the headland is indicated by a palisade underlying the early historic defences, but evidence of agriculture, post-dating the Iron Age use of the promontory and preceding the early historic phase of fortification (Edwards and Ralston, 1978: 208–9), suggests that any relationship between the two structural phases was largely fortuitous. Radiocarbon dates for Green Castle place the construction of its principal defences firmly within the second half of the first millennium AD.

Ring-forts and circular homesteads

The term 'ring-fort' has declined in popularity to describe small, enclosed settlements that are found in various parts of Scotland, including a notable distribution in Perthshire (Fig. 9.4). The class is used in Ireland, as we have observed, as an umbrella for small enclosures, broadly between 15 and 60 metres in diameter, the surrounding walls of which may be of earth with external ditch, or of stone, generally without an accompanying ditch. Despite the name their function need not have been primarily defensive. The chronology of ring-forts in Ireland is predominantly early historic, with some early Iron Age antecedents. In eastern Scotland the principal concentration of sites of this class is found in western Perthshire, notably in Strathtummel and Glen Lyon (Stewart, 1969), exemplified by the stone ring-fort above Balnacraig, Fortingall at Dun Geal. The smaller ring-forts might conceivably have been roofed structures, but most are too large for this to have been realistic, and at Dun Geal there are stone foundations indicative of smaller structures backed against the inner wall of the ring-fort in a manner that certainly recalls the western Irish ring-forts.

One of the earliest modern investigations of the Perthshire ring-forts was Watson's excavations at Borenich in Strathtummel (Fig. 9.4, 3; Watson, 1915). Internally he found

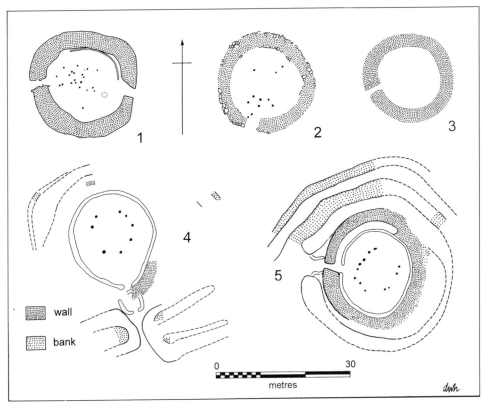

Figure 9.4 Ring-forts of Perthshire. 1, Queen's View; 2, Litigan; 3, Borenich East; 4, Aldclune site 2; 5, Aldclune site 1. Drawings by D. W. Harding, adapted from Taylor (1990), Watson (1915) and Hingley *et al.* (1997).

hearths and some paving, with an undiagnostic material assemblage including a spindle-whorl, bone implements and a fragment of quern. Subsequent work at two further sites was reported by Taylor (1990). At Litigan (Fig. 9.4, 2) a small ring-fort with stone wall 3 metres thick enclosed a circular area some 15 metres in diameter. Internally postholes and a hearth indicated domestic occupation, which, on the basis of a single radiocarbon date might be assigned to the later first millennium AD. The second ring-fort, at the Queen's View (Fig. 9.4, 1), commanding an extensive outlook over Strathtummel, was of much the same proportions. It appears to have had two entrances, the original seemingly blocked in a secondary phase of occupation. Two layers of paving through the surviving entrance, and three hearths within the interior, suggest that the site was occupied over successive periods. A scatter of postholes in the interior and an arc of ring-groove around the north-eastern perimeter of the enclosure are indicative of a roofed building. As at Litigan the material assemblage included fragments of rotary quern, not in themselves closely dateable, but, together with a yellow, opaque glass bead and stone cup, not inconsistent with occupation in the first millennium AD.

Both Stewart and Taylor questioned the utility of the term 'ring-fort', on the grounds that most sites were not obviously located or built with tactical defence in mind. In fact though frequently overlooked from higher ground, sites like Dun Geal, Litigan and the Queen's View do command extensive outlooks, and are tactically well sited in relation to pasture, and to oversee the passage of traffic along these important routes. Stewart was surely right to stress the importance of ring-forts in the context of a pastoral economy in which cattle-raiding was doubtless endemic. Archaeologists quite properly have wished to avoid the implication that they were introduced into central and eastern Scotland as an extension of settlement of Dál Riata in the west until the character and dating of the sites themselves had been more reliably established.

More recent excavation of two related ring-forts or fortified homesteads at Aldclune by Blair Atholl might have been expected to clarify the issue of chronology, but in some respects has only compounded the complexity of the problem (Hingley *et al.*, 1997). The sites occupied a prominent ridge overlooking the river Garry, and appear to have had their origins in the late first millennium BC. By the opening centuries of the first millennium AD the dominant building was a circular house, set behind a double-ditched earthwork extending around its northern circuit where access was easiest (Fig. 9.4, 5). The building itself was of unusual construction, involving a combination of stone walling, penannular ring-groove and post-ring. The sequence of structural episodes was not resolved beyond doubt by excavation. Initial assessments of the dating of the site may have been prejudiced by the discovery in the post-occupational debris of a fine, ninth-century penannular brooch, and required radical review when radiocarbon dates indicated much earlier origins for the settlement. The earlier structure (Site 2; Fig. 9.4, 4) was probably built and occupied at the end of the first millennium BC; the later ring-fort (Site 1; Fig. 9.4, 5) appears to have been constructed between the second and third centuries AD. The problem with the three relevant dates is that they are either from contexts that give only a *terminus post quem* for the site's construction and occupation, or for material that could be residual from the earlier occupation nearby. Given that the building is itself of more than once phase, occupation could have extended significantly into the first millennium AD. Whilst it is possible to point to differences between Aldclune and other ring-forts, it is clear that there is a long-standing tradition in this region of defended homesteads from later prehistoric into early historic times.

Settlements and domestic buildings

Accepting the current evidence that souterrains generally did not remain in use beyond the third century, it is nevertheless important to note that souterrain settlements apparently continued in occupation after the demise of souterrains themselves. Watkins believed that this might indicate progressive centralisation of power, with grain storage on a sizeable scale being transferred from local to regional level as part of a process of social and political development in the mid-first millennium AD. Wainwright equally stressed occupational continuity after the abandonment of the souterrains at Carlungie and Ardestie (Wainwright, 1963). Yet the structural remains at these sites (Fig. 9.5) suggest that a process of change was already under way at Ardestie and Carlungie before the abandonment of souterrains in the late second or early third centuries AD. Because of their small size and rather irregular construction, the agglomerated stone structures at both these sites have been regarded as workshops or ancillary stores (Watkins, 1984a: 77–8), rather than the primary dwellings of the site's occupants, which were presumed to have been larger, timber-built structures along the lines of those inferred at Newmill.

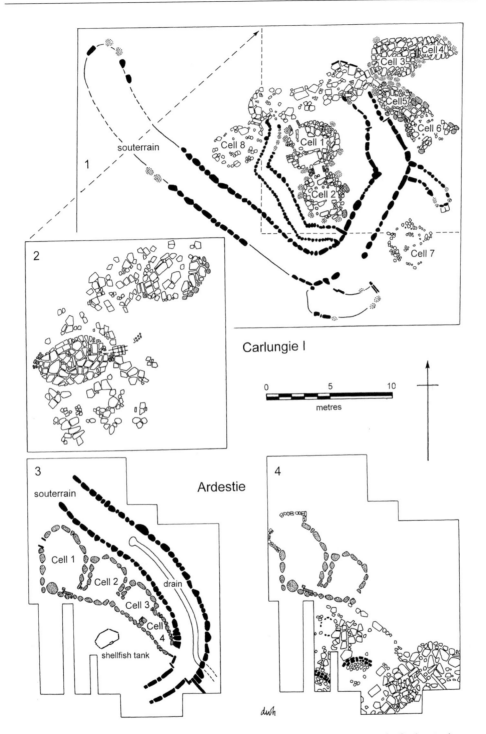

Figure 9.5 Souterrain settlements in Angus. 1, Carlungie I souterrain phase; 2, Carlungie I post-souterrain phase; 3, Ardestie souterrain phase; 4, Ardestie post-souterrain phase.

In fact the Carlungie and Ardestie buildings would be entirely in keeping with the kind of small, agglomerated cellular buildings which characterise the post-monumental phase of architecture in the Northern and Western Isles, among which some at any rate must have been used as domestic houses. The post-souterrain phases at Carlungie and Ardestie, however, are represented by even more ephemeral structural remains, as a result of agricultural damage, and are in consequence of the kind which might easily have evaded recognition or adequate recording on many excavations. They should not be dismissed as evidence of insubstantial occupation, however, and at Carlungie the oval, stone-walled, post-souterrain buildings were in fact larger in area than the cellular buildings contemporary with the souterrain.

With notable exceptions like Carlungie and Ardestie, the dominant medium of construction was evidently timber, which leaves the clearest archaeological traces where the foundations are earth-fast in postholes or bedding trenches. One reason why foundations of domestic buildings might have been archaeologically more ephemeral would be the adoption of rectangular plans, allowing alternative construction techniques such as the use of sill-beams, at or only marginally below ground level, into which upright timbers would be jointed. Alternatively the log-cabin method of construction may entail the use of some vertical posts, but so minimally as to render recognition of plans more contentious. Rectangular buildings could nevertheless have been built using a wall-trench, the rectilinear equivalent of a ring-groove, as at Thornybank, Midlothian. Alternatively, they could have been partially sunk into the ground in the manner of Anglo-Saxon *Grubenhäuser*, which should be readily detectable, despite the absence of postholes to support the roof other that those at either gable ends. At what point rectangularity in domestic architecture came to replace the older prehistoric tradition of circular building remains unclear, but certainly in the Atlantic Iron Age sub-rectangular plans appear alongside the circular tradition by the middle of the first millennium AD.

One regional group of rectangular buildings for which a pre-Improvement date was indicated by their stratigraphic relationships in the landscape is the so-called Pitcarmick house, named after a type-site in north-east Perthshire (RCAHMS, 1990: 12–13). Ranging in length from 10 to 30 metres overall, these buildings are of sub-rectangular plan, having rounded ends or slightly bowing walls. Internally they may have sunken floors at their narrower end, prompting the suggestion of use as a byre. Typically, lesser units are attached to the main building, in a manner reminiscent of early modern black-house settlements in the Hebrides. Excavation of the larger of two such buildings investigated at North Pitcarmick (*DES*, 1993: 102–3, 1994: 87–8, 1996: 141) revealed a sequence of structural phases, of which the latest yielded sherds of thirteenth-century date. Radiocarbon samples from both houses nevertheless indicated occupation in the later first millennium AD, with the possibility that the origins of the type originated somewhat earlier.

Air-photography may contribute to the identification of new sites that could radically change the picture of early historic settlement in eastern Scotland, but air-photography cannot furnish dates. Maxwell (1987: 33–4) was rightly cautious in assigning an early historic context to a series of rectangular crop-marks, potentially indicative of timber structures averaging some 25 metres in length by 9 metres in width, which had been located variously from the estuary of the Forth through Strathearn and Tayside to the Moray Firth. Generally occurring in isolation, one site at Lathrisk in Fife had several such structures in close proximity. Their similarity in plan to the timber halls of the Yeavering and Doon Hill type, especially the apparent annexes occasionally visible at one end, certainly prompts an early historic attribution. But the lesson of Balbridie, where a site of apparently similar plan proved through radiocarbon dating to be Neolithic, has quite properly induced a reluctance to burn fingers twice.

Continuity from earlier settlement types into the mid-first millennium is certainly in evidence in eastern Scotland. At Easter Kinnear in north-east Fife excavations at two adjacent sites, called Easter Kinnear and Hawkhill to distinguish them (Driscoll, 1997), demonstrated that the semi-subterranean or scooped and revetted form of house continued to be built into the early historic period. Recognised as amorphous 'blobs' from air-photography, these buildings, which proved to be sub-circular, oval or tending towards sub-rectangular in plan, could be founded more than a metre into the ground, revetted and sometimes paved with substantial, water-worn boulders. There was no evidence for primary furniture such as hearths, and it remains arguable whether the floor of the building was originally subterranean, or whether this represents storage space below a suspended floor at ground level. The Easter Kinnear house was subsequently filled in, and a series of post and wattled rectilinear buildings was constructed on the same foundations. The artefactual assemblage was hardly definitive, but radiocarbon dates suggest an occupation in the sixth and seventh centuries AD. The Hawkhill settlement was assumed to be broadly contemporary, though here the sequence culminated in a rectangular, stone-built long-house of the eleventh or twelfth century. Evidently there were changes afoot in domestic building by the mid-first millennium AD, the long-standing tradition of roundhouses in their various divergent forms giving way to structures which archaeologically may leave rather more ephemeral traces than the earth-fast roundhouses of the earlier Iron Age. Function is not easy to determine with confidence, but there is every reason to suppose that these scooped foundations represent domestic structures or groups of domestic structures.

Symbol-stones and symbol-ornamented artefacts

There can be few systems of archaeological classifications as enduring as the basic division of symbol-stones into Class I, Class II and Class III. Devised by Joseph Anderson for his Rhind Lectures of 1892, the scheme was published in 1903 in *The Early Christian Monuments of Scotland*, with a comprehensive catalogue by Romilly Allen. The typology was simple enough. Class I stones were essentially undressed monoliths with incised symbols, abstract or animal motifs. Class II stones were cross-slabs, the same symbols combining with but not intruding upon a central cross, the whole being executed in relief. Class III maintained the cross, but omitted the other symbols; these stones fall beyond the scope of the present study. Essentially the typological sequence was seen as corresponding to a chronological progression from around the seventh to the twelfth centuries, a perception that has remained substantially unchanged, with a concession to the possibility of the series starting in the sixth century. There have, of course, been numerous important contributions over many years, both to issues of classification and to the study of the stylistic origins and affinities of the symbols, mainly from an art-historical perspective. Specialists and non-specialists alike have also been absorbed with the question of the 'meaning' of symbol-stones in a way that, rightly or wrongly, has seldom pre-occupied students of earlier Celtic art, or indeed of the arts of early Christian Ireland.

A first issue that needs to be addressed is the date of the symbol-stones. Unfortunately, too few have any archaeological context that might illuminate the question of dating, and in consequence most assessments hitherto have necessarily relied heavily on art-historical considerations, or inferences based upon supposed historical associations. The relatively late dating of the appearance of Class I stones is in part a legacy of Anderson's assumption that their absence from the west must imply that their appearance post-dates the historical emergence of the kingdom of Dál Riata in the fifth century, an inference which has been rightly rejected as a total *non sequitur* (Laing and Laing, 1984). A major consideration in the chronological debate has been the obvious affinities between certain animal or bird motifs on incised stones and similar representations in the Northumbrian school of early gospel books, notably the *Echternach Gospels*, the *Book of Durrow* and Corpus Christi MS 197. Stevenson (1955b) saw the symbols as derived from the gospels; Isabel Henderson (1967) inferred a reciprocal influence of the stones on manuscript art. A direct debt of one to the other cannot be ruled out, of course, in which case we might enquire by what mechanisms such influences were transmitted. Equally it is possible that both drew inspiration from an older or common pool of imagery involving late Roman and Germanic contributions, thereby qualifying simplistic derivations and chronological inferences. Laing and Laing (1984) argued that distinctive motifs, like triskeles, interlace, key and trumpet patterns, which are represented in the Northumbrian manuscripts, were found more frequently on Class II stones rather than on Class I stones or related artefacts. If Class I stones were earlier than Class II, then it seemed logical to infer that they were also earlier than the manuscripts.

A second crucial consideration is the distribution of symbol-stones (Fig. 9.6), and the location of the earliest examples. The distribution of Class I stones is concentrated notably in Aberdeenshire, Strathspey and the Moray Firth region. There is also a significant group in Angus and Perthshire centred on Strathmore, but despite attempts to equate them with a supposed 'Pictish heartland' in this area, the archaeological distribution most logically argues for their origins north of the Dee. In fact, that northern concentration equates most closely with the earlier distribution of decorated glass beads of Guido's Class 13, while the overall distribution of Class I stones reflects the earlier distribution of massive armlets and related bronzes. Like the massive armlets, symbol-stones could be regarded as an expression of identity and autonomy on the part of communities capable of considerable technical and artistic sophistication.

The motifs employed on Class I stones are either abstract symbols or animal images. The human form or narrative scenes do not appear until Class II. Some of the abstract motifs of the Class I repertory – scrolls, peltae, simplified palmette or lotus leaves, ring-and-dot, arc and circle – are part of the common sub-stratum of early Celtic art, the survival of which into the post-Roman period need excite no special comment, other than to underline the native Celtic ancestry of the symbol-stones and their makers. Yet there are others, abstract geometrical shapes like the Z-rod or V-rod, which have no such long-standing antecedents. Symbols resembling everyday objects like combs, mirrors or hammers likewise do not figure as motifs in earlier Celtic art, though earlier Iron Age types might well have been the models on which the symbols were based rather than contemporary types (Thomas, A. C., 1984: 178). The iconography of birds and beasts certainly has a long antecedent history in the earlier Iron Age of Britain and Europe, and on coinage of the pre-Roman Iron Age alone horses, boars, bulls, birds of various kinds and snakes are not uncommon. It is not necessary to invoke direct derivation since the

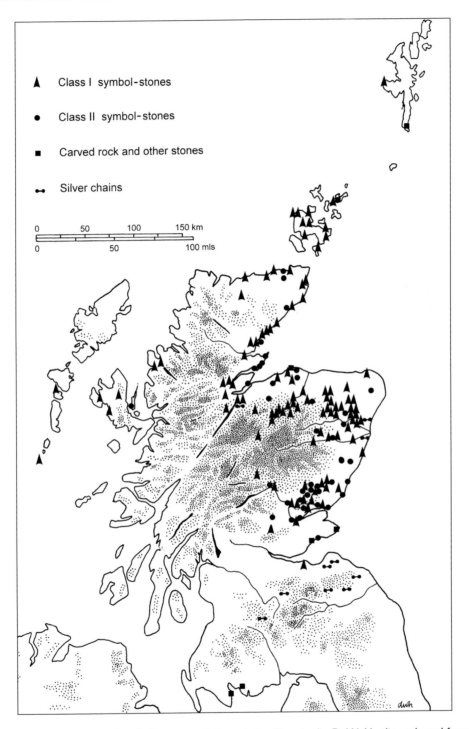

Figure 9.6 Distribution of symbol-stones and silver chains. Drawing by D. W. Harding, adapted from Foster (1996), Breeze, A. (1998) and NMRS.

style of rendering these creatures differs significantly, but the veneration of the Celtic zoo and its mythological or ritual significance could well have been sufficiently enduring to reappear in modified guise on the symbol-stones.

As to the idea of erecting a standing stone, as a memorial to the dead or as a declaration of identity, stone stele, ornamented or plain, are known in the pre-Roman Iron Age of Central and Western Europe, notably in the La Tène phase in Brittany and in Ireland. Within Roman and sub-Roman Britain there is ample evidence for the erection of inscribed stones of various types more specifically in funerary contexts (Thomas, A. C., 1984: 173–4). We should certainly distinguish between the medium of display on the one hand and the artistic style or motifs of the symbols themselves on the other, but both potentially could have had their roots in the pre-Roman Celtic heritage. There remains the problem of time-lag, why there should be an apparent gap of several centuries between the collapse of the Roman world and the resurgence of native artistic practices and symbolism. That hiatus is probably more apparent than real, and to overcome it, it has sometimes been suggested that earlier Class I symbols might have been carved on wooden totems, or even painted on stone, in effect in media that have simply not survived. An appealing alternative might be to imagine that the symbols were transmitted over generations in the form of body-painting, perhaps displayed at special ceremonies or festivals, or as aggressive expressions of identity in battle. Alternatively, the dilemma could be eased by allowing a less compressed chronology for the symbol-stones. But in the absence of definitive archaeological dating by context or reliable associations, the onus of proof evidently lies with those who acknowledge the logic of an earlier start for symbol-stone art to demonstrate their case beyond reasonable doubt. In the meantime, the debate tends to amount to little more than the affirmation or counter-affirmation of authoritative but unprovable opinion.

Whilst it is possible that some Class I symbol-stones were earlier than the conventional, conservative dating, it is equally probable that their currency extended into and overlapped with that of Class II. The fact that the same symbols were incorporated also into the design of Class II stones, on which, apart from the cross itself, biblical imagery clearly proclaims a Christian context, has been taken to indicate that the pagan symbolism was subsumed within the Christian repertory, a process that would not be without parallel. Apart from the cross itself, Christian imagery includes biblical scenes, such as Daniel and the lions (Meigle No. 2) or David in various guises. The cross itself may be embellished with interlace or related patterns, as at Glamis, Angus, while abstract symbols, animals and human figures occupy the panels between. The reverse side may display a fuller narrative scene of hunting or battle, as in the case of the Aberlemno churchyard cross-slab, or the later Aberlemno roadside slab. The cross on the latter is executed in higher relief with raised bosses in a style which reaches its culmination in the early ninth century in works like the Hilton of Cadboll, Ross-shire, stone, which R. B. K. Stevenson described (1955b: 116) as more like the page of a manuscript than a carving in stone.

The range and variety of ornament on Class II stones is considerably greater than on Class I, but echoes of early Celtic themes remain present if elusive, not only in the spiral and triskeles but also in the occasional exotic beast. Interlaced animals like those flanking the Aberlemno cross plainly have a Germanic pedigree, but opposed fantastic creatures like those on the Brodie slab or Meigle No. 26 have echoes of the early Celtic fashion for dragon pairs in similar confrontation. Equally the human head flanked by two animal heads at the top of the cross recalls the earlier Celtic adoption of the voracious beast theme, while the centaur on the same cross-slab is another classical image which is adopted by the Celtic artist on pre-Roman Iron Age coinage. Strikingly different from the traditions of earlier Celtic art is the portrayal of the human form, or the depiction of narrative scenes. The themes depicted nevertheless reflect an older Celtic tradition in which aristocratic pursuits like hunting and fighting are prominent.

The temptation to make simplistic and probably false equations between archaeological evidence and historical traditions is nowhere better demonstrated than in the conventional reading of the scene on the back of the Aberlemno churchyard stone (Fig. 9.7) as a commemoration of the battle of Nechtansmere in AD 685. Rival Picts and Northumbrians are identified on the basis of their helmets, and one horseman, together with the figure over which hovers a carrion bird, is even identified as the defeated Northumbrian king Ecgfrith. The fact that the stone is normally assigned on art-historical grounds to nearly a century after the date of the battle is no impediment to the equation of the scene with one specific historical event, even as a distant folk memory.

An important additional element on some symbol-stones and cross-slabs is the addition of ogham inscriptions. Ogham is generally reckoned to have developed in Ireland in the fourth century AD, and not to have been transmitted to Scotland until the seventh century. Since it was a phenomenon originally of southern Ireland not widely adopted in the north, the role of the historical settlement of Dál Riata in its introduction to Scotland has been challenged (Ritchie, A., 1987). Instead it may have been introduced at the same time as the spread of Christianity through the subsequent activities of Irish missionaries.

Figure 9.7 Aberlemno, Angus, churchyard cross-slab, reverse side. Photograph by the Royal Commission on the Ancient and Historical Monuments of Scotland. Copyright reserved. Reproduced by kind permission.

It is not impossible, of course, that symbols and ogham inscriptions were not contemporary but successive: as Ritchie (Ritchie, A., 1989: 20) observed, 'on symbol stones and cross-slabs [ogham] can look very much an afterthought – almost a footnote'. Many prestigious works of early Celtic art are demonstrably composite pieces, and on several of the later symbol-stones there is evidence of re-working or alterations, or re-use of earlier stones. For the most part the ogham inscriptions themselves on epigraphic grounds are generally regarded as belonging to the second half of the first millennium AD.

Often quoted as the earliest reliable archaeological context for a Class I symbol-stone is the slab found incorporated face down in paving in a sixth-century context at Pool, on Sanday in Orkney. By definition this provides not a date but a *terminus ante quem* for the carving and use of the stone for its original purpose, which could therefore have been significantly earlier than its sixth-century secondary context. Other associations are more equivocal. At Burghead, for example, radiocarbon dates suggest that the fort may have been constructed between the fourth and sixth centuries, but the bulls are normally dated on art-historical grounds to the seventh century, and are therefore arguably from a developed phase of the settlement. Likewise at Garbeg, the association of symbol-stone with incised crescent and V-rod and the barrow remains unproven, though the balance of probability is surely that the stone was originally a grave-marker. The burial is not closely dated, of course, but cemeteries of this kind in eastern Scotland appear from radiocarbon dates to belong between the early and mid-first millennium AD.

The date of portable artefacts bearing symbols can only be determined by their associations, and here again the record is regrettably defective. The Norrie's Law hoard has provoked particular controversy, its conventional seventh-century dating being based essentially on art-historical assessments that are not beyond dispute (Laing and Laing, 1984; Graham-Campbell, 1991). Assuming the hoard to be a genuine association, the youngest artefact in the group obviously provides a *terminus post quem* for the date of deposit. But the objects in the hoard could have been old when buried, treasured over many generations after the date of manufacture and use. It is therefore significant that the oval plaques with double-disc, Z-rod and dog's head should be in pristine condition, and by implication not long in circulation, by comparison for instance with the silver spiral ring. Nevertheless, among the key associations, the spiral bossed plaque with trumpet motifs need not be nearly as late as the seventh century, and dating the hand-pins quite so late is becoming problematic in the light of dated contexts elsewhere.

One striking class of artefacts, on some of which symbols are engraved, is the heavy silver chain, of which a dozen examples are known in a distribution that concentrates south of the Firth of Forth (Fig. 9.6; Henderson, I., 1979). Plainly objects of luxury and high status, perhaps even royal regalia, their find-spots are unfortunately not informative and their dating in consequence is hardly closely defined beyond the mid-first millennium AD or slightly later.

A Pictish postscript

The origins of the Picts is an issue of enduring fascination, and for some is as problematic as their eventual disappearance is mysterious. It is a commonplace that the first documented reference to the Picts is in a late Roman poem of AD 297 by Eumenius. Eumenius in fact attributed his Picts to an earlier context, contemporary with Caesar, so that it is probable that the term was known from the early Roman period. The use of 'proto-

Pictish' to span the period to which Eumenius was referring and the date of his writing would therefore not be unreasonable. It would be unrealistic anyway to imagine that the first documented reference coincided with the very first use of the term, and we may therefore reasonably look to the ancestry of 'Picts' within those groups that made up the Caledonian federation at the time of the Roman advance north. A later panegyricist, writing around 310, referred to 'Caledones and other Picti' in association, suggesting that the Picts were not an independent group, but a general term for the people north of the Roman frontier. The probability is that 'Picti', the 'painted ones', was derived from Roman army slang for 'war-painted savages', in much the same way that 'redskins' was used for native Americans. Ammianus Marcellinus, writing in the later fourth century, claims that the Picts were made up of two tribes, the Dicalydones and the Verturiones, which again suggests that Pict was either a supra-tribal name or was a generalisation for different native groups.

Most authorities acknowledge that the historical Picts in earliest sources referred to all the natives north of the Roman frontier (Smyth, 1984; Ritchie, A., 1989: 6; Foster, 1996: 11–12). It is in archaeological usage that the term has been confined to a more restricted geographical zone, a supposed 'Pictish heartland' in eastern Scotland, though even here internal sub-divisions have to be recognised. As Smyth has cogently argued, there is no historical basis for regarding symbol-stones or even Pit- place-names as specifically or exclusively Pictish, other than in the sense that they occur in Scotland north of the Forth–Clyde line in the period in question. Joseph Anderson in his Rhind Lectures (1881) made no attribution of the symbol-stones to the Picts, treating them instead as late Celtic, and only later adopting the Pictish assignation (Allen and Anderson, 1903). Daniel Wilson (1851) had certainly identified symbol-stones as Pictish, but in the context of a native origin rather than as the product of settlement by the Norse or of Dál Riata Gaels. Picts, of course, are documented in later king-lists and chronicles, which record their presence in eastern Scotland, but these do not demand their identification as an ethnic or archaeological entity distinct from their neighbours. The consequence of the text-led approach is that we end up looking for Pictish burials (Close-Brooks, 1984), Pictish houses (Ralston, 1997), or sites named in historical documents, whose identification on the ground may be extremely tenuous (see Ralston, 1987: 17 on Dun Foither). In collecting and synthesising the archaeological data it would be preferable to categorise it simply as 'later Iron Age' or 'early historic', on the grounds that, though anodyne, the terms do not pre-judge the issue of historical correlations.

The 'heartland' of the Picts from the mid-first millennium AD is generally inferred in the first instance from the distribution of Pit- and related place-names (Fig. 8.9). If the pit- or pett- element actually was related linguistically to Picts, the equation would be secure, but this is not generally accepted. It is agreed that it refers to a unit of land, which almost certainly would have been fundamental to the social order in the early historic period throughout Northern Britain, even if this particular denotation was exclusive to one particular region. The equation of Picts and symbol-stones is probably too deeply embedded in archaeological doctrine to dislodge, but there is nothing intrinsically that proclaims them as Pictish, other than in the generalised sense indicated by the late Roman sources. We have already noted that Class I stones, generally regarded as the earliest, in fact have a particular concentration significantly further north than the conventional centre of southern Pictland. An alternative suggestion (Driscoll, 1988a: 229), that the northern distribution represents a concentrated effort to bring the north under southern rule, may be regarded as special pleading, in the face of the normal inference that the densest distribution represents the focus of the phenomenon.

Earlier structural classes whose archaeological distributions correspond to the same presumed southern heartland include souterrains (Maxwell, 1987) and unenclosed timber roundhouse settlements (Maxwell, 1989: Fig. 6.5), though neither type could be regarded as exclusive to this group or region. Souterrains in particular, as we have seen (Fig. 7.6) have significant concentrations elsewhere in Northern Britain, corresponding in effect to the broader Roman definition of Picts. Silver chains are predominantly distributed *beyond* the territory normally assigned to the Picts. Linguistically, Pictish was regarded by Kenneth Jackson (1955) as a variant of Gallo-Britonnic, and the Picts therefore may be regarded linguistically (and perhaps still archaeologically) as Celtic. Differences between the Pictish language and the Gallo-Brittonic of the Votadini to the south should not be magnified into a major linguistic and cultural watershed on account of a relatively short-lived political anomaly of the mid-second century AD. Jackson also believed he could detect a sub-stratum of an older indigenous language that was not Celtic and not even demonstrably Indo-European. This enquiry was in part prompted by the 'Pictish Problem' in the first place, since older elements in topographical names could doubt-less be detected elsewhere without fundamentally undermining our perception of the native communities of Iron Age Britain. The demise of the Picts and Pictish language by the tenth century, therefore, perhaps might occasion less surprise if the assumed archaeological associations of the Picts were examined more rigorously in the first place.

Chapter 10

Argyll and Atlantic Scotland

There is no immutable threshold for defining the transition from earlier to later Iron Age that would be equally applicable to all regions of Northern Britain. In the Atlantic North and West, an obvious horizon is the decline of monumental buildings, the dismantling of broch towers and the construction within or around them of secondary buildings of lesser proportions. This may have taken place between the second and third centuries AD, in a process that need not have been synchronous across Atlantic Scotland. The position of wheelhouses in the sequence is pivotal. Though Armit (1996) described their internal architecture as preserving the tradition of monumentality, wheelhouses are the very antithesis of the external display of monumentality represented by brochs. Because their occupation still appears generally to have been successive to brochs, they will be here considered as a trailer to the later Iron Age in Atlantic Scotland.

Wheelhouses

The distribution of wheelhouses concentrates primarily in the Western Isles, with some notable outliers in the Shetlands. Their apparent absence on Orkney, and their absence in Argyll and the Inner Hebrides still requires explanation. Their layout in plan (Fig. 10.1) comprises a circular outer wall, from which project inwards radial piers in the manner of the spokes of a wheel, but truncated to leave a central space within the interior, around which the piers divide the perimeter into a series of individual cells. Sill-stones at the front edges of the cells may reinforce the division between central and peripheral space. Paving is not uncommon, and the central space may include a hearth, often of distinctive U-shaped or three-sided, open-ended plan, or a stone-lined trough. Within the cells there may be aumbries, or box-like cavities, within the walls. Access was through a single, main entrance, sometimes with external passage to prevent blockage by wind-blown sand. Wheelhouses appear to have been 'solitary homesteads' in Armit's phrase (1996: 144), sometimes with subordinate structures adjacent to them, but not apparently occurring in 'village' clusters. In the case of upstanding, upland sites like Clettraval, North Uist, and Tigh Talamhanta, Allasdale, Barra, the enclosure may have been contemporary, but the machair location of most wheelhouses would preclude the recognition of any comparable boundary. Occasionally wheelhouses are built into the collapsed debris of previous structures. Only in a limited number of instances are they completely free-standing at ground level, with double-sided walls. The majority are simply built with a revetment wall against the sand backing up to 2 metres into the machair.

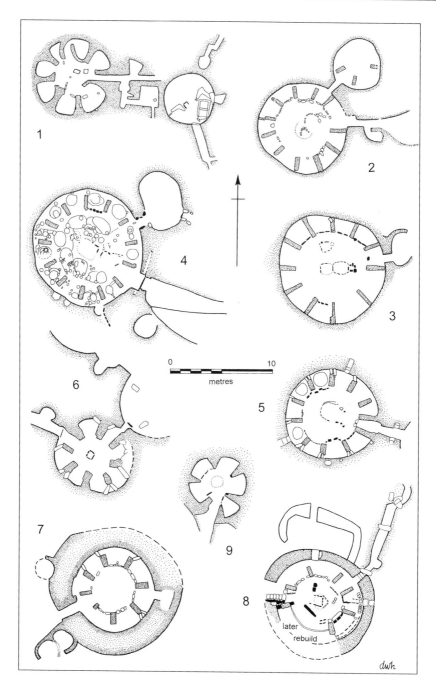

Figure 10.1 Wheelhouses, plans. 1, Bac Mhic Connain, North Uist; 2, A'Cheardach Bheag, South Uist; 3, A'Cheardach Mhor, South Uist; 4, Sollas, North Uist; 5, Kilphedir, South Uist; 6, Cnip, Lewis; 7, Clettraval, North Uist; 8, Tigh Talamhanta, Barra; 9, Old Scatness, Shetland. Drawings by D. W. Harding, adapted from Beveridge (1931), Young and Richardson (1960), Fairhurst (1971), Campbell (1991), Lethbridge (1952), Armit (1992), Scott (1948), Young (1953), Dockrill (1998).

From pioneer fieldwork in the Western Isles, two principal sub-groups of wheelhouses were recognised, those in which the radial piers abutted or were bonded into the outer perimeter wall, and those in which they were detached from the perimeter wall, the latter being known aisled roundhouses. In some instances, the aisle between pier and perimeter wall was blocked in a secondary phase. In fact, though the piers may be free-standing in ground-plan, they were bonded into the outer wall a metre or so above floor level, initially by a pair of long slabs set to form a Y, above which the roof of the cells could be progressively covered by slabbing or corbelling. The significance of the aisle in terms of internal movement must, therefore, have been minimal.

There is a considerable disparity in size and layout of wheelhouse settlements. The Cnip wheelhouse was 7 metres in internal diameter, with just eight radial piers; Sollas was 11 metres in diameter, for which thirteen piers were necessary. The later wheelhouse at nearby Udal South was apparently approaching the same size. The curiously conjoined wheelhouses B and C at Foshigarry were badly eroded by the sea and by later settlement even before Beveridge's excavation, but on the basis of his plan, building C, if its full diameter is projected on the basis of the surviving arc of walling, would have attained between 13 and 15 metres. Large but not excessive in terms of Southern British timber roundhouses, this is beyond the normal maximum of wheelhouse diameters. The abnormal disparity in roundhouse geometry, particularly in the ratio between the perimeter cells and the central court, must raise the question whether the centre in all cases was fully roofed over. Among more complex settlements the two buildings at Foshigarry could hardly have co-existed as wheelhouses; in fact on plan they seem to anticipate the figure-of-eight plans of later Pictish-period buildings. Structure D at Bac Mhic Connain is another that departs from the normal symmetry of wheelhouses, with its perimeter cells showing the irregularities that might be associated with the much earlier courtyard houses at Jarlshof, or some of the more cellular post-broch structures at Old Scatness. The lesson would appear to be that we should beware the seductive sin of creating strict architectural typologies, where in reality we may be dealing with the progressive and occasionally erratic development of roundhouses over a prolonged period of time. In effect, as with brochs, there is the danger that archaeological classification, based upon details of architectural typology, will create the myth of a 'true' wheelhouse, parallel to the self-fulfilling construct of a 'true' broch.

Externally semi-subterranean wheelhouses would have merged in the wind-blown sand into their machair environment. The possibility of livestock wandering on to the roof to graze, alluded to in Irish sources, however improbable in other circumstances, might have been a real risk with such buildings. From an interior perspective, however, they would have presented an imposing elevation, which would have been enhanced by their architectural details. At Cnip the height from original floor level to apex must have been in the order of 5 or 6 metres, which would have given the impression of a towering vault within the relatively confined interior. The radial piers progressively widen from basal course upwards, whilst the use of facing slabs at Jarlshof (Fig. 10.2b) against horizontal coursing set just far enough back to accommodate the width of the facing stone, is a deliberately ornamental rather than functional device. Most elaborate of all was the roofing of the peripheral cells. Only two examples survive intact, one at Jarlshof in Shetland (Fig. 10.2a), where the use of tabular flagstones facilitated the task, the other at Cnip in west Lewis (Fig. 10.3), where the more intractable Lewisian gneiss presented an altogether more formidable challenge for the builders. The Jarlshof technique involves

(a)

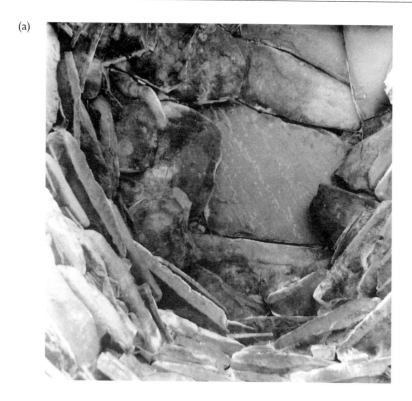

(b)

Figure 10.2 Jarlshof, Shetland, wheelhouses. a, wheelhouse 2, cell roof; b, wheelhouse 1, interior. Photographs by D. W. Harding and I. M. Blake.

Figure 10.3 Cnip, Lewis, cells of wheelhouse 1. Photograph by D. W. Harding.

the initial corbelling of courses of the cell walls, above which large slabs progressively converge, like a camera's aperture diaphragm, until it can be bridged with a single slab. The Cnip roof, preserved in two cells of the latest phase of re-use, entails the use of chunky, undressed gneiss, cruder at first sight but evidently durable over nearly two millennia. Support for the roof of corbelled peripheral cells of wheelhouses would have been required on the inner edge of the cells, which Sir Lindsay Scott at Clettraval deduced could have been provided by an arrangement of cantilevered stone architraves.

The assumption of total roofing, as with brochs, is not one that has been universally agreed. In Atlantic Scotland, where an unroofed court would rapidly fill with wind-blown sand, practicality must argue in favour of a totally roofed reconstruction in the majority of cases. Captain Thomas' (Thomas, F. W. L., 1870) sketch of Usinish, despite his textual observation that the central court was open with only the peripheral cells corbelled, actually shows a central stone vault of quite unrealistic proportions. Perhaps surprisingly for someone who advocated the lesser 'pent', or inward-sloping, annular roof for brochs, Hamilton (1956: 204) revived the notion of a full stone vault for the Jarlshof wheelhouses. Citing the internal diameter of the early Christian corbelled cells at Eileach an Naoimh on the Garvellach islands as comparable to the diameter of the inner court of the Jarlshof wheelhouses, he believed, rather optimistically, that the wheelhouses could have sustained the weight of a totally stone-vaulted roof on their perimeter walls and radial piers.

By contrast, Lethbridge (1952) imagined an altogether more flimsy use of the Kilphedir wheelhouse, which now seems equally improbable at the other extreme. The comparison with 'the regulation army bell tent . . . 16 feet in diameter and . . .

designed to house three officers, seven sergeants or fifteen men with their equipment' seems ludicrously anachronistic, and the idea that the surrounding wall was devised by 'a nomadic people settling down to semi-permanent life' in order to 'prevent cattle from falling over the guy ropes or rubbing against the tent' now beggars belief. But it is a salutary reminder of just how 'primitive' Iron Age communities were believed to have been just a couple of generations ago, against all the evidence of their structural and material remains.

The improbability of Lethbridge's primitivist reconstruction should not distract us from the real problems that reconstruction of wheelhouses poses. That the perimeter cells could be stone-roofed is demonstrated by the survival of examples that were. Scarcity of timber may have been one factor in the development of the wheelhouse plan, since its radial piers certainly reduced the span of timbers required to roof the central court. Straw, reed or heather thatch would presumably have been available for that purpose. Turf as a roofing material would perhaps have been feasible, provided a regular fire was maintained within the building to prevent it collapsing as a sodden mass, but for longer spans its greater weight might have required additional roof support. For this there is little evidence in the form of earth-fast postholes, which is not to say that timber supports could not have been ground-based on flags as heel-stones. The one problem posed by this form of reconstruction is the interface between central cone and the vaults of the peripheral cells. Though there is archaeological evidence for drains, there is no specific provision for dealing with this problem. Armit's reconstruction of the Cnip wheelhouse (1992: Ill. 6.13) overcomes this problem by building up the inner edge of the peripheral cells, so that the rafters lap over their roofs in a broadly continuous slope. Whether this would be viable in practice still requires empirical demonstration.

Wheelhouse settlements are often more heterogeneous than the simplified selection of 'classic' examples might suggest. Sites like Foshigarry were evidently occupied over a long period, and underwent substantial structural modifications. Despite the internal height of wheelhouses there is no evidence for intermediate floors or loft-levels for storage, other than in the hybrid 'aisled roundhouses' of Jarlshof and Old Scatness. Any such additional capacity as was required, therefore, had to be created by lateral expansion, which doubtless accounts for the complexity of surrounding structures of some wheelhouse plans, not all of which need be regarded as secondary. The many amorphous, cellular appendages to wheelhouses occasionally included souterrains, or linear passages in Armit's (1992) terminology. Some souterrains were manifestly secondary, as at Bruthach a Tuath, Benbecula (ibid.: 90), at Foshigarry (Beveridge, 1930) or at Cnip (Harding and Armit, 1990). There are, however, examples of souterrains in the Western Isles that do appear to have been integral to wheelhouse construction, at Tigh Talamhanta and possibly at Usinish (Thomas, F. W. L., 1870).

The constructional problems posed by free-standing buildings like Clettraval (Scott, 1948) and Tigh Talamhanta (Young, 1953) must have been of a different order altogether. With their double-faced walls these buildings are effectively solid-walled roundhouses, within which radial piers dictate the internal ground plan of a wheelhouse. They might be regarded as simple Atlantic roundhouses at one end of a spectrum with complex Atlantic roundhouses or brochs at the other, among which some also display a radial division of internal space. In fact, their radial plans may have more to do with the social division of space than with architectural typology. If social division of space was the key criterion, then the apparent anomaly of the absence of wheelhouses in Orkney may be substantially qualified. Several roundhouses on Orkney betray elements of radial division, notably at Calf of Eday and Howmae Brae, North Ronaldsay, but equally in the secondary occupation of the Burrian broch, North Ronaldsay. The fact that these divisions are frequently achieved by means of edge-set slabs rather than piers, not necessarily to the same height as the radial piers of western wheelhouses, need not mean that the structural types are not related, if social division of space was the key. An example from Skaill (Buteux, 1997) evidently did have radial walls rather than simply edge-set slabs. In fact, building techniques may be expected to vary regionally, reflecting adaptability to local resources. Social conventions might be expected to display a wider currency in Atlantic Scotland, even though their physical expression will have been affected by local considerations.

The total absence of wheelhouses from the Inner Hebrides, on the other hand, is more difficult to account for, since proximity to the Western Isles must have encouraged regular interaction across the Minch in later prehistory. MacKie argued that the secondary roundhouse at Dun Mor Vaul on Tiree could have been an aisled wheelhouse, on the basis of massive lintels around the perimeter of the roundhouse that he believed were the bonding stones of an aisled structure. But excavation revealed no trace of the diagnostic radial piers, and had wheelhouses really been a regular feature of the Iron Age landscape of the Inner Hebrides, chance finds from erosion by wind or sea would surely have exposed their distinctive structural remains. In fact, contact between the two regions appears to have been limited in the Iron Age in terms of structural types and material assemblages.

The case for a ritual function for wheelhouses has been argued on the basis of evidence from Sollas in North Uist (Campbell, 1991). The ritual activities focused upon a series of animal burials, principally of sheep, but also including cremated remains of cattle, found within a series of intersecting pits, numbering around 150 in total, in the interior of the wheelhouse. These pits were disposed in two groupings, one around the perimeter of the central space, the others confined within the peripheral cells; only the entrance 'cell' was devoid of pits. Cell 9, diametrically opposite the main entrance, seems to have attracted a particular concentration of burials. Most convincing as ritual deposits are those in which a whole or near-whole articulated skeleton has been buried, though in one instance the dismembered remains were packed so neatly into the pit as to suggest very careful deposition of the defleshed remains. In some cases the skull and feet were missing, prompting the suggestion that they may have been removed with the skins for a 'heads and hooves' ritual (Piggott, S., 1962) prior to deposition of the remainder of the skeleton. Animal burials were not the only deposits that were potentially of ritual significance; in one instance a broken quern with central perforation had been placed over a small pit, suggesting the possibility that libations were poured through it to the cavity below.

The fact that none of the pits underlay any of the structural walls of the wheelhouse was a clear indication that they were cut after the latter were built. They may reasonably be associated with the initial use of the wheelhouse, though the complexity of intersecting stratigraphy suggests a considerable sequence of activity. Above the pits was a sequence of occupation levels, apparently associated with central hearths, again representing an indeterminate period of subsequent activity. In some instances the pits were clearly sealed by these later levels; in others the nature of the pit-filling precluded an unequivocal assessment of the stratigraphy. There was also some structural modification, and it may be an oversimplification to regard the ritual activity on the site as predominantly belonging to the earlier of these phases. The most convincing as ritual deposits are those from the smaller pits, rather than from the larger, earlier pits, so that the practice of ritual deposition may have been protracted over the life of the wheelhouse.

Sollas is unusual in the density of deposits of apparently ritual character, but votive deposits or even more specifically foundation deposits are not unusual in wheelhouses for which a normal domestic function may otherwise be inferred. Most striking among other settlements are the human burials at Hornish point, South Uist (Barber *et al.*, 1989), found in four pits immediately underlying a structure with radial piers that is undoubtedly related to the wheelhouse class. The human remains were those of a juvenile, possibly male, whose skeleton had been cut up and deposited in portions in each of the four pits, accompanied in three by remains of cattle and sheep, which had likewise been treated as a deliberate deposition. It is possible that the child's remains had been exposed before burial, and the excavator was inclined to regard this not as a foundation burial so much as the abnormal burial of a social outcast. Armit (1996: 156), on the other hand, noting the general absence of Iron Age cemeteries or burials in the Western Isles, suggested that excarnation may have been the norm, which happened to coincide in this instance with the construction of the wheelhouse and the requirement for a foundation deposit.

A clear demonstration of foundation rituals comes from Cnip, Lewis, where behind the wall of the unfinished second wheelhouse was found the skull of a great auk and a whole pottery vessel. Other examples of this kind doubtless exist, but whereas pits in the floor are likely to be recognised by excavators, archaeologists seldom engage in the systematic dismantling of structural walls. The arc of red deer jawbones around the hearth at A' Cheardach Bheag, and the hoard of cattle teeth found in one of the wheelhouse's peripheral cells (Fairhurst, 1971) were clearly deliberate collections, which were presumably intended to serve a votive purpose. The cache of seals' teeth from the later secondary occupation at Beirgh could conceivably have been intended for ornament, though none was perforated for suspension, but cattle teeth seem an unlikely choice for this purpose. On the other hand, the arc of cattle teeth around the secondary roundhouse hearth at Dun Bharabhat closely resembles the deposit from A' Cheardach Bheag, and suggests a magical or supernatural motivation. What is clear from these comparisons is that votive deposits are not unique to wheelhouses, but the scale of the Sollas pit-deposits, together with the abnormal diameter of the building, must raise the question whether this site served particular ritual purposes. Sharing a common building plan or common architectural devices is no guarantee of common function, though in general the evidence of the Atlantic Iron Age argues against specific sites serving a ritual purpose in a way that might be maintained for other periods.

In some cases, in Shetland and in the Western Isles, wheelhouses are demonstrably secondary to Atlantic roundhouses. The older classic model is the Jarlshof sequence (Fig. 10.4; Hamilton, 1956). Here the aisled roundhouse of the immediately post-broch phase represents a transitional form, having a scarcement as well as unbonded radial piers. The scarcement implied the possibility of an upper floor level, or at least a mezzanine or gallery, and the presence in the perimeter wall of an aumbry above the scarcement reinforced the idea of an upper level. The radial piers were regarded as a secondary introduction, not to create peripheral cells in the manner of a wheelhouse, but to provide additional support for the roof. They certainly show no sign of progressive outward

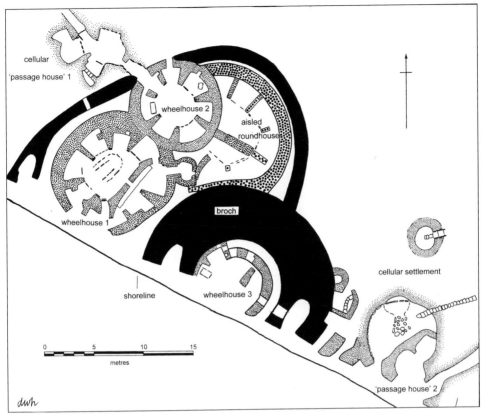

Figure 10.4 Jarlshof, Shetland, broch and post-broch settlement, plan. Drawing by D. W. Harding, adapted from Hamilton (1956).

curvature with height, as is characteristic of the later wheelhouses at Jarlshof, but the contiguous paving of their bays on the other hand enhances the appearance of a conscious differentiation between central and peripheral space.

The fully developed wheelhouses that succeeded the aisled roundhouse at Jarlshof were essentially free-standing structures, with two-faced walls around most of their circuit. The radial piers of these buildings are bonded into their perimeter walls, and they corbel inwards with height to facilitate roofing with stone slabs, still preserved in the cells of wheelhouse 2. The apex of the peripheral cells survive to a height of around 3 metres from the floor, so that, with the addition of a conical roof to the central area, the total height of the building could have been of the order of 5 metres. There was no evidence of any upper or mezzanine level, other than a loft compartment above the entrance passage. Notwithstanding the structural weaknesses that emerged with time, these buildings are feats of considerable technical sophistication and architectural pretension. The aisled roundhouse is an obvious step towards the achievement of that developed class of wheelhouse.

If the reconstruction of the Jarlshof 'hybrid' aisled roundhouse remains an enigma, the structure itself is no longer unique. More recent excavations on the northern perimeter of Sumburgh Airport at Old Scatness (Dockrill, 1998; 2003) have revealed in the post-broch sequence a building (Structure 14) which displays the same combination of scarcement, aumbry and radial piers. At least three radial piers survived to the same level as the scarcement, suggesting to the excavator, as to Hamilton at Jarlshof, that the building could have had an upper floor. These piers were of elongated rectangular plan, in contrast to the shorter, triangular shape of later wheelhouse piers. The fact that one pier partly blocked an aumbry in the outer wall also suggested the possibility of more than one phase of construction in the building. Radiocarbon and archaeomagnetic dates for this aisled roundhouse indicates its occupation in the later first millennium BC, providing the earliest reliable dating for the appearance of wheelhouses or related structures. Old Scatness also features a pair of wheelhouses (Structures 6 and 11) that have decidedly triangular radial piers with signs of incipient corbelling in elevation. These, like the Jarlshof wheelhouses, also include the embellishment of vertical slabs facing the inner edge of the radial piers. The discovery of a discarded slab with carving of a bear-symbol on its face has prompted the suggestion that it could have been an ornamental façade for just such a pier. The internal occupation of these buildings was intensive, and in Structure 6 in particular was represented by a series of superimposed floors and hearths. AMS radiocarbon dates, archaeomagnetic dates and optically stimulated luminescence dating all point to the probability that the later phases of these buildings belonged to a period much later than is conventionally assigned to the currency of wheelhouses, in the second half of the first millennium AD. In fact the upper levels of Structure 11 yielded a significant assemblage of Norse artefacts, indicating unprecedented re-use or longevity of occupation.

In the Western Isles the Beirgh sequence suggests an alternative model of development. It seems probable that initially the secondary re-occupation of the reduced shell of the complex Atlantic roundhouse was a simple roundhouse. At Beirgh this was a structure revetted into rubble around the inner broch wall, but with re-entrant gaps to provide access into the ground-floor galleries and cells of the former broch. In effect, the roundhouse had a series of peripheral cells, created by re-use of the earlier intra-mural structures. The rising water table at Beirgh, however, required that the floor level should be raised periodically, so that in due course the intra-mural cells of the former broch were no longer accessible. Only at this stage, it appears on present evidence, were radial piers introduced into the roundhouse in order to re-create the internal division of space that would approximate to the archaeological definition of a wheelhouse. Quite evidently this would have resulted in a reduction in the overall space available, and it may well be that it was at this stage that the external structures were developed in compensation.

Site sequences like Jarlshof need not in principle preclude the use of wheelhouses at an earlier date, contemporary with Atlantic roundhouses. Once again the problem is compounded by the undiagnostic nature of earlier material assemblages (Harding, 1995; forthcoming, a). A late dating for wheelhouses was argued by R. B. K. Stevenson (1955a), though much of the material in question may have been derived from secondary contexts on wheelhouse sites. Both saddle-querns and rotary querns are found, either within undifferentiated occupation debris or sometimes incorporated into the walls themselves, so that the position of wheelhouses relative to the period of 'quern replacement' (Caulfield, 1978) is therefore hard to assess. Beads are hardly closely dateable between the closing centuries of the first millennium BC and the early or mid-first millennium AD. On the basis of its ceramic assemblage, which included applied cabled ornament and a variety of stamped and incised wares, but notably did not include arcaded ornament of everted-rim vessels in the Clettraval style, we might wonder whether, *contra* Sir Lindsay Scott (Young, 1953: 104), Tigh Talamhanta, Barra, might not have been among the earlier wheelhouse settlements in the Western Isles.

In his analysis of the Sollas evidence Armit argued (1996: 145) that occupation levels that survive for archaeological examination most likely relate to the closing stages of the site's use, so that the data are necessarily biased towards late dating. Whilst this may seem like special pleading, it is probably true that evidence of the earliest occupation on a site will have been obliterated by re-use if not simply by periodic cleaning and maintenance. For this reason the *terminus post quem* centring on the late fifth century BC (GU-2754: 2370+/– 130 BP), obtained from bone in the votive deposit behind the wall of wheelhouse 2 at Cnip, though only a single uncorroborated date, might be of potential significance. Cnip yielded a series of eighteen radiocarbon dates, but the excavator still regarded the dating of its first phase as ambiguous. Phase 2 was fairly securely dated to the mid- to late-first century AD, so by implication the earliest wheelhouse could have been constructed in the closing centuries of the first millennium BC. Much the same could have been true of Sollas. The radiocarbon dates there pointed to a span of occupation between the first and third centuries AD, but none was from an unequivocally primary context. Whilst Campbell believed that the smaller pits, which were cut through the filling of the earlier, larger series, were not long removed from the primary occupation, this conclusion is certainly open to challenge. The dates from Hornish Point, South Uist, centring on the fifth and fourth centuries BC were recognised by the excavator as probably prejudiced by the marine reservoir effect, and are not therefore reliable testimony of early dating of wheelhouses.

As regards the Udal, until such time as the site is adequately published and the stratigraphic and contextual data are available for critical review, it is obviously prudent to reserve judgement. But the excavator has claimed that the wheelhouses there had their origins in the later Bronze Age (Crawford, n.d.: 8–9). In a long sequence of occupation of Udal South the final wheelhouse phases apparently produced three radiocarbon dates centring on the first century AD. Crawford compared the later Bronze Age phase of activity, apparently represented by bronze working and buildings of piered construction, to the late Bronze Age settlement at Jarlshof, raising the possibility that buildings allied to the wheelhouse originated in structures of the earlier 'courtyard' class. The social-use-of-space rather than the architectural-typology model would certainly lead to the expectation of an older tradition of building in which the defining factor was the division of central from peripheral areas.

In sum, the case for an early Iron Age origin of wheelhouses is far from demonstrated, but cannot altogether be ruled out. On the other hand, the secondary occurrence of wheelhouses in Atlantic roundhouse sequences is undeniable. Where wheelhouses in the Western Isles in particular have been investigated in the past, their multi-period character and probable longevity of use is apparent. Recent evidence from Shetland, notably from Old Scatness, certainly argues for the survival of a cellular wheelhouse variant into the later first millennium AD. At Scalloway (Sharples, 1998) the post-broch occupation included the introduction of radial piers of a distinctive V-shaped design, which the excavator dated there to the fifth and sixth centuries AD. The issue of chronology is important, not least in the debate regarding social reconstruction in the Atlantic Iron Age, in which the relationship between brochs and wheelhouses in any inferred social hierarchy is one of the more contentious issues. At present it seems probable that the currency of the two settlement types may have overlapped, but it is difficult to see them as representing different social levels within a coterminous system.

Post-broch settlement in the Western Isles

In both the Northern and Western Isles the immediately post-broch occupation frequently takes the form of a roundhouse, built within the courtyard of the inner broch wall (Fig. 10.5). In some cases the broch walls were apparently deliberately reduced, perhaps in part to provide building material for the new construction and in part to consolidate the remains of the broch tower. Where the roundhouse wall actually abuts the inner broch wall, as at Dun Mor Vaul, we might question why it was necessary to create a new wall-face at all, constricting internal space to no obvious advantage, when the original broch walls appeared to be perfectly serviceable. At Carn Liath (Fig. 10.6a) the rebuilt secondary wall seems unnecessarily to reduce space within a serviceable broch wall, and at Mousa (Fig. 10.6b) the surviving broch structure must surely have remained in use. The implication might be that the re-facing was a symbolic as well as a physical break with the past, even though functional features of the Atlantic roundhouse were re-used, such as its entrance or perhaps its intra-mural galleries. The transition was evidently one of some significance. Post-broch structures cease to be monumental on the scale of the Atlantic roundhouses, and in floor area their single-storeyed construction cannot have matched a quarter of the potential of a tower with multiple floors and intra-mural galleries. In compensation, expansion beyond the walls of the broch may have been necessary, as was probably the case at Beirgh. What the catalyst for this major change was, and whether it was synchronous across Atlantic Scotland, remains a puzzle. Major demographic disruption or innovation hardly seems to be implied in the material assemblage and can probably be discounted. In any event, the question, 'what brought about the demise of the brochs?' should surely be addressed in conjunction with the question, 'what prompted their construction and development in the first place?' Whatever circumstances demanded a display of monumentality either no longer pertained, or the need was met by other means.

An informative post-broch settlement sequence survived in the Loch na Beirgh, in west Lewis (Harding and Gilmour, 2000). Because it has not proved possible to complete the excavation of this uniquely preserved sequence, crucial information regarding the primary phases of occupation, and the earliest post-broch structures, remain to be investigated. The later settlement sequence, however, extending from around the second century AD to the Norse incursions of the ninth or thereabouts, has been recorded in detail. A unique facet of the Beirgh environment was the progressive silting of the loch and the consequential rise in the water table, which obliged successive generations of occupants to raise their internal floor levels, thus preserving more completely than is usual the underlying structural foundations and associated occupation deposits. The consequence of this process is not only a deeper than usual vertical stratigraphy, from which the occupational sequence could be unravelled, but the inundation of the lowest deposits, in which organic materials are unusually well preserved.

The early post-broch occupation at Beirgh, as we have seen, focused on a roundhouse, built within the broch walls, but utilising some of its still accessible intra-mural galleries, until such time as the rising water level rendered that impractical. At this stage radial

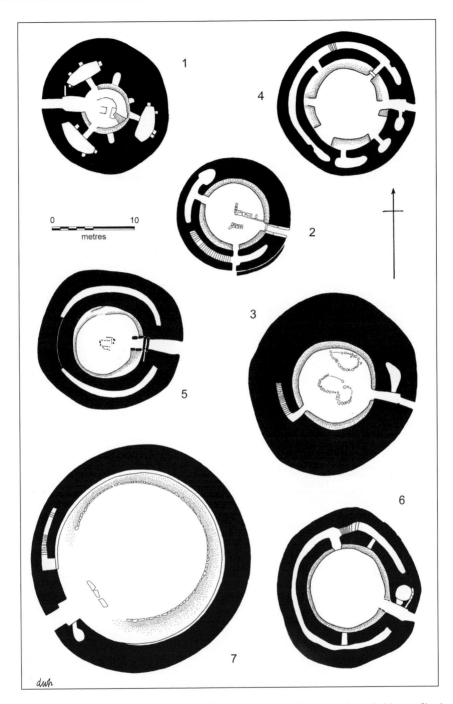

Figure 10.5 Complex Atlantic roundhouses with secondary roundhouses, plans. 1, Mousa, Shetland; 2, Yarrows, Caithness; 3, Carn Liath, Sutherland; 4, Beirgh, Lewis; 5, Dun Cuier, Barra; 6, Dun Mor Vaul, Tiree; 7, Ardifuar, Argyll. Drawings by D. W. Harding, adapted from RCAMS (1946), RCAHMS (1911), Joass (1890), Love (1989), Young (1956), MacKie (1974), RCAHMS (1988).

piers were constructed, giving the building an internal division of space akin to that of a wheelhouse. The complexities of the Beirgh roundhouse phase remain to be clarified. Its end is marked stratigraphically by one of the few contexts that extends across the whole of the site's interior, a thick layer of laid peat covering the roundhouse occupation

(a)

(b)

Figure 10.6 'Post-broch' secondary structures. a, Carn Liath, Sutherland; b, Mousa, Shetland. Photographs by D. W. Harding and I. M. Blake.

and providing the foundations for the next major structural phase, characterised by multiple, small, cellular units. The contrast between the roundhouse, which, however modified, occupied the former broch interior in its entirety, and the cellular suite of buildings, could not be greater and must signify some important shift in function or change in social pattern. The early cellular phase yielded debris from bronze working, which suggests industrial activity in close proximity. The use of external space, probably initiated already in the roundhouse phase of occupation, was probably extended in the cellular phase. The dating of the cellular phase is assigned to a span between the early third and late sixth centuries AD.

In terms of construction techniques, the cellular phase is particularly characterised by the use of edge-set slabs, as single-sided facing of debris from previous buildings or as double-sided facing of a free-standing wall. In either instance slab-revetted foundations commonly formed the base for a wall of drystone coursing, which progressively corbelled inwards to create either a completely corbelled roof to the smaller cells, or partly corbelled eaves for an organic roof of timber and thatch. Partial corbelling, though inherently unstable unless firmly braced by the roof timbers, seems to be well attested by the structural remains from Beirgh and other sites in the Western Isles, and is paralleled in more recent buildings such as the *cleitan* of St Kilda (RCAHMS, 1988a). Corbelled cells of this kind are particularly difficult to recognise archaeologically unless the excavator is expressly looking for them, or is familiar with their residual characteristics, since their courses are progressively set back with depth, and at first sight appear more like collapsed masonry than a conventional wall-face. Secondary occupation characterised by this kind of construction can easily have been missed or misinterpreted in older excavations in Atlantic Scotland and Ireland. Reference to amorphous sections of masonry at Cahercommaun, Co. Clare (Hencken, 1938), for example, almost certainly indicates secondary occupation, from which much of the Early Christian material might have derived rather than from the primary occupation of the stone fort.

The cellular phase at Beirgh nevertheless exhibits several different types of structure, utilising a combination of stone and timber. Structure 5 was unique in having the timbers of its twin door-posts still *in situ*, with their lower, earth-fast sections still intact below floor level. The fact that the only surviving evidence of its sub-circular plan was a kerb of small edge-set slabs suggests that its walls as well as its roof may have been of organic materials. Similar foundations of small, edge-set slabs characterised one circular building at Close ny chollagh on the Isle of Man (Gelling, 1958), where the two more substantial roundhouses used a combination of edge-set boulders and horizontal coursing in the manner of the cellular and later phases at Beirgh. The Manx promontory fort from its material associations would appear to have been occupied around the first century AD. Structures of wattled construction from Deer Park Farms in Co. Antrim could provide a possible parallel for the superstructure of these less substantial buildings at Beirgh. Alternatively, as Gilmour has suggested, the cellular settlement in its earlier stages at any rate could still have had an overarching roof, so that the surviving foundations may delineate activity areas rather than independently roofed buildings.

By the later cellular phases, at any rate, structures 1a and 1b were quite evidently a pair of fully stone-corbelled cells. At one stage in their use these cells formed part of a shamrock-shaped unit, with an open court bounded by the re-used wall of the earlier roundhouse (Fig. 10.7, 2). The hearths were characteristically of open-ended, three-sided plan. The similarity with the Pictish-period 'shamrock' from Gurness, Orkney (Fig.

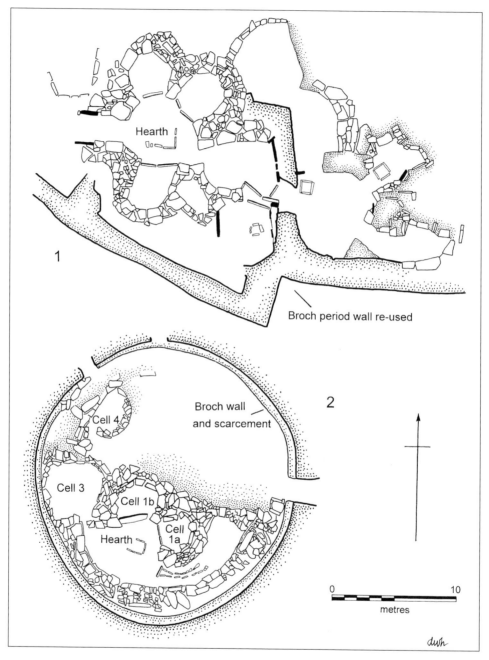

Figure 10.7 Cellular 'shamrock' structures, plans. 1, Gurness, Orkney; 2, Beirgh, Lewis. Drawings by D. W. Harding, adapted from Hedges (1987) and Harding and Gilmour (2000).

10.7,1), is striking, even down to the sill-stones that marked the entrance into the cells. Two adjacent cells, structures 3 and 4, may have had part corbelled, part timber and thatch roofs; both included slumped stonework that was generally indicative of partial corbelling. A further novelty of the late cellular phase at Beirgh was a short souterrain-like structure leading out of the 'shamrock', which, like some souterrains in eastern Scotland, had a drain running axially down its length. In fact, the Beirgh 'shamrock' should perhaps be seen as including cell 3 and the souterrain, as well as cells 1a and 1b with the open court, its quadrifoliate plan being simply compressed by the constraint of the encircling broch wall.

The final stage of occupation at Beirgh, dated broadly by artefacts to the seventh–eighth centuries AD, is represented by the culmination of cellular construction, the so-called figure-of-eight, or 'ventral' house (Fig. 10.8, 3). The Beirgh example, which itself overlay some intermediate structures of which only amorphous arcs of walling survived, occupies the whole of the former broch interior. It still retained the line of the broch entrance as its entrance passage, though because of the progressive rise in occupation levels its paving would have been approximately at the level of the capstones over the original broch entrance. The interior divides into a main cell, with central hearth and twin aumbries or recesses diametrically opposite the entrance, and a secondary cell to the north, compressed into a kidney shape by the former broch walls. At one stage in its use, a third, smaller cell just inside the entrance passage occupied the same relative position as an earlier cell of the cellular occupation period, perhaps a later derivative of the guard-cell of a broch. The figure-of-eight building used massive edge-set slabs to revet the debris of earlier collapsed masonry, above which in places several horizontal courses survived, in sections plainly demonstrating a tendency to partial corbelling. How such a structure was roofed, however, remains a matter of conjecture. Roofing each cell independently may have proved problematic, and it is possible that these buildings had an overall hipped roof, as was inferred for the experimental reconstruction of the Bostadh house, just across the water on Great Bernera.

Dating the later Iron Age occupation is aided by artefactual evidence, which fortunately included several diagnostic types, rather than upon radiocarbon samples alone. Two penannular brooches came from levels immediately preceding the construction of the final figure-of-eight house, and a pair of copper alloy tweezers was found on the floor of the house itself. Pipe-bowl shaped crucibles likewise suggested a date-span in the seventh to ninth centuries, but unlike its northern counterparts, Beirgh yielded no trace of Norse occupation, despite evidence of Norse burials on the Bhaltos peninsula.

In summary, therefore, Beirgh suggests a threefold post-broch sequence, from round-house, to cellular buildings and finally to figure-of-eight or ventral house. This sequence also accords broadly with a progression in ceramic styles (Fig. 10.9), with incised linear or impressed ornament in decline with the transition to the cellular phase, in which applied cabled bands, together with a variety of applied circlets and horseshoes pre-dominated among decorated wares. Finally the late cellular, figure-of-eight phase sees only undecorated pottery of essentially slack-profiled form, corresponding to Lane's (1990) 'plain wares' from the Udal, North Uist. The changes in building typology would seem to indicate radical social change, but in some details the successive phases unexpectedly preserve the spatial pattern of earlier phases. The internal divisions in the functional and social use of space of earlier roundhouses may have been effected with partitions that did not leave structural evidence in the archaeological record, so that the contrast with

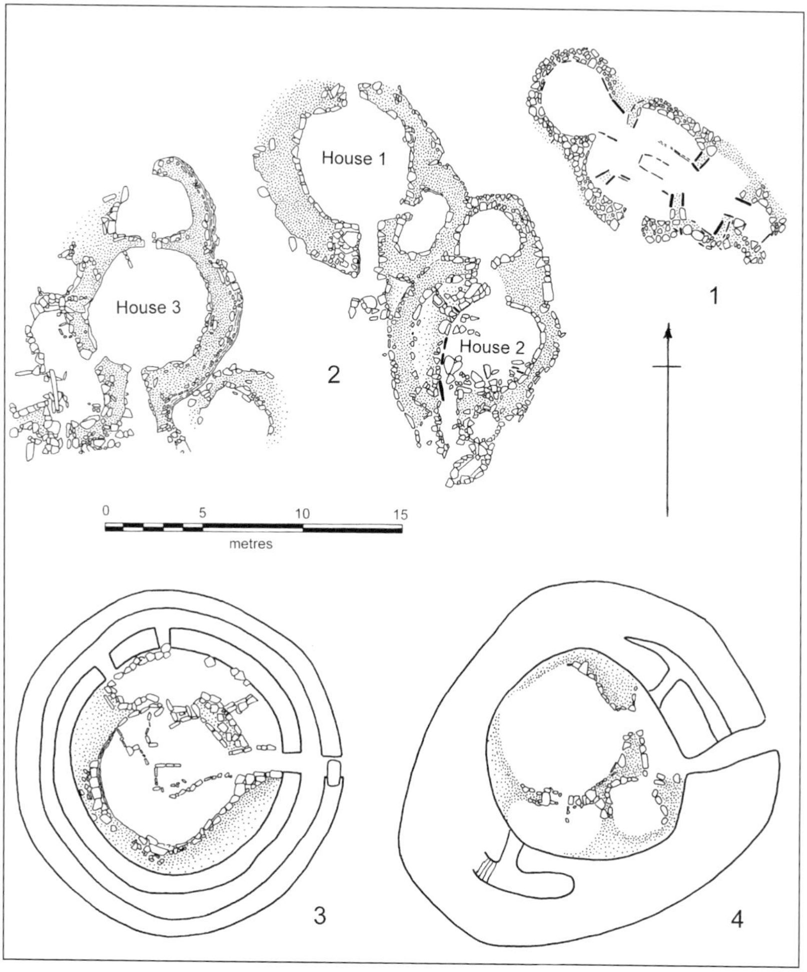

Figure 10.8 Late ventral or figure-of-eight houses, plans. 1, Buckquoy, Orkney; 2, Bostadh, Great Bernera, Lewis; 3, Beirgh, Lewis; 4, Dun Vulan, South Uist. Drawings by D. W. Harding, adapted from Ritchie, A. (1977), Neighbour and Burgess (1996), Harding and Gilmour (2000), Parker Pearson and Sharples (1999).

the more formalised sub-divisions of the cellular phase may be more apparent than real. In any event, from the longer chronological perspective, it could be the monumental Atlantic roundhouses that were exceptional, rather than their archaeologically more ephemeral antecedents and successors.

The neighbouring sites of the Bhaltos peninsula broadly endorse, and in some measure amplify, this model sequence. At Dun Bharabhat the situation was evidently complicated by the structural collapse of the early complex Atlantic roundhouse. It is perhaps surprising that no attempt was made to re-face its inner walls in the construction of the secondary roundhouse, which, on the basis of the limited radiocarbon dates available, could have taken place rather earlier than the demise of monumentality elsewhere. The external structures at Bharabhat, located on the annexe on the opposite side from the

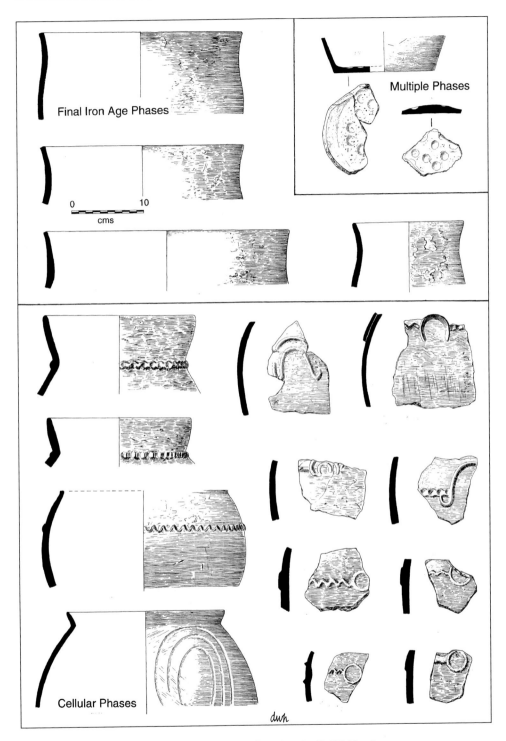

Final Iron Age Phases

Multiple Phases

0   10
cms

Cellular Phases

Figure 10.9 Beirgh, Lewis, later Iron Age pottery. Drawings by D. W. Harding.

causeway and in part revetted into the collapsed debris of the roundhouse, were cellular in form, displaying the characteristic combination of edge-set slabs and horizontal drystone coursing. Radiocarbon dates from samples taken from the annexe margins, though not associated directly with these structures, indicate continuing occupation of the site into the first half of the first millennium AD.

Cnip introduces the additional dimension of a classic wheelhouse into the Bhaltos sequence. Here the radiocarbon dates are less conclusive than we might wish, but they can be taken to indicate that the wheelhouse was still in occupation in the opening centuries AD, which would be broadly coterminous with the roundhouse or wheelhouse phase at Beirgh. Thereafter Cnip too sees the appearance of cellular structures with edge-set slabs revetting the sand and with horizontal coursing above. The principal house of the immediately post-wheelhouse phase had its vertical slabbing graded to its highest point directly opposite the entrance, providing a focus in much the same way as the twin recesses did in the later figure-of-eight building at Beirgh. The final phase at Cnip was a linear building, wider than a souterrain, and incorporating two of the surviving cells of the earlier wheelhouse as its terminal focus. Linear building is exemplified still more clearly at Tungadale, Skye (Miket, 2002; Fig. 10.10, 1), and might be regarded as an early variant on the rectilinear plan that represents a major innovation of the early historic period.

The Bostadh settlement exemplifies a later Iron Age site in which the cellular plan is not constrained by pre-existing bounds. Whilst its buildings provide good parallels for the Beirgh figure-of-eight plan (Fig. 10.8, 2), with free-standing rather than revetted walls, the open settlement permitted lateral expansion into more complex forms. The structures are thus multi-cellular, or ventral with accretions, rather than being simple figures-of-eight, in a way that conveys convincingly the fact that they represent the culmination of a sequence of cellular building. They also include a variety of structural features such as aumbries, and micro-analysis of deposits may warrant the identification of different activities in the subordinate cells. One important difference from Beirgh is that the latest levels, though somewhat ephemeral, indicated Norse settlement.

Metalworking is also attested in the sub-shamrock-shaped structure at Eilean Olabhat, North Uist (Armit, 1996: Fig. 9, 10). The construction of the building involved similar techniques and features to the Beirgh cellular sequence, including the use of corbelling or partial corbelling. Evidence for metalworking, including crucible fragments and fragments of moulds for pins and brooches, suggests a slightly later date, spanning perhaps the sixth and seventh centuries AD. One mould appears to have been for casting an ornament with a triskele motif, comparable to an example from Dunadd. Dating of the earlier, sub-circular buildings that underlay the Eilean Olabhat 'shamrock', however, remains problematic, as indeed is their function, which was probably domestic in spite of various indications of ritual deposits.

Post-wheelhouse occupation at A' Cheardach Mhor (Young and Richardson, 1960) evidently took the form of cellular structures, and though incomplete in plan their associations broadly endorse the sequence outlined above for Beirgh. Three ephemeral cellular phases were recognised (Phases 2, 3 and 4) with a final, rectilinear structure (Phase 5) for which a Norse date is possibly implied by the presence of worked steatite. Of the cellular structures, those of Phase 4 included arcs of walling comprising edge-set slabs with up to two courses of stone-work above. As regards finds, Phase 2 yielded an everted-rim vessel with applied wavy cordon and fillets; Phase 3 was characterised by plain wares

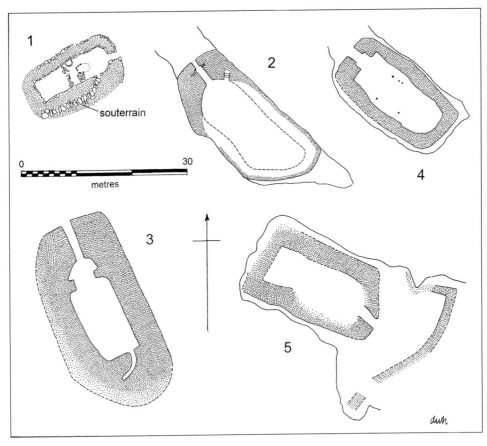

Figure 10.10 Rectangular building plans in the Atlantic west. 1, Tungadale, Skye; 2, Dun Grugaig, Skye; 3, Dun Totaig, Skye; 4, Dun Fhinn, Argyll; 5, Dun Mucaig, Argyll. Drawings by D. W. Harding, adapted from Armit (1996), RCAHMS (1928), (1971), (1975), MacSween (1985), Miket (2002).

comparable to that from the later occupation at Dun Cuier. Phase 4 produced little occupation debris, but artefactual finds did include a cast bronze pin with loose, wire ring-head, which might be dated between the sixth and eighth centuries AD (Fanning, 1983).

Among other cellular settlements in the Western Isles the Udal was plainly an important example, not least because of the presence of at least seven such cellular units. These appear to include bicameral, 'figure-of-eight' variants as well as multi-cellular structures. Pottery included Lane's 'plain ware', and cellular occupation appears to have continued until it was succeeded by Norse settlement in the ninth century AD. Among other discoveries, Ceann nan Clachan, North Uist (Armit and Braby, 2002) appears to be essentially a figure-of-eight plan with additional lateral cells; its dating is now reported to be later Iron Age, rather than earlier.

Finally, Dun Vulan, South Uist, presents a close analogy in its sequence with Beirgh, its final phase being a figure-of-eight that must overlie several intermediate structural phases following the abandonment of the original complex Atlantic roundhouse. Dun

Vulan, however, is also important for its rectangular stone platforms, confirmed as early to mid-first millennium AD by a series of radiocarbon dates. It is not clear that these structures were necessarily for domestic occupation rather than for use as ancillary buildings. The wheelhouse settlements at Clettraval and Tigh Talamhanta also included rectangular buildings that were regarded by their excavators as barns, which, together with other lesser structures, made up the farmstead complex. A parallel might be cited in the rectangular 'wags' of Caithness, which were also regarded by their excavators essentially as animal byres. In some instances, however, these rectangular structures were probably successive to, rather than contemporary with, the circular homesteads.

From fieldwork over the past twenty years a convincing sequence of post-broch occupational evidence has emerged from which it is possible to argue a progressive development from wheelhouses or allied roundhouses to cellular buildings culminating in the figure-of-eight or ventral plans of the latest Iron Age. This sequence gains broad endorsement from excavated evidence in the Northern Isles. The structural components of cellular construction plainly do have older antecedents, however, as examples in the Inner Hebrides and the Northern Isles testify. At Cladh Hallan, South Uist, structures of cellular character have been dated to the late Bronze Age or early Iron Age (Marshall et al., 1999). Rectilinear buildings stand aside but parallel to this sequence, but should not be equated too simplistically with any inferred historical episode of settlement.

Argyll and the Inner Hebrides

At Dun Mor Vaul, Tiree, the post-broch roundhouse represents the latest substantial structure on the site, though several ephemeral structures in the external court could conceivably be the fugitive remains of a later, cellular phase of occupation. The technique of edge-set slab construction, combined with drystone coursing or not, certainly formed one of the traits of later Iron Age settlement in Argyll. Ritchie's excavations at Machrins, Colonsay (Ritchie, J. N. G., 1981) revealed four single-roomed 'houses' or 'cells', all of which were defined by edge-set slabs, within which a sequence of hearths belied their apparently unsubstantial construction. Radiocarbon analysis of bone from the settlement gave a date centred on AD 800, which would be broadly consistent with the artefactual associations of an adjacent long-cist burial. At the other end of the chronological spectrum, a hut-circle excavated in 1976 at Ardnave, Islay, was constructed with 'orthostats angled against the thrust of the dune, and upper courses of drystone walling' (RCAHMS, 1984: 127). This was essentially the same technique as is used in the Western Isles, except that the drystone construction at Ardnave was less obviously coursed, with more rounded boulders. No dating evidence was recovered from this house, but an adjacent and possibly related site yielded evidence of later prehistoric occupation. The technique is plainly suited to structures whose foundations are revetted either into sand or into the collapsed rubble of earlier buildings, and as such may be typical without being diagnostic of any given period.

For mainland Argyll a similar sequence of structural development to that of the Western Isles might be inferred, given that it is extremely unlikely that secondary, ephemeral, cellular structures would have been recognised in older excavations. Even at Rahoy, Childe noted stonework that in retrospect might well have been part of a later, secondary re-occupation. Cellular structures could have formed part of the secondary occupation at Kildalloig, or in the smaller fort at Dun Mac Sniachan. Clearly secondary is the penannular arc of edge-set slabs at Ardifuar, mid-Argyll (Christison *et al.*, 1905), some with integral drystone coursing, revetted into the earth and rubble between it and the original dun walls, with which the secondary cell is noticeably not concentric. In fact the early excavators recognised that the site was multi-period, a conclusion that is endorsed by the material finds, despite the absence of proper stratigraphic record. Apart from undiagnostic finds such as whetstones, polishing stones and perforated discs, the excavations yielded a fragment of samian ware and a sherd subsequently recognised as E-ware, plainly indicative of occupation continuing through the first half of the first millennium AD.

Among the Argyll duns modern excavation and radiocarbon dating has confirmed the first millennium AD construction and occupation of Kildonan in Kintyre. Though Kildonan is by no means the most irregular of galleried duns in the Argyll *Inventories*, its sub-triangular plan is quite alien to the early Iron Age tradition of circular or sub-circular plans. Elements of Atlantic roundhouse architecture are certainly present, though in a form not at all characteristic of complex Atlantic roundhouses themselves. The entrance is rebated for a door with bar-holes, but its passage is much wider than in an Atlantic roundhouse. There is a form of intra-mural gallery leading away from the entrance passage on its south side, but open at both ends, and quite unlike an Atlantic roundhouse guard-cell. Finally there is a gallery with access to upper levels, but this is by means of a double staircase set against a continuous 'median wall face' which extends around the entire enclosure. Excavations by Fairhurst (1939) and Peltenburg (1984, 1982: 207–8) have conclusively shown that this was the product of secondary refacing of the dun wall, rather than an integral device for internally strengthening the original wall. Earlier material was very abraded, and radiocarbon dates for samples recovered by Peltenburg from below a hearth of the second of the site's four principal phases calibrated between the seventh and ninth centuries AD. Whilst there must always remain the residual possibility that the earliest occupational evidence has been obliterated by subsequent activity, the strong probability is that Kildonan was a mid-first millennium AD foundation. Once again it is apparent that complex architecture is not itself chronologically diagnostic of the earlier Iron Age, and that in some regions similar building traditions persisted into the early historic phase.

An important innovation of the early historic period, as we have remarked, is the rectangular or sub-rectangular building plan. In mainland Argyll the only example to have been excavated is the remarkable stack site on the west coast of Kintyre at Dun Fhinn (Fig. 10.10, 4). This building, enclosing an area some 14 metres by 6, was almost certainly a roofed rectangular house; internal postholes, formerly considered as supports for internal timber ranges (RCAHMS, 1971: 83), could equally have supported a fully roofed aisled structure. Dating of the site's construction and initial occupation is based upon the material assemblage from the primary floors, which included samian scraps, two penannular brooches and a blue glass 'dumb-bell' bead, all of which would be consistent with an occupation in the second or third centuries AD. Very similar in topographic location, plan and size is the undated rectangular Dun Mucaig, Seil, which differs only in having an outwork on its eastern, accessible flank. Dun Grugaig on Skye might also afford an analogy for the building at Dun Fhinn, less regular in its rectangular plan, but of very similar dimensions and sharing the use of door-checks in its entrance passage. Admittedly Dun Fhinn lacks galleries or scarcement, but so too would Dun Grugaig had it survived only to the height of Dun Fhinn's wall foundations. Both could easily have been roofed structures. Far from being one of the earliest of the proto-brochs, as MacKie suggested (1991: 168), Dun Grugaig might well belong instead to the early historic period. There are several other sites, less well preserved, on Skye which might belong to this same category of rectangular, roofed promontory duns, including Dun Ila, Dun Beag, Torrin, and possibly Dun Pharuig (MacSween, 1985).

Stack sites are not uncommon in the Atlantic north and west, wherever the topography has created opportunity for defensive reinforcement. In some instances sites which were built on narrow-necked promontories may now survive only as stacks through marine erosion. Some are so precipitate that it is hard to imagine their use as domestic habitation sites, other than as temporary refuges. Caisteal a' Mhorair, North Tolsta, is one such example on Lewis. Located less than 100 metres from the cliff-edge, and overlooked by it, its summit is occupied by a rectilinear building with subordinate chamber, suggesting occupation in the early historic, rather than in the later prehistoric Iron Age. Similarities with the stack site at Luchruban (the 'Pigmies Isle') west of the Butt of Lewis, where the buildings suggested an early Christian occupation (Thomas, A. C., 1971: 85–6), raise the possibility that some of these stacks were used as ecclesiastical settlements or eremetic sanctuaries.

The crucial question remains, what significance should be attached to the introduction of rectangular plans? Any simplistic equation with settlement of Argyll by Dál Riata should probably be resisted, even though some coastal sites, allied perhaps to those of Argyll, might be cited in Donegal and elsewhere in Northern Ireland. Rectangularity is no more endemic to the later prehistoric building traditions of Ireland than it is to any other part of the insular north-west of Europe. Yet there does appear to be a crucial distinction between sites with a longer tradition of settlement that have been re-occupied and sites where rectangular buildings represent an innovation or complete break in the local settlement tradition. Influence from the Romanised parts of Britain should probably not be over-rated. The dating of rectangular structures in the west to the opening centuries AD on the other hand would exclude neither of these connections.

Dunadd and nuclear forts in the west

Since R. B. K. Stevenson's pioneering study of Dalmahoy (1949b), the term 'nuclear fort', as we have seen, has been associated primarily with sites of the early historic period. Because of their requirement for a citadel as their focal point on the summit, with a series of lesser enclosures looping away from that nucleus to create a hierarchical structure, the sites selected tended to be particularly craggy or precipitous of access, and were generally not locations that had commended themselves for occupation in the earlier Iron Age.

The early historic occupation and role of Dunadd (Fig. 10.11) and related nuclear forts has been amply demonstrated by excavation. Earlier excavations at Dunadd had unfortunately not recognised the stratigraphic sequence of activity on the site, but investigations in 1980–81 confirmed that there may have been two phases of Iron Age occupation, which were dated by radiocarbon to the early and middle Iron Age, based upon a stone-built rampart on the summit (Lane and Campbell, 2000). The evidence for occupation is admittedly ephemeral, but saddle-querns from the older excavations and some undiagnostic artefacts could have derived from later prehistoric activity on the site. The early Mediaeval occupation began somewhere between the fourth and sixth centuries AD, extending towards the end of the millennium, and even possibly for a short period

Figure 10.11 Dunadd, Argyll, from the north. Photograph by D. W. Harding.

thereafter. During this period the early historic defences were successively constructed to complete the plan of a fully developed nuclear fort by the seventh century or thereabouts. The site has thus been conventionally regarded as a major centre of the Dál Riata, possibly the *caput regionis* of Adomnán's seventh-century record. From the time of Captain Thomas' report (1878), and recognition of the rock-cut footprint and basin, Dunadd has been regarded as an inauguration place of kings of Dál Riata, and accorded primacy among the Dark Age centres of the region.

Alcock (1981: 167; Alcock *et al.*, 1989) had argued that nuclear forts, together with Feachem's sub-group of citadel forts, which he subsumed within 'a single broad class' on the grounds that it was the 'hierarchical organisation of space' that mattered rather than the arrangement of their enclosure plans, were essentially an innovation of the early historic period. Dundurn at any rate he was able to demonstrate was a foundation of the early historic period, with no evidence for re-use of an earlier Iron Age fortified citadel, a model which he believed applied generally (1989: 211). Whilst the Dunadd evidence is hardly sufficient grounds for contesting this view, it seems always possible that later foundations might favour sites whose geographical or topographical advantages had attracted earlier settlement. If the Dalriadic settlement of Argyll represented a radical change, bringing with it a fundamentally new political and social order, then we might indeed expect that this would reflect itself in distinctive field monuments and a break in settlement continuity. But current thinking increasingly favours the view that the radical nature of this process has been overestimated. Conversely, if the roots of cross-Channel connections go back much further, then the settlement of Dál Riata documented historically may have been no more than a change in ruling élite, with less obvious consequences in the archaeological settlement record.

Elsewhere in Argyll there are instances of smaller sites, like Little Dunagoil on Bute, where the settlement might have been ordered into a series of enclosures descending from the summit on the 'nuclear' model. Little Dunagoil (Marshall, 1964) was possibly occupied from the sixth century AD. The origins of the adjacent early Christian site of St Blane's are also commonly attributed to the sixth century, though archaeological support for this early foundation is sparse.

Crannogs in Argyll and the Inner Hebrides

Five miles east of Dunadd lies Loch Glashan, where the lowering of the waters in 1960 for hydro-electric operations provided an opportunity for some superficial examination of a crannog, from which an exceptionally rich assemblage of organic artefacts was recovered (RCAHMS, 1988: no. 354; Earwood, 1990). Of the crannog structures themselves only a limited area was examined, and what was described as its substructure of brushwood and timber was almost certainly only the latest in a deeper sequence of deposits. Though some of the timbers appear to have been laid, and evidently displayed structural joints, their interpretation as a rectangular building seems rather tentative in view of the limited area opened. The date of the occupation represented, however, is hardly in doubt. An E-ware vessel and penannular brooch indicate a span between the sixth and eighth or early ninth centuries. One fragment of a lathe-turned bowl quite closely resembled a common E-ware form. The wooden containers recovered from the site include several rectangular troughs or ashets, one nearly a metre in length and suitable for serving the largest salmon in style. In addition, there were several objects that could have been oars or paddles, and several 'spatulae', too small to have served as paddles, unless as votive miniatures or toys, which could have been used for a variety of domestic purposes. A crucible and fragments of slag indicated metalworking on site, and more than a dozen rotary querns were included in the domestic assemblage. Fragments of leather were identified as the remnants of shoes and clothing. The survival of organic remains in such waterlogged conditions serves to underline the very partial picture that is left from terrestrial excavation.

Iona and Celtic Christianity

We have already considered briefly the spread of Roman Christianity from Northumbria. The other major tradition was represented by Celtic monastic Christianity in the west. Adomnán's *Life of Columba*, written in the later seventh century, records the founding of a monastic community at Iona in 563, but there were doubtless other missions that did not register so prominently in recorded history. The site of the earliest church at Iona has not been identified archaeologically, and it may lie under the mediaeval abbey.

Excavations between the late 1950s and 1979 nevertheless have traced evidence of the early settlement to the south-west of the abbey, where structural and material evidence of ancillary activities date from the seventh century, and possibly from the time of Columba. Barber (1981) certainly believed that he had uncovered a section of ditch of the Columban *vallum* on the basis of radiocarbon dates. In fact these afford a long and continuous span at one sigma from the fourth century to AD 1000 and after, and from the evidence of air-photography and from geophysical survey it is probable that the monastic enclosure was modified substantially over that period. The extant traces (Fig. 10.12) probably cover a much larger area to the north than would have been enclosed by the early *vallum*. From the later eighth century the high crosses of St Martin and St John survive intact.

According to Adomnán, Columba extended his mission to the Picts, apparently meeting Bridei, son of Maelchon, somewhere near Inverness. It is likely that the monastic community at Iona founded daughter houses elsewhere in the west, and several possible religious sites have been identified, such as the sub-circular enclosure with internal cells at Sgor nam Ban-naomha, the 'rock of the holy women', on Canna, and Cladh a' Bhearnaig, Kerrera, in the Firth of Lorn. There were doubtless other missions in the west, conventionally associated with the names of various saints, but the dating of individual sites without excavation is problematical. In the Western Isles North Rona became an important centre, with Luchruban, north Lewis, perhaps one of its satellites. The church

Figure 10.12 Iona monastic settlement, air-photograph. Photograph by D. W. Harding.

of Saint Blane's at Kingarth, Bute, is reputed to have early origins, and the beehive cells and possibly elements of enclosure at Eileach an Naoimh in the Garvellach islands may have been founded as an early monastic retreat. How these monastic communities integrated with the local, secular population is a question that needs to be addressed (Hunter, J. R., 2002).

Caithness, Sutherland and the Northern Isles

The building of secondary roundhouses within the shell of brochs or complex Atlantic roundhouses seems to have been equally in evidence in the north-eastern mainland of Scotland. One striking example at Carn Liath (Fig. 10.5; Fig. 10.6a) on the Sutherland coast has already been noted; here a secondary wall-facing within the broch interior could indeed be contemporary with some of the structural accretions around the outside of the former tower. The broch at Yarrows, Caithness, likewise has a very obvious secondary roundhouse within its circuit. Less conspicuous examples occur in Caithness, notably at the Keiss and other brochs investigated by Tress-Barry in the late nineteenth century.

At Crosskirk (Fairhurst, 1984) there was substantial re-organisation of both the Atlantic roundhouse and its external structures around the second century AD, including the construction of an elaborate external passage, accessible by means of several sets of steps from adjacent flagged platforms. The function of this structure was not clear, but its layout conforms to that of the linear structure of the latest phase at Cnip, including the reduction in its width by the insertion of additional facing on one side. Interesting though this complex sequence is, however, it stands unique, and hardly therefore affords a model for the region.

The site that really deserves that accolade is one that has not been well served by its mid-twentieth-century excavators, the so-called 'wag' settlement at Forse, Caithness (Fig. 10.13; Curle, 1941, 1946, 1948). Here there is a sequence of substantial buildings including Atlantic roundhouse, rectangular houses and figure-of-eight structures, all of which were regarded by Curle as variant forms of 'wags', or agricultural contemporaries of brochs. Gilmour's reinterpretation certainly seems more probable on the basis of the surviving field evidence. The earliest visible structure of any significance is the 'circular wag', in reality a complex Atlantic roundhouse, of which most of the inner wall had been removed by later reconstruction. The internal diameter of this building would thus have been around 9 metres, rather than 47 feet (or some 14 metres) as Curle believed. Its original entrance, in accordance with the prevailing convention, was south of east, and access to upper floors was gained by means of an intra-mural staircase within a gallery on the north side. At a later stage, a secondary entrance was opened through the outer wall adjacent to the foot of the staircase, direct access to the interior through the original gallery entrance being blocked in favour of a new opening in that gallery's butt end. Robbing of the stonework of the inner broch wall reduced the structures flanking this secondary northern entrance to the appearance of a 'tower', which MacKie (1975: 224) compared to the blockhouses of the Shetland forts.

The sub-rectangular 'wags' at Forse are plainly secondary, as is the figure-of-eight building labelled structures C and D by Curle. Despite the excavator's belief that the second figure-of-eight (structures O and P; Fig. 10.13, 2) was earlier than the circular dun, it too could belong to the later, post-broch occupation. The better preserved of the two sub-rectangular houses (Fig. 10.13, 3) had five surviving pillar-stones aligned along

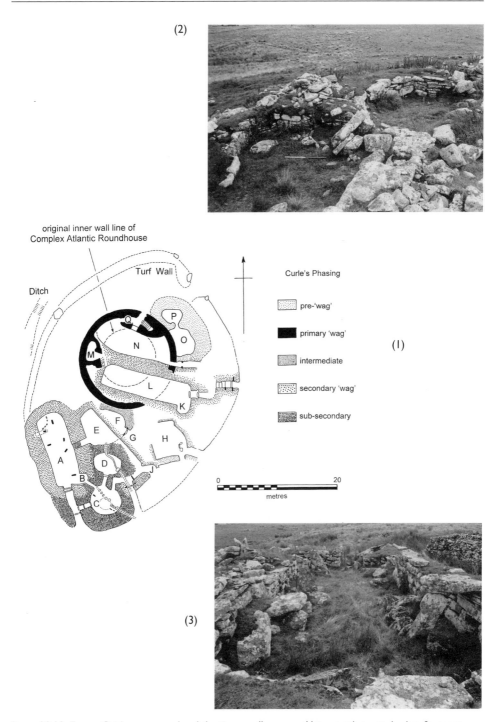

(2)

original inner wall line of
Complex Atlantic Roundhouse

Ditch

Turf Wall

Curle's Phasing

pre-'wag'

primary 'wag'

intermediate

secondary 'wag'

sub-secondary

(1)

0   20
metres

(3)

Figure 10.13 Forse, Caithness, complex Atlantic roundhouse and later settlement. 1, plan; 2, structures O and P; 3, structure A. Photographs by D. W. Harding; drawing by D. W. Harding, adapted from Curle (1941).

its long axis, one of which still supports a lintel from the external wall. Much the same form of building was found adjacent to a circular dun at Langwell, Berriedale, Caithness, also investigated by Curle in the course of researching the Caithness *Inventory* (RCAHMS, 1911). A similar structure again had been investigated still earlier by Joseph Anderson at Yarrows. The appearance created by the pillar stones and lintels of a series of stalls evidently predetermined the assumption that the building was a byre, and the failure to recognise chronological depth at Forse resulted in the idea that here were the farm buildings of nearby broch-dwellers. Whether stock was brought into the rectangular building cannot be determined with certainty, but that possibility should not exclude the likelihood that this was a habitation site, just as more recent black houses had provision for both. The size of the Forse buildings are of the same order as the oblong buildings from Argyll and Skye, and their perimeter 'stalls' could be regarded as a translation of perimeter cells of a wheelhouse into a rectangular plan. The figure-of-eight buildings included hearths, always taken as the hallmark of human habitation. Buildings C and D are unquestionably later additions, even if O and P are not demonstrably so. Evidence for intermediate cellular construction may well have been missed in areas left unexcavated. MacKie (1975: 224) suggested that the novelty of rectangular building was introduced by Iron Age settlers from Scandinavia, though the lack of any evidence of exotic material culture makes this notion implausible. The adoption of rectangular architecture was evidently more widespread in the early historic period than can be explained by episodes of colonisation, either in the west or the north-east.

Orkney and Shetland provide a number of sites where there was evidently a complex sequence of post-broch occupation, not always readily understood on the basis of older excavations. Among more recent investigations, the Howe on Mainland Orkney affords an extremely complex but informative post-broch sequence. By the fifth–sixth centuries, a new type of building, sub-rectangular in plan with apsidal ends, and distinguished by stalled partitions down its long axis in much the same fashion as the wags of Caithness, was built over the levelled debris of earlier structures on the south-west side of the former broch enclosure. There is no reason to suppose that this building was not the primary domestic structure of the farmstead at this stage. In turn, this building too fell into decay, and the focus of settlement once more reverted to the cellular complex on the east side of the site in the later sixth and seventh centuries. The final stage in the Phase 8 occupation saw the construction over the derelict stalled building of a figure-of-eight structure, or what the excavator preferred to term a 'clover-leaf' building on account of its having additional cellular elements (Smith, B. B., 1994: 116). The central element of this house is more like a waisted oval in plan, not unlike the building at Red Craig, Birsay (Morris, 1996), than a figure-of-eight in which access between the cells is through a quite constricted entrance gap. This settlement continued to be occupied into the ninth century AD, when remnants of rectangular buildings on top of the mound may indicate the presence of Norse settlers.

The Howe sequence may not provide an invariable model for post-broch settlement in Orkney, but it shows that cellular building, including multi-cellular or figure-of-eight plans, together with rectilinear and even stalled, wag-like buildings, are part of the architectural mix, and it provides some indication as to where these building types might belong within the first millennium sequence. Among older excavations the most controversial is Gurness on the northern Mainland. The principal debate centres on whether the external structures are part of a contemporary layout with the broch tower, as they appear to have been initially at the Howe, or whether they represent an entirely secondary accretion around the derelict broch. A second issue was whether the broch itself had undergone radical alteration around the second century AD, as a result of which its walls were substantially reduced. Hedges (1987) favoured a progressive view of the site's occupation, in which the extra-mural village was integral to the original design and changes within the broch were cumulative rather than radical. MacKie (1994) re-asserted the older conventional view (RCAMS, 1946) that the external buildings were secondary to the broch occupation, and that the broch interior itself had been radically redesigned at a comparatively early stage. MacKie's case for viewing much of the internal layout as secondary is convincing, as is his belief that the primary occupation deposits almost certainly still lie intact beneath the secondary paving. As regard the extra-mural village, some of the structures currently on display clearly extend over the edge of the inner ditch. But it is also clear, as Hedges pointed out, that the present layout must be composite, showing evidence of later walls abutting earlier, buildings that have been extended, and paving that has been resurfaced. In effect, the tell-like mound that presented itself to the excavators in 1929 was the product of a succession of structures of which the broch was probably, though not demonstrably, the earliest, and of which Norse long-houses, given scant consideration by the excavators, were apparently among the latest. The defensive enclosure, the entrance through which is aligned directly on the broch entrance, has always been regarded as integral to the broch settlement, and the wide space between ditch and broch walls was presumably intended for occupational activity. Though the surviving exposed structures are doubtless largely the product of secondary, post-broch occupation, therefore, they were probably successive to earlier external buildings dating from the broch period.

Salvaging the inadequate record of the 1930s excavations, Hedges was at least able to throw some light on the nature of the later Iron Age occupation at Gurness. Unlike more ephemeral structures that were simply destroyed, the 'shamrock' (Fig. 10.7, 1) was removed and rebuilt away from its original location. It had five principal cells grouped around its central court, though in fact it merged with a series of other cellular buildings described as an annexe, almost certainly representing cumulative construction. All were built into the remains of the pre-existing structures, with no recorded stratigraphic separation suggesting any significant break in occupation. Overlying this complex was one of the probable Norse long-houses. Occupation of the site in this post-broch, pre-Norse period was not, however, restricted to the south side of the enclosure. Along its northern perimeter, bordering the shore, a series of cellular structures, all removed by the excavators, testify to a post-broch occupation of some intensity.

If the Iron Age archaeology of the Northern Isles has been dominated by the prominence of brochs and their site sequences, a new perspective was afforded by excavations at Pool on Sanday (Hunter, J. R., 1990, 1997) and by the publication of earlier excavations at Skaill on the Deerness peninsula of Mainland Orkney (Buteux, 1997). On neither site is there evidence of a broch in the immediate vicinity. So the roundhouses on both sites, dating to the first half of the first millennium AD, represent not simply a trend away from the tradition of monumental architecture but a parallel development of settlement away from the focal centres represented by the broch 'villages'. At Pool the layout of Structure 18 once again reflects the division between central and peripheral space, marking the division with low orthostats (Hunter, J. R. 1997: 12, Fig. 4), while at Skaill the underlying plan of the roundhouse suggested a radial arrangement around a central 'service area' (Buteux, 1997: 51). This pattern, as we have seen, is characteristic of some brochs and reaches its most formal expression in the design of wheelhouses. Both roundhouses had smaller circular annexes or workshops, which seems to anticipate the more formal figure-of-eight plans of the later first millennium AD.

Around the middle of the first millennium AD both Pool and Skaill underwent a major structural change. At Skaill the reorganisation was especially radical, the roundhouse settlement being paved over and replaced by apparently rectangular structures of which only the truncated remains survived. Circularity of plan survived only in a small structure with porched entrance, which was interpreted by the excavator as a shrine, but which could equally have served a more mundane purpose. At Pool extensive paving was also a prominent feature of the modified settlement, with cellular structures of various forms and interconnecting passages. In due course a large sub-rectangular building or courtyard was a prominent feature, as the settlement reached its maximum extent, before its progressive decline and contraction in the eighth century and into the Norse period. These structural sequences are also matched by changes in both pottery styles and the non-ceramic assemblages. In particular, bone pins, bone combs (Foster, 1990) and penannular brooches are diagnostic of the seventh and eighth centuries, and are widely represented across Atlantic Scotland. Buteux, however, has argued that the significant changes in settlement layout at Skaill, and by implication the changes in the social order which they represent, must be dated closer to the sixth century, perhaps triggered by political developments in the Pictish kingdom of Orkney, alluded to in historical sources.

The important interface between later Iron Age ('Pictish') occupation and evidence of Norse colonisation and settlement was illuminated by excavations at Buckquoy (Ritchie, A., 1977). In its earlier occupation cellular buildings were the norm, including plans that broadly equated with the Gurness 'shamrock', constructed characteristically using both drystone coursing and vertical slabs. Though lacking diagnostic associations, this phase of settlement was assigned to the seventh century AD or thereabouts. In contrast to these cellular plans, in which the individual cells clustered around the central hearth, the later building (house 4; Fig. 10.8, 1) was of extended figure-of-eight plan. The cellular elements were in linear disposition, with a three-sided hearth in the largest of the cells, aligned down the spinal axis of the building. This phase was dated to the eighth century on the basis of an ogham-inscribed spindle-whorl and other artefacts. For Orkney Buckquoy house 4 remains the model 'figure-of-eight' plan, though variations on the theme such as those from Birsay and Red Craig may be broadly contemporary. This later Iron Age settlement was in turn succeeded by several phases of rectilinear Norse buildings, which, despite the radical change in architectural fashion, lacked any truly diagnostic Scandinavian artefacts. Together with results of excavations at Birsay, Pool and Skaill among others, this has led to a realisation that the Norse settlement of Orkney was a complex process of integration with the native 'Pictish' communities which, in the early stages at any rate, resulted in a significant measure of co-existence and integration. Buteux (1997: 262) has proposed a threefold process of Norse settlement, a 'pioneer stage' of raiding, trading and perhaps over-wintering followed by a 'consolidation stage' in which more permanent settlements were established alongside those of the Picts before eventually an 'establishment stage' resulted in the effective replacement of Pictish traditions and material culture. This model still does not wholly satisfy the archaeological evidence for the apparent continuity of 'Pictish' assemblages and their subsequent total eradication, but this intriguing issue lies beyond the main scope of the present study.

For Shetland our understanding of the post-broch settlement sequence has progressed substantially as a result of recent field research, amplifying the evidence available from Jarlshof and avoiding the need to become embroiled in the contradictions of Clickhimin. We have already remarked the importance of the Old Scatness sequence (Fig. 10.14; Dockrill, 1998, 2003) not only for the dating of complex Atlantic roundhouses but also for its aisled roundhouse (Structure 14) and wheelhouses with distinctive triangular piers (Structures 6 and 11). A roundhouse with projecting piers (Structure 12) was evidently part of a group of conjoined and related buildings. Contiguous and accessible from it was a building, the western wall of which was divided by a series of parallel piers, reminiscent of the stalled rectangular wags of Caithness. Sub-phases of activity are obviously represented within this western group of buildings, but their combination of circular and rectilinear building plans is not inconsistent with post-broch sequences elsewhere.

Characteristically late Iron Age in plan are the structures built within the central area of the Atlantic roundhouse (Structure 7), comprising five cells clustered around a central hearth from which they are divided, as in the 'shamrocks', by low sills or partition walls. Connected to this area is an external group of later cellular buildings to the east of the Atlantic roundhouse, though here again containing intrusive Norse artefacts in their later phases. Built into an earlier complex of cellular buildings Structure 5 was of figure-of-eight plan, constructed using both upright slabs and intermediate horizontal drystone coursing. In the centre of the main cell was a three-sided or horseshoe-shaped hearth defined by edge-set slabs, its open end facing the entrance. Dating suggests a late Iron Age occupation for the building (between AD 600 and 900), though its upper filling again contained material of Norse type. Old Scatness therefore has a dual importance, not only in furnishing potentially the most reliably dated structural sequence from the earlier Iron Age, but also casting new light on the fascinating interface between later Iron Age 'Pictish' occupation and Norse in Atlantic Scotland.

Material culture of the later Iron Age

One reason for adopting here the minimalist division between earlier and later Iron Ages is that any finer classification based upon structural sequences would almost certainly not accord with any based upon material classification and dating. There need, of course, be no presumption that significant changes in structural types and artefactual assemblages should march hand in hand, and even in the case of apparently radical political or demographic change, such as the Norse raids and settlement, the archaeological record may be far from straightforward in reflecting that change.

Current convention divides the later Iron Age in Atlantic Scotland into LIA I and LIA II, spanning the period from the late third or early fourth centuries AD to the late eighth or early ninth. The threshold between the sub-phases falls around the early seventh century, and is based essentially upon the dating of two key artefactual types, hipped pins and composite, double-sided combs. Both pins and combs are represented among earlier assemblages, of course, but it is the distinctive hipped variant of pin, with short bone or metal shaft and various forms of head, and the combs of Types A and B, Foster's Groups 5 and 6 (Foster, 1990), that predominate in the LIA II sub-phase. A third type, the penannular brooch, likewise has a longer chronology from the earlier Iron Age, though some of its most distinctive, developed variants also fall within the later period. The typology of penannular brooches has been subjected to particular debate, but a

Figure 10.14 Old Scatness, Shetland. Photograph copyright J. Dockrill, University of Bradford and Shetland Amenity Trust, reproduced by kind permission.

significant proportion of the Atlantic Scottish brooches can still be assigned with reasonable confidence to the LIA II sub-phase. All of these several types are found commonly on broch sites from the Western and Northern Isles, but from the secondary, post-broch phases of occupation that are not infrequently those levels least well recognised on older excavations.

Metal types of the LIA I sub-phase include handpins, so named because their end plate is shaped like a hand with projecting fingers. Since R. B. K. Stevenson's pioneer study (1955a), it has been generally accepted that these developed progressively from ring-headed pins with beaded moulding, through an intermediate proto-handpin in which the beads may be reduced to just three above a crescentic plate, as in the Norrie's Law silver examples. The typology, though very conventional, is probably sound, but the dating of the pins within the developmental sequence is more controversial. The conventional dating of handpins would have placed them between the fifth and eighth centuries AD, but moulds from dated contexts at both Beirgh and Eilean Olabhat indicate their manufacture rather earlier, perhaps between the third and fifth centuries. Proto-handpins consequently should be somewhat earlier still. This re-assessment of the Scottish series would not be incompatible with more recent evidence for the dating of handpins in Ireland. It would, however, place handpins firmly within the LIA I sub-phase rather than later, with their origins in the opening centuries of the first millennium AD, the 'middle' Iron Age in the threefold system.

A second major class of artefact for which there is an increasing number of moulds in Scotland is the so-called spearbutt, a cast bronze shaped not unlike a door-knob and assumed to have served as a ferrule on the rear end of a spear. The plainest variant is known simply as a door-knob spearbutt, while a version with mouldings is named after the type-site of Lisnacrogher in Co. Antrim. Hitherto regarded as archetypally Irish, and dated around the turn of the first millennium, these objects have now been recognised from a much wider distribution zone, including examples from Roman sites in Southern Britain (Heald, 2001). Crucially the only known moulds for such spearbutts have been from Scottish sites, including Traprain Law, Dunagoil, Dun Mor Vaul, Beirgh, Gurness and Mine Howe. Ironically, there is still no comparable evidence of manufacture in Ireland, even though spearbutts occur there in much greater numbers. Once again, however, the radiocarbon-dated structural sequence at Beirgh has prompted a review of the dating of spearbutts, suggesting their manufacture there from the third to fifth centuries AD rather than in the 'middle' Iron Age. The association at Dun Mor Vaul of a door-knob spearbutt mould with Roman glass of second- or third-century date could still be accommodated just within this span. Independent dating evidence for the Lisnacrogher type is still lacking, but if the two types were not at least concurrent to some degree then their coincidence at Dunagoil (Fig. 5.21, 39–40) would be the more remarkable.

In sum, there does indeed appear to be an increase in the production or survival of distinctive artefact types, notably but by no means exclusively in personal or costume accessories like pins and brooches, in the period following the demise of monumental architecture. This could well reflect changing patterns in the expression of social identity from fixed and communal monuments to portable and personal artefacts. Whether assumptions of social status based upon the presence of metalwork or metalworking debris can reasonably be sustained remains an issue of debate.

Part 5

Review and conclusion

Chapter 11

Settlement and society

Continuity and change

Settlement and enclosure

Settlement evidence is predominant in the earlier Iron Age over much of Northern Britain, with the important qualification that dating sites in the absence of radiocarbon samples has proved problematic in many upland regions for want of a diagnostic material assemblage. The pattern in the later Iron Age is more variable, with marked regional disparities in the nature of the evidence.

Major enclosed sites, including hillforts, are not nearly as numerous or densely distributed as in Southern Britain. Some, like Mam Tor or Eildon Hill were evidently in use from the later Bronze Age, though not necessarily as permanent habitations. In the widely dispersed pattern of settlement that characterises much of Northern Britain in later prehistory, conspicuous landmarks like Ingleborough or Tap o' Noth might well have been chosen deliberately for their dominating position in the landscape as centres of periodic communal assembly. The defensive role of hillforts remains equivocal, though the presence of siegeworks at Burnswark, and the record of Roman historians for Southern Britain indicates that they could have served as defensive refuges. Not all these sites were abandoned during the Roman interlude: Traprain Law and Castle O'er evidently continued in occupation, presumably by diplomatic negotiation with the Roman authorities.

In the later Iron Age, some hillforts almost certainly were re-occupied. Others, like Dunadd and Dundurn, embody an innovative form of nuclear enclosure, though the hierarchical structure may already have been latent in earlier Iron Age citadels. Larger terrain enclosures are known in the earlier Iron Age, of which Stanwick approximates to the Southern British *oppidum* model. Not all enclosed sites have man-made perimeter works around their entire circuit, but even in promontory forts and headland forts there can be no doubt that confinement or exclusion was the objective. The precipitate nature of some northern and western promontory sites again raises doubts regarding the function of such sites as domestic settlements.

Lesser enclosed sites, sometimes with multiple roundhouses like High Knowes B, Hayhope Knowe or Gibb's Hill might be thought of as protected villages. In such cases, groups of households, perhaps of collateral kin, may be inferred, even acknowledging that not all the surviving buildings need have been from contemporaneous occupation. The broch 'villages' of Orkney are likewise community settlements, but with the implication of a hierarchical relationship to the broch that is absent from the majority of other settlement types.

Individual enclosed sites with a single large roundhouse or pair of buildings of the kind represented at West Brandon, High Knowes A or Greenbrough may be described as 'homesteads', and were presumably occupied by a single nuclear family. This form accords with the *Einzelhof* concept typified by the type-site at Little Woodbury, Wiltshire. Crannogs might also be regarded as single-family homesteads, some of which may have had perimeter fencing in addition to being enclosed by water.

Open settlements are the least well-documented class of field monument, except where they survived above the zone of destruction in various upland locations from the second millennium. Examples have been excavated of the early Iron Age at Douglasmuir, and of the later Iron Age at Easter Kinnear. In the Western Isles wheelhouses in the machair appear to have been unenclosed, though occasional free-standing upland examples may have had contemporary enclosures. Exposure by excavation in advance of development of open settlements in the lowlands of south-east Scotland and north-east England encourages the belief that more may have been missed elsewhere. Unenclosed sites are not necessarily the lowest in the social hierarchy; brochs like Carloway are unenclosed, yet monumental in their scale of construction.

An important consideration therefore is the question of enclosure. For many years Iron Age studies have been concerned almost exclusively with enclosed settlements, of which hillforts, regarded almost as an archetype of the insular Iron Age, represented the apex of the social pyramid. As we have seen, an older view saw an ordered progression towards enclosure through increasingly complex or labour-intensive structural stages. What the purpose was of enclosure, and why it was only achieved progressively over time, was never explained. One consequence was certainly to blind us from the complexity of the settlement mix at any given time. Enclosure of a settlement might be desirable for several reasons. Most obvious among functionalist interpretations would be protection from thieves or predators, or on a larger scale for communal defence against raiders or aggressive neighbouring communities. Equally important might be to assert one's identity and to define the nodal points of a settlement. The idea of defining personal or communal space by enclosure is endemic in human society as much as it is in other social animals. This was probably not achieved solely by the construction of walls or ditches. Even across open ground or open water around crannogs an intruder would doubtless be aware of encroaching on someone else's space, which can be marked in various ways. At Dun an Sticer on North Uist, for example, access is controlled by a network of causeways in stages across the water. For this reason defining enclosure, or conversely recognising an 'open' settlement, could be difficult, since archaeologically elusive markers could have been as potent as earthworks in proclaiming liminality. In any settlement that includes adjacent fields with trackways between them, like those of upland Perthshire, the concept of enclosure and the controlling of access is in any case endemic to the layout of the agricultural pattern in the landscape. We might therefore distinguish between *dedicated* enclosure, like a hillfort rampart, and *implicit* enclosure, of the kind that controls access through surrounding fields or natural barriers.

Enclosure on a landscape scale too might be undertaken for various reasons. Once again defining limits and asserting rights to territory is an obvious political motive. This might be accentuated by economic considerations in time of population growth with consequent intensification of agriculture, or climatic deterioration during which marginal uplands were no longer viable and there was increasing demand for prime land. Agricultural practice itself may require landscape boundaries, between arable and pastoral. One or more of these may combine in prompting the construction of extensive systems like those of the North York moors or even the intensive networks of the Lothian plain. Their creation would nevertheless require an authority and resources of manpower beyond the household scale, so that these works should signify social organisation on a regional basis. Defining territory, locally and regionally, is fundamental to social identity, and is much more ancient than the Iron Age. Extending that principle to individual settlements or domestic enclosures simply combines the basic assertion of identity with practical advantages for controlling access and movement of people and livestock, and for defining areas allocated to specific purposes or activities.

Houses and households

Following Hingley (1992) we may suggest that the basic unit of society in the Northern British Iron Age was the *household*. Irish vernacular sources have various terms for 'household' or 'farmstead' that do not equate directly with a kinship group, since they would also include servants. It is arguable whether a household, based on a substantial timber roundhouse like West Brandon, might include a nuclear family unit only with its sub-ordinates, and whether a broch tower by contrast might have been occupied by an extended family group. The number of individuals involved would be complicated if polygyny was practised, or if adoption or fosterage were a regular part of the social system. Among sites that appear to have been for permanent occupation, some homesteads are effectively made up of a single household, a single residential unit or paired unit. In the case of paired units it might be tempting to see the secondary element as the residence of a cadet group, such as a married son, or of servants or estate workers, or even of dual 'ownership'. But equally it could simply have been functionally different from the main building.

Conventional classification has invariably distinguished buildings on the basis of their architectural plans and construction techniques. In consequence, brochs are seen as different from crannogs, and wheelhouses are different from cellular houses. Most obviously circular plans stand in contrast to rectangular, and for most of prehistory distinguish the Atlantic settlement tradition from that of Central or Northern Europe. Closer architectural sub-division would distinguish ring-groove plans from ring-ditch houses, or brochs from wheelhouses. If instead we give priority to the social use of space, the division between central or communal space and peripheral, personal or functionally specific space, seems to be common across these categorical boundaries. It could even be argued that the central–peripheral contrast extends in the early historic period into a rectangular version of the same apparent order. Barrett (1981) referred to the *structuring principles* whereby social order was translated into the internal division of space. In the case of brochs this almost certainly introduced a vertical dimension, with several floor levels offering a physical hierarchy of space, as well as the more common horizontal divisions. Factors bearing upon those structuring principles will have included gender and age considerations, as well as practical functions of sleeping, eating and working. Attempts have been made to read these social factors from the distribution of artefacts or micro-debris of human activity, but we must be sure in doing so that we have correctly interpreted the taphonomy of deposition.

Within the various groups it is commonly assumed that the most striking, monumental buildings were the residences of élite families, on the simple argument that their construction would have required control of substantial resources, notably stone and timber, and authority to marshal the manpower needed to build them. If, however, Atlantic roundhouses represented the apex of a hierarchical settlement system, other, lesser contemporary settlements might be expected in proximity, representing the lower or non-land holding orders. In the Northern Isles the 'broch villages' might reflect a social spectrum if the broch itself and surrounding buildings were in contemporary occupation. In Orkney we have seen the possibility of separate settlement development in the post-broch era on sites that on the one hand had broch towers as their original focus and on the other on sites that did not. For Shetland, Dockrill (Turner and Dockrill, forthcoming) has recently proposed a similar distinction between brochs that were the focus of nuclear villages and those that may have been strategically located between a group of lesser, dispersed dependent settlements. In the Western Isles contemporary lesser settlements have yet to be identified, assuming that wheelhouses are for much of their occupation successive to, rather than concurrent with, brochs. Armit (2002: 24) preferred to see Atlantic roundhouses as residences not just of social élites but of free land-holders below the highest rank, 'analogous to the tenant farmers of the post-medieval period'.

In fact, though there is considerable diversity in roundhouse design and construction between regions in the British Iron Age, there is remarkably little evidence within any settlement of social distinction being expressed in terms of house size or elaboration. The facile inference that the chief's house should be larger than the rest seems to be based on an entirely anachronistic capitalist conception of status. In the construction of Atlantic roundhouses it need not follow that those who commanded resources and manpower would only exercise that authority on their own behalf. It would be consistent with what is known of Celtic society from other sources and regions that patronage would be exercised on behalf of subordinate social groups in a system that bound the latter with reciprocal obligations, which might extend over several generations. This then raises in an earlier Iron Age context questions regarding the nature of possession and inheritance, particularly in areas like Atlantic Scotland, where monumental buildings had a potential endurance of centuries rather than decades. No doubt obligations and debts could be inherited as well as assets and entitlements. The nature of land-holding also bears upon the issue of monumentality. If brochs were intended to assert identity and to legitimise entitlement to land, whose identity and entitlement was being asserted, the occupants', the social superior's, the community's or kinship group's collectively? Within the dispersed settlement pattern of Atlantic Scotland it need not follow that society was egalitarian rather than hierarchical, and the apparent absence of lesser categories of settlement contemporary with the brochs is probably still partly a factor of archaeological invisibility. But any assumption that a broch might be regarded as the capital asset of its owner-occupier must surely be anachronistic, and community or kin control of land and buildings seems more likely.

The assumption that monumental buildings like brochs were occupied without break over many generations has recently been challenged (Cowley, 2003). Though they plainly had the capacity for longevity of use, and in some cases evidently were occupied over several centuries, it is hard to demonstrate archaeologically that occupation was unbroken. Had their roofs not been maintained, sites like Beirgh might have been expected to show intermittent layers of windblown sand, but the probability on many sites is that later occupation or re-occupation would largely eliminate evidence for earlier use. With the passing of monumentality, did the household order disintegrate, revert to later Bronze

Age forms of cellular or courtyard building, or mutate while still preserving its essential elements in a reconfigured structure? The disadvantage of the roundhouse concept, compared to rectangular plans, is its limited capacity for expansion. The broch towers achieved this monumentally in vertically superimposed floors, but in the horizontal plane the only options are building a second structure adjacent or conjoined to the first, or aggregating less regularly a series of adjacent cells, as seen on some wheelhouse settlements. The formalisation of the principle of cellular aggregation is seen in the shamrocks or ventral houses of the later Iron Age.

Domestic structures: recognition and interpretation

The shorthand term 'house' is almost universally applied to Iron Age buildings, irrespective of the archaeological evidence for their use. Even excluding the possibility of ritual or ceremonial functions, within a normal agricultural homestead it may be hard on the basis of structural plans alone to distinguish domestic houses from barns and byres, or roofed buildings from open corrals. Conventional reconstructions of Iron Age timber roundhouses, exemplified by the reconstruction of the Pimperne and Longbridge Deverill houses at the Butser Ancient Farm in Hampshire, were based essentially upon ground-plans of earth-fast postholes. They further assumed that the roofing material was straw or reed thatch, for which tradition demanded a pitch of 45 degrees in order to be weather-proof. Quite plainly in Northern British roundhouses other materials than timber and straw thatch may be employed, including stone, turf or earth for walls and heather thatch or turf for roofs. In consequence other constructional techniques are in evidence, not simply posthole substitutes, such as a continuous ring-grooves, but ring-ditches or hollowed-out foundations, and because these materials and techniques imply a different elevation profile, ground-plans need not accord with Southern British roundhouse geometry. The classic Little Woodbury or Pimperne ground-plan had its weight-bearing circle of postholes much closer to the perimeter wall than to the mid-point between it and the centre of the house. This was almost certainly because this ratio broadly equalises the surface areas of the roof within and beyond the weight-bearing circle. The central four-poster at Little Woodbury is unlikely to have been an essential element in supporting the roof. Its purpose may have been constructional, like a scaffolding frame, or may have been related to the support of an upper or mezzanine floor, or simply formed a framework around the hearth for suspending pots, spits or foodstuffs for curing.

In Northern Britain there is ample evidence of house-plans in which the post-rings do conform to conventional roundhouse geometry, on the basis of which we may reasonably infer a conical thatched roof of straw, reed or perhaps heather. There are, nevertheless, anomalous plans, like Monymusk, with large internal four-poster settings, proportionately rather larger than the classic Little Woodbury four-posters. We might be tempted to conclude that such structures were not roofed houses, but served some other purpose, such as excarnation platforms. Yet we must guard against the assumption that domestic architecture should conform to a Southern British structural norm. At Butser Reynolds recognised the probability that alternatives to the Wessex norm existed in Southern Britain too. He concluded that minimally a roundhouse could be based upon a solitary central posthole, the structure being largely built of turf (Reynolds, 1979: 42–5). Ironically, his own experiments had demonstrated that for any roundhouse larger than a bell-tent a central post was redundant, so that the ultimate extension of this logic should have been that roundhouses could be built without any postholes whatsoever. For larger buildings, like the Scotstarvit roundhouse, with its diameter in the order of 18 metres, or like the even larger, multi-ringed building at Navan fort in County Armagh, a simple conical roof pitched at 45 degrees is surely improbable. Reynolds accepted a lower pitch of 30 degrees as feasible for a turf roof, provided a fire was maintained internally to prevent it becoming sodden. Other commentators have assumed a lower pitch for houses in Northern Britain without adequate justification, and Bersu's reconstruction of the Ballacagen house on the Isle of Man certainly envisaged a very low pitch (Bersu, 1977: Pl. III). The corollary of a lower pitch must be the need for stronger roof support, most obviously in the form of multiple post circles. It need not follow, however, that the additional internal support required should manifest itself in the form of earth-fast postholes. Heel-stones or internal paving would serve perfectly adequately as support for posts on which the principal thrust is vertically downward.

In the case of multi-ringed structures built on this principle, like the Navan 'temple', the Manx roundhouses or perhaps roundhouses like Scotstarvit, there is no obvious threshold of size beyond which roofing becomes unsustainable. But with the larger, multi-ringed plans an alternative would be to revert to the concept of the penannular or annular ridge-roof building, advanced for Grahame Clark's structure at West Harling, Norfolk (Clark and Fell, 1953), which, with a diameter in the order of 22 metres, was unlikely to have sustained a conical roof. On the same principle, rejecting the lean-to reconstructions of brochs that could perfectly well have sustained complete roofs does not mean that the annular ridge-roofed principle could not have been applicable to exceptionally large stone-built variants like Edin's Hall.

Social structure

Roman sources describe a tribal geography of Northern Britain. How real was this in the earlier Iron Age? Evidence suggests little centralisation of power or social unity at regional level, beyond what would have been implicit in kinship ties. Historical records suggest names for Southern Britain that may approximate to a tribal structure, but for Northern Britain the evidence is much more equivocal, with names like Brigantes or Picti not necessarily corresponding to any clearly defined grouping. A move towards greater cohesion apparently came in the later Iron Age, though doubtless in different degrees in different parts of Northern Britain.

It would be dangerous to infer from documentary sources, classical or later Irish or Welsh, that there was a pan-European or even a north-western Celtic social order that was uniform through space and time. Even within Atlantic Europe there could have been significant variations of custom. Nor need systems that prevailed in the Mediaeval period have had their origins in the earlier Iron Age. In particular, the model of a threefold hierarchy, with king at the apex and with progressively subordinate nobles and free farmers (Cunliffe, 1983: Fig. 94) is hard to support in the archaeological record, and is doubtless a simplification of a much more complex social structure anyway. Nevertheless, models derived from early historic Ireland and Wales are surely as relevant to Iron Age Northern Britain as might be models drawn from ethnographic contexts more remote in distance and time. Scholars have rightly sounded warnings regarding the use of epic literature, with its formulaic conventions, or early Irish and Welsh legal tracts, themselves subject to rewriting and liberal editing by successive scribes over hundreds of years. Yet a rigorous analysis of these legal sources (Charles-Edwards, 1993) suggests that there were underlying recurrent elements in the social order that might reasonably be regarded as having a considerable antiquity, perhaps deriving from earlier Iron Age traditions. The window on the Iron Age may be of distorted glass, but, like all historical sources, treated with due qualification, it may yet afford the archaeologist useful insights.

In the first place we should question whether Iron Age society in Northern Britain was nearly as rigidly stratified as is normally inferred for Southern Britain or Continental Europe. From a Wessex perspective it is easy to imagine hillforts functioning as *capites*, but in Northern Britain hillforts in some regions are hardly represented, and in others are distributed too densely overall, whilst being individually on an insufficient scale, to represent this hierarchical structure. Furthermore there is little evidence in terms of material assemblages to indicate the high status of hillforts in contrast to lesser home-steads. Status need not be reflected in portable artefacts, of course, and was much more likely to have been measured principally in land-holding or stock-holding. Until the emergence in the early historic period of larger political entities, with high kings or dominant lineages, hierarchy was probably less accentuated, which is not to assume that society was egalitarian in a modern political sense. Hierarchy within and between lineages, and the probable existence of clientship within and between communities, was doubtless based upon an established order within kin groups, linked to land and stock-holdings. But this will have been a dynamic system, with inherent dangers of what Charles-Edwards (1993) has called 'downward social mobility' as well as the upward alternative.

In the Irish model the importance of the *túath*, a social unit with territorial conno-tations, and the threefold hierarchical order is conventionally stressed (Powell, 1958/1980). Ranks below free farmers are seldom discussed, following Caesar's dismissal of all below the *equites* and *druides* as being of no account (*dBG*, VI: 13). The Old Irish laws suggest, however, that there may have been grades among the non-free, with a rank of semi-free above slavery. Status evidently was linked to land-holding, and if a lineage was unable to sustain the land requirements of a freeman then it might be relegated to the status of semi-free (Charles-Edwards, 1972).

Before the seventh century, Ireland evidently had a social structure based upon kinship made up of lineages comprising the agnatic descendants of the great-grandfather of the youngest generation of the group (ibid.). With the passage of generations lineages split in a process of segmentation, creating daughter lineages that might or might not super-sede the parent lineage. The status of freeman or free farmer was dependent on the holding of land, not just in Celtic society, but in Anglo-Saxon too. Anyone whose holding through partitive inheritance fell below that qualifying threshold might forfeit free status, and be forced into bonds of clientship. Inherited land was evidently transferred on the principle of agnatic division among sons of recognised liaisons, though acquired land could be disposed of by the individual, or by the kin group in redistribution to members of the group whose status as freemen was at risk. Even so, there were considerable complexities in matters relating to polygynous offspring, to adopted and fostered sons, and in the relationship between linear and collateral kin, with some significant differences of legal custom between Ireland and Wales. In consequence we should not transpose the detail of land ownership or inheritance of the early historic period from cognate areas into the earlier Iron Age of Northern Britain. But it seems reasonable to suggest that land was basically controlled by kindred rather than individuals, and that inheritance of land was essentially through agnatic male descendants. In essence the system of partitive inheritance militates in favour of downward social mobility if the male offspring surviving to adulthood exceeds one in any generation, or three in two generations, unless additional land is acquired to enhance the kin holding. This doubtless encouraged aggressive acquisition of land or stock from neighbouring communities. Extinction of the lineage can be avoided by adopting a son into full membership of the kin, but adopted sons or polygynous sons will otherwise increase the consequences of division.

Possible systems of inheritance have recently been discussed by Armit (forthcoming, b) in the context of Atlantic roundhouses and the transition to wheelhouses. Armit rightly argued that the stability and longevity of the broch landscape in Atlantic Scotland was hardly consistent with a normal system of partitive inheritance, which would surely have resulted in greater fragmentation of land-holding, and consequent 'downward social mobility', than is witnessed archaeologically. The incentive to acquire additional land to compensate for impoverishment resulting from land division might well have triggered political instability between neighbouring communities, but is hardly in evidence archaeologically. The replacement of larger roundhouses in south-west Scotland by a group of smaller houses, as at Boonies, might indicate divisions in inheritance, whilst the unit villas of Roman Britain have been regarded potentially as evidence of dual ownership. But there is little evidence in Atlantic Scotland of similar divisions that might be attributed to partitive inheritance. If land was held by a larger kin group, and title passed elsewhere within the kindred on the death of the former holder, then another broch site might for a generation assume primacy within the district. Armit adapted the idea of 'redistributive partible inheritance' (Charles-Edwards, 1972) to explain the Atlantic roundhouse phenomenon, based on a broadly egalitarian ideology and with the ownership of land similarly vested in the kin group. He argued that it was the breakdown of this system and the emergence of certain lines of descent that prompted the decline of the brochs and the shift to wheelhouses and other settlement forms. The demise of monumental Atlantic roundhouses, and their replacement by structures of rather different, cellular character, could be the archaeological manifestation of some fairly radical change within the social order. The economic success represented by Atlantic roundhouses may have resulted in a self-destructive increase in the number of surviving sons of the dominant lineage, if not a demographic increase in the population at large, with the result that the system was unable to sustain itself and collapsed. This certainly seems more plausible than to see a radical change in social patterns as the result of the very limited introduction of Roman goods in Atlantic Scotland (Sharples, 2003) or of a series of environmental catastrophes in the first millennium AD (Baillie, 2000).

At the top of the social hierarchy, lordship or kingship in historical Celtic societies was determined not by primogeniture but by choice from those eligible within dominant lineages. The important hierarchy therefore was not so much within the lineages, but between them. The model therefore is more complex than might appear, and that much more difficult to detect archaeologically. Furthermore, the system would have been subject to dynamic change over time, as a result of factors of inheritance, kinship alliances, marriages, repayment of social debts, competition and feuds, so that 'fixing' it at any given point in time in the archaeological record will be extremely difficult.

One regional variation that has commonly been inferred from documentary sources is the matrilineal system attributed to the Picts, which has been vigorously challenged by Smyth (1984) as wholly mythical. Bede, the earliest written source of this idea, includes it in his account of the origin myth of the Picts, who, far from being indigenous in Scotland as archaeologists would now believe, are said to have come from Scythia via Ireland, a notion that would strain the credulity of the most ardent diffusionist. Not having brought any women with them, the Picts allegedly sought wives from the Irish, who only agreed subject to the condition that in cases of dispute inheritance should be established through the female line. It is not my purpose here to argue the merits of this debate. What is worth remarking, however, is that Bede's account actually required the matrilineal principle only to operate in the event that the royal succession should be in dispute, which must imply that it would be the exception rather than the rule. Yet Duncan (1992: 48) dismissed this crucial point as arising from Bede's ignorance of Pictish practice, since the matrilineal principle among the Picts, though unique in Europe, has become accepted wisdom. Whether Bede's account repeats Irish propaganda intended to bolster political claims in Scotland need not concern us: the point of interest is that documentary sources should not predetermine archaeological interpretations, nor should they be accepted or rejected according to the preferred standpoint of the commentator.

Ritual, ceremonial and the archaeology of death

The interpretation of archaeological sites as ritual *foci* is currently quite fashionable, whereas to a previous generation it was regarded as being on the very limits of archaeological inference (Hawkes, 1954), and sometimes satirically parodied as the last refuge when all rational explanations were wanting. The reason for caution was understandable, since it was considered that mute artefacts in the context of non-literate prehistoric societies could only exceptionally cast light upon spiritual beliefs and social rituals. Ethnographic models might arguably afford insights into cognate systems, but even so it is important that we should recognise the limits of inference of archaeological evidence. Disquiet at the contemporary fashion for invoking ritual explanations arises from the cavalier disregard of those limits, too frequently paraded in the popular presentation of archaeology, but now deeply embedded in academic archaeology as well. Too often archaeologists simply assert, without reference to the evidential basis, however tenuous, that prehistoric societies believed this or that, so that archaeological synthesis becomes closer to creative fiction than to rational deduction or reasoned inference.

For the Celtic Iron Age generally there are very few sites that as a class might be regarded as potentially cultic or ceremonial, even as henge monuments or stone circles of the Neolithic or Bronze Age might be. Across Continental Europe there are sites for which a ritual function has been reasonably inferred from their exceptional deposits, like the enclosure with 2,000 broken weapons in its ditch at Gournay-sur-Aronde or the immense ossuary at Ribemont-sur-Ancre in Picardy (Brunaux, 1988). The ditched enclosures or *Viereckschanzen* of Central and Western Europe have been regarded as cultic on the grounds that they lack normal domestic structures and assemblages, and contain shafts in which special deposits have been found. In other instances natural sites may have been the focus of ritual, as indicated by hundreds of wooden images and carvings deposited at the source of the river Seine and at Chamalières in the Auvergne. Springs, rivers, lakes and bogs attracted apparently votive hoards or even human sacrifices widely throughout Celtic and Germanic Europe. Where the sheer scale or abnormality of the deposit defies normal interpretation, a ritual explanation presents itself by default. But it is hard to codify the conditions for recognising ritual deposition in less dramatic circumstances. In early Iron Age ritual contexts there are no recognisable formal furnishings like altars or inscribed dedications, as are found in the classical world, or icons like crosses in the Christian era to signify a ritual purpose. Artefacts like torcs may have had a special significance, the 'leaf-crown' motif in sculpture and metalwork may have been a symbol of divinity, and recurrent motifs in La Tène art, like the triskele, may have had occult significance, but these inferences are hardly amenable to empirical demonstration.

The one formal ritual context that can leave tangible traces in the archaeological record is burial, but even so there is a significant absence of evidence in many regions and periods during the Iron Age in Northern Britain, from which we can only deduce that disposal of the dead was by some ritual that did not lead to interment in a recognisable form. Where burials like the limited number of late pre-Roman sword burials are known, these plainly represented a highly selective and unrepresentative rite. Only perhaps in the case of the cemeteries of the Arras group of eastern Yorkshire, or in the long-cist cemeteries of the later Iron Age in eastern Scotland, might we reckon to have identified a regular mode of disposal of the dead. The absence of a recurrent burial type for much of Iron Age Britain could be the outcome of the widespread adoption of a rite like cremation and scattering that leaves no archaeological trace. But there need be no presumption that funerary practices should involve a single, widespread and archaeologically recognisable rite, when regional diversity and variable practices within a community may have been the custom (Wait, 1985).

Of the two pan-European practices that accord reasonably with ritual activity, watery deposits and shafts into the ground are both represented in Northern Britain. The ironwork hoards of southern Scotland could be matched elsewhere in Britain, and on a grander scale in Central Europe. Shafts into the underworld may range from relatively modest pits at Newstead, matched widely by examples throughout Celtic Britain and Europe (Ross, 1968; Piggott, S., 1978), to the more formal flights of steps represented at Mine Howe, Orkney, and perhaps at Burghead into the Christian era. The existence of other sites whose function was predominantly ritual is hinted at by excavations at An Dunan in the Western Isles. In a society in which ritual was doubtless implicit as well as codified, it may be difficult to isolate cult practices in a domestic context. The burials beneath the foundations at Sollas or behind the wheelhouse wall at Cnip certainly suggest ritual, as do the arrangements of animal bones or teeth around the hearths at Dun Bharabhat, A' Cheardach Mhor and A' Cheardach Bheag. But whether cosmological significance can legitimately be read into the deposition of surviving artefacts from house floors is more debatable, and depends crucially upon taphonomic factors and the reliability of the residual pattern as an index of the pattern in use.

Communal ritual may well have been one of the functions of major hillforts in those regions where such larger centres existed. Numerous hillforts in Southern Britain were sought out in the late Roman period for the construction of Romano-Celtic temples, perhaps suggestive of older ritual associations. Prominent landmarks like Ingleborough, Yeavering Bell, Traprain Law or Tap o' Noth may well have been used for seasonal gatherings or religious festivals among other communal purposes. Promontory forts and headland forts, especially where their perilously precipitate location seems unduly hazardous for normal occupation, could perhaps have served some ritual purpose. Enclosure evidently served a variety of different purposes in later prehistory and early history, and the association of sites, large and small, simple or complex, into a single category of hillforts has undoubtedly been an oversimplification of archaeological classification.

Culture contact and culture change

Most theoretical texts on archaeology discuss trade and exchange as if this were the only form of culture contact or mechanism for material innovation. In fact there are a number of possible agencies short of full-scale migration or invasion, some suggested by documentary sources, that could have been influential in triggering cultural or material innovations. Fosterage, for example, the outplacing of sons or cadet members of a high-ranking family during years of education and training, or the exchange of professional skilled men, craftsmen, technicians, poets or seers could have resulted in the transmission of ideas between ruling élites or their entourages that might account, for example, for technical or stylistic changes in high-status metalwork. Mercenary service, sometimes evidently in quite remote, foreign parts, or diplomatic missions by envoys, whose role may be closely related to trade by *mercatores*, could equally have made a disproportionate impact among small but influential ruling groups. Finally, hostages or slaves, the former at least probably of higher status, and potentially influential, or acts of raiding or piracy, could have resulted in the displacement from their area of origin of both ideas and artefacts.

High-status metalwork in southern Scotland like the Cairnmuir gold torc terminal are so manifestly of south-eastern English origin that diplomatic gift or high-status exchange seem the most likely explanations. The Balmaclellan collar, on the other hand, shows distinctive south-western stylistic traits in a form that is unknown in the south-west of England. Here we might speculate whether a craftsman from south-west England might not have been working for a south-western Scottish patron as a result of negotiated exchange of specialists. The Stichill collar likewise displays a combination of styles and techniques with both Irish and south-western English affinities, suggesting composite input rather than a simple import from a southern source. Nor should we assume that Southern Britain was the furthest extent of diplomatic or trading contacts with Northern Britain. The western seaways were evidently being exploited in the early historic period, with the import of Mediterranean or Continental pottery and glass to major centres in western Britain and Ireland, but it remains unclear whether western Scotland was receiving such imports directly or through down-the-line contacts with south-western Britain. For the earlier Iron Age archaeological distributions like that of Hallstatt or Hallstatt-derived swords suggest that direct maritime contacts across the North Sea route with Continental Europe, in Haselgrove's 'North-west European Hallstatt Interaction Sphere', were well established by later prehistory. The Newbridge chariot-burial is thus particularly intriguing in view of its affinities with the Continental series rather than those of eastern Yorkshire. Could this have been the burial of a Continental prince in fosterage with a southern Scottish aristocratic kin group, or the result of a diplomatic marriage anticipating by more than a millennium the Auld Alliance?

Invasion or population movement on any significant scale has been discredited since the 1960s as an explanation of archaeological culture change, even though classical and later historical sources suggest that population mobility was endemic in Iron Age and early historic Europe. A couple of generations later it should now be possible to take a more objective view. Acknowledging that archaeologists in the political environment of the mid-twentieth century tended to explain culture change too simplistically, it is plain that migration or invasion should not be excluded from the wider spectrum of options. Short of DNA testing or related biogenetic techniques for identifying immigrant groups, it might be hard to distinguish an influential but numerically limited ruling élite, for example, in terms of their impact on the archaeological record. So was the Northern British Iron Age indigenous or is there archaeological evidence for external settlement or colonisation? Fluctuations in climatic patterns through later prehistory and the early historic period may well have curtailed seaborne traffic from time to time, but an overall pattern of culture contact seems more probable than one of cultural isolation.

To sustain a case for immigration, however, we might expect in optimum circumstances to show a range of types, relating to settlement, funerary practice or material culture, and among the last perhaps several different variants, whether ceramic or metalwork or both, which were demonstrably novel in the local context. Second, we should expect to be able to point to a place of origin, where these types could equally be found in recurrent association. Yet even in the case of the Arras culture the selective nature of the innovative package compared to assemblages in any putative Continental homeland is such as to qualify our interpretation. Furthermore a convincing Continental homeland for this particular version of the funerary rite remains hard to demonstrate. The fact is that optimum circumstances seldom pertain, and the archaeological record alone is seldom likely to be sufficient to demonstrate beyond reasonable doubt the case for population movement. Refugee movements, as in the aftermath of the Roman Conquest of southern England, even including influential members of former ruling dynasties, are unlikely to have made a substantial impact in the archaeological record, though their presence could account for some exotic imports of high-status metalwork. Such negotiated settlement might well have resulted from diplomatic liaisons of much longer standing, but their impact archaeologically would be hard to estimate.

More probable than colonisation from the south, other than in the special circumstances of displacement by Roman annexation, are long-standing links between communities across the North Channel. Again archaeologically it is difficult to adduce evidence for population movement on any scale, in the earlier or later Iron Age, with or without the support of documentary sources. In part this may be because political change could involve a change in ruling élite without major population change, and in part because across Atlantic Scotland and the Irish Sea province a broad cultural continuum may have minimised the impact archaeologically of regional changes. Caesar referred to the Gaulish chief Diviciacus, who had ruled on both sides of the Channel. Equally it is possible that longer-standing diplomatic liaisons if not political dominion could have united communities on both sides of the North Channel in the earlier Iron Age.

Romanisation

The discussion of Romanisation, acculturation of Britain under the Roman occupation, has in recent years rightly come under radical review. The older conventional view of Richmond, Frere and Salway, sometimes called 'interventionist', has been challenged by the so-called 'non-interventionist' view of Millett and others. The key to an understanding of the relationship between Roman and native is to appreciate that there could have been no single, static, universal concept of what it was to be Roman, as was formerly implied by scholars who pronounced what 'Rome' did or believed in matters of political, military or imperial policy. Issues of individual identity, what Britons believed themselves to be, or how their behaviour patterns may have changed under Roman occupation, are hard to infer from archaeological evidence alone, and historical sources do not include a native social anthropology of Roman Britain. The presence of sherds of samian pottery does not necessarily tell us whether natives regarded it as valuable tableware or not, but Romans in Rome would hardly have regarded this mass-produced ware as anything special.

A logical question arising from this debate is whether we should even be considering the issue of Romanisation? The answer is that the old polarisation of Roman and native, as epitomised in the title of the volume of essays, *Roman and Native in North Britain*, edited by Ian Richmond in 1958, and in four of its six constituent chapters, is now rightly regarded as obsolete. The process of ethnic and cultural fusion resulting from the annexation of Britain into the Empire was more mutually complex than was implied by the model of unalloyed Roman civilisation being imposed upon a barbarian society that was receptive or resistant according to inclination or perversity. Certainly the archaeologist should be concerned with material culture as an expression of social role and identity, but these are areas in which extreme caution must be exercised if archaeological interpretation is not to become academically discredited as sociological dilettantism.

Because of the inevitable effects of dynamic interaction, the older notion that when the legions withdrew the natives heaved a collective sigh of relief and reverted once more to traditional Celtic customs is simply naïve. It is impossible to believe that anyone was not immeasurably affected by three and a half centuries of Roman imperial presence in Britain, not excluding the Romans themselves. The most critical impact of Roman occupation must have been upon the structure and fabric of native society. Even if the native aristocracies were persuaded to adopt Roman living styles and to accept a measure of political or administrative responsibility in the new province, their authority would have derived from the occupying regime, and the traditional bonds of obligation between rulers and dependants would inevitably have been eroded or completely destroyed. It was this that survived beyond the Roman frontier, so that when John Mann (1974) observed that at one level the emergence of a Scottish nation was the legacy of Rome, it was a legacy forged not just by the unification of northern tribes in opposition to Rome, but by the fact that their traditional social structure had not been fractured by subjugation within the Empire. In fact, the history of the northern frontier, despite its Roman perspective, contains sufficient information for us to infer that the political and military campaign north of Hadrian's Wall was little short of a disaster, with no consistent policy being sustained for any length of time, and a succession of disruptions, which in any impartial account would be described as defeats. Not surprisingly, therefore, any legacy was largely negative. There was no significant legacy of literacy or artistic tradition, no legacy of urbanisation, monetary economy or diocesan administration, and only a limited legacy of Roman Christianity. The fact that the question is asked at all, indeed, tells us more about the presumptions of archaeologists and historians than it does about Roman and native in Iron Age Britain.

Archaeology and the historical paradigm

How far could the Roman presence in Northern Britain, as historically documented, be sustained on the basis of archaeology alone? A Roman military presence in Northern Britain would be indisputable, simply because the structures along, behind and beyond the frontier are unique and not amenable to other interpretations, even if the garrisons included native auxiliaries from Britain and elsewhere in the Empire. The episodic nature of Roman occupation in Scotland might be inferred from material remains, though these are not uniformly represented quantitatively over time, and absence of evidence is therefore not invariably evidence of absence. As for the native population at the time of the Roman advance north, there is no clear correlation between archaeological types, habitational, funerary or artefactual, and inferred tribal territories, with the sole exception of the distinctive cemeteries of the Arras series in eastern Yorkshire, sometimes equated with the antecedents of the Parisi of Ptolemy's *Geography*. In Southern Britain, some ceramic 'style zones' (Cunliffe, 1991) might represent incipient territories, but the closest correlations have been inferred, not always without challenge, on the basis of coin distributions, particularly those on which rulers and mints are named. The absence of coinage precludes even this basis of assessment north of the Trent. In consequence it is impossible to offer archaeological support for a unified tribe of Brigantes, or even a looser Brigantian confederacy, and the suspicion must be that contemporary reports were merely indicating that much of northern England was populated by hostile highlanders. The Parisi are recorded only by Ptolemy in the second century AD, who located them north of the Humber. Any link between this name and the users of cemeteries dating some half a millennium earlier must obviously be tentative, as must any link between them and the Parisii of northern France at the time of Caesar's Gallic campaigns. But the distribution of cemeteries with square-ditched barrows and occasional cart-burials is geographically well defined, and the idea of the introduction of these rites as a result of contact, perhaps by a small but influential group, from an unspecified source in north-eastern Gaul still seems persuasive.

But what of other intrusive groups whose structural and material assemblages were less distinctive and unequivocal than those of the Roman army? At the very end of our time-span, it might be argued that Norse settlers were distinguished by particular building types, burials and artefacts. Yet in Orkney the transition from 'Pictish' to Norse is far from a clear-cut horizon. In the south-east of Scotland and north-eastern England in the post-Roman period, the Anglian expansion is largely predicated on the frame-work of documented history and place-names. Certain building types, like rectangular halls with distinctive architectural features, might be attributed to Anglian settlers, but at both Yeavering and Doon Hill rectangular construction was apparently in evidence among pre-existing native British communities. Cemeteries, as we have seen, become a less reliable index of the Anglian advance with the conversion to Christianity, and diagnostic material artefacts are hardly so profuse as to preclude other possible explanations.

The absence of distinctive settlement or material types that might make up an archaeological distribution coterminous with the historically inferred region of Dál Riata in western Scotland has frequently been remarked. The expectation that archaeological distributions might correlate with the territories of distinct ethnic groups was implicit in the cultural model developed by Gordon Childe, but prehistorians have long since recognised that such simplistic equations are unlikely to be valid, either in principle or in practice. The irony in this instance is that the territory of Dál Riata in its Irish homeland is not recognisable from any unique or diagnostic settlement types or material remains, so that any such expectation in western Scotland seems flawed from the outset. In any event it is becoming increasing clear that connections across the North Channel were of much longer standing than the historical record might imply, and that a commonality of culture across the western seaways would always obscure any particular historical episode, even if such occurred. Cultural inter-action is a cumulative and dynamic process that will always defy definition by the static boundaries of archaeological distributions. Should we therefore expect anything diagnostically indicative of Dál Riata settlers if the historical record conflates a long sequence of events and complex relationships into a simplistic apologue? This does not mean that historical migrations or the transfer of ruling élites from one region to another did not happen; but the documentary record in this instance may well reflect politically fabricated traditions intended to bolster the claims of the Dál Riata dynasty in its rivalry with its neighbours.

So what about the Picts? Like Brigantes, Picti was almost certainly in origin a descriptive name, given to native groups whose ethnic identities or kinship relationships were not implicit in the Roman use of these terms. Yet like the Brigantes, whose name was incorporated later in a regional centre at Aldborough, the name Picti, from unspecific origins, implying painted natives beyond the Pale, also acquired a more particular attribution in the early historic period in historical annals and in recorded king-lists. From these, however, it is clear than the Picts were still divided into numerous separate groups that progressively through the first millennium AD coalesced into two main kingdoms, a northern and a southern. Identifying individual kings and their territorial seats is the prerogative of the historian, but there is no sound reason for believing that we can reliably equate the limited definition of a 'Pictish heartland' with any archaeological distribution, not excluding that of symbol-stones, still less that of souterrains or massive silver chains. Even if such artefacts occurred within this limited definition of Pictish territory, at a time coincident with the existence of these Pictish kingdoms, their distributions in space and time are hardly coterminous with the Pictish heartlands, extending beyond or falling short of both. They might therefore be *descriptive* of Picts in the broader sense of natives beyond the Roman frontier, but they cannot be regarded as *diagnostic* of the Picts in the more limited sense that has become fashionable among historians and archaeologists. Whether any symbol-stones are earlier than the sixth century, or whether antecedents in timber preceded their appearance is immaterial to Pictish origins. Symbol-stones were a statement of identity, whether as memorials, as territorial markers or as expressions of social alliances, and would only have been erected when a community felt the need to make this public statement. As with funerary monuments, that need may have arisen at times of dynamic social or political change. That need may abate, and the role of monuments may mutate with time, as presumably did that of symbol-stones with the advent of Christianity. The dilemma concerning the sudden demise of the Picts therefore is hardly an archaeological problem. Like all other archaeological type-fossils, souterrains, square barrows, symbol-stones or nuclear forts have a limited currency, the ending of which at various stages over a millennium does not represent the mysterious demise of people with whom they were too rigidly identified in the first place.

Northern Britain in the Iron Age: a community of diversity?

In 1964 Hodson attempted a characterisation through recurrent type-fossils of the Southern British Iron Age, typified by the settlement site at Little Woodbury in Wiltshire, distinct from the two cultural groups which he acknowledged were related to the wider La Tène family, the so-called Aylesford and Arras cultures (Hodson, 1964). Whilst the case for the essentially insular character of the Woodbury culture was well made, the type-fossils proposed, namely the permanent large roundhouse, the weaving comb of bone or antler, and the ring-headed pin, together with a 'negative type-fossil', the absence of a regular burial rite, seemed to be a pitifully inadequate representation of a much broader and richer assemblage of weapons, tools and ornaments. Any attempt to characterise the Northern British Iron Age on the basis of material artefacts would probably suffer a similar fate, since for much of the Iron Age the surviving domestic assemblage is minimal, and the absence of burials removes the one context that archaeologically provides the most productive source of material artefacts.

Recognising that absence may be as significant as presence, however, some generalisations may be offered as a preliminary characterisation of the Northern British Iron Age.

- Settlements for the most part are dispersed, and fall into two principal categories, either individual homesteads of a nuclear family or village-sized communities, probably of an extended kin group. Major hillforts or larger enclosed sites analogous to Southern British *oppida* are rare, and where they existed may have served as places of assembly for a much larger dispersed community. The implication is that in Northern Britain political, social or economic organisation on a regional or wider scale was a late Iron Age development, in contrast to the time scheme in Southern Britain or Continental Europe.
- The most recurrent manifestation of domestic settlement, as in Southern Britain, is the roundhouse, with a shift towards rectilinear plans occurring to a limited extent in the later Iron Age. The diversity of plans and construction techniques, however, is considerable, even within the timber or timber-and-stone houses of lowland Scotland and northern England. In Atlantic Scotland monumental building in stone gives way to a more complex set of circular, cellular, ventral or sub-rectangular plans. In this Northern Britain stands firmly in an Atlantic tradition that is represented from the Northern Isles to the Hispanic peninsula, in contrast to the Central and Northern European rectangular building traditions.
- Funerary practices in the earlier Iron Age, with the sole exception of the Arras group of eastern Yorkshire, did not entail in general the deposition of the dead in archaeologically visible burials of a recurrent class. Those burials that have been recognised like the warrior graves of Mortonhall or Alloa, or the small cemetery at Broxmouth, therefore, must have been special in some way, socially or otherwise. By the early historic period, square-ditched cemeteries in eastern Scotland are locally distinctive, and the appearance of long-cist cemeteries coincides in due course with the adoption of Christian burial rites.
- The economic basis of the Northern British Iron Age was variously a combination of pastoralism and agriculture, supplemented by local resources where available. The cereal regime was for large areas of the north a barley monoculture, but arable intensification or extensification can be attested, notably in parts of northern England already before the Roman occupation. In many regions pastoralism was undoubtedly dominant, but not generally to the exclusion of arable cultivation.
- For the earlier Iron Age, in contrast to Southern Britain, much of Northern Britain was effectively aceramic, a characteristic shared with Ireland, and one that can hardly be attributed to cultural isolation or ignorance in view of the exceptional nature of

the pottery assemblage of Atlantic Scotland, and of the Western Isles in particular. Whilst it is easy to infer the use of other materials, wood, leather and textiles for containers, the implication must also be that food preparation was by spit-roasting, or boiling in a communal cauldron that was too valuable to be abandoned to the archaeological record except in votive deposits.

- Material production of other artefacts was largely conducted on a domestic or local scale, with little evidence until the later Iron Age of centralised production on even the scale that characterised the pre-Roman Iron Age in Southern Britain. The material assemblages from domestic settlements from northern England in the pre-Roman period, and from Scotland in the earlier Iron Age, are basic and utilitarian, principally in stone or bone. Artefacts of Hallstatt or La Tène type are comparatively rare, the latter mostly dating from the late first millennium BC. By the early first millennium AD regional patterns are evident in pin and bead production and the localised distribution of distinctive bronze ornaments. Thereafter pins and brooch types conform to recurrent types of wider British and Irish distribution.

- Trade and exchange may be inferred with Southern Britain and beyond, though actual imports are exceptional in the pre-Roman period. Though maritime contacts across the North Sea route and along the western seaways in the earlier Iron Age may be inferred, the absence of specific imports or a suite of cognate material types makes it unlikely that there was any significant element of colonisation from the south or directly from Continental Europe in the earlier Iron Age. A significant distinction in the economic systems of the Northern British Iron Age is indicated by the fact that communities north of the Trent were not coin-using until the historic period. By the sixth century AD there is ample evidence of imported pottery and glass from Continental or Mediterranean Europe, including trade via the Irish Sea to western Scottish centres, but these centres controlling trade were royal or monastic rather than commercial ports or markets as in Anglo-Saxon England.

Two models which have gained prominence in the last twenty years are the World Systems Theory in which it was presumed that there was a Core and a Periphery in cultural relationships, and the Prestige Goods Economy Model, not unrelated to it, since what was regarded as prestigious invariably derived from the presumed core and sustained the social hierarchies operating on the dependent periphery. In the context of Mediterranean relationships with Central and Western Europe in later prehistory, the classical civilisations of Greece and Rome were obviously cast in the role of core, with north Alpine Europe and more especially Atlantic Europe in the role of periphery. Prime examples of this relationship were the appearance of Greek imports in late Hallstatt and early La Tène princely fortifications and burials, or the deposition in lavishly furnished graves of late La Tène in north-eastern Gaul and the Ardennes of wine amphorae and Italic bronze vessels. The former made little or no impact upon Britain; the distribution of the latter includes a group of high-status burials in south-eastern England. These imports were seen as a means whereby local aristocracies sustained their élite status by exercising local control over the trade in luxury goods. This being the case, then the hierarchical dominance of the élite within the social structure would plainly be threatened by any disruption in the supply of exotic goods. This might indeed account for some of the regional shifts over time in the apparent dominance of centres of trans-alpine interaction. Nevertheless, whilst it is conceivable that at certain times control of long-distance exchange may have become a dominant factor in sustaining social hierarchies in Central and Western Europe, it is hard to believe that such hierarchies had not developed in the context of much more complex relationships, among which Greek and Roman imports are merely the most archaeologically visible elements. Nor should it be assumed that the presence or absence of Mediterranean imports was solely determined by the Mediterranean sources. The pattern of imports in north-Alpine and Western Europe clearly indicates that they were not all simply the product of trading initiatives by Greek or Roman entrepreneurs. The distribution in the sixth century BC of Phocaean grey ware and amphorae along the Mediterranean littoral and its immediate hinterland might well accord with a maritime trading pattern. But the appearance of exotic items like the Grächwil hydria or the Vix crater so far from the coast surely argues for other relationships and mechanisms in which the barbarian chieftains of north-Alpine and Western Europe were not simply passive recipients. In these relationships any changes that can be observed archaeologically could as easily have been triggered by native as by Greek agency. The process in any event cannot have been one-way, even though the reciprocated goods – metal ores, hides, slaves or whatever – were not such as to leave traces in the archaeological record.

Whatever the limitations of the core–periphery model might be for characterising the relationship between the Mediterranean and north-Alpine or Western Europe, there can be no doubt that the two zones interacted significantly and even, according to historical sources, violently in the second half of the first millennium BC. Atlantic Europe, including Northern Britain and Ireland but not excluding the lands bordering the western approaches nor the Atlantic coast to the Hispanic peninsula, periodically came into contact with the Mediterranean world. The documented voyage of Pytheas or the Barbary ape from Navan fort in Armagh are indicative of a burgeoning pattern of maritime contacts. This pattern was certainly sustained into the early historic period, with imports from the Mediterranean and Western Europe attested in various parts of Western and Northern Britain and Ireland. This need not mean that Atlantic Europe was any more peripheral to a Mediterranean core than the Mediterranean was peripheral to Atlantic Europe. Both had their reserves of natural resources, both doubtless had developed sophisticated social structures over many generations, and both may be expected to have had their independent orbit of political and economic contacts and alliances. Our perception of the two zones is, of course, immeasurably and indelibly influenced by the fact that the Mediterranean world was literate from an early date, with the result not only that we are much better informed about classical societies than we could ever be from archaeological sources alone, but also that our perception of the ancient world is essentially from the viewpoint of classical civilisation.

In drawing a broad distinction between the Mediterranean world, with its immediate neighbours in north-Alpine and west-Central Europe on the one hand, and Atlantic Europe on the other, it is not my intention to suggest any implicit cultural unity across the Atlantic zone. At certain periods in some regions there may well have appeared distinctive fashions of building or burial, or indeed in material assemblages, which might be the archaeological indicators of a broader community of cultural tradition. The practice of collective burial in megalithic tombs might be cited as an instance, though the regional distinctiveness of different groups defies simplistic explanation of their potential relationships. Metalworking industries of the later Bronze Age are equally distinctive, though the presence of individual types in hoards suggests a good deal of reciprocal exchange between neighbouring Atlantic communities. The predominance throughout later prehistory of the circular ground-plan for domestic buildings in Atlantic Europe is one of the region's most enduring characteristics, even if the local building types, of Scottish brochs and duns, Wessex timber roundhouses, Irish cashels or roundhouses of the Hispanic *castros* and *cividade*, all proclaim their local origins.

To make a case therefore for a common cultural identity across the Atlantic Iron Age, of which Northern Britain was part, might be tempting, but would probably be misguided. Atlantic Europe is not a cultural unity in the Iron Age, though its regions have many characteristics in common that distinguish them from the Central European tradition. Throughout the Iron Age Northern Britain doubtless had contacts, in varying degrees at various times, with both Southern Britain and Continental Europe on the one hand, and Ireland on the other. These contacts could have triggered cultural innovation, and in the most extreme form of Romanisation must have had a lasting impact on the native population, particularly in the disruption of an older social and political order. The process of dynamic change to which these external impulses contributed culminated in the political territories that emerged with documented identities in the early historic period. Even if there is no single Atlantic Iron Age, Northern Britain cannot be dismissed as peripheral to the mainstream of Central and Western Europe. Northern Britain and Atlantic Europe were in another mainstream altogether.

Bibliography

Abbreviations

AA	*Archaeologia Aeliana*
AJ	*Antiquaries Journal*
ArchJ	*Archaeological Journal*
BAR	*British Archaeological Reports*
BMQ	*British Museum Quarterly*
CA	*Current Archaeology*
DAJ	*Durham Archaeological Journal*
DES	*Discovery and Excavation in Scotland*
DyAJ	*Derbyshire Archaeological Journal*
GAJ	*Glasgow Archaeological Journal*
JAS	*Journal of Archaeological Science*
JBAA	*Journal of the British Archaeological Association*
JIA	*Journal of Irish Archaeology*
JRA	*Journal of Roman Archaeology*
JRS	*Journal of Roman Studies*
JRSAI	*Journal of the Royal Society of Antiquaries of Ireland*
JWA	*Journal of Wetland Archaeology*
MA	*Medieval Archaeology*
NA	*Northern Archaeology*
OJA	*Oxford Journal of Archaeology*
PBA	*Proceedings of the British Academy*
PDNHAS	*Proceedings of the Dorset Natural History and Archaeological Society*
PPS	*Proceedings of the Prehistoric Society*
PRIA	*Proceedings of the Royal Irish Academy*
PSAS	*Proceedings of the Society of Antiquaries of Scotland*
RCA(H)MS	*Royal Commission on the Ancient (and Historical) Monuments of Scotland*
SAF	*Scottish Archaeological Forum*
SAR	*Scottish Archaeological Review*
STAR	*Scottish Trust for Archaeological Research*
TAASDN	*Transactions of the Architectural and Archaeological Society of Durham and Northumberland*
TAFAJ	*Tayside and Fife Archaeological Journal*
TBNHS	*Transactions of the Buteshire Natural History Society*
TCWAS	*Transactions of the Cumberland and Westmorland Archaeological Society*
TDGNHAS	*Transactions of the Dumfriesshire and Galloway Natural History and Antiquarian Society*

TGAS   *Transactions of the Glasgow Archaeological Society*
TLCAS   *Transactions of the Lancashire and Cheshire Archaeological Society*
YAJ   *Yorkshire Archaeological Journal*

Abercromby, J., Ross, T. and Anderson, T. (1902) 'Account of the excavation of the Roman Station at Inchtuthill, Perthshire, undertaken by the Society of Antiquaries of Scotland in 1901', *PSAS*, 36, 1901–2: 182–242.

Alcock, L. (1981) 'Early historic fortifications in Scotland', in Guilbert, G. ed. (1981) 150–80.

Alcock, L. (1984) 'A survey of Pictish settlement archaeology', in Friell, J. G. P. and Watson, W. G. eds (1984) 7–41.

Alcock, L. (1987) 'Pictish studies: present and future', in Small, A. ed. (1987) 80–92.

Alcock, L. (1988) 'Bede, Eddius and the forts of the North Britons', Newcastle upon Tyne, Jarrow Lecture 1988.

Alcock, L. (1998) 'From realism to caricature: reflections on insular depictions of animals and people', *PSAS*, 128: 515–36.

Alcock, L. (2003) *Kings and Warriors, Craftsmen and Priests in Northern Britain AD 550–850*, Edinburgh, Society of Antiquaries of Scotland.

Alcock, L. and Alcock, E. A. (1987) 'Reconnaissance excavations on Early Historic fortifications and other royal sites in Scotland 1974–84: 2, Excavations at Dunollie Castle, Oban, Argyll, 1978', *PSAS*, 117: 119–47.

Alcock, L. and Alcock, E. A. (1990) 'Reconnaissance excavations on Early Historic fortifications and other royal sites in Scotland 1974–84: 4, Excavations at Alt Clut, Clyde Rock, Strathclyde 1974–75', *PSAS*, 120: 95–149.

Alcock, L. and Alcock, E. A. (1992) 'Reconnaissance excavations on Early Historic fortifications and other royal sites in Scotland 1974–84: 5, A, Excavations and other fieldwork at Forteviot, Perthshire, 1981; B, Excavations at Urquhart Castle, Inverness-shire, 1983; C, Excavations at Dunnottar, Kincardineshire, 1984', *PSAS*, 122: 215–89.

Alcock, L., Alcock, E. A. and Driscoll, S. T. (1989) 'Reconnaissance excavations on Early Historic fortifications and other royal sites in Scotland, 1974–84: 3, Excavations at Dundurn, Strathearn, Perthshire, 1976–77', *PSAS*, 119: 189–226.

Alcock, L., Alcock, E. A. and Foster, S. M. (1986) 'Reconnaissance excavations on Early Historic fortifications and other royal sites in Scotland, 1974–84: 1, Excavations near St Abb's Head, Berwickshire, 1980', *PSAS*, 116: 255–79.

Alexander, D. ed. (1996) *Prehistoric Renfrewshire: Papers in Honour of Frank Newall*, Edinburgh, Renfrew Local History Forum.

Alexander, D. (2000) 'Later prehistoric settlement in west central Scotland', in Harding, J. and Johnston, R. eds 2000: 157–66.

Alexander, D. (2002) 'An oblong fort at Finavon, Angus: an example of the over-reliance on the appliance of science', in Smith, B. B. and Banks, I. eds (2002) 45–54.

Alexander, D. and Ralston, I. (1999) 'Survey work on Turin Hill, Angus', *TAFAJ*, 5, 1999: 36–49.

Alexander, D. and Watkins, T. (1998) 'St Germains, Tranent, East Lothian: the excavation of Early Bronze Age remains and Iron Age enclosed and unenclosed settlements', *PSAS*, 128, 1998: 203–54.

Allen, D. F. (1961) 'The origins of coinage in Britain: a reappraisal', in Frere, S. S. ed. (1961) 97–308.

Allen, D. F. (1963) *The Coins of the Coritani, Sylloge of Coins of the British Isles 3*, London, British Academy, Oxford University Press, Spink.

Allen, J. R. and Anderson, J. (1903) *The Early Christian Monuments of Scotland*, Edinburgh, Neil and Co./Society of Antiquaries of Scotland.

Allison, P. M. ed. (1999) *The Archaeology of Household Activities*, London, Routledge.

Anderson, J. (1881) *Scotland in Early Christian Times*, Edinburgh, David Douglas.

Anderson, J. (1883) *Scotland in Pagan Times: The Iron Age*, Edinburgh, David Douglas.

Armit, I. ed. (1990) *Beyond the Brochs: Changing Perspectives on the Atlantic Scottish Iron Age*, Edinburgh, Edinburgh University Press.

Armit, I. (1991) 'The Atlantic Scottish Iron Age: five levels of chronology', *PSAS*, 121: 189–226.

Armit, I. (1992) *The Later Prehistory of the Western Isles of Scotland*, Oxford, BAR, Brit. Ser., 221.

Armit, I. (1996) *The Archaeology of Skye and the Western Isles*, Edinburgh, Edinburgh University Press.

Armit, I. (1997a) *Celtic Scotland*, London, Batsford/Historic Scotland.

Armit, I. (1997b) 'Cultural landscapes and identities; a case study in the Scottish Iron Age', in Gwilt, A. *et al.* eds (1997) 248–53.

Armit, I. (1999a) 'Life after Hownam: the Iron Age in south-east Scotland', in Bevan, B. ed. (1999) 65–80.

Armit, I. (1999b) 'The abandonment of souterrains: evolution, catastrophe or dislocation?', *PSAS*, 129: 577–96.

Armit, I. (2000) Review of M. Parker Pearson, N. Sharples with J. Mulville, *Between Land and Sea: Excavations at Dun Vulan, South Uist,* Sheffield, 1999, *Antiquity*, 74: 244–5.

Armit, I. (2002) 'Land and freedom: implications of Atlantic Scottish settlement patterns for Iron Age land-holding and social organisation', in Smith, B. B. and Banks, I. eds (2002) 15–26.

Armit, I. (2003) *Towers in the North: The Brochs of Scotland*, Stroud, Tempus.

Armit, I. (forthcoming, a) 'Floor formation and structured deposition: Cnip wheelhouse, Lewis', *Scottish Archaeological Forum.*

Armit, I. (forthcoming, b) 'Land-holding and inheritance in the Atlantic Scottish Iron Age', in *Tall Stories?*, Proceedings of Conference in Lerwick, July, 2000, Oxford, BAR.

Armit, I. and Braby, A. (1996) 'Ceann nan Clachan', *DES*, 1996: 106.

Armit, I. and Braby, A. (2002) 'Excavation of a burnt mound and associated structures at Ceann nan Clachan, North Uist', *PSAS*, 132: 229–58.

Armit, I., Dunwell, A. and Hunter, F. (1999) *Traprain Law Summit Project, East Lothian: Data Structure Report, 1999*, Edinburgh, privately published professional report.

Armit, I., Dunwell, A. and Hunter, F. (2000) *Traprain Law Summit Project, East Lothian: Data Structure Report, 2000*, Edinburgh, privately published professional report.

Armit, I. and Ralston, I. B. M. (1997) 'The Iron Age', in Edwards, K. and Ralston, I. eds (1997) 169–94.

Ashmore, P. J. (1980) 'Low cairns, long cists and symbol stones', *PSAS*, 110, 1978–80: 346–55.

Ashmore, P. J. (1997) 'Radiocarbon dates from archaeological sites in Argyll and Arran', in Ritchie, G. ed. (1997), 236–83.

Atkinson, R. J. C. and Piggott, S. (1955) 'The Torrs Chamfrein', *Archaeologia*, 96: 197–235.

Baillie, M. (2000) *Exodus to Arthur: Catastrophic Encounters with Comets*, London, Batsford.

Banks, I. (2000) 'Excavation of an Iron Age and Romano-British enclosure at Woodend Farm, Johnstonebridge, Annandale, 1994 and 1997', *PSAS*, 130: 223–81.

Barber, J. (1981) 'Excavations on Iona, 1979', *PSAS*, 111: 282–380.

Barber, J. (1985) 'The pit alignment at Eskbank Nurseries', *PPS*, 51: 149–66.

Barber, J., Halstead, P., James, H. and Lee, F. (1989) 'An unusual Iron Age burial at Hornish Point, South Uist', *Antiquity*, 63: 773–8.

Barclay, G. (1980) 'Newmill and the souterrains of Southern Pictland', *PSAS*, 110, 1978–80: 200–8.

Barclay, G. (1995) 'What's new in Scottish prehistory?', *SAR*, 9/10: 3–14.

Barclay, G. (1999) 'Cairnpapple revisited: 1948–1998', *PPS*, 65: 17–46.

Barley, M. W. and Hanson, R. P. C. (1968) *Christianity in Britain 300–700*, Leicester, Leicester University Press.

Barrett, J. C. (1981) 'Aspects of the Iron Age in Atlantic Scotland. A case study in the problems of archaeological interpretation', *PSAS*, 111: 205–19.

Barrett, J. and Bradley, R. eds (1980) *Settlement and Society in the British Late Bronze Age*, Oxford, BAR Brit. Ser. 83.

Barrett, J., Fitzpatrick, A. and Macinnes, L., eds (1989) *Barbarians and Romans in North-West Europe, from the Later Republic to Late Antiquity*, Oxford, BAR Internat. Ser., 471.

Benton, S. (1931) 'The excavations of the Sculptor's Cave, Covesea, Morayshire', *PSAS*, 65, 1930–1: 177–216.

Bernelle, A. ed. (1992) *Decantations: A Tribute to Maurice Craig*, Dublin, Lilliput Press.

Bersu, G. (1940) 'Excavations at Little Woodbury, Wiltshire, part 1', *PPS*, 6: 30–111.

Bersu, G. (1948) '"Fort" at Scotstarvit Covert, Fife', *PSAS*, 82, 1947–8: 241–63.

Bersu, G. (1977) *Three Iron Age Round Houses in the Isle of Man*, ed. C. A. R. Radford, Isle of Man, Manx National Museum and National Trust.

Beswick, P. (1987) 'Wincobank hillfort: radiocarbon dates', *Bull. Prehist. Res. Section, Yorks. Arch. Soc.*, Leeds, no page nos.

Beswick, P. and Coombs, D. (1986) 'Excavations at Portfield Hillfort, 1960, 1970 and 1972', in Manby, T. and Turnbull, P. eds (1986) 137–79.

Bevan, B. (1997) 'Bounding the landscape: place and identity during the Yorkshire Wolds Iron Age', in Haselgrove, C. ed. (1997) 181–91.

Bevan, B. (1999) 'Northern exposure: interpretative devolution and the Iron Ages in Britain', in Bevan, B. ed. (1999) 1–19.

Bevan, B. ed. (1999) *Northern Exposure: Interpretative Devolution and the Iron Ages in Britain*, Leicester, University of Leicester Arch. Mon., 4.

Bevan, B. (2000) 'Peak practice: whatever happened to the iron age in the southern Pennines?', in Harding, J. and Johnston, P. eds (2000) 141–55.

Beveridge, E. (1905) *Coll and Tiree*, Edinburgh, William Brown.

Beveridge, E. (1911) *North Uist*, Edinburgh, William Brown.

Beveridge, E. (1930) 'Excavation of an earth house at Foshigarry and a fort, Dun Thomaigh in North Uist', *PSAS*, 65, 299–357.

Beveridge, E. (1931) 'Earth houses at Garry Iodrach and Bac Mhic Connain in North Uist', *PSAS*, 66: 32–67.

Bewley, R. H. (1986). 'Survey and excavation in the Solway Plain, Cumbria (1982–4)', *TCWAS*, 86: 19–40.

Bewley, R. H. (1992) 'Excavations on two crop-mark sites in the Solway Plain, Cumbria, Ewanrigg Settlement and Swarthy Hill, 1986–1988', *TCWAS*, 92: 23–47.

Bewley, R. H. (1993) 'Survey and excavation at a crop-mark enclosure, Plasketlands, Cumbria', *TCWAS*, 93: 1–18.

Bewley, R. H. (1994) *Book of Prehistoric Settlements*, London, Batsford/English Heritage.

Bewley, R. H. (1998) 'Survey and excavations of a cropmark enclosure at Edderside, Cumbria, 1989–90', *TCWAS*, 98: 107–17.

Blake, B. (1959) 'Excavations of native (Iron Age) sites in Cumberland 1956–58', *TCWAS*, 59: 1–14.

Blundell, J. D. and Longworth, I. H. (1967) 'A Bronze Age hoard from Portfield Farm, Whalley, Lancs', *BMQ*, 32: 8–14.

Boulton, G. S., Peacock, J. D. and Sutherland, D. G. (1991) 'Quaternary', in Craig, G. Y. ed. (1991) 503–43.

Bowden, M. C. B., Mackay, D. A. and Blood, N. K. (1989) 'A new survey of Ingleborough Hillfort, North Yorkshire', *PPS*, 55: 267–71.

Bowen, E. G. (1972) *Britain and the Western Seaways*, London, Thames and Hudson.

Bowen, H. C. and Fowler, P. J. eds (1978) *Early Land Allotment*, Oxford, BAR, Brit. Ser. 48.

Bradley, R. J. (1984) *The Social Foundations of Prehistoric Britain, Themes and Variations in the Archaeology of Power*, London and New York, Longman.

Bradley, R. J. (1987) 'Time regained: the creation of continuity', *JBAA*, 140: 1–17.

Branigan, K., ed. (1980) *Rome and the Brigantes: The Impact of Rome on Northern England*, Sheffield, Dept of Prehistory and Archaeology, University of Sheffield.

Branigan, K. and Foster, P. eds (1995) *Barra: Archaeological Research on Ben Tangaval*, Sheffield, Sheffield Academic Press.

Breeze, A. (1998) 'Pictish chains and Welsh forgeries', *PSAS*, 128, 481–4.

Breeze, D. (1989) 'The impact of the Roman Army on North Britain', in Barrett, J. *et al.* eds (1989) 227–34.

Breeze, D. (1994) 'The imperial legacy – Rome and her neighbours', in Crawford, B. ed. (1994) 13–19.

Breeze, D. and Dobson, B. (2000) *Hadrian's Wall*, 4th edn London, Penguin Books.

Brewster, T. C. M. (1963) *The Excavation of Staple Howe*, Malton, East Riding Arch. Res. Comm.

Brewster, T. C. M. (1981) 'The Devil's Hill', *CA*, 76: 140–1.

Brown, M. (1983) 'New evidence for Anglian settlement in East Lothian', *SAR*, 2, 2: 156–63.

Bruce, J. (1900) 'Notes of the discovery and exploration of a pile structure on the north bank of the river Clyde, east from Dumbarton Rock', *PSAS*, 34, 1899–1900: 437–62.

Bruce, J. (1908) 'Report and investigations upon the Langbank pile dwelling', *TGAS*, 5: 43–53.

Bruck, J. (1995) 'A place for the dead; the role of human remains in Late Bronze Age Britain', *PPS*, 61: 245–78.

Bruneux, J. L. (1988) *The Celtic Gauls: Gods, Rites and Sanctuaries*, London, Seaby.

Burgess, C. B. (1970) 'Excavations at the scooped settlement Hetha Burn I, Hethpool, Northumberland', *TAASDN*, ns 2: 1–26.

Burgess, C. B. (1974) 'The Bronze Age', in Renfrew, C. ed. (1974) 165–232.

Burgess, C. B. (1984) 'The prehistoric settlement of Northumberland: a speculative survey', in Miket, R. and Burgess, C. eds (1984) 126–75.

Burgess, C. M. G. (1999) 'Promontory enclosures on the Isle of Lewis, the Western Isles, Scotland', in Frodsham, P. *et al.* eds (1999) 93–104.

Burgess, C. M. G. and Church, M. (1997) *Coastal Erosion Assessment, Lewis: A Report for Historic Scotland*, Edinburgh, privately published professional report.

Burgess, C. M. G., Church, M. and Gilmour, S. M. D. (1998) *Uig Landscape Survey: Second Interim Report*, Edinburgh, privately published professional report.

Burt, J. R. F. (1997) 'Long Cist Cemeteries in Fife', in Henry, D. ed. (1997) 64–6.

Buteux, S. (1997) *Settlements at Skaill, Deerness, Orkney. Excavations by Peter Gelling of the Prehistoric, Pictish, Viking and Later Periods, 1963–1981*, Oxford, BAR Brit. Ser. 260.

Butler, R. M. ed. (1971) *Soldier and Civilian in Roman Yorkshire*, Leicester, Leicester University Press.

Calder, C. S. T. (1963) 'Cairns, Neolithic houses and burnt mounds in Shetland', *PSAS*, 96, 1962–3: 37–86.

Callander, J. G. (1931) 'Excavation of an earth house at Foshigarry and a fort, Dun Thomaidh, in North Uist, by the late E. Beveridge', *PSAS*, 65, 1930–1: 299–357.

Callander, J. G. (1932) 'Earth houses at Garry Iochdrach and Bac Mhic Connain in North Uist by the late E. Beveridge', *PSAS*, 66, 1931–2: 32–66.

Campbell, E. (1991) 'Excavations of a wheelhouse and other Iron Age structures at Sollas, North Uist by R. J. C. Atkinson in 1957', *PSAS*, 121: 117–73.

Campbell, E. (1996a) 'The archaeological evidence for external contacts: imports, trade and economy in Celtic Britain A.D. 400–800', in Dark, K. ed. (1996) 83–96.

Campbell, E. (1996b) 'Trade in the Dark Age West: a peripheral activity?', in Crawford, B. ed. (1996) 79–91.

Campbell, E. (2000) 'A review of glass vessels in western Britain and Ireland AD 400–800', in Price, J. ed. (2000) 33–46.

Card, N. and Downes, J. (2003) 'Mine Howe – the significance of space and place in the Iron Age', in Downes, J. and Ritchie, A. eds (2003): 11–19.

Carson, R. A. G. and Kraay, C. M. eds (1978) *Scripta Nummaria Romana: Essays Presented to Humphrey Sutherland*, London.

Carter, S. P. (1994) 'Radiocarbon dating evidence for the age of narrow cultivation ridges in Scotland', *Tools and Tillage*, 7: 83–91.

Carter, S. P. and Hunter, F. (2003) 'An Iron Age chariot burial from Scotland', *Antiquity*, 77: 531–5.

Carter, S. P., McCullagh, R. P. J. and MacSween, A. (1995) 'The Iron Age in Shetland: excavations at five sites threatened by coastal erosion', *PSAS*, 125: 429–83.

Casey, P. J. (1984) 'Roman coinage of the fourth century in Scotland', in Miket, R. and Burgess, C. eds (1984) 295–304.

Caulfield, S. (1977) 'The beehive quern in Ireland', *JRSAI*, 107: 104–38.

Caulfield, S. (1978) 'Quern replacement and the origins of brochs', *PSAS*, 109: 129–39.

Challis, A. J. and Harding, D. W. (1975) *Later Prehistory from the Trent to the Tyne*, Oxford, BAR, 20.

Champion, S. (1995) 'Hillfort Study Group visit to the Isle of Man, 21–24 April 1995: Guide', privately circulated.

Chapman, J. C. and Mytum, H. C. (1983) *Settlement in North Britain 1000BC–AD 1000*, Oxford, BAR, Brit. Ser. 118.

Chapman, M. (1992) *The Celts: The Construction of a Myth*, New York, St Martin's Press and London, Macmillan.

Charles-Edwards, T. M. (1972) 'Kinship, status and the origin of the hide', *Past and Present*, 56: 3–33.

Charles-Edwards, T. M. (1993) *Early Irish and Welsh Kinship*, Oxford, Clarendon Press.

Childe, V. G. (1935a) *The Prehistory of Scotland*, London, Kegan Paul.

Childe, V. G. (1935b) 'Excavation of the vitrified fort of Finavon, Angus', *PSAS*, 69, 1934–5: 49–80.

Childe, V. G. (1945) *Scotland before the Scots*, Soc. Ant. Scot. Rhind Lectures for 1944, London, Methuen.

Childe, V. G. and Thorneycroft, W. (1938a) 'The vitrified fort at Rahoy, Morvern, Argyll', *PSAS*, 72, 1937–8: 23–43.

Childe, V. G. and Thorneycroft, W. (1938b) 'The experimental production of the phenomena distinctive of vitrified forts', *PSAS*, 72, 1937–8: 44–55.

Christison, D., Anderson, J. and Ross, T. (1905) 'Report on the Society's excavations of forts on the Poltalloch Estate, Argyll, in 1904–5', *PSAS*, 39, 259–322.

Church, M. (2002) 'The archaeological and archaeobotanical implications of a destruction layer at Dun Bharabhat, Lewis', in Smith, B. B. ed. (2002) 67–75.

Church, M., forthcoming. 'The botany of brochs – twenty years on', *SAF*.

Clack, P. A. G. (1982) 'The Northern Frontier: farmers in the military zone', in Miles, D. ed. (1982) 377–402.

Clack, P. A. G. and Haselgrove, S. eds (1982) *Rural Settlement in the Roman North*, Durham, CBA Regional Group 3.

Clark, J. G. D. and Fell, C. I. (1953) 'The Early Iron Age site at Micklemoor Hill, West Harling, Norfolk, and its Pottery', *PPS*, 19: 1–40.

Clarke, D. V. (1970) 'Bone dice and the Scottish Iron Age', *PPS*, 36: 214–32.

Clarke, D. V. (1971) 'Small finds of the Atlantic Province: problems of approach', *SAF*, 3: 22–54.

Close, R. S. (1972) 'Excavation of Iron Age hut circles at Percy Rigg, Kildale', *YAJ*, 44: 23–31.

Close-Brooks, J. (1984) 'Pictish and other burials', in Friell, J. G. P. and Watson, W. G. eds (1984) 87–114.

Close-Brooks, J. (1986) 'Excavations at Clatchard Craig, Fife', *PSAS*, 116: 117–84.

Coggins, D. (1985) 'Settlement and farming in Upper Teesdale', in Spratt, D. and Burgess, C. eds (1985) 163–75.

Coggins, D. (1986) *Upper Teesdale: The Archaeology of a North Pennine Valley*, Oxford, BAR Brit. Ser. 150.

Coles, J. M. and Simpson, D. D. A. (1968) *Studies in Ancient Europe: Essays Presented to Stuart Piggott*, Leicester, Leicester University Press.

Collingwood, R. G. (1933) 'Prehistoric Settlement near Crosby Ravensworth', *TCWAS*, 33: 201–26.

Collingwood, R. G. (1938) 'The hill-fort on Carrock Fell', *TCWAS*, 38: 32–41.

Collingwood, R. G. and Richmond, I. A. (1969) *The Archaeology of Roman Britain*, London, Methuen.

Collingwood, W. G. (1908) 'Report on a exploration of the Romano-British settlement at Ewe Close, Crosby Ravensworth', *TCWAS*, 8: 355–68.

Collis, J. (1997) 'Celtic myths', *Antiquity*, 71: 195–201.

Cook, M. (1999) 'Aspects of the funerary rituals of the pre-Christian Iron Age in Scotland', Edinburgh, MA Dissertation, University of Edinburgh, Department of Archaeology.

Cool, H. E. M. (1982) 'The artefact record: some possibilities', in Harding, D. W. ed. (1982) 92–100.

Coombs, D. G. (1982) 'Excavations at the hillfort of Castercliff, Nelson, Lancashire 1970–71', *TLCAS*, 81: 111–30.

Coombs, D. G. and Thompson, F. H. (1979) 'Excavation of the Hill Fort of Mam Tor, Derbyshire, 1965–69', *DyAJ*, 99: 7–51.

Corder, P. and Hawkes, C. F. C. (1940) 'A panel of late Celtic ornament from Elmswell, East Yorkshire', *AJ*, 20: 338–57.

Cowie, T. G. (1978) 'Excavations at the Catstane, Midlothian, 1977', *PSAS*, 109, 1977–8: 166–201.

Cowley, D. (1996) 'Square barrows in Dumfries and Galloway', *TDGNHAS*, 71: 107–13.

Cowley, D. (2000) 'Site morphology and regional variation in the later prehistoric settlement of south-west Scotland', in Harding, J. ed. (2000) 167–76.

Cowley, D. (2003) 'Changing places – building life spans and settlement continuity in northern Scotland', in Downes, J. and Ritchie, A. eds (2003) 75–81.

Cowley, D. and Brophy, K. (2001) 'The impact of aerial photography across the Lowlands of South-West Scotland', *TDGNHAS*, 75: 47–72.

Craig, D. (1997) 'The provenance of the Early Christian inscriptions of Galloway', in Hill, P. (1997) 614–19.

Craig, G. Y. ed. (1991) *Geology of Scotland*, 3rd edn, London, The Geological Society.

Cramp, R. J. (1960) 'The Anglian sculptured crosses in Dumfriesshire', *TDGNHAS*, 38, 1959–60: 9–20.

Craw, J. H. (1931) 'Excavations of a cairn at Drumelzier, Peeblesshire', *PSAS*, 65: 363–72.

Crawford, B. ed. (1994) *Scotland in Dark Age Europe*, St Andrews, St John's House Papers 5.

Crawford, B. ed. (1996) *Scotland in Dark Age Britain*, St Andrews, St John's House Papers 6.

Crawford, I. (n.d.) *The West Highlands and Islands: A View of 50 Centuries: The Udal (N. Uist) Evidence*, Cambridge, Great Auk Press.

Crawford, I. and Selkirk, A. (1996) 'The Udal', *CA*, 147: 84–94.

Creighton, J. (2001) 'The Iron Age–Roman transition', in James, S. and Millett, M. eds (2001) 4–11.

Crone, A. (1993) 'Crannogs and chronologies', *PSAS*, 123: 245–54.

Crone, A. (2000) *The History of a Scottish Lowland Crannog at Buiston, Ayrshire 1989–90*, Edinburgh, STAR Mon. 4.

Cunliffe, B. W. (1983) *Danebury: Anatomy of an Iron Age Hillfort*, London: Batsford.

Cunliffe, B. W. (1991) *Iron Age Communities in Britain*, 3rd edn London, Routledge.

Cunliffe, B. (2001) *The Extraordinary Voyage of Pytheas the Greek*, London, Allen Lane Penguin.

Cunliffe, B. and Rowley, T. eds (1978) *Lowland Iron Age Communities in Europe*, Oxford, BAR, Internat. Ser. (suppl) 48.

Curle, A. O. (1905) 'Descriptions of the fortifications on Ruberslaw, Roxburghshire, and notices of Roman remains found there', *PSAS*, 39, 1904–5: 219–32.

Curle, A. O. (1910) 'Notice of some excavation on the fort occupying the summit of Bonchester Hill, parish of Hobkirk, Roxburghshire', *PSAS*, 44, 1909–10, 225–36.

Curle, A. O. (1921) 'The broch of Dun Troddan, Gleann Beag, Glenelg, Inverness-shire', *PSAS*, 55: 83–94.

Curle, A. O. (1923) *The Traprain Treasure*, Glasgow, Maclehose, Jackson and Co.

Curle, A. O. (1936) 'Account of the excavation of an Iron Age smeltery and of an associated dwelling and tumuli at Wiltrow in the parish of Dunrossness, Shetland', *PSAS*, 70, 1935–6: 153–69.

Curle, A. O. (1941) 'An account of the partial excavation of the "wag" or galleried building at Forse, in the Parish of Latheron, Caithness', *PSAS*, 80: 11–25.

Curle, A. O. (1946) 'The excavation of the 'wag' or prehistoric cattlefold at Forse, Caithness, and the relation of "wags" to brochs, and implications arising therefrom', *PSAS*, 80, 1945–6: 11–25.

Curle, A. O. (1948) 'The "wag" of Forse, Caithness. Report of further excavation made in 1947 and 1948', *PSAS*, 82, 1947–8: 275–85.

Dalland, M. (1992) 'Long cist burials at Four Winds, Longniddry, East Lothian', *PSAS*, 122: 197–206.

Daniels, R. (1988) 'The Anglo-Saxon monastery at Church Close, Hartlepool, Cleveland', *ArchJ*, 145: 158–210.

Dark, K. A. ed. (1996) *External Contacts and the Economy of Late Roman and Post-Roman Britain*, Woodbridge, Suffolk, Boydell.

Dark, K. A. (2000) *Britain and the End of the Roman Empire*, Stroud, Tempus.

Davies, G. and Turner, J. (1979) 'Pollen diagrams from Northumberland', *New Phytologist*, 82: 783–804.

Dent, J. S. (1982) 'Cemeteries and settlement patterns of the Iron Age on the Yorkshire Wolds', *PPS*, 48: 437–57.

Dixon, T. N. (1982) 'A survey of crannogs in Loch Tay', *PSAS*, 112: 17–38.

Dixon, T. N. and Andrian, B. (1995) 'Underwater archaeology in Scotland', *SAR*, 9/10: 26–35.

Dobson, J. (1907) 'Urswick stone walls', *TCWAS*, 7: 72–94.

Dockrill, S. J. (1998) 'Northern exposure: phase 1 of the Old Scatness excavations, 1995–8', in Nicholson, R. A. and Dockrill, S. J. eds (1998) 59–80.

Dockrill, S. J. (2003) 'Broch, wheelhouse and cell: redefining the Iron Age in Scotland', in Downes, J. and Ritchie, A. eds (2003): 82–94.

Dockrill, S. J., Bond, J. M. and Batt, C. M. (forthcoming) 'Old Scatness: the first millennium AD', in Nicholson, R. A. and Turner, V. eds (forthcoming).

Downes, J. and Lamb, R. (2000) *Prehistoric Houses at Sumburgh in Shetland, Excavations at Sumburgh Airport 1967–74*, Oxford, Oxbow.

Downes, J. and Ritchie, A. eds (2003) *Sea Change: Orkney and Northern Europe in the later Iron Age AD 300–800*, Balgavies, Pinkfoot Press.

Driscoll, S. T. (1988a) 'Power and authority in Early Historic Scotland: Pictish symbol stones and other documents', in Gledhill, J. *et al.* eds (1988) 215–36.

Driscoll, S. T. (1988b) 'The relationship between history and archaeology: artefacts, documents and power', in Driscoll, S. T. and Nieke, M. eds (1988) 162–88.

Driscoll, S. T. (1991) 'The archaeology of state formation in Scotland', in Hanson, W. and Slater, E. eds (1991) 81–111.

Driscoll, S. T. (1997) 'A Pictish settlement in north-east Fife: the Scottish Field School of Archaeology excavations at Easter Kinnear', *TAFAJ*, 3: 74–118.

Driscoll, S. T. and Nieke, M. eds (1988) *Power and Politics in Early Medieval Britain and Ireland*, Edinburgh, Edinburgh University Press.

Dumayne-Peaty, L. (1998) 'Human impact on the environment during Iron Age and Romano-British times: Palynological evidence from three sites near the Antonine Wall', *JAS*, 25: 203–14.

Duncan, A. A. M. (1992) *Scotland: The Making of the Kingdom*, Edinburgh, Mercat Press.

Dunning, G. C. (1934) 'The swan's neck and ring-headed pins of the Early Iron Age in Britain', *ArchJ*, 91: 269–95.

Dunwell, A. (1999) 'Edin's Hall fort, broch and settlement, Berwickshire (Scottish Borders): recent fieldwork and new perceptions', *PSAS*, 129: 303–58.

Earwood, C. (1990) 'The wooden artefacts from Loch Glashan crannog, Mid Argyll', *PSAS*, 120: 79–94.

Edwards, K. and Ralston, I. (1978) 'New dating and environmental evidence from Burghead Fort, Moray', *PSAS*, 109: 202–10.

Edwards, K. and Ralston, I. B. M. eds (1997) *Scotland: Environment and Archaeology, 8000BC–AD 1000*, Chichester, Wiley.

Ellis, C. (2001) 'Braehead (Govan parish) prehistoric enclosure', *DES*, ns 2: 49–50.

Ellis, P. (1993) *Beeston Castle, Cheshire: excavations by Laurence Keen and Peter Hough, 1968–85*, London, English Heritage.

Erdrich, M., Giannotta, K. M. and Hanson, W. S. (2000) 'Traprain Law: native and Roman on the northern frontier', *PSAS*, 130: 441–56.

Fairhurst, H. (1939) 'The galleried dun at Kildonan Bay, Kintyre', *PSAS*, 73: 185–228.

Fairhurst, H. (1971) 'The wheelhouse site at A' Cheardach Bheag on Drimore Machair, South Uist', *GAJ*, 2: 72–106.

Fairhurst, H. (1984) *Excavations at Crosskirk Broch, Caithness*, Edinburgh, Soc. Ant. Scot. Mon., 3.

Fairhurst, H. and Taylor, D. B. (1971) 'A hut-circle settlement at Kilphedir, Sutherland', *PSAS*, 103, 1970–1: 65–99.

Fairless, K. J. and Coggins, D. (1980) 'Excavations at the early settlement site of Forcegarth Pasture North 1972–74', *TAASDN*, 5: 31–8.

Fairless, K. J. and Coggins, D. (1986) 'Excavations of the early settlement site of Forcegarth Pasture South 1974–75', *DAJ*, 2: 25–40.

Fanning, T. (1983) 'Some aspects of the bronze ringed pin in Scotland', in O'Connor, A. and Clarke, D. V. eds (1983) 324–42.

Faull, M. L. ed. (1984) *Studies in Late Anglo-Saxon Settlement*, Oxford, Oxford Univ Dept Ext. Studs.

Feachem, R. W. (1955) 'Fortifications', in Wainwright, F. T. ed. (1955) 66–86.

Feachem, R. W. (1959) 'Glenachan Rig Homestead, Cardon, Peeblesshire', *PSAS*, 112, 1958–9: 15–24.

Feachem, R. W. (1960) 'The Palisaded Settlements at Harehope, Peebleshire. Excavations, 1960', *PSAS*, 93, 1959–60: 174–91.

Feachem, R. W. (1961) 'Unenclosed platform settlements', *PSAS*, 94, 1960–1: 79–85.

Feachem, R. W. (1963) *A Guide to Prehistoric Scotland*, London, Batsford.

Feachem, R. W. (1966) 'The Hill-Forts of Northern Britain', in Rivet, A. L. F. ed. (1966) 59–88.

Ferrell, G. (1997) 'Space and society in the Iron Age of north-east England', in Haselgrove, C. and Gwilt, A. eds (1997) 228–38.

Field, N. H. (1965) 'Romano-British settlement at Studland, Dorset, by N. H. Field, with a note on the term "cottage" by Professor C. F. C. Hawkes', *PDNHAS*, 87: 142–207.

Fitts, R. L., Haselgrove, C. C., Lowther, P. C. and Willis, S. H. (1999) 'Melsonby revisited: survey and excavation 1992–95 at the site of discovery of the "Stanwick", North Yorkshire, Hoard of 1843', *DAJ*, 14–15: 1–52.

Fitzpatrick, A. (1994) 'Outside in: the structure of an early Iron Age house at Dunston Park, Thatcham, Berkshire', in Fitzpatrick, A. and Morris, E. L. eds (1994) 68–72.

Fitzpatrick, A. (1997) 'Everyday life in Iron Age Wessex', in Haselgrove, C. and Gwilt, A. eds (1997) 73–86.

Fitzpatrick, A. and Morris, E. L. eds (1994) *The Iron Age in Wessex: Recent Work*, Salisbury, Trust for Wessex Archaeology.

Fojut, N. (1982) 'Towards a geography of Iron Age Shetland', *GAJ*, 9: 38–59.

Fojut, N. (1998) 'How did we get here? Shetland studies to 1995', in Nicholson, R. A. and Dockrill, S. J. eds (1998) 1–41.

Foster, P. (1995) 'Excavations at Allt Chrisal', in Branigan, K. and Foster, P. eds (1995) 49–160.

Foster, S. (1989) 'Analysis of spatial patterns in buildings as an insight into social structure', *Antiquity*, 63: 40–50.

Foster, S. (1990) 'Pins, combs and chronology of Later Atlantic Iron Age settlement', in Armit, I. ed. (1990) 143–74.

Foster, S. (1996) *Picts, Gaels and Scots: Early Historic Scotland*, London, Batsford/Historic Scotland.

Foster, S. and Smout, T. C. eds (1994) *The History of Soils and Field Systems*, Aberdeen, Scottish Cultural Press.

Fowler, E. (1963) 'Celtic metalwork of the fifth and sixth centuries AD: a re-appraisal', *ArchJ*, 120: 98–160.

Fowler, P. J. ed. (1975) *Recent Work in Rural Archaeology*, Bradford-on-Avon, Moonraker.

Fox, C. (1932/38) *The Personality of Britain*, Cardiff, National Museum of Wales.

Fox, C. and Hyde, H. (1939) 'A Second Cauldron and an Iron Sword from the Llyn Fawr Hoard, Rhigos, Glamorganshire', *AJ*, 19: 369–404.

Frere, S. S. ed. (1961) *Problems of the Iron Age in Southern Britain*, London, CBA Occ. Ppr 11.

Frere, S. S. (1967/98) *Britannia: A History of Roman Britain*, London, Routledge.

Friell, J. G. P. and Watson, W. G. eds (1984) *Pictish Studies: Settlement, Burial and Art in Dark Age North Britain*, Oxford, BAR, Brit. Ser. 125.

Frodsham, P. (1999) 'Forgetting *Gefrin*: Elements of the Past in the Past at Yeavering', in Frodsham, P. *et al.* eds (1999) 191–207.

Frodsham, P., Topping, P. and Cowley, D. eds (1999) *We were always chasing time. Papers presented to Keith Blood, Northern Archaeology*, 17/18, Newcastle upon Tyne, Northern Archaeology Group.

Fulford, M. (1989) 'Roman and Barbarian: the economy of Roman frontier systems', in Barrett, J. *et al.* eds (1989) 81–95.

Gannon, A. R. (1999) 'Challenging the past: the resurvey of Braidwood Hillfort', in Frodsham, P. *et al.* eds (1999) 105–91.

Gates, T. (1983) 'Unenclosed settlements in Northumberland', in Chapman, J. and Mytum, H. C. eds (1983) 103–48.

Gates, T. and O'Brien, C. F. (1988) 'Cropmarks at Milfield and New Bewick and the recognition of Grubenhäuser in Northumberland', *AA*, 5th ser., 16: 1–9.

Gelling, P. (1958) 'Close ny chollagh: an Iron Age fort at Scarlett, Isle of Man', *PPS*, 24: 85–100.

Gelling, P. (1972) 'The hillfort on South Barrule and its position in the Manx Iron Age', in Lynch, F. and Burgess, C. B. eds (1972) 285–92.

Gelling, P. (1977) 'Excavations at Pilsdon Pen, Dorset, 1964–71', *PPS*, 43: 263–86.

Gentles, D. (1993) 'Vitrified forts', *CA*, 133: 18–20.

Gillam, J. (1958) 'Roman and native, A.D. 122–197', in Richmond, I. A. ed. (1958) 60–90.

Gilmour, S. (2000) 'First millennia settlement development in the Atlantic West', in Henderson, Jon C. ed. (2000) 155–70.

Gilmour, S. (2002) 'Mid-first millennium BC settlement in the Atlantic West?', in Smith, B. B. and Banks, I. eds (2002) 55–66.

Gilmour, S. (forthcoming) 'Complex Atlantic roundhouses – chronology and complexity', in Nicholson R. A. and Turner, V. eds (forthcoming).

Gilmour, S. and Cook, M. (1998) 'Excavations at Dun Vulan: a reinterpretation of the reappraised Iron Age', *Antiquity*, 72: 327–37.

Gledhill, J., Bender, B. and Larsen, M. T. eds (1988) *State and Society: The Emergence and Development of Social Hierarchy and Political Centralization*, London/Boston, Unwin Hyman.

Graham-Campbell, J. (1991) 'Norrie's Law, Fife: on the nature and dating of the silver hoard', *PSAS*, 121: 241–59.

Graham-Campbell, J., Close-Brooks, J., Laing, J. and Laing, L. R. (1976) 'The Mote of Mark and Celtic interlace', *Antiquity*, 50: 48–53.

Green, M. ed. (1995) *The Celtic World*, London, Routledge.

Gregory, R. (2001) 'Excavation at Hayknowes Farm, Annan, Dumfriesshire', *TDGNHAS*, 75: 29–46.

Greig, C., Greig, M. and Ashmore, P. J. (2000) 'Excavation of a cairn cemetery at Lundin Links, Fife, in 1965–6', *PSAS*, 130: 585–636.

Greig, J. C. (1971) 'Excavations at Cullykhan, Castle Point, Troup, Banffshire', *SAF*, 3: 15–21.

Greig, J. C. (1970) 'Excavations at Castle Point, Troup, Banffshire', *Aberdeen University Review*, 43, 274–83.

Greig, J. C. (1972) 'Cullykhan', *CA*, 32: 227–31.

Guido, M. (1974) 'A Scottish crannog re-dated', *Antiquity*, 48: 54–5.

Guido, M. (1978) *The Glass Beads of the Prehistoric and Roman Periods in Britain and Ireland*, London, Society of Antiquaries/Thames and Hudson.

Guilbert, G. ed. (1981) *Hill-Fort Studies: Essays for A. H. A. Hogg*, Leicester, Leicester University Press.

Gwilt, A. and Haselgrove, C. eds (1997) *Reconstructing Iron Age Societies; New Approaches to the British Iron Age*, Oxford, Oxbow Monographs 71.

Hachmann, R. (1976) 'The problem of the Belgae seen from the Continent', *Bull. London Univ. Inst. Arch.*, 13: 117–38.

Haggarty, A. and Haggarty, G. (1983) 'Excavations at Rispain Camp, Whithorn, 1978–81', *TDGNHAS*, 58: 21–51.

Hale, A. (1999) 'Marine crannogs', unpublished PhD thesis, University of Edinburgh, Department of Archaeology.

Hale, A. (2000) 'Marine crannogs: previous work and recent surveys', *PSAS*, 130: 537–58.

Halliday, S. P. (1982) 'Later prehistoric farming in south-east Scotland', in Harding, D. W. ed. (1982) 57–91.

Halliday, S. P. (1983) 'Cord Rig Survey Project', privately circulated typescript.

Halliday, S. P. (1985) 'Unenclosed upland settlement in the east and south-east of Scotland', in Spratt, D. and Burgess, C. eds (1985) 231–51.

Halliday, S. P. (1986) 'Cord rig and early cultivation in the Borders', *PSAS*, 116: 584–5.

Halliday, S. P. (1993) 'Marginal agriculture in Scotland', in Smout, T. C. ed. (1993) 64–78.

Halliday, S. P. (1995) 'The Borders in prehistory', in Omand, D. ed. (1995) 21–37.

Halliday, S. P. (1999) 'Hut circle settlements in the Scottish landscape', in Frodsham, P. *et al.* eds (1999) 49–66.

Halliday, S. P. (forthcoming) 'Settlement, territory and landscape; the later prehistoric landscape in the light of the survey of Eastern Dumfriesshire', *TDNHAS*.

Halliday, S. P., Hill, P. and Stevenson, J. B. (1981) 'Early agriculture in Scotland', in Mercer, R. ed. (1981) 55–65.

Hamilton, J. R. C. (1956) *Excavations at Jarlshof, Shetland*, Edinburgh, HMSO.

Hamilton, J. R. C. (1968) *Excavations at Clickhimin, Shetland*, Edinburgh, HMSO.

Hanson, W. S. (1989) 'The nature and function of Roman frontiers', in Barrett, J. *et al.* eds (1989) 55–61.

Hanson, W. S. and Campbell, D. B. (1986) 'The Brigantes: from clientage to conquest', *Britannia*, 17: 73–89.

Hanson, W. S. and Slater, E. A. eds (1991) *Scottish Archaeology: New Perceptions*, Aberdeen, Aberdeen UP.

Harbison, P. (1971) 'Wooden and stone *Chevaux-de-frise* in Central and Western Europe', *PPS*, 37: 195–225.

Harding, A. F. (1981) 'Excavations in the prehistoric ritual complex near Milfield, Northumberland', *PPS*, 47: 87–136.

Harding, D. W. (1973) 'Round and rectangular: Iron Age houses, British and Foreign', in Hawkes, C. F. C. and S. C. eds (1973) 43–62.

Harding, D. W. ed. (1976) *Hillforts, Later Prehistoric Earthworks in Britain and Ireland*, London, Academic Press.

Harding, D. W. (1979) 'Air survey in the Tyne-Tees region, 1969–79', in Higham, N. J. ed. (1979a) 21–30.

Harding, D. W. ed. (1982) *Later Prehistoric Settlement in South-East Scotland*, Edinburgh, University of Edinburgh, Department of Archaeology Occasional Paper No 8.

Harding, D. W. (1984a) 'The function and classification of brochs and duns', in Miket, R. and Burgess, C. eds (1984) 206–20.

Harding, D. W. (1984b) *Holme House, Piercebridge: Excavations, 1969–70. A Summary Report*, Edinburgh, Univ. Edinburgh Dept Arch. Project Paper No. 2.

Harding, D. W. (1990) 'Changing perspectives in the Atlantic Iron Age', in Armit, I. ed. (1990) 5–16.

Harding, D. W. (1995) 'Atlantic Scotland and the Western Seaways', lecture given to X Intern. Congress Celtic Studies, Edinburgh, privately circulated; see also Harding, D. W. (forthcoming, a).

Harding, D. W. (1997) 'Forts, duns, brochs and crannogs: Iron Age settlements in Argyll', in Ritchie, G. ed. (1997) 118–40.

Harding, D. W. (2000a) 'Crannogs and island duns', *OJA*, 19: 301–17.

Harding, D. W. (2000b) *The Hebridean Iron Age: Twenty Years' Research*, Edinburgh, Univ. Edinburgh Dept Arch. Occ. Ppr. 20.

Harding, D. W. (2001) 'Later prehistory in South-East Scotland: a critical review', *OJA*, 20: 355–76.

Harding, D. W. (2002) 'Torrs and the early La Tène Ornamental Style in Britain and Ireland', in Smith, B. B. and Banks, I. eds (2002) 191–204.

Harding, D. W. (forthcoming, a). 'Atlantic Scotland and the Western Seaways', in Harding, D. W. and Gillies, W. eds (forthcoming).

Harding, D. W. (forthcoming, b) 'The Atlantic Scottish Iron Age: external relations reviewed', Nicholson, R. A. and Turner, V. eds (forthcoming).

Harding, D. W. (forthcoming, c) 'Dunagoil, Bute, re-instated', *TBNHS*.

Harding, D. W. and Armit, I. (1990) 'Survey and excavation in West Lewis', in Armit, I. ed. (1990) 71–107.

Harding, D. W., Blake, I. M. and Reynolds, P. J. (1993) *An Iron Age Settlement in Dorset: Excavation and Reconstruction*, Edinburgh, Univ. Edin. Dept Arch. Mon. Ser. 1.

Harding, D. W. and Dixon, T. N. (2000) *Dun Bharabhat, Cnip: An Iron Age Settlement in West Lewis, Vol. 1 Structures and Material Culture*, Edinburgh, Calanais Research Series 2, Edinburgh University Department of Archaeology.

Harding, D. W. and Gillies, W. (forthcoming, a) *Celtic Connections* Vol. 2, Proceedings of X International Congress of Celtic Studies, Edinburgh 1995, Edinburgh, Edinburgh University Department of Archaeology Mon. Ser. 2.

Harding, D. W. and Gillies, W. (forthcoming, b) 'Archaeology and Celticity', in Harding, D. W. and Gillies, W. eds (forthcoming, a)

Harding, D. W. and Gilmour, S. M. D. (2000) *The Iron Age Settlement at Beirgh, Riof, Isle of Lewis: Excavations, 1985–95, Vol.1, The Structures and Stratigraphy*, Edinburgh, Calanais Research Series 1, Edinburgh University Department of Archaeology.

Harding, J. and Johnston, R. eds (2000) *Northern Pasts: Interpretations of the Later Prehistory of Northern England and Southern Scotland*, Oxford, BAR, Brit. Ser. 302.

Harris, J. (1984) 'A preliminary survey of hut circles and field systems in SE Perthshire', *PPS*, 114: 199–216.

Haselgrove, C. (1980) 'A cropmark site on Strawberry Hill, Shadforth, Co. Durham', *TAASDN*, 5: 39–43.

Haselgrove, C. (1982a) 'Indigenous settlement patterns in the Tyne-Tees lowlands', in Clack, P. A. G. and Haselgrove, S. eds (1982) 57–104.

Haselgrove, C. (1982b) 'Wealth, prestige and power: the dynamics of Late Iron Age political centralisation in south-eastern England', in Renfrew, C. ed. (1982) 79–88.

Haselgrove, C. (1984) 'The later Pre-Roman Iron Age between the Humber and the Tyne', in Wilson, P. R. *et al.* eds (1984) 9–26.

Haselgrove, C. (1996) 'The Iron Age', in Newman, R. ed. (1996) 61–74.

Haselgrove, C. (1999) 'Iron Age societies in Central Britain: retrospect and prospect', in Bevan, B. ed. (1999) 253–78.

Haselgrove, C. and Allon, V. L. (1982) 'An Iron Age settlement at West House, Coxhoe, County Durham', *AA*, 5th ser. 10: 25–51.

Haselgrove, C. and Gwilt, A. eds (1997) *Reconstructing Iron Age Societies*, Oxford, Oxbow Mon. 71.

Haselgrove, C., Lowther, P. C. and Turnbull, P. (1990) 'Stanwick, North Yorkshire, Part 3: Excavations on earthwork sites 1981–86', *ArchJ*, 147: 37–90.

Haselgrove, C. and McCullagh, R. (2000) *An Iron Age Coastal Community in East Lothian: The Excavation of Two Later Prehistoric Enclosure Complexes at Fishers Road, Port Seton, 1994–5*, Edinburgh, STAR Mon. 6.

Haselgrove, C., Turnbull, P. and Fitts, R. L. (1990) 'Stanwick, North Yorkshire, Part 1: Recent research and previous archaeological investigations', *ArchJ*, 147: 1–15.

Hawkes, C. F. C. (1948) *Archaeology and the History of Europe: an Inaugural Lecture Delivered before the University of Oxford on 28 Nov. 1947*, Oxford, Clarendon Press.

Hawkes, C. F. C. (1954) 'Archaeological theory and method: some suggestions from the Old World', *American Anthropologist*, 56: 155–68.

Hawkes, C. F. C. (1959) 'The ABC of the British Iron Age', *Antiquity*, 33: 170–82.

Hawkes, C. F. C. (1961) 'The ABC of the British Iron Age', in Frere, S. S. ed. (1961) 1–16.

Hawkes, C. F. C. (1977) *Pytheas. Europe and the Greek Explorers*, Oxford, Blackwell.

Hawkes, C. F. C. and Hawkes, S. C. eds (1973) *Greeks, Celts and Romans: Studies in Venture and Resistance*, London, Dent.

Hayes, R. H. (1966) 'A Romano-British site at Pale End, Kildale', *YAJ*, 41: 687–700.

Hayes, R. H. (1983) *Levisham Moor Archaeological Investigations, 1957–78*, Helmsley, North York Moors National Park Committee and Scarborough Archaeological and Historical Society.

Hayes, R. H., Hemingway, J. E. and Spratt, D. A. (1980) 'The distribution and lithology of beehive querns in Northeast Yorkshire', *JAS*, 7: 297–324.

Heald, A. (2001) 'Knobbed spearbutts of the British and Irish Iron Age: new examples and new thoughts', *Antiquity*, 75: 689–96.

Heald, A. and Jackson, A. (2001) 'Towards a new understanding of Iron Age Caithness', *PSAS*, 131: 129–48.

Hedges, J. W. (1987) *Bu, Gurness and the Brochs of Orkney*, Oxford, BAR, Brit. Ser., 163–5.

Hencken, H. (1936) 'Ballinderry crannog no. 1', *PRIA*, 43C: 103–239.

Hencken, H. (1938) *Cahercommaun: A Stone Fort in Co. Clare*, Dublin, Royal Society of Antiquaries of Ireland.

Hencken, H. (1942) 'Ballinderry crannog no. 2', *PRIA*, 47C: 1–76.

Hencken, H. (1950) 'Lagore crannog: an Irish royal residence of the seventh to tenth century AD', *PRIA*, 53C: 1–248.

Henderson, I. (1967) *The Picts*, London, Thames and Hudson.

Henderson, I. (1979) 'The silver chain from Whitecleugh, Shieldholm, Crawfordjohn, Lanarkshire', *TDGNHAS*, 54: 20–8.

Henderson, Jon (1998a) 'Islets through time: the definition, dating and distribution of Scottish crannogs', *OJA*, 17: 227–44.

Henderson, Jon (1998b) 'A survey of crannogs in the Lake of Menteith, Stirlingshire', *PSAS*, 128: 273–92.

Henderson, Jon ed. (2000) *The Prehistory and Early History of Atlantic Europe, Papers from a session held at the European Association of Archaeologists Fourth Annual Meeting in Göteborg 1998*, Oxford, BAR, Internat. Ser. 861.

Henderson, Julian (1991) 'Industrial specialisation in Late Iron Age Britain and Europe', *ArchJ*, 148: 104–48.

Henry, D. ed. (1997) *The Worm, the Germ and the Thorn: Pictish and Related Studies presented to Isabel Henderson*, Balgavies, Angus, Pinkfoot Press.

Henshall, A. S. (1956) 'The long cist cemetery at Lasswade, Midlothian', *PSAS*, 89, 1955–6: 252–83.

Heslop, D. H. (1984) 'Initial excavations at Ingleby Barwick, Cleveland', *DAJ*, 1: 23–34.

Heslop, D. H. (1987) *The Excavation of an Iron Age Settlement at Thorpe Thewles, Cleveland*, London, CBA Res. Rep. 65.

Higham, N. (1978) 'Early field survival in North Cumbria', in Bowen, H. C. and Fowler, P. J. eds (1978) 119–26.

Higham, N. ed. (1979a) *The Changing Past: Some Recent Work in the Archaeology of Northern England*, Manchester, Univ. Manchester Dept Extra-Mural Studies.

Higham, N. (1979b) 'An aerial survey of the Upper Lune Valley', in Higham, N. ed. (1979a) 31–8.

Higham, N. (1979c) 'Continuity in North West England in the first millennium AD', in Higham, N. ed. (1979a) 43–52.

Higham, N. (1980a) 'Native settlement West of the Pennines', in Branigan, K. ed. (1980) 41–7.

Higham, N. (1980b) 'Dyke systems in Northern Cumbria', *Bull. Board of Celtic Studs.*, 28, Nov. 1978: 142–55.

Higham, N. (1981) 'Two enclosures at Dobcross Hall, Dalston', *TCWAS*, 81: 1–6.

Higham, N. (1982) 'The Roman impact upon rural settlement in Cumbria', in Clack, P. A. G. and Haselgrove, S. eds (1982) 105–22.

Higham, N. (1983) 'A Romano-British farm site and field system at Yanwath Wood near Penrith', *TCWAS*, 83: 49–58.

Higham, N. (1986) *The Northern Counties to AD 1000*, London, Longman.

Higham, N. (1989) 'Roman and native in England north of the Tees: acculturation and its limitations', in Barrett, J. *et al.* eds (1989) 153–74.

Higham, N. and Jones, G. D. B. (1975) 'Frontier, forts and farmers: Cumbrian aerial survey 1974–5', *ArchJ*, 132: 16–53.

Higham, N. and Jones, G. D. B. (1983) 'The excavation of two Romano-British farm sites in North Cumbria', *Britannia*, 14: 45–86.

Hill, J. D. (2001) 'Romanisation, gender and class: recent approaches to identity in Britain and their possible consequences', in James, S. and Millett, M. eds (2001) 12–18.

Hill, P. (1979) *Broxmouth Hillfort Excavations, 1977–78: an Interim Report*, University of Edinburgh Department of Archaeology Occasional Paper No. 2.

Hill, P. (1982a) 'Settlement and chronology', in Harding, D. W. ed. (1982) 4–43.

Hill, P. (1982b) 'Broxmouth Hill – fort excavations, 1977–78', in Harding, D. W. ed. (1982) 141–88.

Hill, P. (1983) 'Survey and excavations at Hut Knowe North, Hownam, Roxburghshire, June 4th–10th, 1983', privately circulated typescript.

Hill, P. (1997) *Whithorn and St Ninian: The Excavation of a Monastic Town, 1984–91*, Stroud, Whithorn Trust.

Hingley, R. (1989) *Rural Settlement in Roman Britain*, London, Seaby.

Hingley, R. (1992) 'Society in Scotland from 700 BC to AD 200', *PSAS*, 122, 1992: 7–54.

Hingley, R., Moore, H. L., Triscott, J. E. and Wilson, G. (1997) 'The excavation of two later Iron Age fortified homesteads at Aldclune, Blair Atholl, Perth & Kinross', *PSAS*, 127: 407–66.

Hodson, F. R. (1964) 'Cultural groupings within the British pre-Roman Iron Age', *PPS*, 30: 99–110.

Hogg, A. H. A. (1965) 'Rheged and Brigantia', *Antiquity*, 39: 53–5.

Hogg, A. H. A. (1972) 'Hill-forts in the coastal area of Wales', in Thomas, A. C. ed. (1972) 11–23.

Hogg, A. H. A. (1975) *Hill-Forts of Britain*, London, Hart-Davis MacGibbon.

Hope-Taylor, B. (1977) *Yeavering: An Anglo-British Centre of Early Northumbria*, London, HMSO.

Hope-Taylor, B. (1980) 'Doon Hill', *CA*, 72: 18–19.

Hunter, F. (1996) 'Recent Roman Iron Age metalwork finds from Fife and Tayside', *TAFAJ*, 2: 113–25.

Hunter, F. (1997) 'Iron Age hoarding in Scotland and northern England', in Gwilt, A. and Haselgrove, C. eds (1997) 108–33.

Hunter, F. (1998) 'Discussion of the artefact assemblage', in Main, L. (1998) 393–401.

Hunter, F. (2001a) 'Roman and native in Scotland: new approaches', *JRA*, 14: 289–309.

Hunter, F. (2001b) 'The Carnyx in Iron Age Europe', *AJ*, 81: 77–108.

Hunter, F. (2002) 'Birnie: buying peace on the Northern Frontier', *CA*, 181: 12–16.

Hunter, F. (2003) 'An Iron Age chariot burial from Scotland', *Antiquity*, 77: 531–5.

Hunter, J. R. (1986) *Rescue Excavations on the Brough of Birsay 1974–82*, Edinburgh, Soc. Ant. Scot. Mon. Ser. 4.

Hunter, J. R. (1990) 'Pool, Sanday: a case study for the Late Iron Age and Viking periods', in Armit, I. ed. (1990) 175–93.

Hunter, J. R. (1996) *Fair Isle: The Archaeology of an Island Community*, Edinburgh, HMSO/Historic Scotland.

Hunter, J. R. (1997) *A Persona for the Northern Picts*, Rosemarkie, Groam House Museum Trust.

Hunter, J. R. (2002) 'Saints and sinners: the archaeology of the late Iron Age in the Western Isles', in Smith, B. B. and Banks, I. eds (2002) 129–38.

Inglis, J. (1987) 'Patterns in stone, patterns in population: symbol stones seen from beyond the Mounth', in Small, A. ed. (1987) 73–9.

Inman, R., Brown, D. R., Goddard, R. E. and Spratt, D. A. (1985) 'Roxby Iron Age settlement and the Iron Age in north-east Yorkshire', *PPS*, 51: 181–213.

Jackson, D., Harding, D. W. and Myres, J. N. L. (1969) 'The Iron Age and Anglo-Saxon site at Upton, Northants', *AJ*, 49: 202–21.

Jackson, K. H. (1955) 'The Pictish language', in Wainwright, F. T. ed. (1955) 129–66.

James, S. (1999) *The Atlantic Celts. Ancient People or Modern Invention*, London, British Museum Press.

James, S. and Millett, M. eds (2001) *Britons and Romans: Advancing an Archaeological Agenda*, London, CBA Res. Rep. 125.

Joass, J. M. (1890) 'The brochs of Cinn Trolla, Carn Liath and Craig Carrilo in Sutherland, with notes on other northern brochs', *Archaeologia Scotica*, 5: 95–130.

Jobey, G. (1959) 'Excavations at a native settlement at Huckhoe, Northumberland', *AA*, 4th ser., 37: 217–78.

Jobey, G. (1960) 'Some rectilinear settlements of the Roman period in Northumberland, part 1', *AA*, 4th ser., 38: 1–38.

Jobey, G. (1962) 'An Iron Age homestead at West Brandon, Durham', *AA*, 4th ser., 40: 1–34.

Jobey, G. (1964) 'Enclosed stone-built settlements in North Northumberland', *AA*, 4th ser., 42: 41–64.

Jobey, G. (1965) 'Hillforts and settlements in Northumberland', *AA*, 4th ser., 43: 21–64.

Jobey, G. (1966a) 'A field survey in Northumberland', in Rivet, A. L. F. ed. (1966) 89–110.

Jobey, G. (1966b) 'Homesteads and settlements in the frontier area', in Thomas, A. C. ed. (1966) 1–14.

Jobey, G. (1968) 'A radiocarbon date for the palisaded settlement at Huckhoe', *AA*, 4th ser., 46: 293–5.

Jobey, G. (1970) An Iron Age settlement at Burradon, Northumberland', *AA*, 4th ser., 48: 51–95.

Jobey, G. (1971) 'Excavations at Brough Law and Ingram Hill', *AA*, 4th ser., 49: 71–93.

Jobey, G. (1973) 'A Romano-British settlement at Tower Knowe, Wellhaugh, Northumberland', *AA*, 5th ser., 1: 55–79.

Jobey, G. (1974) 'Excavations at Boonies, Westerkirk and the nature of Romano-British settlement in eastern Dumfriesshire', *PSAS*, 105, 1972–4: 119–40.

Jobey, G. (1976) 'Traprain Law: a summary', in Harding, D. W. ed. (1976) 191–204 and 436–8.

Jobey, G. (1977) 'Iron Age and later farmsteads at Belling Law, Northumberland', *AA*, 5th ser., 5: 1–38.

Jobey, G. (1978a) 'Burnswark Hill', *TDGNHAS*, 53: 57–105.

Jobey, G. (1978b) 'Iron Age and Romano-British settlements on Kennel Hall Knowe', *AA*, 5th ser., 6: 1–28.

Jobey, G. (1980a) 'Green Knowe unenclosed platform settlement and Harehope cairn', *PSAS*, 110, 1978–80: 72–113.

Jobey, G. (1980b) 'Unenclosed platforms and settlements of the later second millennium BC in North Britain', *SAF*, 10: 12–26.

Jobey, G. (1983) 'A note on some northern palisaded settlements', in O'Connor, A. and Clarke, D. V. eds (1983) 197–205.

Jobey, G. and Tait, J. (1966) 'Excavations on palisaded settlements and cairnfields at Alnham, Northumberland', *AA*, 4th ser., 44: 5–48.

Johnston, D. A. (1994) 'Carronbridge, Dumfries and Galloway: the excavation of Bronze Age cremations, Iron Age settlements and a Roman camp', *PSAS*, 124: 233–92.

Jones, G. D. B. (1975) 'The North-Western interface', in Fowler, P. J. ed. (1975) 93–106.

Jones, G. D. B. and Wooliscroft, D. J. (2001) *Hadrian's Wall from the Air*, Stroud, Tempus.

Jope, E. M. and Jacobsthal, P. (2000) *Early Celtic Art in the British Isles*, Oxford, Clarendon Press.

Kendrick, J. (1982) 'Excavations at Douglasmuir, 1979–80', in Harding, D. W. ed. (1982), 136–40.

Kendrick, J. (1995) 'Excavation of a Neolithic enclosure and an Iron Age settlement at Douglasmuir, Angus', *PSAS*, 125: 29–67.

Kilbride-Jones, H. (1938) 'Glass armlets in Britain', *PSAS*, 72: 366–95.

King, A. (1978) 'Early agriculture in Craven, North Yorkshire', in Bowen, H. C. and Fowler, P. J. eds (1978) 109–14.

King, A. (1987) 'The Ingleborough Hillfort, North Yorkshire', *Bulletin of the Prehistory Research section, Yorkshire Arch. Soc.*, Leeds, no page nos.

Laing, L. (1973a) 'The Angles in Scotland and the Mote of Mark', *TDGNHAS*, 50: 37–52.

Laing. L. (1973b) 'The Mote of Mark', *CA*, 4: 121–4.

Laing, L. (1975a) *Settlement Types in Post-Roman Scotland*, Oxford, BAR, Brit. Ser. 13.

Laing, L. (1975b). 'The Mote of Mark and the origins of Celtic interlace', *Antiquity*, 49: 98–108.

Laing, L. and Laing, J. (1984) 'The date and origin of the Pictish symbols', *PSAS*, 114: 261–78.

Laing, L. and Laing, J. (1986) 'Scottish and Irish metalwork and the '*conspiratio barbarica*', *PSAS*, 116: 211–21.

Lamb, R. G. (1980) *Iron Age Promontory Forts in the Northern Isles*, Oxford, BAR, Brit. Ser. 79.

LaMotta, M. W. and Schiffer, M. B. (1999) 'Formation processes of house floor assemblages', in Allison, P. M. ed. (1999) 19–29.

Lane, A. (1987) 'English migrants in the Hebrides: 'Atlantic Second B' revisited', *PSAS*, 117: 47–66.

Lane, A. (1990) 'Hebridean pottery: problems of definition, chronology, presence and absence', in Armit, I. ed. (1990) 108–30.

Lane, A. (1994) 'Trade, gifts and cultural exchange in Dark-Age western Scotland', in Crawford, B. ed. (1994) 103–15.

Lane, A. and Campbell, E. (2000) *Dunadd, An Early Dalriadic Capital*, Oxford, Cardiff Studs in Arch., Oxbow Books.

Lethbridge, T. (1952) 'Excavations at Kilphedir, South Uist, and the problem of the brochs and wheel-houses', *PPS*, 18: 176–93.

Long, C. D. (1988) 'The Iron Age and Romano-British settlement at Catcote, Hartlepool, Cleveland', *DAJ*, 4: 13–35.

Longley, D. (1982) 'The date of the Mote of Mark', *Antiquity*, 56: 132–4.

Love, P. (1989) 'Recent excavations at Carn Liath Broch, Golspie, Sutherland', *GAJ*, 15, 1988–9: 157–69.

Lowe, C. (1991) 'New light on the Anglian "Minster" at Hoddom; recent excavations at Hallguards Quarry, Hoddom, Annandale and Eskdale District, Dumfries and Galloway Region', *TDGNHAS*, 66: 11–36.

Lowe, C. (1993) 'Hoddom', *CA*, 135: 82–92.

Lowe, C. (1999) *Angels, Fools and Tyrants: Britons and Anglo-Saxons in Southern Scotland*, Edinburgh, Historic Scotland.

Lynch, F. and Burgess, C. B. eds (1972) *Prehistoric Man in Wales and the West: Essays in Honour of Lily F. Chitty*, Bath, Adams and Dart.

Lynn, C. J. (1983) 'Some "early" ring-forts and crannogs', *JIA*, 1: 47–58.

Lynn, C. J. (1986) 'Lagore, County Meath, and Ballinderry No. 1, County Westmeath crannogs; some possible structural reinterpretations', *JIA*, 3: 69–73.

McCarthy, M. (2000) 'Prehistoric settlement in northern Cumbria', in Harding, J. and Johnston, R. eds (2000) 131–40.

McCarthy, M. (2002) 'Rheged: an Early Historic kingdom near the Solway', *PSAS*, 132: 357–82.

McCullagh, R. (1992) 'Lairg', *CA*, 131: 455–9.

MacDonald, J. (1891) *Place Names in Strathbogie with Notes Historical, Antiquarian and Descriptive*, Aberdeen, Wyllie.

MacGregor, M. (1962) 'The Early Iron Age metalwork from Stanwick, N.R. Yorks, England', *PPS*, 28, 17–57.

MacGregor, M. (1976) *Early Celtic Art in North Britain*, Leicester, Leicester University Press.

Macinnes, L. (1982) 'Pattern and purpose: the settlement evidence', in Harding, D. W. ed. (1982) 57–74.

Macinnes, L. (1984) 'Brochs and the Roman occupation of lowland Scotland', *PSAS*, 114: 235–50.

Macinnes, L. (1989) 'Baubles, bangles and beads: trade and exchange in Roman Scotland', in Barrett, J. *et al.* eds (1989) 108–16.

MacKay, G. (1980) 'A study of pit-alignments in Scotland', Edinburgh, MA dissertation, Dept of Archaeology, University of Edinburgh.

MacKie, E. W. (1965a) 'The origin and development of the broch and wheelhouse building cultures of the Scottish Iron Age', *PPS*, 31: 93–146.

MacKie, E. W. (1965b) 'Brochs and the Hebridean Iron Age', *Antiquity*, 39: 266–78.

MacKie, E. W. (1969a) 'Radiocarbon dates and the Scottish Iron Age', *Antiquity*, 43: 15–26.

MacKie, E. W. (1969b) 'The historical context of the origin of brochs', *SAF*, 1: 53–9.

MacKie, E. W. (1971) 'English migrants and Scottish brochs', *GAJ*, 2: 39–71.

MacKie, E. W. (1974) *Dun Mor Vaul, an Iron Age Broch on Tiree*, Glasgow, Glasgow University Press.

MacKie, E. W. (1975) *Scotland: An Archaeological Guide*, London, Faber and Faber.

MacKie, E. W. (1976) 'The vitrified forts of Scotland', in Harding, D. W. ed. (1976) 205–35.

MacKie, E. W. (1980) 'Dun an Ruigh Ruaidh, Lochbroom, Ross and Cromarty; excavations in 1968 and 1978', *GAJ*, 7: 32–89.

MacKie, E. W. (1982) 'Excavations at Leckie broch, Stirlingshire, 1970–78: an interim report', *GAJ*, 9: 60–72.

MacKie, E. W. (1987) 'Review of Hedges, *Bu, Gurness and the Brochs of Orkney', Antiquity*', 61: 492–4.

MacKie, E. W. (1991) 'The Iron Age semi-brochs of Atlantic Scotland: a case study in the problems of deductive reasoning', *ArchJ*, 148: 149–81.

MacKie, E. W. (1994) 'Gurness and Midhowe brochs in Orkney: some problems of mis-interpretation', *ArchJ*, 151: 98–157.

MacKie, E. W. (1995) 'The Early Celts in Scotland,' in Green, M. ed. (1995) 654–70.

MacKie, E. W. (1997) 'Dun Mor Vaul revisited: fact and theory in the reappraisal of the Scottish Atlantic Iron Age', in Ritchie, G. ed. (1997) 141–80.

MacKie, E. W. (2000) 'Excavations at Dun Ardtreck, Skye, in 1964 and 1965', *PSAS*, 130: 301–412.

McOmish, D. (1999) 'Wether Hill and Cheviot Hillforts', in Frodsham, P. *et al.* eds (1999) 113–21.

MacSween, A. (1985) *The Brochs, Duns and Enclosures of Skye, Northern Archaeology*, 5/6, Newcastle, Northern Archaeology Group.

Main, L. (1998) 'Excavation of a timber round-house and broch at the Fairy Knowe, Buchlyvie, Stirlingshire, 1975–8', *PSAS*, 128: 293–418.

Manby, T. G. (1980) 'Bronze Age settlement in eastern Yorkshire', in Barrett, J. and Bradley, R., eds (1980) 307–70.

Manby, T. G. and Turnbull, P. eds (1986) *Archaeology in the Pennines: Studies in Honour of Arthur Raistrick*, Oxford, BAR, Brit. Ser. 158.

Mann, J. C. (1974) 'The Northern Frontier after AD 369', *GAJ*, 3: 34–42.

Manning, W. H. (1972) 'Ironwork hoards in Iron Age and Roman Britain', *Britannia*, 3: 224–50.

Manning, W. H. (1981) 'Native and Roman metalwork in northern Britain: a question of origins', *SAF*, 11, (Early Technology in North Britain): 52–61.

Marshall, D. N. (1964) 'Report on excavations at Little Dunagoil', *TBNHS*, 16: 1–69.

Marshall, P., Mulville, J., Parker Pearson, M. and Ingram, C. eds (1999) *The Late Bronze Age and Early Iron Age Community at Cladh Hallan, South Uist; Excavations in 1999*, Sheffield, Sheffield University Dept of Prehistory and Archaeology.

Matthews, K. J. (1999) 'The Iron Age of North-West England and Irish sea trade', in Bevan, B. ed. (1999) 173–96.

Maxwell, G. S. (1969) 'Duns and forts – a note on some Iron Age monuments of the Atlantic Province', *SAF*, 1: 41–6.

Maxwell, G. S. (1976) '*Casus belli*: native pressures and Roman policy', *SAF*, 7, 31–49.

Maxwell, G. S. (1987) 'Settlement in Southern Pictland – a new overview', in Small, A. ed. (1987) 31–44.

Maxwell, G. S. (1989) *The Romans in Scotland*, Edinburgh, Mercat Press.

Maxwell, G. S. (1992) 'Aerial survey in South-East Perth', *CA*, 131: 451–4.

Megaw, J. V. S. and Megaw, R. (2001) *Celtic Art, from its Beginnings to the Book of Kells*, London, Thames and Hudson.

Mercer, R. J. ed. (1981a) *Farming Practice in British Prehistory*, Edinburgh, Edinburgh University Press.

Mercer, R. J. (1981b) 'The excavation of an earthwork enclosure at Long Knowe, Eskdale, Dumfriesshire', *TDGNHAS*, 56: 38–72.

Mercer, R. J. (1985) 'Over Rig excavation and field survey, Eskdalemuir, Dumfriesshire, south-west Scotland', *Univ. Edin. Dept Arch. Ann. Rpt*, 31: 19–22.

Mercer, R. J. (1987) 'The Hillfort Studies Group: the Northern Cheviots', Edinburgh, typescript handbook for the Spring, 1987 meeting of the Hillforts Studies Group.

Mercer, R. J. (1991) 'The Highland Zone: reaction and reality 5000BC–2000AD', *PBA*, 76: 129–50.

Mercer, R. J. and Tipping, R. (1994) 'The prehistory of soil erosion in the Northern and Eastern Cheviot Hills, Anglo-Scottish Borders', in Foster, S. and Smout, T. C. eds (1994) 1–25.

Miket, R. (2002) 'The souterrains of Skye', in Smith, B. B. and Banks, I. eds (2002) 77–110.

Miket, R., and Burgess, C. eds (1984) *Between and Beyond the Walls: Essays on the Prehistory and History of Northern Britain in Honour of George Jobey*, Edinburgh, John Donald.

Miles, D. ed. (1984) *The Romano-British Countryside: Studies in Rural Settlement and economy*, Oxford, BAR, Brit. Ser. 103.

Millett, M. (1990) *The Romanization of Britain*, Cambridge, Cambridge University Press.

Morris, C. D. (1996) 'From Birsay to Tintagel: a personal view', in Crawford, B. ed. (1996) 37–78.

Morris, E. (1985) 'Prehistoric salt distributions: two cases from western Britain', *Bull. Board Celtic Studs*, 32: 336–79.

Morrison, I. (1985) *Landscape with Lake Dwellings*, Edinburgh, Edinburgh University Press.

Mowat, R. J. C. (1996) *The Logboats of Scotland*, Oxford, Oxbow Mon. 68.

Munro, R. (1882) *Ancient Scottish Lake-Dwellings or Crannogs*, Edinburgh, David Douglas.

Munro, R. (1893) 'Notes on crannogs or lake-dwellings recently discovered in Ayrshire', *PSAS*, 27, 1892–3: 211–22.

Munro, R. (1905) *Archaeology and False Antiquities*, London, Methuen.

Murray, D. M. and Ralston, I. (1997) 'The excavation of a square-ditched barrow and other cropmarks at Boysack Mills, Inverkeilor, Angus', *PSAS*, 127: 359–86.

Mytum, H. (1992) *The Origins of Early Christian Ireland*, London, Routledge.

Neal, D. S. (1974) *The Excavation of the Roman Villa at Gadebridge Park, Hemel Hempstead, 1963–8*, London, Soc. Ant. London Res. Comm. Rpt 31, Thames and Hudson.

Neal, D. S. (1978) 'The growth and decline of villas in the Verulamium area', in Todd, M. ed. (1978) 33–58.

Neal, D. S. and Selkirk, A. (1983) 'Gorhambury', *CA*, 87: 115–21.

Neighbour, T. and Burgess, C. (1996) 'Traigh Bostadh', *DES*, 1996: 113–14.

Nevell, M. (1989) 'Great Woolden Hall Farm: excavations on a late prehistoric/ Romano-British native site', *Greater Manchester Arch. Journ.*, 3: 35–44.

Newman, R. (1984) 'The problems of rural settlement in Northern Cumbria in the pre-conquest period', in Faull, M. L. ed. (1984) 155–76.

Newman, R. ed. (1996) *The Archaeology of Lancashire: Present State and Future Priorities*, Lancaster, Lancaster University Archaeology Unit.

Nicholson, R. A. and Dockrill, S. J. eds (1998) *Old Scatness Broch, Shetland: Retrospect and Prospect*, Univ. Bradford/Shetland Amenity Trust/NABO, Bradford Arch. Sc. Res. 5., NABO Mon. 2.

Nicholson, R. A. and Turner, V. eds (forthcoming) *Tall Stories?* Proceedings of a conference held in Lerwick, Shetland, July, 2000, Oxford, Oxbow Books.

Nicolaisen, W. F. H. (1976) *Scottish Place-Names: Their Study and Significance*, London, Batsford.

Nicoll, E. H. (1995) *A Pictish Panorama*, Balgavies, Angus, Pinkfoot Press.

Nieke, M. (1988) 'Literacy and power: the introduction and use of writing in Early Historic Scotland', in Gledhill, J. *et al.* eds (1988) 237–52.

Nieke, M. (1990) 'Fortifications in Argyll: retrospect and future prospect', in Armit, I. ed. (1990) 131–42.

Nisbet, H. (1994) 'Excavations of a vitrified dun at Langwell, Strath Oikel, Sutherland', *GAJ*, 19: 51–74.

Nisbet, H. (1996) 'Craigmarloch hillfort, Kilmacolm', in Alexander, D. ed. (1996) 43–58.

O'Brien, C. (1982) 'Excavations at Thirlings, *Univ. Durham and Newcastle Arch. Reports for 1981*, 5: 44–5.

O'Brien, C. and Miket, R. (1991) 'The early Medieval settlement of Thirlings, Northumberland', *DAJ*, 7: 57–91.

O'Connor, A. and Clarke, D. V. eds (1983) *From the Stone Age to the 'Forty-Five: Studies Presented to R. B. K. Stevenson*, Edinburgh, John Donald.

Omand, D. ed. (1995) *The Borders Book*, Edinburgh, Birlinn.

Oswald, A. (1997) 'A doorway on the past: practical and mystic concerns in the orientation of roundhouse doorways', in Haselgrove, C. and Gwilt, A. eds (1997) 87–95.

Owen, O. (1992) 'Eildon Hill North', in Rideout, J.S., Owen, O.A. and Halpin, E. (1992) 21–72.

Owen, O. and Lowe, C. (1999) *Kebister: The Four-thousand-year-old Story of One Shetland Township*, Edinburgh, Soc. Ant. Scot. Mon. 14.

Palk, N. (1984) *Iron Age Bridle-bits from Britain*, Edinburgh, Univ. Edin. Dept Arch. Occ. Ppr, 10.

Parker Pearson, M. and Sharples, N. (1999) *Between Land and Sea, Excavations at Dun Vulan, South Uist*, Sheffield, Sheffield Academic Press.

Parker Pearson, M., Sharples, N. and Mulville, J. (1996) 'Brochs and Iron Age society: a reappraisal', *Antiquity*, 70: 57–68.

Parker Pearson, M. and Sydes, R. E. (1997) 'The Iron Age enclosures and prehistoric landscape of Sutton Common, South Yorkshire', *PPS*, 63: 221–59.

Parry, M. L. (1985) 'Upland settlement and climatic change; the Medieval Evidence', in Spratt, D. and Burgess, C. eds (1985) 35–49.

Peltenburg, E. (1982) 'Excavations at Balloch Hill, Argyll', *PSAS*, 112: 142–214.

Peltenburg, E. (1984) 'Kildonan Dun, Kintyre', *DES*, 1984: 23.

Perry, D. R. (2000) *Castle Park, Dunbar: Two Thousand Years on a Fortified Headland*, Edinburgh, Soc. Ant. Scot. Mon. 16.

Piggott, C. M. (1948) 'Excavations at Hownam Rings, Roxburghshire, 1948', *PSAS*, 82, 1947–8: 193–225.

Piggott, C. M. (1949) 'The Iron Age settlement at Hayhope Knowe, Roxburghshire: excavations, 1949', *PSAS*, 83, 1948–9: 45–67.

Piggott, C. M. (1950) 'The excavations at Bonchester Hill, 1950', *PSAS*, 84, 1949–50: 113–36.

Piggott, C. M. (1953) 'Milton Loch Crannog I: a native house of the 2nd century AD in Kirkcudbrightshire', *PSAS*, 87, 1952–3: 134–52.

Piggott, S. (1948) 'The excavations at Cairnpapple Hill, West Lothian, 1947–48', *PSAS*, 82: 68–123.

Piggott, S. (1950) 'Swords and Scabbards of the British Early Iron Age', *PPS*, 16: 1–28.

Piggott, S. (1951) 'Excavations in the broch and hill-fort of Torwoodlee, Selkirkshire, 1950', *PSAS*, 85, 1950–1: 92–117.

Piggott, S. (1953a) 'Three metalwork hoards of the Roman period from Southern Scotland', *PSAS*, 87, 1952–3: 1–50.

Piggott, S. (1953b) 'A Late Bronze Age hoard from Peeblesshire', *PSAS*, 87, 1952–3: 175–86.

Piggott, S. (1958a) 'Native economies and the Roman occupation of North Britain', in Richmond, I. A. ed. (1958) 1–27.

Piggott, S. (1958b) 'Excavations at Braidwood Fort, Midlothian and Craig's Quarry, Dirleton, East Lothian', *PSAS*, 91, 1957–8: 61–77.

Piggott, S. (1962) 'Heads and hoofs', *Antiquity*, 36: 110–18.

Piggott, S. (1966) 'A scheme for the Scottish Iron Age', in Rivet, A. L. F. ed. (1966) 1–16.

Piggott, S. (1978) 'Nemeton, temenos, bothros: sanctuaries of the ancient Celts', in *I Celti e la loro cultura nell'epoca pre-Romana e Romana nella Britannia*, Rome, Accademia Nazionale dei Lincei/ British Academy: 37–54.

Piggott, S. (1983) 'The National Museum of Antiquities and archaeological research', in O'Connor and Clarke, D. V. eds (1983) 4–8.

Pococke, M. and Miket, R. (1976) 'An Anglo-Saxon cemetery at Greenbank, Darlington', *MA*, 20: 62–74.

Pollock, D. (1997) 'The excavation of Iron Age buildings at Ironshill, Inverkeilor, Angus', *PSAS*, 127: 339–58.

Pollock, R. (1992) 'The excavation of a souterrain and roundhouse at Cyderhall, Sutherland', *PSAS*, 122: 149–60.

Powell, T. G. E. (1958/80) *The Celts*, London, Thames and Hudson.

Powell, T. G. E., Fell, C. I., Corcoran, J. X. W. P. and Barnes, F. (1963) 'Excavations at Skelmore Heads near Ulverston', *TCWAS*, 63: 1–30.

Powlesland, D., Haughton, C. and Hanson, J. (1986) 'Excavations at Heslerton, North Yorkshire, 1978–82', *ArchJ*, 13: 414–54.

Price, J. ed. (2000) *Glass in Britain and Ireland AD 350–1100*, London, British Museum.

Proudfoot, E. (1996) 'Excavations at the long cist cemetery on Hallow Hill, St Andrews, Fife', *PSAS*, 126: 387–454.

Raftery, B. (1972) 'Irish hill-forts,' in Thomas, C. ed. (1972) 37–58.

Raftery, B. (1982) 'Knobbed spearbutts of the Irish Iron Age', in Scott, B. G. ed. (1982) 75–92.

Raftery, B. (1984) *La Tène in Ireland: problems of origin and chronology*, Marburg, Veröffentlichung des Vorgeschichtlichen Seminars Marburg, Sonderband 2.

Raftery, B. ed. (1995a) *Sites and Sights of the Iron Age, Essays on Fieldwork and Museum Research presented to Ian Mathieson Stead*, Oxford, Oxbow Monograph 56.

Raftery, B. (1995b) 'The conundrum of Irish Iron Age pottery', in Raftery, B. ed. (1995a), 149–56.

Raistrick, A. (1937) 'Prehistoric cultivation at Grassington', *YAJ*, 33: 166–74.

Raistrick, A. (1939) 'Iron Age settlements in west Yorkshire', *YAJ*, 34: 115–50.

Raistrick, A. and Chapman, S. E. (1929) 'Lynchet groups in Upper Wharfedale', *Antiquity*, 3: 165–81.

Ralston, I. (1980) 'The Green Castle and the promontory forts of North-East Scotland', *SAF*, 10: 27–40.

Ralston, I. (1986) 'The Yorkshire Television vitrified wall experiment at East Tullos, City of Aberdeen District', *PSAS*, 116: 17–40.

Ralston, I. (1987) 'Portknockie: promontory forts and Pictish settlement in the North-East', in Small, A. ed. (1987) 15–26.

Ralston, I. (1997) 'Pictish homes', in Henry, D. ed. (1997) 18–34.

Ralston, I. and Armit, I. (1997) 'The Early Historic period', in Edwards, K. and Ralston, I. eds (1997) 217–39.

Ralston, I., Sabine, K. and Watt, W. (1983) 'Later prehistoric settlement in North-east Scotland: a preliminary assessment', in Chapman, J. C. and Mytum, H. C. eds (1983) 149–74.

Ralston, I. and Smith, J. S. (1983) 'High altitude settlement on Ben Griam Beg, Sutherland', *PSAS*, 113: 636–8.

Ramm, H. (1980) 'Native settlements East of the Pennines', in Branigan, K. ed. (1980) 28–41.

RCAHMS (1911) *Third Report and Inventory of Monuments and Constructions in the County of Caithness*, Edinburgh, HMSO.

RCAHMS (1915) *Sixth Report and Inventory of Monuments and Constructions in the County of Berwick*, Edinburgh, HMSO.

RCAHMS (1924) *Eighth Report with Inventory of Monuments and Constructions in the County of East Lothian*, Edinburgh, HMSO.

RCAHMS (1928) *Ninth Report with Inventory of Monuments and Constructions in the Outer Hebrides, Skye and the Small Isles*, Edinburgh, HMSO.

RCAHMS (1929) *Inventory of the Monuments and Constructions in the Counties of Midlothian and West Lothian*, Edinburgh, HMSO.

RCAHMS (1933) *Inventory of the Monuments and Constructions of Fife, Kinross and Clackmannan*, Edinburgh, HMSO.

RCAMS (1946) *Twelfth Report with an Inventory of the Ancient Monuments of Orkney and Shetland*, Edinburgh, HMSO.

RCAHMS (1956) *An Inventory of the Ancient and Historical Monuments of Roxburghshire*, Edinburgh, HMSO.

RCAHMS (1957) *An Inventory of the Ancient and Historical Monuments of Selkirkshire*, Edinburgh, HMSO.

RCAHMS (1967) *Peeblesshire: an Inventory of the Ancient Monuments*, Edinburgh, HMSO.

RCAHMS (1971) *Argyll: An Inventory of the Ancient Monuments, Vol. 1, Kintyre*, Edinburgh, HMSO.

RCAHMS (1975) *Argyll: An Inventory of the Ancient Monuments, Vol. 2, Lorn*, Edinburgh, HMSO.

RCAHMS (1978) *Lanarkshire: An Inventory of the Prehistoric and Roman Monuments*, Edinburgh, HMSO.

RCAHMS (1980) *Argyll: An Inventory of the Ancient Monuments, Vol. 3, Mull, Tiree, Coll and Northern Argyll*, Edinburgh, HMSO.

RCAHMS (1982) *Argyll: An Inventory of the Monuments, Vol. 4, Iona*, Edinburgh, HMSO.

RCAHMS (1984) *Argyll: An Inventory of the Monuments, Vol. 5, Islay, Jura, Colonsay and Oronsay*, Edinburgh, HMSO.

RCAHMS (1988) *Argyll: An Inventory of the Monuments, Vol. 6, Mid Argyll and Cowal, Prehistoric and Early Historic Monuments*, Edinburgh, HMSO.

RCAHMS (1988a) *Buildings of St Kilda*, Edinburgh, HMSO.

RCAHMS (1990) *North-East Perth: An Archaeological Landscape*, Edinburgh, HMSO.

RCAHMS (1992) *Argyll: An Inventory of the Monuments, Vol. 7, Mid Argyll and Cowal, Medieval and Later Monuments*, Edinburgh, HMSO.

RCAHMS (1994) *South-East Perth: An Archaeological Landscape*, Edinburgh, HMSO.

RCAHMS (1997) *Eastern Dumfriesshire: An Archaeological Landscape*, Edinburgh, HMSO.

RCAHMS (2000) 'Special surveys', in *DES*, 2000: 105 and Fig. 37.

RCHME (1936) *An Inventory of the Historical Monuments of Westmorland*, London, HMSO.

Rees, A. R. (1997) 'Thornybank, near Dalkeith (Newton parish), long-cist, pit-alignment, ring-groove, rectilinear structure', *DES*, 1997: 53.

Rees, A. R. (1999) 'Thornybank cemetery', *DES*, 1999: 113–14.

Rees, A. R. (2002) 'A first millennium AD cemetery, rectangular Bronze Age structure and late prehistoric settlement at Thornybank, Midlothian', *PSAS*, 132: 313–56.

Rees, T. (1998) 'Excavation of Culhawk ring-ditch house, Kirriemuir, Angus', *TAFAJ*, 4: 106–28.

Renfrew, C. ed. (1974) *British Prehistory: A New Outline*, London, Duckworth.

Renfrew, C. (1987) *Archaeology and Language: The Puzzle of Indo-European Origins*, London, Jonathan Cape.

Renfrew, C. and Shennan, S. eds (1982) *Ranking, Resource and Exchange*, Cambridge, Cambridge University Press.

Reynolds, D. M. (1982) 'Aspects of later prehistoric timber construction in south-east Scotland', in Harding, D. W. ed. (1982) 44–56.

Reynolds, N. (1980) 'Dark Age timber halls and the background to excavation at Balbridie', *Settlements in Scotland 1000BC–AD 1000, SAF*, 10: 41–60.

Reynolds, P. J. (1979) *Iron Age Farm*, London, British Museum.

Reynolds, P. J. (1993) 'Experimental reconstruction', in Harding, D. W. *et al.* (1993) 93–113.

Richardson, G. G. S. (1977) 'A Romano-British farmstead at Fingland', *TCWAS*, 77: 52–9.

Richmond, I. A. (1925) *Huddersfield in Roman Times*, Huddersfield, Tolson Memorial Museum.

Richmond, I. A. ed. (1958) *Roman and Native in North Britain*, Edinburgh/London, Nelson.

Richmond, I. A. (1968) *Hod Hill Volume Two: Excavations Carried Out between 1951 and 1958*, London, British Museum.

Rideout, J. S. (1996) 'Excavation of a promontory fort and a palisaded homestead at Lower Greenyards, Bannockburn, Stirling, 1982–5', *PSAS*, 126: 199–269.

Rideout, J. S., Owen, O. A. and Halpin E. (1992) *Hillforts of Southern Scotland*, Edinburgh, Historic Scotland/ AOC.

Ritchie, A. (1977) 'Excavation of Pictish and Viking Age farmsteads at Buckquoy, Orkney', *PSAS*, 108, 1976–7: 174–227.

Ritchie, A. (1987) 'The Picto-Scottish interface in material culture', in Small, A. ed. (1987) 59–67.

Ritchie, A. (1989) *Picts*, Edinburgh, HMSO/Historic Scotland.

Ritchie, A. (1994) *Perceptions of the Picts: from Eumenius to John Buchan*, Inverness, Groam House Museum.

Ritchie, A. (1995) 'Meigle and lay patronage in Tayside in the 9th and 10th centuries AD', *TAFAJ*, 1: 1–10.

Ritchie, A. (2003) 'Paganism among the Picts and the conversion of Orkney', in Downes, J. and Ritchie, A. eds (2003): 3–10.

Ritchie, J. N. G. (1981) 'Excavations at the Machrins, Colonsay', *PSAS*, 111: 263–81.

Ritchie, J. N. G. ed. (1997) *The Archaeology of Argyll*, Edinburgh, Edinburgh University Press.

Ritchie, J. N. G. and Lane, A. (1980) 'Dun Cul Bhuirg, Iona, Argyll', *PSAS*, 110, 1978–80: 209–29.

Ritchie, J. N. G. and Ritchie, A. (1991) *Scotland: Archaeology and Early History*, 2nd edn, Edinburgh, Edinburgh University Press.

Ritchie, W. (1985) 'Inter-tidal and sub-tidal organic deposits and sea level changes in the Uists, Outer Hebrides', *Scottish Journ. Geology*, 21, 2: 161–76.

Rivet, A. L. F. (1958) *Town and Country in Roman Britain*, London, Hutchinson.

Rivet, A. L. F. ed. (1966) *The Iron Age in North Britain*, Edinburgh, Edinburgh University Press.

Rivet, A. L. F. and Smith, C. (1979) *The Place-names of Roman Britain*, London, Batsford.

Robertson, A. (1970) 'Roman finds from non-Roman sites in Scotland: more Roman 'drift' in Caledonia', *Britannia*, 1: 198–226.

Robertson, A. (1975) 'The Romans in North Britain: the coin evidence', in Temporini, H. ed. (1975) 364–426.

Robertson, A. (1978) 'The circulation of Roman coins in North Britain: the evidence of hoards and site-finds from Scotland', in Carson, R. A. G. and Kraay, C. M. eds (1978), 186–216.

Robertson, A. (1983) 'Roman coins found in Scotland, 1971–1982', *PSAS*, 113: 405–48.

Rodwell, W. (1978) 'Buildings and settlements in south-east Britain in the late Iron Age', in Cunliffe, B. W. and Rowley, T. eds (1978) 25–42.

Ross, A. (1968) 'Shafts, pits, wells – sanctuaries of the Belgic Britons?', in Coles, J. and Simpson, D. D. A. eds (1968) 255–85.

Ross, A. (1970) *Everyday Life of the Pagan Celts*, London, Batsford.

Roth, H. (1974) 'Ein Ledermesser der Atlantischen Bronzezeit aus Mittelfranken', *Archäologisches Korrespondenzblatt*, 4, 1: 37–48.

Rutherford, A. and Ritchie, G. (1974) 'The Catstane', *PSAS*, 105, 1972–4: 183–8.

Rynne, E. (1991) 'Dún Aengusa – Daingean nó Teampall?' *Archaeology Ireland*, 5: 19–21.

Rynne, E. (1992) 'Dún Aengus and some similar Celtic ceremonial sites', in Bernell, A. ed. (1992) 196–207.

Sanderson, D. C. W., Placido, F. and Tate, J. O. (1988) 'Scottish vitrified forts: TL results from six study sites', *Nuclear Tracks and Radiation Measurements*, 14, No [1/2]: 307–16, Oxford, Pergamon.

Sands, R. and Hale, A. (2001) 'Evidence of later prehistoric use of the Firth of Clyde from marine crannogs', *JWA*, 1: 41–3.

Schoenwetter, J. (1982) 'Environmental archaeology of the Peckforton Hills', *Cheshire Arch. Bull.*, 8: 10–11.

Scott, B. G. ed. (1982) *Studies on early Ireland, Essays in Honour of M. V. Duignan*, Belfast, Association of Young Irish Archaeologists.

Scott, Sir Lindsay (1947) 'The problem of the brochs', *PPS*, 13: 1–37.

Scott, Sir Lindsay (1948) ' Gallo-British colonies: the Aisled Roundhouse culture in the North,' *PPS*, 14: 46–125.

Scull, C. (1991) 'Post-Roman Phase 1 at Yeavering: a reconsideration', *MA*, 35: 57–63.

Scull, C. and Harding, A. F. (1990) 'Two early Medieval cemeteries at Milfield, Northumberland', *DAJ*, 6: 1–30.

Sharples, N. (1998) *Scalloway: A Broch, Late Iron Age Settlement and Medieval Cemetery in Shetland*, Oxford, Oxbow Mon. 82.

Sharples, N. (2003) 'From monuments to artefacts: changing social relationships in the later Iron Age', in Downes, J. and Ritchie, A. eds (2003), 151–65.

Sheffield (1999) *Allt Chrisal, T17: A Preliminary Report on the Excavation of Iron Age and Later Structures, 1996–1999*, Sheffield, Sheffield University Department of Prehistory and Archaeology.

Shepherd, I. A. G. (1983) 'Pictish settlement patterns in North-East Scotland', in Chapman, J. C. and Mytum, H. C. eds (1983) 327–56.

Shepherd, I. A. G. and Shepherd, A. (1995) 'The Sculptor's Cave, Covesea, Moray: from Bronze Age ossuary to Pictish shrine?', *PSAS*, 125: 1194–5.

Simpson, D. D. A. (1969) 'Excavations at Kaimes Hillfort, Midlothian', *GAJ*, 1: 7–28.

Small, A. ed. (1987) *The Picts: A New Look at Old Problems*, Dundee, Dundee University/Dundee City Council.

Small, A. (1969) 'Burghead', *SAF*, 1: 61–8.

Small, A. and Cottam, M. B. (1972) *Craig Phadrig: interim report on 1971 excavation*, Dundee, Univ. Dundee Dept Geog. Occ. Ppr., 1.

Smith, A. (1995) 'The excavation of Neolithic, Bronze Age and Early Historic features near Ratho, Edinburgh', *PSAS*, 125: 69–138.

Smith, B. B. ed. (1994) *Howe: Four Millenia of Orkney Prehistory*, Edinburgh, Soc. Ant. Scot. Mon. 9.

Smith, B. B. and Banks, I. eds (2002) *In the Shadow of the Brochs: The Iron Age in Scotland*, Stroud, Tempus.

Smith, I. (1991) 'Sprouston, Roxburghshire: an early Anglian centre of the eastern Tweed Basin', *PSAS*, 121: 261–94.

Smith, J. T. (1978) 'Villas as a key to social structure', in Todd, M. ed. (1978) 149–86.

Smith, J. T. (1997) *Roman Villas: A Study in Social Structure*, London, Routledge.

Smith, R. A. (1927) 'Pre-Roman remains at Scarborough', *Archaeologia*, 78: 179–200.

Smout, T. C. ed. (1993) *Scotland since Prehistory: Natural Change and Human Impact*, Aberdeen, Scottish Cultural Press.

Smyth, A. (1984) *Warlords and Holy Men: Scotland AD 80–1000*, London, Edward Arnold.

Spearman, R. M. (1990) 'The Helmsdale bowls, a re-assessment', *PSAS*, 120: 63–78.

Spratt, D. (1978) 'Prehistoric field and land boundary systems in the North York Moors', in Bowen, H. C. and Fowler, P. J. eds (1978) 115–18.

Spratt, D. (1982) 'The Cleave Dyke system', *YAJ*, 54: 33–52.

Spratt, D. (1989) *Linear Earthworks of the Tabular Hills, Northeast Yorkshire*, Sheffield, Sheffield University Department of Archaeology and Prehistory.

Spratt, D. and Burgess, C. eds (1985) *Upland Settlement in Britain: The Second Millennium BC and After*, Oxford, BAR Brit. Ser. 143.

Spratt, D. and White R. F. (1986) 'Further information on the Cleave Dyke system', *YAJ*, 58: 195–7.

Stead, I. M. (1965) *The La Tène Cultures of eastern Yorkshire*, York, Yorkshire Philosophical Society.

Stead, I. M. (1968) 'An Iron Age hill-fort at Grimthorpe, Yorkshire, England', *PPS*, 34: 148–90.

Stead, I. M. (1972) 'Beadlam Roman villa: an interim report', *YAJ*, 43: 178–86.

Stead, I. M. (1976) *Excavations at the Winterton Roman Villa and other Roman sites in north Lincolnshire 1958–1967*, Department of the Environment Arch. Rpts 9, London, HMSO.

Stead, I. M. (1979) *The Arras Culture*, York, Yorkshire Philosophical Society.

Stead, I. M. (1991) *Iron Age Cemeteries in East Yorkshire*, London, English Heritage/British Museum.

Steer, K. A. (1956) 'The Early Iron Age homestead at West Plean', *PSAS*, 89, 1955–6: 227–51.

Steer, K. A. and Keeney, G. S. (1947) 'Excavations in two homesteads at Crock Cleugh, Roxburghshire', *PSAS*, 81, 1946–7: 138–57.

Stevenson, J. B. (1984) 'Garbeg and Whitebridge: two square-barrow cemeteries in Inverness-shire', in Friell, J. G. P. and Watson, W. G. eds. (1984) 145–50.

Stevenson, R. B. K. (1949a) 'Braidwood Fort, Midlothian: the exploration of two huts', *PSAS*, 83, 1948–9: 1–11.

Stevenson, R. B. K. (1949b) 'The nuclear fort at Dalmahoy, Midlothian, and other Dark Age capitals', *PSAS*, 83, 1948–9: 186–98.

Stevenson, R. B. K. (1952) 'Long cist burials, particularly those at Galson (Lewis) and Gairloch (Wester Ross), with a symbol stone at Gairloch', *PSAS*, 86, 1951–2: 106–14.

Stevenson, R. B. K. (1955a) 'Pins and the chronology of Brochs', *PPS*, 21: 282–94.

Stevenson, R. B. K. (1955b) 'Pictish art' in Wainwright, F. T. ed. (1955) 97–128.

Stevenson, R. B. K. (1956) 'Native bangles and Roman glass', *PSAS*, 88, 1954–6: 208–21.

Stevenson, R. B. K. (1966) 'Metalwork and some other objects in Scotland and their cultural affinities', in Rivet, A. L. F. ed. (1966) 17–44.

Stewart, M. (1969) 'The ring forts of Central Perthshire', *Trans. Proc. Perthshire Soc. Nat. Science*, 12: 21–32.

Strickertsson, K., Placido, F. and Tate, J. O. (1988) 'Thermoluminescence dating of Scottish vitrified forts', *Nuclear Tracks and Radiation Measurements*, 14, No. 1/2, Oxford, Pergamon: 317–20.

Strickertsson, K., Sanderson, D., Placido, F. and Tate, J. (1987) 'Thermoluminescence dating of Scottish vitrified forts: new results and a review', Glasgow Archaeological Sciences Meeting, 1987.

Suddaby, I. (1995) 'Practical Aspects of Archaeology with reference to Iron Age Drystone Structures in Atlantic Scotland', Edinburgh, Univ. Edinburgh Dept Arch. MA dissertation.

Taylor, D. B. (1990) *Circular Homesteads in North-west Perthshire*, Dundee, Abertay Historical Society Publications 29.

Taylor, J. (2001) 'Rural society in Roman Britain, in James, S. and Millett, M. ed. (2001) 46–59.

Temporini, H. (1975) *Aufstieg und Niedergang der Römischen Welt, II, 3*, Berlin, de Gruyter.

Thomas, A. C. (1959) 'Imported pottery in dark-age western Britain', *MA*, 3: 89–111.

Thomas, A. C. (1960) 'Excavations at Trusty's Hill, Anwoth, Kirkcudbright, 1960', *TDGNHAS*, 38, 1959–60: 58–70.

Thomas, A. C. (1961) 'The animal art of the Scottish Iron Age and its origins', *ArchJ*, 118: 14–64.

Thomas, A. C. ed. (1966) *Rural Settlement in Roman Britain*, London, CBA Res. Rep. 7.

Thomas, A. C. (1968) 'The evidence from North Britain', in Barley, M. and Hanson, R. P. C. eds (1968) 93–122.

Thomas, A. C. (1971) *The Early Christian Archaeology of North Britain*, London and Glasgow, Oxford University Press.

Thomas, A. C. ed. (1972) *The Iron Age in the Irish Sea Province*, London, CBA Res. Rpt, 9.

Thomas, A. C. (1984) 'The Pictish Class I symbol stones', in Friell, J. G. P. and Watson, W. G. eds (1984) 169–88.

Thomas, A. C. (1992) 'The early Christian inscriptions of southern Scotland', *GAJ*, 17: 1–10.

Thomas, F. W. L. (1870) 'On the primitive dwellings and hypogea of the Outer Hebrides', *PSAS*, 7: 153–95.

Thomas, F. W. L. (1878) 'Dunadd, Glassary, Argyllshire: the place of inauguration of Dalriadic kings', *PSAS*, 13, 1877–8: 28–47.

Thomas, F. W. L. (1890) 'On the duns of the Outer Hebrides', *Archaeologia Scotica*, 5: 365–415.

Thomas, G. D. (1988) 'Excavations at the Roman civil settlement at Inveresk, 1976–7', *PSAS*, 118: 139–76.

Thorneycroft, W. (1933) 'Observation of hut-circles near the eastern border of Perthshire, North of Blairgowrie', *PSAS*, 67, 1932–3: 187–203.

Thorneycroft, W. (1948) 'Further observations on hut-circles', *PSAS*, 80, 1945–6: 131–5.

Tinkler, B. N. and Spratt, D. A. (1978) 'An Iron Age enclosure on Great Ayton Moor, North Yorkshire', *YAJ*, 50: 49–56.

Tipping, R. (1997) 'Pollen analysis and the impact of Rome on native agriculture around Hadrian's Wall', in Haselgrove, C. and Gwilt, A. eds (1997) 239–47.

Todd, M. (1978) *Studies in the Romano-British Villa*, Leicester, Leicester University Press.

Todd, M. (1985) 'The Falkirk hoard of denarii; trade or subsidy?', *PSAS*, 115: 229–32.

Tooley, M. J. (1974) 'Sea-level changes during the last 900 years in north-west England', *Geographical Journal*, 140: 18–42.

Topping, Patrick G. (1985) 'Later prehistoric pottery from Dun Cul Bhuirg, Iona, Argyll', *PSAS*, 115: 199–209.

Topping, Patrick (1986) 'Neutron activation analysis of later prehistoric pottery from the Western Isles of Scotland', *PSAS*, 52: 105–29.

Topping, Patrick (1987) 'Typology and chronology in the Later Prehistoric pottery assemblages of the Western Isles', *PSAS*, 117: 67–84.

Topping, Peter (1989) 'Early cultivation in Northumberland and the Borders', *PPS*, 55: 161–79.

Topping, P. and McOmish, D. (2001) 'Summary Report on the excavations at Wether Hill, Northumberland: 2000', *Northumberland Archaeological Group Newsletter*, Oct. 2001: 1–7.

Toynbee, J. M. C. (1964) *Art in Britain under the Romans*, Oxford, Clarendon Press.

Triscott, J. (1982) 'Excavations at Dryburn Bridge, East Lothian', in Harding, D. W. ed. (1982) 117–24.

Tuohy, T. (1999) *Prehistoric Combs of Antler and Bone*, Oxford, BAR, Brit. Ser. 285.

Turnbull, P. (1983) 'Excavations at Rillington, 1980', *YAJ*, 55: 1–9.

Turner, V. and Dockrill, S. (forthcoming) 'Continuity or change: exploring the potential', in Nicholson, R. A. and Turner, V. (forthcoming).

Van der Veen, M. (1992) *Crop Husbandry Regimes: An Archaeobotanical Study of Farming in northern England 1000 BC–AD 500*, Sheffield, Sheffield Arch. Mon. 3.

Varley, W. J. (1935) 'Maiden Castle, Bickerton: preliminary excavations, 1934', *Liverpool Univ. Annals Arch. Anth.*, 22: 97–110.

Varley, W. J. (1936a) 'Further excavations at Maiden Castle, Bickerton, 1935', *Liverpool Univ. Annals Arch. Anth.*, 23: 101–12.

Varley, W. J. (1936b) 'Maiden Castle, Bickerton: a summary of the results of the excavations of 1934 and 1935', *Chester Arch. Soc.*, 31: 113–21.

Varley, W. J. (1950) 'Excavations of the Castle Ditch, Eddisbury, 1935–38', *Trans. Hist. Soc. Lancashire and Cheshire*, 102: 1–68.

Varley, W. J. (1964) *Cheshire before the Romans*, A History of Cheshire, Vol. 1, Chester, Cheshire Community Council.

Varley, W. J. (1976) 'A summary of the excavations at Castle Hill, Almondbury, 1939–72', in Harding, D. W. ed. (1976) 119–32.

Vyner, B. (1988) 'The hill-fort at Eston Nab, Eston, Cleveland', *ArchJ*, 145: 60–98.

Vyner, B. and Daniels, R. (1989) 'Further investigation of the Iron Age and Romano-British settlement site at Catcote, Hartlepool, Cleveland, 1987', *DAJ*, 5: 11–34.

Waddington, C. (1998) 'Humbleton Hill Hillfort Survey', *NA*, 15/16: 71–82.

Wainwright, F. T. ed. (1955) *The Problem of the Picts*, Edinburgh, Nelson.

Wainwright, F. T. (1963) *The Souterrains of Southern Pictland*, London, Routledge and Kegan Paul.

Wait, G. (1985) *Ritual and Religion in Iron Age Britain*, Oxford, BAR, Brit Ser., 149.

Walker, J. (2003) 'The dating of timber halls from the aerial photograph record: a selective site analysis', Edinburgh, Edinburgh University Archaeology MA Hons dissertation.

Warner, R. (1980) 'Irish souterrains: Later Iron Age Refuges', *Archaeologica Atlantica*, 3, 81–99.

Warner, R. B. (1983) 'Ireland, Ulster and Scotland in the Earlier Iron Age', in O'Connor, A. and Clarke, D. V. eds (1983) 160–87.

Waterman, D. (1997) *Excavations at Navan Fort 1961–71, County Armagh*, ed. C. J. Lynn, Northern Ireland Archaeological Monographs 3, Belfast, Stationery Office.

Watkins, T. F. (1980a) 'Excavation of an Iron Age open settlement at Dalladies, Kincardineshire', *PSAS*, 110, 1979–80: 122–64.

Watkins, T. F. (1980b) 'Excavation of a settlement and souterrain at Newmill, near Bankfoot, Perthshire', *PSAS*, 110, 1978–80:165–208.

Watkins, T. F. (1984a) 'Where were the Picts? An essay in settlement archaeology', in Friell, J. G. P. and Watson, W. G. eds (1984) 63–86.

Watkins, T. F. (1984b) *Rullion Green 1983: Report on the 1983 Season of Excavations*, Edinburgh, Univ. Edin. Dept Arch. Project Paper No. 1.

Watkins, T. F. (1986) *Rullion Green, 1984: Report on the 1984 Season of Excavations*, Edinburgh, Univ. Edin. Dept Arch. Project Paper No. 3.

Watkins, T. F. and Murray, J. (1990) *Rullion Green, 1985: Report on the 1985 Season of Excavations*, Edinburgh, Univ. Edin. Dept Arch. Project Paper, No. 11.

Watkins, T. F. and Selkirk, A. (1992) 'Doughnuts and bananas: the Leuchars cropmark project', *CA*, 131: 472–4.

Watson, W. J. (1915) 'Circular forts in Lorne and North Perthshire with a note on the excavation of one at Borenich, Loch Tummel', *PSAS*, 59, 1914–15: 17–34.

Watson, W. J. (1926) *The History of the Celtic Place-names of Scotland*, Edinburgh, reprinted Shannon, Irish Univ. Press 1973.

Webster, G. A. (1971) 'A hoard of Roman military equipment from Fremington Hagg', in Butler, R. M. ed. (1971) 107–25.

Webster, J. (1999) 'Here Be Dragons! The continuing influence of Roman attitudes to northern Britain', in Bevan, B. ed. (1999) 21–32.

Webster, R. A. (1971) 'A morphological study of Romano-British settlements in Westmorland', *TCWAS*, 71: 65–74.

Webster, R. A. (1972) 'Excavation of a Romano-British settlement at Waitby, Westmorland', *TCWAS*, 72: 66–73.

Wedderburn, L. and Grime, D. (1984) 'The cairn cemetery at Garbeg, Drumnadrochit', in Friell, J. G. P. and Watson, W. G. eds (1984) 151–68.

Welfare, H., Topping, P., Blood, K. and Turnbull, P. (1990) 'Stanwick, North Yorkshire, Part 2: A summary description of the earthworks', *ArchJ*, 147: 16–36.

Wheeler, R. E. M. (1931) 'Prehistoric Scarborough', in Rowntree, A. (ed), *A History of Scarborough*, London and Toronto, Dent, 9–33, with Appendix, 'The "Linear Earthworks" of the Scarborough District', 34–39.

Wheeler, R. E. M. (1943) *Maiden Castle, Dorset*, Oxford, Res. Comm. Soc. Ant. London Res. Rep., 12, Oxford University Press.

Wheeler, R. E. M. (1954) *The Stanwick Fortifications, North Riding of Yorkshire*, Oxford, Res. Comm. Soc. Ant. London Rep. 17, Oxford University Press.

Whimster, R. (1981) *Burial Practices in Iron Age Britain: A Discussion and Gazetteer of the Evidence c. 700BC–AD43*, Oxford, BAR, Brit. Ser. 90.

Whittaker, C. R. (1989) 'Supplying the system: frontiers and beyond', in Barrett, J. C. *et al.* eds (1989) 64–80.

Whittington, G (1975) 'Placenames and the settlement pattern of dark-age Scotland', *PSAS*, 106, 1974–5: 99–110.

Whittle, A., Keith-Lucas, M., Milles, A., Noddle, B., Rees, S. and Romans, J. (1986) *Scord of Brouster. An Early Agricultural Settlement on Shetland*, Oxford, Oxford Univ. Comm. Arch. Mon., 9.

Willis, S. (1998) 'Samian pottery in Britain: exploring its distributional and archaeological potential', *ArchJ*, 155: 82–133.

Willis, S. (1999) 'Without and within: aspects of culture and community in the Iron Age of north-eastern England', in Bevan, B. ed. (1999) 81–110.

Wilson, D. (1851) *Archaeology and Prehistoric Annals of Scotland*, Edinburgh, Constable.

Wilson, D. R. (1966) 'Roman Britain in 1965', *JRS*, 56: 207.

Wilson, P. R., Jones, R. F. J. and Evans, D. M. eds (1984) *Settlement and Society in the Roman North*, Leeds, School of Archaeological Sciences, Univ. Bradford and Roman Antiquities Section, Yorkshire Arch. Soc.

Woolf, G. (1998) *Becoming Roman: The Origins of Provincial Civilization in Gaul*, Cambridge, Cambridge University Press.

Wrathmell, S. and Nicholson, A. (1990) *Dalton Parlours Iron Age Settlement and Roman Villa*, Wakefield, Yorkshire Archaeology 3.

Wright, R. P. and Gillam, J. (1951) 'Second Report on Roman Buildings at Old Durham', *AA*, 4th ser. 29: 203–12.

Young, A. (1953) 'An aisled farmhouse at Allasdale, Isle of Barra', *PSAS*, 87, 1952–3: 80–105.

Young, A. (1956) 'Excavations at Dun Cuier, Isle of Barra, Outer Hebrides', *PSAS*, 89, 1955–6: 290–327.

Young, A. (1966) 'The sequence of Hebridean pottery,' in Rivet, A. L. F. ed. (1966) 45–58.

Young, A. and Richardson, K. (1960) "A' Cheardach Mhor, Drimore, South Uist', *PSAS*, 93, 1959–60: 135–73.

Young, M. (2002) 'A consideration of the use of space in a Late Iron Age figure-of-eight domestic dwelling at Bostadh beach, Isle of Lewis', Edinburgh, Edinburgh University Hons. Archaeology MA dissertation.

Index